THE MORMON✝JESUS

The

MORMON✣JESUS

A BIOGRAPHY

John G. Turner

THE BELKNAP PRESS OF HARVARD UNIVERSITY PRESS
Cambridge, Massachusetts, and London, England
2016

First printing

Library of Congress Cataloging-in-Publication Data

Names: Turner, John G., author.
Title: The Mormon Jesus : a biography / John G. Turner.
Description: Cambridge, Massachusetts : The Belknap Press of Harvard
University Press, 2016. | Includes bibliographical references and index.
Identifiers: LCCN 2015039201 | ISBN 9780674737433 (alk. paper)
Subjects: LCSH: Jesus Christ—Mormon interpretations. | Jesus Christ—In the
Book of Mormon. | Mormon Church—History. | Mormon
Church—Doctrines—History.
Classification: LCC BX8643.J4 T87 2016 | DDC 232.088/2893—dc23
LC record available at http://lccn.loc.gov/2015039201

CONTENTS

✢

THE MORMON ✤ JESUS

INTRODUCTION

EVERY YEAR IN MID-JULY, Jesus comes down from the heavens onto a hillside in bucolic western New York State. It is the climactic scene of the Hill Cumorah Pageant, an annual production performed by volunteers belonging to the Church of Jesus Christ of Latter-day Saints (LDS Church). In performances that begin just after nightfall, audiences watch the story of an ancient people, their encounter with Jesus Christ, and the visit of an angel to an American prophet.

In 1937, a group of Mormons first performed what was then called *America's Witness for Christ* on a hill a few miles south of the village of Palmyra. In the intervening decades, the production and cast have become as large as the massive, multitiered stage now used. Today's pageant includes a script penned by science fiction author Orson Scott Card, a sound track featuring the Mormon Tabernacle Choir, pyrotechnics and other special effects, and elaborate battle scenes.

The pageant brings to life the church's founding scripture, the Book of Mormon. After a processional that brings the entire cast of hundreds on the stage, the drama begins with the story of Lehi, an Israelite who receives visions of Jesus Christ and then sails for the New World before Jerusalem's destruction at the hands of the Babylonians. Lehi and his son Nephi have visions of Jesus Christ's future life and ministry. Lehi's descendants divide into two warring groups, named, respectively, for his righteous son Nephi and his rebellious son Laman.

The indisputable star of the show, however, is Jesus Christ. After his ascension from Jerusalem, the Christian savior appears to the Nephites and Lamanites. Fitted with wires invisible to the audience, he materializes in a blaze of light above the stage and slowly descends. He announces

The Hill Cumorah Pageant, 2011. (Photograph by Carolyn Cole. Copyright © 2011, *Los Angeles Times*. Reprinted with permission.)

that he has died for the sins of the world. Jesus tenderly invites children to come and sit around him. He founds a church. Then, he ascends back up to his Father in heaven.

Jesus Christ's ministry ushers in a brief era of peace. Eventually, however, the Nephites and Lamanites resume their warfare, and the wicked gradually exterminate the righteous. The surviving Nephites take refuge in the land of Cumorah, where a climactic battle takes place. Among the last surviving Nephites are Mormon and his son Moroni, who bury the records of their people in a hillside. In the final scene, Moroni returns to earth as an angel in the United States of the 1820s. He leads a young man named Joseph Smith to that same hillside, where Smith retrieves a set of golden plates. Smith translates the writings on the plates, publishes their contents as the Book of Mormon, and founds a church destined to spread across the earth.

Each year, tens of thousands of people come to watch the pageant. For the church, the pageant is both a celebration of its sacred history and a missionary opportunity. Cast members and missionaries circulate among the crowds before and after the show, looking for opportunities to talk to non-Mormons. Those who stop at the visitors' center next to the hill see an eight-foot statue of Jesus Christ. Trees have been painted on the walls surrounding the statue; visitors learn that when Joseph Smith was around fifteen years old, God and Jesus Christ appeared to him in a nearby grove of woods.

The pageant's claims do not go unchallenged. For years, protesters—conservative evangelicals convinced that Mormonism is a dangerous cult—also have come to the Hill Cumorah. Until recently, they proffered anti-Mormon literature from behind a rope as pageant-goers made their way to the hillside. The church recently built a parking lot adjacent to the pageant grounds, which keeps the protesters at a greater distance. Using bullhorns, they shout slogans that question Joseph Smith's character and carry signs criticizing Mormon theology. They insist that Mormons are not Christians.

It is a strange sideshow to the drama on the stage. The hundreds of friendly, polite Latter-day Saint cast members vastly outnumber the protesters and are certainly more winsome exponents of their faith. Still, the scene points to the long-contested place of Mormonism within the landscape of American religion. The pageant and the visitors' center, moreover, make plain the current trajectory of the LDS Church and the way it wishes to be understood. The figure of Jesus towers—literally, in this case—over everything else.[1]

According to the Gospel of Mark, Jesus asks his disciples a question while they are traveling: "Whom do men say that I am?"[2] The disciples report many different opinions. Some people identify Jesus as the reincarnation of John the Baptist, as Elijah (Elias in the King James Version), or as another prophet.

"But whom say ye that I am?" Jesus presses them. Peter affirms that Jesus is "the Christ," a Greek translation of the Hebrew "messiah," meaning "the anointed one."

In the decades after Jesus's death, New Testament authors employed a host of titles and names for him. He was "the savior." He was "rabbi," "teacher," and "Lord." He was the "firstborn of every creature," the "firstborn son" of Mary, and the "firstborn from the dead." He was "Son of

David," "Son of Man," and "Son of God." He was "the word of God" and the "lamb of God." He was the alpha and omega, the beginning and the end. He was the church's bridegroom. New Testament writers identify him as a prophet, an apostle, and a high priest.

Christians spent the next several centuries clarifying—and often disagreeing about—the meaning of these claims about Jesus, their Christ and Lord. What was his relationship to God? What was the relationship between his humanity and his divinity? Did he have a human nature and a divine nature, or one nature that incorporated both? Consensus was elusive. Some Christians believed that because Jesus was God's "first-born," there would have been a time prior to the Son of God's existence. Others bitterly opposed any proposals that would detract from Jesus Christ's full divinity and co-eternity with God. As is true of early Christian scriptures, ritual, and theology more broadly, there was a remarkable diversity of belief about the person of Jesus and the meaning of his life, death, and resurrection.

Backed by the Roman emperor Constantine, the early fourth-century Council of Nicaea affirmed that Jesus Christ and God the Father were "consubstantial," of the same substance or essence, that the Son of God was just as eternal and divine as his Father. The mid-fifth-century Council of Chalcedon further asserted that the "Lord Jesus Christ" was "consubstantial with the Father as regards his divinity, and the same consubstantial with us as regards his humanity . . . one and the same Christ, Son, Lord, Only-begotten."[3] Though dissent continued in some quarters for centuries, these creedal positions eventually achieved broad assent, becoming the foundation for how Christian theologians and hierarchs understood Jesus Christ and the relationship among Father, Son, and Holy Spirit.

The great ecumenical councils narrowed the range of acceptable opinion about Jesus Christ. Even during the height of European Christendom, however, church and civil leaders were hard pressed to extinguish what they perceived to be heresies. For example, between the twelfth and fourteenth centuries, some southern European Christians known as Cathars (from a Greek word meaning "the pure") dissented from the Nicaean and Chalcedonian understanding of Jesus Christ. Cathars were dualists who believed that an evil God, Satan, had created the material realm, whereas a good God had created the spiritual realm. Within this framework, some Cathars understood Jesus as a lesser form of divinity (such as an angel) or as not fully human.[4] For centuries, Catholic and Protestant governments and hierarchies alike sought to extirpate such expressions of theological dissent and heresy.

The era of Christendom is now long over. Because of increased religious freedom and the proliferation of indigenous forms of Christianity in Africa, Asia, and Latin America (often led by prophets and visionaries), contemporary Christianity more closely resembles the theological diversity of its earliest centuries.[5] Thus, Christians are still formulating new answers—and reviving old answers—to the question Jesus posed to his disciples about his identity.

Who is Jesus? What does it mean for him to be the Christ? What is the meaning of his life, death, and resurrection? What did he look like? Was he meek or muscular? How did he live? Was he convivial or ascetic? Christians and others have constructed a "kaleidoscopic variety" of responses to such questions.[6] This book examines one new, distinctive set of answers. *The Mormon Jesus* chronicles how Latter-day Saints have understood and experienced Jesus Christ from the church's earliest years to the present. It is not a simple matter of new doctrine brought forth by Joseph Smith Jr. and his successors. Instead, the Mormon Jesus has a history of change and variety over the course of the church's nearly two-hundred-year history. This is his biography.

The Mormon Jesus begins with the making and remaking of scripture. The Book of Mormon and Joseph Smith's own revision and expansion of the King James Bible proclaimed the divinity of Jesus Christ and his central role in creation and human salvation across time and geography. Most distinctively, early Mormon scripture wrote the Son of God into the Old Testament and into the religion of ancient peoples who lived many centuries before the birth of Jesus. In many respects, though, American Protestant readers found in the Book of Mormon a Jesus who was familiar to them, a major reason for the book's appeal and ongoing usefulness as a missionary tool.

Early Mormons experienced Jesus through dramatic personal encounters with him. For them, Jesus was not confined to the pages of ancient scripture. Instead, he appeared to human beings through visions in the here and now. Smith himself had several significant visions of Jesus Christ, and he taught church members that they too could see their savior, not just in a future heaven, but on earth. Accordingly, early Mormons thirsted to see the face of Jesus, and they also prized the words that he spoke through his latter-day prophet. Joseph Smith dictated scores of revelations—divine messages and commandments—that came primarily as the words of Jesus Christ. Over time, though, early Mormon forms of religious ecstasy subsided, and by the twentieth century, the place of visions and revelations within the church had changed. Instead of seeing Jesus Christ in visions, most church members contented themselves with anticipations of eternity. Ongoing revelation currently proceeds through the talks of high-ranking church leaders, not through the translation of scriptures or the promulgation of divine commandments.

In Joseph Smith's early revelations, Jesus Christ repeatedly promised that he would soon return to the earth, and beginning in 1831 many of Smith's followers gathered to Jackson County, Missouri, to await their savior's appearance as the earth's millennial king. After their expulsion from Jackson County and then from Missouri as a whole, the Mormons gradually lengthened their timetable for Jesus's return. During the early years of the church, moreover, the Mormon rejection of existing Christian creeds paved the way for a burst of creative thought, a revolution of existing Christian metaphysics. The result was a distinctively Mormon christology, a Jesus no longer bound by the contours and limits of Protestant theology.

As Joseph Smith laid out new ideas about the relationship between God, Jesus Christ, and human beings, he introduced rituals designed to bind them together for eternity. Latter-day Saint temple ordinances prompted Mormons to reconsider aspects of Jesus's cosmic and mortal existence. By the early twentieth century, Latter-day Saint leaders identified Jesus Christ with the "Jehovah" of the Old Testament and the temple endowment ceremony. Also, nineteenth-century Mormon leaders taught that while on earth, Jesus had married, and had taken more than one woman as his wife.

Jesus is ubiquitous within contemporary Mormonism, a visible presence in church publications and in artwork on the walls of meetinghouses, temples, and homes. These paintings have portrayed Jesus as a gloriously white savior, and, for much of the twentieth century, Mormon leaders and artists criticized existing depictions of Jesus Christ as insufficiently masculine. The proliferation of Jesus-centered artwork, moreover, reflects the church's desire for outsiders to recognize Mormonism as Christian, a public relations campaign the church has waged with persistence but mixed success over the last several decades.

In the year 2000, the LDS Church's First Presidency and the Quorum of the Twelve Apostles released "The Living Christ," their "testimony" about Jesus Christ in celebration of his birth "two millennia ago." According to "The Living Christ," Jesus Christ is the creator of the earth and the redeemer of humankind. While on earth, he spread peace and goodwill, healed the sick, gave sight to the blind, and raised the dead. At the heart of his work of redemption, he died for everyone. "He gave His life to atone for the sins of all mankind," church leaders testified. "His was a great vicarious gift in behalf of all who would ever live upon the earth." Eventually, the Son of God will return to earth "and reign as Lord of Lords, and every knee shall bend and every tongue shall speak in worship before Him." The savior of all will then judge all people according to their works and "desires." "He is the light, the life, and the hope of the world," Mormon leaders proclaimed. These tenets would resonate with many Christians.

Teachings particular to Mormonism also appeared in "The Living Christ." The statement identified the Christian savior as "the Great Jehovah of the Old Testament." Church leaders further asserted that Jesus Christ taught "the reality of our premortal existence, the purpose of our life on earth, and the potential for the sons and daughters of God in the life to come." "The Living Christ" informed readers that the resurrected Jesus had "ministered" to his "'other sheep' . . . in ancient America," and that he and God the Father had "appeared to the boy Joseph Smith, ushering in the long-promised 'dispensation of the fulness of times.'" The statement proposed an intimate connection between Jesus Christ and the authority of contemporary church leaders. "We declare in words of solemnity that His priesthood and His Church have been restored upon the earth," they testified, identifying themselves as "His duly ordained Apostles." Mormon doctrine about Jesus Christ, thus, connects to Latter-day Saint teachings about priesthood, restoration, and authority.[7]

The LDS Church takes great pains to emphasize the central importance it places upon Jesus Christ. In 1995, the church unveiled a new logo,
a three-line design with the church's full name. The middle line consisted
of an enlarged "JESUS CHRIST." McGray Magleby, the chief designer,
explained that the goal was to give the new logo "more of a Christian
base." The message was for outsiders and members alike. "I think because
of our emphasis on the key words Jesus Christ," he explained, "it will be
in the minds of the member . . . to try to be as much like him [Jesus
Christ] as we can." The new logo reflects the contemporary church's
assertion of its Christian identity.[8]

Historian of American Catholicism Robert Orsi defines religion as
"a network of relationships between heaven and earth involving humans
of all ages and many different sacred figures together."[9] The Latter-day
Saints assiduously maintain such networks, performing rituals in their
temples designed to save, exalt, and bind together families across generations. They also anticipate their reunion with their Heavenly Father
(and, though seldom discussed, a Mother in Heaven). Jesus Christ oc-
cupies a pivotal role in this network of family relationships. It is his suffering and death that enables human resurrection and, for those who
mirror his faithfulness to God's commandments, exaltation to glory,
power, and godhood. He is Christ, Lord, savior, "Elder Brother," and—
especially for Mormon children—friend.

Indeed, from their years in Primary (the Latter-day Saint children's
auxiliary), Mormons are taught to love, revere, and imitate Jesus Christ.
The church's *Friend* magazine for children very much resembles a Mormon
version of *Highlights*, replete with jokes, hidden pictures, mazes, and rec-
ipes for yoghurt parfait. It also teaches Mormon doctrine. In 2015, the
magazine guided children through the Articles of Faith, a set of core
church teachings written in 1842. "We believe in God, the Eternal Father,
and in His son Jesus Christ, and in the Holy Ghost," states the first article. The *Friend* included this letter from Taelor and Owen T., ages ten
and seven:

> One day my little brother's friend was at our house. He
> asked who the picture of Jesus was in my room. He asked if
> it was Heavenly Father. My brother and I told him it was

Jesus. This friend said that Heavenly Father and Jesus were the same person. We told him that Heavenly Father, Jesus, and the Holy Ghost were three different people. I was glad we shared a little bit of the gospel with him.[10]

That Jesus Christ and God the Father are two divine beings is understood as part of a uniquely Latter-day Saint gospel. At an early age, Mormon children are taught not only to love Jesus (the same issue of the *Friend* encouraged them to understand Jesus as a "friend" and to serve him by serving others) but also to understand the way that their doctrine differs from that of other Christians.

Renowned historian of American religion Sydney Ahlstrom once confessed that "the great story of Mormonism . . . persistently escapes definition." Was Mormonism a sect, a church, a new religion, or a people? Ahlstrom threw up his hands and left the question unresolved.[11]

For many nineteenth-century Americans, the LDS Church's exact classification was beside the point. Mormonism was not a "religion," let alone a Christian church. Instead, the Mormon prophet Joseph Smith and his church were prime examples of fraud, delusion, lechery, and treason, traits antithetical to religion properly understood.[12]

In 1860, Representative Thomas Nelson of Tennessee argued for the criminalization of territorial polygamy and the revocation of the Utah Territory's incorporation of the church. Responding to arguments that the U.S. Constitution protected Latter-day Saint practices, Nelson denied that Mormonism was a religion:

> The framers of the Constitution . . . did not mean to
> dignify with the name of religion a tribe of Latter Day
> Saints disgracing that hallowed name, and wickedly
> imposing upon the credulity of mankind. When the
> characters and position of the distinguished men who
> framed that instrument are remembered, it is more than
> probable that by the term religion they meant only to
> convey the idea of a belief founded upon the precepts of the

Bible . . . surely they never intended that the wild vagaries of
the Hindoo or the ridiculous mummeries of the Hottentot
should be ennobled by so honored and sacred a name.[13]

Nelson—and many other Americans—believed that Mormonism had
nothing in common with Christianity.

In 1890, the U.S. Supreme Court upheld the disincorporation of the
LDS Church and the seizure of its assets. Justice Joseph Bradley considered Mormon polygamy a barbaric "blot on our civilization." The
Mormon plea for religious freedom was pure sophistry. "No doubt the
Thugs of India," he held, "imagined that their belief in the right of as-
sassination was a religious belief, but their thinking so did not make it
so." Mormonism was not a genuine "religion" worthy of either constitutional protection or respect, and it was certainly not a species of Christianity. If anything, it resembled a form of Asiatic barbarism.[14]

In 1893, a group of mostly Protestant organizers convened a World's
Parliament of Religions in conjunction with that year's Chicago World's
Fair. In addition to Protestant, Catholic, and Orthodox Christians, they
invited Buddhists, Hindus, Muslims, Jews, and even Zoroastrians. The
congress cast a fairly wide net, but it did not extend an invitation to the
LDS Church. The organizers similarly ignored a variety of indigenous
religions and had only the token presence of Native Americans and African Americans.

Mormon representative B. H. Roberts met with parliament organizer
Charles Carroll Bonney and conveyed his church's desire to participate.
Countering Bonney's objections about plural marriage, Roberts pointed
out that many of the other religions invited to the congress also encouraged or tolerated polygamy. It was a rather personal issue for Roberts, who
had three wives and had once been imprisoned for "unlawful cohabita-
tion." Eventually, Roberts was given permission to read a paper at the
congress. Before he could do so, Muslim representative Alexander
Russell Webb pitched the congress into a tizzy of outrage by publicly
defending polygamy. In response, the organizers promptly moved
Roberts's planned speech to a small side room. Roberts refused to be
shunted off to the obscure venue and never delivered his talk. Bonney
publicly explained that the LDS Church "was not admitted to the Par-

liament of Religions . . . for the reason that its disclaimer of a practice forbidden by the laws of the country had not become sufficiently established to warrant such admission." Three years earlier, in 1890, church president Wilford Woodruff had advised Latter-day Saints to obey federal laws against polygamy. For Bonney, though, polygamy defined Mormonism and made it something other than a religion or church deserving public respect. Mormon exclusion from the parliament rankled church leaders for many years.[15]

As the LDS Church distanced itself from polygamy, many Americans gradually came to admire Mormon patriotism, work ethic, and devotion to family. Though most knew little of Mormon beliefs or practices, non-Mormons gradually conceded the essentially religious character of the church. When a similar World's Congress of Religious Philosophies was held in conjunction with the 1915 San Francisco World's Fair, conveners extended what Latter-day Saint Apostle James Talmage termed "a very cordial invitation to the Church to be represented on their program." Behind the scenes, the Congress's organizers were not of one mind about the invitation, but Mormonism appeared as part of "Christian Day."[16] The LDS Church was on a rocky path toward greater acceptance within Christian America.

One group of American Protestants remained dogged in its opposition to Mormonism, however. An essay in the early twentieth-century *The Fundamentals* (which gave conservative Protestantism a new and soon pejorative name) denounced Mormonism as "strongly anti-American," "anti-Christian," "downright heathenism," and "positively Satanic."[17] For these evangelicals (as many fundamentalists renamed themselves after 1945), Mormonism was the prime example of a dangerous "cult." For the rest of the twentieth century, evangelical publishing houses issued a host of pamphlets and books warning Christians—and Latter-day Saints— about the theological deviancy of the LDS Church.

Evangelical authors such as Walter Martin objected to Latter-day Saint beliefs in an embodied God; in Jesus Christ as a distinct, divine being; in the existence of a Heavenly Mother; in the necessity of both baptism and rituals particular to the LDS Church for the full extent of heavenly glory; and in the principle of ongoing revelation, symbolized by the Book of Mormon and prophetic revelations. Mormonism posed a danger because Latter-day Saints represented their church as Christian, in the process duping gullible inquirers. "Of all the major cults extant in the melting pot of religions called American," warned Martin, "none is more subtle or dangerous to the unwary soul than The Church of Jesus Christ of Latter-day Saints." Martin cautioned naive individuals that the "menace of Mormonism is the fact that it coats most cleverly large doses of error with a thin layer of sugary half-truths."[18]

In 1982, evangelical churches began showing a film designed to warn their members against the threat posed by the Latter-day Saints. *The God Makers* was produced by former Latter-day Saint Ed Decker and evangelical countercult author Dave Hunter (author of *The Cult Explosion*).[19] The film presented an animated summary of Mormon beliefs, including the family history of God the Father (identified as the Elohim of the Hebrew Bible) and his son Jesus. Elohim, who has "endless celestial sex" on a planet near a star named Kolob, calls a council of his spirit children, including Jesus and his brother Lucifer. In order to facilitate his children's progression to godhood, Elohim decides to create Earth. Lucifer presents himself as humanity's savior, recommending that all of Elohim's spirit children obtain salvation and become gods. By contrast, according to the film's narrator, "the Mormon Jesus suggests giving man his freedom of choice as on other planets." Jesus's plan prevails, and the rebellious Lucifer revolts against Elohim along with one-third of his siblings. Denied a body, Lucifer becomes the devil, and the other rebels become demons. Undeterred, Elohim proceeds with his plans for Earth.

> Elohim and one of his goddess wives came to earth as Adam and Eve. Thousands of years later, Elohim, in human form once again, journeyed to earth from the starbase Kolob, this time to have sex with the Virgin Mary, in order to provide Jesus with a physical body. Mormon apostle Orson Pratt taught that after Jesus Christ grew to manhood, he took at least three wives, Mary, Martha, and Mary Magdalene. Through these wives, the Mormon Jesus, from whom Joseph Smith claimed direct descent, supposedly fathered a number of children before he was crucified.

The God Makers contends that the "Mormon Jesus" is not the Jesus Christ other Christians love and worship. While the film's depiction of Elohim and Jesus reflects certain teachings of nineteenth-century church leaders, it was not an accurate representation of the way that most late twentieth-century Latter-day Saints understood either their Heavenly Father or Jesus Christ.

Although *The God Makers* raised doctrinal objections to Mormonism, its critique went far beyond theology. *The God Makers* impugned the LDS Church for its treatment of discontented members, alleging that institutional pressure and the theology of eternal families made it difficult for disaffected members to leave and that bishops persuaded believing spouses to divorce partners who had lost their faith. Mormons were victims, driven to suicide at alarming rates. Mormonism was a dangerous, even "Satanic" cult. Decker's ministry, Saints Alive in Jesus, provided literature, hotlines, and counseling for individuals considering leaving the LDS Church. Although many nonevangelical religious leaders criticized the film as religious bigotry, it shaped the opinions of a generation of American evangelicals about the LDS Church.[20]

Meanwhile, the LDS Church expanded significantly in the years following World War II. In 1947, the church counted its one-millionth member. Today, claimed church membership around the world tops fifteen million. Only a minority (roughly 6.5 million) of the church's members reside in the United States, and less than a third of those American Mormons live in Utah.[21]

While it alarmed evangelicals, the church's spectacular growth intrigued many scholars of religion. In the mid-to-late nineteenth century, historians and other scholars had dismissed the Latter-day Saints as an example of fraud and immorality. A hundred years later, Mormonism garnered unprecedented and far more respectful attention.

In the 1980s, historian Jan Shipps argued with great sophistication that Mormonism is a "new religious tradition," developed out of Christianity akin to the way that early Christianity emerged out of Judaism. According to Shipps, Mormonism thus was sui generis—a unique species of religion—despite "manifest parallels to other forms of Christian restorationism." As Shipps noted, Joseph Smith's biographer Fawn Brodie once commented that Mormonism "was a real religious creation, one intended to be to Christianity as Christianity was to Judaism: that is, a reform and a consummation." Shipps concluded that with the family rather than the individual as its "unit of salvation," with a goal of eternal progression toward godhood rather than eternity in the presence of God and Jesus Christ, and with distinctive scriptures, rituals, and a history of persecution, "Mormonism differs from traditional Christianity in much the same fashion that traditional Christianity, in its ultimate emphasis on the individual, came to differ from Judaism." Shipps readily acknowledged that the Saints understood themselves to be members of Christ's restored—and only—church. The Mormons "maintained," Shipps wrote elsewhere, "that their way of being Christian was the only legitimate way to be Christian." Still, her analogy between early Mormonism and early Christianity suggested that Mormonism had definitively separated itself from its Christian antecedents.[22]

Also in the mid-1980s, Protestant sociologist Rodney Stark predicted that Mormonism would "become a major world faith," the first "world religion" to arise since Islam. Given the relative lack of documentation about the early years of Christianity or Buddhism, Stark relished the chance to observe a new religion's rise. Analyzing past rates of LDS growth, Stark projected that with a growth rate of 30 percent per decade (historically below the LDS average), there would be upwards of sixty million Mormons in 2080. Assuming a 50 percent rate of growth (above the historical average), Stark pegged 2080 membership at a remarkable 265 million. In 2004, Stark observed that actual church membership had thus far slightly exceeded the high end of his projections. A decade later, Mormon membership no longer exceeded Stark's "high projection," but fell somewhere in between his "high" and "low" projections.[23]

As scholar of religion Jonathan Z. Smith notes, it "is impossible to escape the suspicion that a world religion is . . . a tradition that has achieved sufficient power and numbers to enter our history to form it, interact with it, or thwart it."[24] Indeed, Stark's descriptor of "world religion" connotes that Mormonism is both important and distinctive. Not surprisingly, therefore, some Latter-day Saints greeted Stark's argument positively, primarily because his projections coincided with Mormon missionary hopes. Gaining status as a "new religious tradition" or "world religion" suggests a certain organizational accomplishment and public acceptance. After all, most Americans do not regard Islam, Buddhism, or Hinduism as "cults." For scholars seeking to establish the importance of their subject matter, moreover, the classification of Mormonism as a "new religion" or "world religion" has a certain appeal. At the same time, Mormonism can only be a "world religion" or "a new religious tradition" if it is something other or more than a branch of Christianity.

The Latter-day Saints themselves have been of two minds about claiming space for themselves within the broader world of Christianity.

From the start, Joseph Smith and his followers issued biting critiques of Christianity's existing forms. For example, the Book of Mormon draws a firm line between members of Jesus Christ's true church and all others. An angel tells Lehi's son Nephi that "there is, save it be, two churches: the one is the church of the Lamb of God, and the other is the church of the Devil," also termed the "mother of abominations," "the whore of all the earth," the "great and abominable church," and the "mother of harlots."[25] Until recently, many Latter-day Saints identified the "great and abominable church" as the Catholic Church, akin to the way that Protestants had long interpreted the Book of Revelation's "whore of Babylon" with Rome's "great apostasy." A central teaching of the LDS Church, however, is that *all* other Christian churches are in apostasy, having abandoned over time many of the "plain and precious" scriptures, ordinances, and doctrines of God. In the canonical account of Joseph Smith's early visionary experiences, Jesus Christ tells him to "join none of them, for they were all wrong" and "that all their creeds were an abomination in his sight." Thus, for Latter-day Saints, Protestants, Catholics, and any other Christians belong to apostate churches. Christian apostasy is the LDS Church's raison d'être.

At times, Latter-day Saints have professed friendship toward all and recognized Jesus Christ as a figure that connected them with their Protestant antagonists. "I will ask no man to believe as I do," assured Joseph Smith in an 1843 speech contrasting Latter-day Saints and Presbyterian teachings. "Do you believe in Jesus Christ, etc.? So do I. Christians

should cultivate the friendship of each other and will do it."[26] But Smith
was not always so irenic. In December 1834, William McLellin recorded
in his journal that "President Smith preached . . . three hours in Kirt[land]
during which he exposed the Methodist Dicipline in its black deformity
and called upon the Elders in the power of the spirit of God to expose
the creeds & confessions of men—His discourse was animated and
Pointed, against all Creeds of men."[27] Smith's contemporaries and successors often repeated such criticisms.

Mormons have embraced a strong sense of themselves as a people set
apart. Following language in the Book of Mormon, they called other
Americans and Europeans "Gentiles," a term of opprobrium as well as
description. As Jan Shipps explains, the Saints were God's new Israelites, recapitulating the experiences of persecution, deliverance, and exodus of the ancient Hebrews.[28] Through patriarchal blessings, church
members learned that they had Israelite blood, usually of the tribe of
Ephraim. Especially in the nineteenth century, this was more than meta-
phorical. Joseph Smith had taught that powerful spiritual and physical manifestations often accompanied the conversion of a Gentile to
Mormonism because the Holy Ghost would "purge out the old blood
and make him actually the seed of Abraham."[29] During their exodus,
the Saints saw themselves as reliving the sacred history of the former
Israelites. The trek across the plains and mountains was a rite of passage
for tens of thousands of Saints, and the pioneering experiences of
migration and settlement fashioned the Mormons into a people and a
"near nation."[30] In the nineteenth century, the divide was wide between
Saint and Gentile, between New Israel and its Protestant antagonists.

Recent Mormon leaders have balanced a broader sense of Christian
identity with distinctive Latter-day Saint claims and doctrine. "We are
part of the great community of Christians," church president Gordon B.
Hinckley proclaimed in 1997, "and yet we are a peculiar people. . . . We
are somewhat peculiar in our doctrine." Hinckley noted that Latter-day
Saint beliefs diverge from ancient traditions and creeds.[31] "They say we
do not believe in the traditional Christ of Christianity," Hinckley explained in 2002. "There is some substance to what they say." Hinckley
contrasted "the almost infinite discussions of men trying to arrive at
a definition of the risen Christ" with Mormonism's acceptance of

direct, modern revelation.[32] The church maintains its belief that other Christian churches are in apostasy, a key part of the Latter-day Saint missionary handbook.

Thus, the church wants other churches to recognize its Christian claims, but it simultaneously insists that all of those other churches are in apostasy. "Mormons insist on the need for a gospel restoration," observes Latter-day Saint scholar Terryl Givens, "but then feel the sting of being excluded from the fold of Christendom they have just dismissed as irredeemably apostate."[33] Mormons want to have it both ways. Indeed, the church's coherence and growth depend on having it both ways.

How, then, should scholars classify Mormonism? Because Mormonism emerged within the context of American Protestantism, is it one of those many "species" of Protestantism? Or is Mormonism its own separate "genus" of Christianity? Or its own "order" within the larger framework of Abrahamic religions? Or, because Mormon scriptures speak of a plurality of gods and the possibility of human deification, is Mormonism its own "class" of religion?

It is important to note that over the past two centuries a number of churches have laid claim to the label "Mormon." For example, for a century after its 1860 establishment, the Reorganized Church of Jesus Christ of Latter Day Saints (RLDS, and *Latter Day Saints* rather than *Latter-day Saints*) articulated a restorationist identity as Christ's one true church led by a descendant of Joseph Smith. The "Prairie Saints"[34] or "Josephites," as distinguished from the Utah "Mountain Saints" or "Brighamites," rejected polygamy (and denied that Joseph Smith Jr. had practiced it) and—after some uncertainty—did not adopt the distinctive rituals Smith had introduced during the last several years of his life. Renamed the Community of Christ in 2001, it is the second largest of the churches that trace their origins to Joseph Smith and the Book of Mormon. In recent decades, the Community of Christ has mostly shed its Mormon identity in favor of a broader Christian self-understanding. Unlike the LDS Church, the Community of Christ has sought and attained membership in the National and World Councils of Churches, a sign that the church now privileges an ecumenically Christian identity over a Mormon sense of self. At the other end of the "Mormon" spectrum, there are fundamentalist churches that persist with the practice of polygamy. In this book, the Community of Christ and fundamentalist Mormons serve as bases for comparison rather than as objects of examination in their own right. *The Mormon Jesus* keeps its focus on the numerically dominant Salt Lake City-based LDS Church.

Certainly there are many things that set the Latter-day Saints apart from other branches of Christianity, such as additional scriptures; ongoing revelation through current prophets; a belief that God the Father and Jesus Christ are two separate, material, embodied divine beings; the belief that certain rituals are required for human exaltation to godhood; and the performance of proxy rituals to save and exalt the dead. There are antecedents, some widespread and some rare, for a good number of Mormon beliefs and practices, but collectively, these and other tenets maintain ecclesiastical space between Mormonism and other Christian churches.

At the same time, the prominence of Jesus Christ in Mormon scriptures, thought, and culture place the Latter-day Saints within most common and commonsense definitions of Christianity.[35] Whereas few followers of Jesus two centuries after his lifetime insisted that they were Jews, Mormons today unabashedly proclaim their fidelity to Jesus Christ and call themselves Christians. Most Mormon scriptures either place a central importance on Jesus Christ or deliver God's instructions in his voice. Especially in light of the church's pronounced emphasis on Jesus Christ over the past several decades, the contemporary LDS Church is a new genus of Christianity rather than a new religious tradition or a new world religion.[36] Mormon Christianity is not Catholic, Protestant, or Orthodox. Instead, the Latter-day Saints have charted their own Christian course.

✣

CHAPTER ONE

ANOTHER TESTAMENT
OF JESUS CHRIST

"HELLO, WOULD YOU LIKE to change religions and have a free book written by Jesus?" asks missionary Arnold Cunningham in the Broadway smash *The Book of Mormon: The Musical*.

Since its publication in 1830, the Book of Mormon has become one of the most widely distributed works of American literature, with more than 150 million copies printed. For millions of believers across the United States and around the world, it is a work of scripture alongside the Bible. Joseph Smith once referred to the Book of Mormon as "the most correct of any book on earth and the keystone of our religion."[1]

At the same time, the scripture has found little respect beyond the ranks of the faithful. Non-Mormons who dip into its pages and encounter its archaic, King James-style language often agree with Mark Twain that it is "chloroform in print."[2] The Broadway musical that bears its name lampoons many aspects of Mormonism but pays scant attention to the scripture itself, other than to identify its protagonists as "Jews who met with Christ" in America. The book's contents and the story of its publication, however, are both remarkable in their complexity, a complexity that has often obscured—at least for outsiders—the Book of Mormon's central message.

Like the Bible, the Book of Mormon is divided into individual books, fifteen in this case. It chronicles the histories of several peoples who inhabit parts of the New World, including the warring Nephites and Lamanites to whom Jesus Christ appears following his ascension from Jerusalem. The scripture's penultimate book (the Book of Ether) narrates the experiences of a cluster of families living at the time of the Tower of Babel, when "the Lord confounded the language of the people" and scattered them across the earth. This story's central character is a man identified only as "the brother of Jared," who cries unto "the Lord" and pleads with God not to confound his people's language. God spares them from linguistic confusion. He instructs them to venture into the wilderness and build enclosed barges so that they might travel to a "land of promise" across "many waters." God promises the people that they shall be "free from bondage, and from captivity . . . if they will but serve the God of the land, which is Jesus Christ." The people reach the coast, where they remain for several years.

As the people prepare for their voyage, the brother of Jared climbs a mountain, fashions sixteen glass-like stones out of a rock, and again cries out "unto the Lord." He asks the Lord to touch the stones, that they would "shine forth unto us in the vessels which we have prepared, that we may have light while we shall cross the sea." The Lord grants this request, stretches out his finger, and touches the stones one at a time. The brother of Jared "saw the finger of the Lord; and it was as the finger of a man, like unto flesh and blood." Shocked by this sight, the brother of Jared collapses to the ground. When the Lord asks him to explain his fear, he explains that he "knew not that the Lord had flesh and blood." Then he asks the Lord to show himself fully. After the brother of Jared affirms his faith, the Lord reveals his identity:

> I am he who was prepared from the foundation of the
> world to redeem my people. Behold, I am Jesus Christ.
> I am the Father and the Son. In me shall all mankind have
> life, and that eternally, even they who shall believe on my
> name; and they shall become my sons and daughters.

The Lord further explains that what the brother of Jared beholds is "the body of my spirit; and man I have created after the body of my spirit." He promises that he will eventually appear to his people "in the flesh."

Jesus then tells the brother of Jared not to share what he has seen with his people but instead to prepare a record for others to find in the future. The Lord commands him to write in a language that others cannot interpret without the use of two stones. "I will cause in mine own due time," Jesus promises, "that these stones shall magnify to the eyes of men these things which ye shall write."

Meanwhile, the people finish their barges, the brother of Jared places one of the consecrated, luminous stones in each vessel, and the people float to the promised land. Their descendants suffer from strife, rebellion, and the machinations of an oath-bound "secret combination." Sons succeed their fathers as kings. A prophet named Ether foretells the coming of Christ and the eventual establishment of a "New Jerusalem," and he warns a king named Coriantumr that if he does not repent, he will become the last of his people. Coriantumr does not repent, and wickedness and rebellion continue unabated. Two million men die, and also their wives and children. In the end, all of the Jaredites perish, and Ether buries the records of his people, inscribed on twenty-four plates of pure gold.[3]

These plates are discovered several hundred years later by the Nephites. Then, around four centuries after the life of Jesus, a Nephite prophet named Moroni edits the Jaredite record and incorporates it into the history of his own people.[4] Moroni laments that the Nephites also have dwindled because of wickedness and unremitting warfare. He recalls that "Christ shewed himself unto our fathers, after that he had risen from the dead." Moroni adds that he too has "seen Jesus, and that he hath talked with me face to face." Finally, he encourages his future readers "to seek this Jesus of whom the prophets and apostles have written." Like Ether, alone and full of mourning, Moroni buries his ancestors' records, including the history of the Jaredites.[5]

According to Joseph Smith, these ancient records lay buried for another fourteen hundred years. Then, an angel—Moroni, returned to earth—appeared to him, showed him a set of golden plates, and instructed him to translate them. In 1830, Smith published the Book of Mormon, whose title page announced that the book contained the records of the Nephites, their enemies the Lamanites, and the Jaredites. It was an

audacious way for the untutored, twenty-four-year-old Smith to introduce himself to the world.

The book's title page explained that the "Lamanites," understood as
the native peoples of North America, were "a remnant of the House of
Israel." Smith later commented that the ancestors of the American Indians "were principally Israelites. . . . The remnant are the Indians that
now inhabit this country." Such ideas had long circulated among white
Americans and Europeans. Partly out of desire to unite the lineage of
all human beings within biblical narrative, many Europeans and Americans had connected American Indians with the "ten lost tribes of
Israel," those who disappear from biblical history after the Assyrian
conquest of the northern kingdom of Israel in the late eighth century.
The Book of Mormon departed from the lost tribes theory by instead
tracing American Indian ancestry to a single family of Israelites. Even if
the details were original, the theory that American Indians were of Israelite ancestry was familiar to Joseph Smith's contemporaries.[6]

Joseph Smith's early followers took the Book of Mormon to Indians,
informing them that the book contained the history of their ancestors
and that they could be redeemed and brought back to their ancient faith.
The initial response from Indians was underwhelming. For the most
part, therefore, the book found an audience among North American
and then European Protestants. In its pages those readers found some
distinctive ideas about Jesus Christ, such as the above-mentioned
teaching that Jesus had a spiritual body prior to his mortal life. Moreover, they learned that many ancient peoples—long before the birth of
Jesus—were Christians. Still, the focus of early Mormon missions was
not the introduction of new teachings about Jesus Christ. Through the
Bible and the Book of Mormon, Joseph Smith and his followers sought
to convince potential converts that they had finally found true Christianity, the true church of Jesus Christ.

Born in 1805 in Vermont, Joseph Smith Jr. was the fifth of eleven
children, nine of whom lived to at least young adulthood. In 1816, the
family moved to western New York, purchasing a farm that straddled
the townships of Palmyra and Manchester. As his family struggled to

maintain ownership of its farm, Smith was busy helping to clear land, plant and harvest crops, and produce maple syrup.

Smith and his early supporters came of age in the midst of what was very nearly a national obsession with Jesus. While a host of diverse religious groups took root in the fertile cultural soil of the early republic, evangelical Protestantism was the closest thing to an unofficial American religion. As religious freedom expanded in the wake of the American Revolution, new, aggressively evangelistic forms of Protestantism thrived. Methodist and Baptist churches grew exponentially. Church membership as a whole rose dramatically. Millions of Americans experienced emotional conversions (and often reconversions, as they were born again and again) at camp meetings, in urban revivals, and within shrouded plantation arbors. Evangelicals proclaimed their love for Jesus in hymns, prayers, and books. They confessed their sins, sang about Jesus Christ's bloody death on the cross, saw him in visions and dreams, reveled in his gracious forgiveness, and surrendered their lives to him.[7]

Smith grew up in a visionary household on the religious margins of this evangelical culture. Evangelicalism influenced the Smith family, but Joseph Smith, his parents, and siblings mostly kept Protestant churches at arm's length. Joseph Smith Sr. had a host of spiritual dreams and visions, which his wife Lucy Mack Smith later recorded. In one such dream, he arrived at a meetinghouse to find the door shut. The doorkeeper told him he had come too late. He felt that he was perishing, that his "flesh" was "wither[ing]" on his bones. While he was wracked with despair and desperation, an angel attended him and asked him if he had done what he could to obtain entrance into heaven. It occurred to him to cry out in agony: "Oh lord I beseech Thee in the name of Jesus christ to forgive my sins." Immediately, his flesh began to be restored. The angel instructed Smith Sr. that he "must plead the merits of Jesus" to gain salvation and a heavenly reward. Clearly, the elder Smith agonized about the state of his soul, but he found no lasting spiritual peace. He never joined any Protestant church.[8]

Lucy Mack Smith, along with several of the couple's children (not including Joseph Jr.), eventually became a member of Palmyra's Presbyterian church. She had no deep attachment to the denomination and its doctrines, however. Joseph Smith Jr.'s ancestors also included a maternal grandfather (Solomon Mack), who had published an account of his evangelical conversion, and a paternal grandfather (Asael Smith), who was drawn to Enlightenment-era skepticism and to Universalism, the belief that all people would be saved.

Joseph Smith's family fostered skepticism about religious institutions, but for the most part the Macks and Smiths were not skeptical about Jesus. They disagreed about the extent of the salvation wrought by Jesus's sacrifice, but they believed that he was the Son of God, the savior of the world, and that through him one might find forgiveness. Once, when an illness forced her to contemplate death, Lucy Mack Smith felt that "it seemed to me as though there was a dark and lonely chasm between myself and Christ that I dare not attempt to cross."[9] That chasm stood between the Smith family and any institutional form of Christianity, indeed between them and an elusive Jesus. The Smiths were unsure whether any church reflected Jesus Christ's teachings and mission. Joseph Smith Jr. grew up in a home suffused with spiritual practices. Bible reading, prayer, visions, and magical objects (including the use of divining rods and seer stones for the detection of buried treasures) informed his spiritual understandings and hopes. The Smiths sought glimpses of God and Jesus; they also searched for purported riches buried in the New York countryside.[10]

Smith later recalled that when he was around the age of twelve, he became concerned over the "welfare of his soul." He read at least some of the Bible and began to pray. Given the surrounding culture of evangelical revivalism, it is not surprising that Smith's thoughts turned in these directions. Given the example of his ancestors, it is also not surprising that, instead of joining one of the Protestant churches in his vicinity, Smith began to narrate remarkable visions.

As Smith matured into manhood, he prayed while again troubled at the state of his soul. Smith told the story of what happened next many times, gradually adding more detail. While he prayed, an angel—dazzlingly white—appeared and stood before him. Smith subsequently identified the angel as Moroni, the last of the Nephite prophets.[11] According to a history Smith began preparing for publication in 1838, Moroni informed him that nearby there were engraved plates of gold containing "the fullness of the everlasting Gospel . . . as delivered by the

Saviour to the ancient inhabitants." In order to translate the writing on the plates, he would need an interpretive device, two stones in silver bows that were fastened to a breastplate, buried with the plates. Moroni returned twice more that night, each time repeating the same message. When he went out to work the next day, he fell "helpless to the ground, and for a time [was] quite unconscious of anything." While Smith was in this apparent trance, the angel appeared again and repeated the message.[12]

After this night and day of visions, Smith found the plates, but he could not obtain them despite his attempts to do so. Moroni explained that Smith needed to purify his motives before he could receive the plates. Not surprisingly, given his participation in quests for buried treasure, Smith conceded that "I had been tempted of the advisary [adversary] and saught the Plates to obtain riches." Moroni told Smith he would have to wait four years. Each year on the same day, they would meet at this place. Should he exercise patience and display purer motives, God would forgive him and allow him to receive the plates.

Smith's parents and siblings assembled to hear him tell what he had seen and heard. It was a curious tale: golden plates containing an ancient record from Jesus Christ, buried in a nearby hillside, but unobtainable for now. Visions of angels and treasures were not strange or incredible in the Smith household, however. The family sat up late listening to Joseph's story. In retrospect, Lucy Mack Smith marveled at the sight of her family "all seated in a circle father mother sons and Daughters listening in breathless anxiety to the teachings of a boy . . . who had never read the Bible through." They believed him and rejoiced together.[13]

Soon more immediate concerns disrupted their joy. Joseph's elder brother Alvin died, and with him the family lost its chief source of economic initiative and hope. The next year, hopelessly behind on their payments, the Smiths lost title to their farm. Fortunately, a local man purchased the land and permitted them to remain as tenants. Joseph Smith Sr. and his namesake visionary traveled to Harmony, Pennsylvania, in the employ of Josiah Stowell, who hired them to search for a Spanish silver mine.

Stowell employed the Smiths because of their reputation for being able to find buried treasures. The younger Joseph Smith was a scryer. He gazed into a seer stone in order to locate lost objects, and his talent had captured the attention of fellow treasure-seekers such as Stowell. In 1826 Joseph Jr. appeared in court to defend himself against charges of disorderliness, of fraudulently claiming to have the power to locate missing items. Smith testified that he indeed possessed the ability to find "hidden treasures in the bowels of the earth" and had done so with some frequency. Nevertheless, he stated that he no longer wanted "anything to do with this business" because it made his eyes sore.[14]

Joseph Smith Jr. never found the supposed silver mine, but while in Harmony he fell in love with Emma Hale, a young woman who lived nearby. Smith's courtship of Emma brought him in contact with the evangelical Protestantism from which his family had long remained aloof. Despite his occasional visionary experiences, Smith as a young man did not appear especially interested in religion. By his mother's account, he had never read the Bible through prior to his first encounter with Moroni. Josiah Stowell's son later recalled Smith as someone who "at that time did not Profess religion." He was neither profane nor pious.[15] Emma, however, came from a Methodist family. Her father disapproved of Smith as a suitor, at least partly because of his occupation as a treasure-seeker. So the couple eloped. After temporarily mending fences with Emma's father, Smith attended Methodist meetings with the Hales in Harmony. Any dalliances with existing churches, however, soon came to an end.

About eight months after his marriage, Smith announced to his family that he had finally obtained the treasure the angel had first shown him four years earlier. What he found, he told his wife, parents, siblings, and a few close friends, was a set of large, heavy, golden plates containing illegible characters and an interpretive device. Lucy Mack Smith later said that the stones looked like "three-cornered diamonds set in glass," which, together with the "silver bows," looked like a pair of "old-fashioned spectacles." Smith's mother once said he possessed the ability to "tear open the bowels of the Earth and drag to light the precious things of the Earth beneath and then extend his search up to the throne of God and bring down the precious [things] of Heaven above." Smith had long sought "hidden treasures" and now had found golden plates. His family had accepted both the validity of his heavenly visions and his enchanted quest for buried riches; they correspondingly accepted something that brought together these two aspects of their religious culture.[16]

The next two years were an adventure in scripture making. For the most part, Smith kept the golden plates to himself, though a number of his relatives and close friends testified that they had both seen and "hefted" them. In fits and starts, besieged by would-be thieves and financial hardship, Joseph Smith brought forth what became the Book of Mormon. Smith wrote in a preface to the book's first edition that he "translated, by the gift and power of God," but this does little to explain how he proceeded.[17]

Smith scried. At first, he apparently used the seer stones contained in the spectacle-like interpretive device. Later, while burying his face in a hat to block out the surrounding light, he peered into another seer stone, a smooth, brown, egg-shaped rock discovered while Smith helped a Palmyra neighbor dig a well in 1822. Smith came to associate these stones with the biblical "Urim and Thummim," divining stones attached to the Israelite high priest's breastplate. Joseph Knight Sr., acquainted with Smith since 1826, recounted that Smith "put the urim and thummim into his hat and Darkned his Eyes." As he gazed into the hat, he would see a sentence appear in "Brite Roman Letters." After he dictated the sentence, it would disappear if the scribe spelled it correctly, which for Knight illustrated the "marvelous" nature of the work. "Thus was the hol [whole] translated," Knight concluded.[18] At least during much of the process, Smith did not even look at the plates, which he sometimes kept wrapped in cloth on a nearby table. They served as an object of inspiration, not as a textual basis for translation. As the LDS Church itself has suggested recently, it is more accurate to think of the Book of Mormon as a "revelation" than as a "translation" in any conventional sense of the term. The editors of the church's ongoing Joseph Smith Papers project describe the scripture as the "most prominent among Joseph Smith's revelatory dictations."[19]

In 1828 Smith dictated about 116 manuscript pages, which were lost after he allowed his scribe and financial backer Martin Harris to take them home to show his skeptical wife. The project stalled. Then, over the span of several months in the spring of 1829, bolstered by the presence of new scribe Oliver Cowdery, Smith dictated what he published the following year as the Book of Mormon. Smith later reported that he had returned the plates to the angel. Regardless of whether Smith revealed a long-hidden ancient text, composed the book himself through a hitherto latent genius, or otherwise obscured its true source, the Book of Mormon added a decided scriptural heft to the visions Joseph Smith had experienced for nearly a decade.

The Book of Mormon begins with Lehi and his family, Israelites living in Jerusalem shortly before the Babylonians conquered it in the early sixth century BCE. The book's characters live in a visionary culture with some resemblance to that of Joseph Smith's family in early nineteenth-century New York. The veil between heaven and earth was thin, and it sometimes disappeared entirely. In the very first chapter of the Book of Mormon, Lehi sees God on his throne surrounded by angels, and sees Jesus descend from heaven with "lustre . . . above that of the sun at noonday." Lehi testifies to the "coming of a Messiah, and also the redemption of the world."[20] As the story proceeds, and Lehi's descendants populate a promised land across the waters, visionary figures repeatedly prophesy of Christ's coming.

The Book of Mormon's prophecies about Jesus Christ are detailed and explicit. For example, an angel teaches Lehi's son Nephi that a virgin "exceeding fair and white . . . is the mother of God." Lehi further learns that the "Lamb of God" will be baptized of a prophet, will have the Holy Ghost come upon him "in the form of a dove," and will cast out demons and heal the sick. The "Son of God" will be "lifted up upon the cross, and slain for the sins of the world." That "Lamb of God," the angel tells Nephi, is "Jesus Christ."[21] Subsequent prophecies, centuries later in the narrative, add that "he [Jesus Christ] shall suffer temptations, and pain of body, hunger, thirst, and fatigue, even more than man can suffer, except it be unto death: for behold blood cometh from every pore."[22] As the generations pass, the Book of Mormon chronicles wars between the descendants of Nephi (the Nephites) and his brother Laman (the Lamanites). The Book of Mormon also contains a theological reinterpretation of Adam's sin ("Adam fell, that men might be; and men are, that they might have joy"),[23] focuses on the preservation of ancient records and genealogies, and foretells the future course of Jews, Gentiles, nations, and churches. Again and again, however, the book returns to prophecies about Jesus Christ. Moreover, hundreds of years before the birth of Jesus,

Alma Baptizes in the Waters of Mormon, by Minerva Teichert, 1949–1951. (Courtesy of Brigham Young University Museum of Art.)

the ancient Americans who accept these prophecies baptize in the name of Christ, pray in the name of Christ, work miracles in the name of Christ, and worship in the name of Christ. As Terryl Givens has commented, the Book of Mormon's protagonists are "pre-Christian Christians."[24]

At first, the Nephites honor the prophecies of Christ, whereas the bloodthirsty, shaven-headed, and dark-skinned Lamanites do not. As the year of Christ's birth approaches, though, many of the Lamanites convert, while the Nephites lapse into wickedness. At the time of Jesus's crucifixion in Jerusalem, there are great tribulations in the New World. Cities sink into the ground and the sea or burn to ashes. Whirlwinds snatch people into the air. Darkness covers the land. The survivors hear a voice: "many great destructions have I caused to come upon this land." The voice is that of "Jesus Christ, the Son of God," the one whom the prophets have long predicted. The people gather together, and the res-urrected Jesus descends out of heaven in a white robe and stands in their midst.[25] It is the climax of the entire scripture.

Jesus Christ Visits the Americas, by John Scott. (© by Intellectual Reserve, Inc.)

The Book of Mormon includes countless predictions of Jesus's grue-some suffering and crucifixion, but in the New World people only see the resurrected, glorified Lord. In the New Testament Gospel of John, the disciple Thomas overcomes his doubts by inspecting the wounds of the resurrected Jesus. In the Book of Mormon, multitudes come for-ward to feel his pierced side, hands, and feet. John Scott's mural painting *Jesus Christ Visits the Americas*, found in many Mormon meetinghouses, shows Jesus with outstretched palms, risen, triumphant, and resplendent.

After the people inspect his wounds and worship him, Jesus gives the prophet Nephi (a later Nephi, who lives long after Lehi's son of the same name) and eleven other disciples the authority to baptize. Jesus gives pre-cise instructions about the manner of baptism. Nephi must "stand in the water" and "immerse them in the water." Jesus instructs them that "there shall be no disputations among you" about baptism. In the Book of Mormon, baptism by immersion is a clear requirement for salvation: "whoso believeth in me, and is baptized, the same shall be saved . . . whoso believeth not in me, and is not baptized, shall be damned." Later pas-sages in the Book of Mormon condemn the practice of infant baptism as wicked, insisting that "all little children are alive in Christ" and need nei-ther baptism nor repentance to bring about their salvation.[26]

Jesus then preaches to the Nephites, repeating many of the messages he preached in Palestine, especially the Sermon on the Mount in the Gospel of Matthew. After these extended sermons, Jesus looks at the people, whose eyes are filled with tears because they want him to remain with them. In return, Jesus tells them that his "bowels is filled with compassion towards you." He asks for them to bring the sick, the lame, the blind. As in Jerusalem, Jesus heals many people. His compassion in the Book of Mormon, however, is more emotional, unrestrained, overflowing. "Bring them hither, and I will heal them," he invites, "for I have compassion upon you; my bowels is filled with mercy." In the New Testament, the sick often seek out Jesus. Here, he commands them to come or be brought. In the New Testament, Jesus rebukes those who would seek to keep children from him. Here, Jesus commands that the children be brought to him. He waits for them all to come. Jesus groans because of the "wickedness of the people of the house of Israel"; then he kneels and prays. When his prayers are finished, he is consumed with joy and weeps and then blesses the children. Afterward, he weeps again. A fire encircles the children, and angels minister to them.[27]

After making plain his love and compassion, Jesus teaches the people to eat bread and drink wine in a passage that resembles the Last Supper discourses found in the New Testament gospels of Mark, Matthew, and Luke. In all three of those texts, Jesus takes bread and then tells his disciples, "This is my body." In Third Nephi, Jesus instead commands them that "this shall ye do in remembrance of my body, which I have shewn unto you."[28] Catholics and others have used the phrase "this is my body" to argue for either transubstantiation (i.e., that the bread and wine become the body and blood of Jesus) or at least the "real presence" of Jesus Christ in the sacramental elements. By contrast, the Latter-day Saints have from the start maintained a strictly "memorialist" view of what they simply term "the sacrament." The sacrament prompts remembrance of Christ's sacrifice but does not actually contain his flesh or his presence.

Having healed and taught a multitude and having ordained his disciples with authority, Jesus ascends into heaven. The next day, however, while Nephi is baptizing "all they whom Jesus had chosen," Jesus reappears. He prophesies at length about the disciples' future and that of the Gentiles, and he informs them that he will eventually return in order to judge the world. The people ask him what they should call "this church." Jesus responds, "how be it my church save it be called in my name?" The people thus form the "church of Christ."[29]

Before his final ascension, Jesus asks his twelve disciples what they desire. Most ask that they might quickly enter his kingdom when they die in old age. Jesus promises them this shall occur when they attain the age of seventy-two. Three of them, however, refuse to state their wish, which is that they would "never taste of death," but live to witness all that Jesus has foretold. These three are caught up into the heavens, transfigured in glory, and are changed so that they will not suffer pain or sorrow in this world. They go forth, preaching and baptizing.[30]

En masse, the Nephites and Lamanites are "all converted unto the Lord," and a time of peace and prosperity ensues. "There were no robbers, nor no murderers," records another prophet, "neither were there Lamanites, nor no manner of Ites; but they were in one, the children of Christ, and heirs to the kingdom of God."[31] After two hundred years, this spiritual unity crumbles, and division between Nephites and Lamanites reemerges. Both peoples eventually slide into wickedness, and the stronger Lamanites wipe out the Nephites.

Within the context of early nineteenth-century American Protestantism, the ideas contained in the Book of Mormon were a mixture of the familiar and the novel. In one of the more striking departures from Protestant beliefs, the scripture predicts that shortly before Christ's Second Coming, the Lamanites—whom Latter-day Saints understood as the American Indians of their day—will become God's agent of judgment against the "Gentiles" who reject the gospel. The Book of Mormon foretells an apocalyptic reversal, as the Europeans who had decimated Indian populations and expelled the survivors from their lands would receive the ultimate comeuppance. "The Father hath commanded me that I should give unto you this land," Jesus Christ promises when he appears to the Nephites. Furthermore, he warns that "if the Gentiles [Americans of European descent] do not repent. . . . Thy hand shall be lifted up upon thine adversaries, and all thine enemies shall be cut off." Elsewhere, Jesus says that "my people" will "tread them down." Redeemed Lamanites and those few others who join Christ's true church would build God's New Jerusalem, the new city of Zion, in North America. As the nineteenth century proceeded, some Mormon leaders continued to take seriously the idea of Indians as God's agents of vengeance. "He'll yet go forth and from his thicket den," wrote the Latter-day Saint poet Eliza R. Snow, "As a young lion, prowl on guilty men—The scourge of justice—vengeance' rod, he'll be, And smite with fearful, savage cruelty." Although the idea of a Mormon-Indian alliance frightened the U.S. government and many non-Mormon western settlers, few Indians were interested in signing up for the role.[32]

Several other Book of Mormon teachings about Jesus Christ were distinctive, such as those that Jesus Christ had a premortal spiritual body, that ancient prophets and peoples possessed detailed knowledge of Jesus Christ long before his birth, and that the postresurrection Jesus made appearances beyond Palestine.[33] The latter two ideas supported a key tenet of the Book of Mormon: human beings in every age and place find salvation in the same way. The Book of Mormon's Jesus Christ is the Lord for all people in all places through all time, and people can read of him in many books. "And because my words shall hiss forth," God explains mockingly, "many of the Gentiles shall say, A Bible, a Bible, we have got a Bible, and there cannot be any more Bible." God remonstrates that "there are more nations than one" and that all peoples merit divine revelation. All of those revelations, however, point human beings toward the same Lord and the same Christ.[34]

American Protestants of Joseph Smith's lifetime agreed that human salvation hinged on faith in Jesus Christ and on his death and resurrection. Beyond that, however, Protestants were bitterly divided about the scope and mechanics of salvation. Mormons joined a host of other mid-nineteenth-century Americans in a fierce rejection of the Calvinist doctrine of election, in which God chooses to save a limited number of elect individuals with a grace they could not even choose to resist. Growing numbers of Americans argued that all human beings could choose to accept or reject God's universal offer of salvation, a belief associated with the Dutch theologian Jacob Arminius and embraced by Methodism and other rapidly growing denominations. At the same time, whether Calvinist or Arminian, most American Protestants sharply contested the teaching of Universalists, who contended that *all* would be saved in the end.

The Book of Mormon's strong sense of human agency and its emphasis on the need for believers to persevere in their faith correlates well with Arminianism, at least in a shared rejection of Calvinist arbitrariness.

Lehi, the scripture's founding patriarch, teaches that because of Jesus Christ's redemptive work, all human beings are "free forever, knowing good from evil; to act for themselves and not to be acted upon." Men and women are free to choose or reject God's offer of salvation. Indeed, the Book of Mormon's exuberant declaration of human free will extends far beyond what most Methodists would have allowed. It asserts that all individuals have the freedom to choose between good and evil, whereas most Methodists would have more thoroughly insisted upon the depravity of human beings prior to their conversion.[35]

The Book of Mormon also repudiates the Calvinist teachings that God's elect cannot resist divine grace and that the elect will necessarily persist in their faith until the end of their lives. For Methodists and other opponents of Calvinism, it was crucial that men and women chose to endure in their faith as part of their response to God's grace. The Book of Mormon Jesus teaches his Nephite disciples that "nothing entereth into his [God's] rest save it be those who have washed their garments in my blood, because of their faith, and the repentance of all their sins, and their faithfulness unto the end." Elsewhere, Jesus promises that "unto him that endureth to the end will I give eternal life." Should they choose to repent, believers must persevere in their faith—an ongoing choice—in order to obtain salvation.[36]

The Book of Mormon rejects Universalism. For example, the first prophet Nephi explains that an "awful Hell" is "the final state" of wicked souls. Curiously, one year prior to the Book of Mormon's publication, Joseph Smith had dictated a revelation—one of scores of divine messages that came through the Mormon prophet during the church's early years—in which Jesus Christ cautioned that "it is not written, that there shall be no end to this torment" and explained that the phrase "eternal damnation" was intended to "work upon the hearts of the children of men."[37] The revelation's suggestion of probationary suffering resembled the teachings of some Universalists. The Book of Mormon itself, however, makes no such allowance. Later Mormon revelations would embrace ideas such as various degrees of heavenly glory, a much less populous hell, and the idea that those who die without hearing the gospel receive an opportunity while they reside in a "spirit prison." These theological developments, however, are also absent from the Book of Mormon.[38]

Finally, the Book of Mormon reflects a Christian Trinitarianism with a twist. A prophet named Abinadi refers to Jesus as "being the Father and the Son; the Father, because he was conceived by the power of God; and the Son, because of the flesh; thus becoming the Father and the Son." "They are one God," Abinadi affirms, "yea, the very Eternal Father of heaven and earth." That same prophet encourages his listeners to teach the people "that redemption cometh through Christ the Lord, which is the very Eternal Father." A similar identification of Jesus Christ as Father and Son appears elsewhere. For example, Jesus tells Jared's brother that he is "the Father and the Son."[39]

Some interpreters of the Book of Mormon find in such passages a resemblance to the teachings of Sabellius,[40] an obscure third-century theologian who contended that the Father, Son, and Holy Spirit were three successive divine manifestations (this school of thought is also called monarchianism or modalism), as opposed to three distinct and eternal "persons," of a single god. The church councils that helped establish the bounds of orthodox belief for most Christian churches rejected such ideas. For the bishops who prevailed at Nicaea and Constantinople, the three persons of the Trinity were both united and distinct.

As in the New Testament, the Book of Mormon's Jesus is distinct from God the Father. After all, while among the Nephites, he prays "unto the Father."[41] Yet in the Book of Mormon there is more of an emphasis on the unity between God the Father and Jesus Christ than on a distinction between the two. In fact, the Book of Mormon's emphasis on divine unity contrasts with Joseph Smith's later understanding of a plurality of gods and his corresponding insistence that the Father and Son are two separate divine beings. In any event, while early Protestant critics lodged many complaints about the Book of Mormon (most often without having read it), none took issue with its descriptions of the Trinity. The scripture's repeated identification of the "Son" with "the Father" reflects the Book of Mormon's unbridled and enthusiastic insistence on Jesus Christ's divinity.

For earlier generations of American Protestants, God the Father, the Lord God Almighty, had been the fulcrum of worship and prayer. For antebellum evangelicals, by contrast, Jesus was the center of religious thought and devotion. "The upshot of this passionate piety," writes historian Richard Fox, "was to minimize the importance of sharp boundaries between Father, Son, and Holy Spirit, and allow 'Jesus' to function as an umbrella term for all three. . . . The Father slipped increasingly into the shadows and the Holy Ghost into a derivative position as the emanation of the Son's spirit."[42] A few voices dissented from this fixation on Jesus Christ. Unitarian preachers such as William Ellery Channing objected that untoward Christian devotion to Jesus was "taking from the Father the supreme affection, which is his due, and transferring it to the Son."[43] Channing complained that most Protestants made Jesus so attractive and vivid that they almost inevitably distracted individuals from the true object of worship, the divine Father. The Jesus-centered piety of evangelicals was to Channing an especially dangerous form of idolatry. Unitarians revered Jesus for his humanity and moral example, but only the Father was the eternal God.

Though they never departed from a robust affirmation of Jesus's divinity, later generations of Mormons came to share some of Channing's concern. For example, twentieth-century Latter-day Saint apostle Bruce McConkie criticized the idea that church members should cultivate a personal relationship with Jesus Christ. The church teaches its members to pray only to their Heavenly Father in the name of Jesus Christ, not directly to the Son of God. Latter-day Saints worship God the Father.

In the Book of Mormon, however, Jesus Christ is the practical center of the Trinitarian godhead. Although Jesus teaches the Nephites to pray "always unto the Father in my name," his disciples also "pray unto Jesus, calling him their Lord and their God."[44] The Book of Mormon rejects any diminution of Jesus's divinity. Indeed, its title page announced that its purpose was "the convincing of the Jew and Gentile that JESUS is the CHRIST, the ETERNAL GOD, manifesting Himself unto all nations." The Book of Mormon presents Jesus as the fully divine Son of God who atoned for humanity's sin with his blood and stood ready to receive anyone who believed in him and was baptized into his church.

At the end of the Book of Mormon, Moroni's parting words maintain that individuals seeking salvation and sanctification will find it in Jesus Christ:

> Yea, come unto Christ, and be perfected in him, and deny
> yourselves of all ungodliness; and if ye shall deny yourselves
> of all ungodliness, and love God with all your might, mind
> and strength, then is his grace sufficient for you, that by his
> grace ye may be perfect in Christ . . . then are ye sanctified
> in Christ by the grace of God, through the shedding of the
> blood of Christ, which is in the covenant of the Father,
> unto the remission of your sins, that ye become holy
> without spot.[45]

Had it come from John Wesley rather than through Joseph Smith, Moroni's message of salvation and holiness might have warmed the hearts of American Methodists. Thus, despite the faith's apparent novelty, there was more resonance than dissonance between the Jesus of the Book of Mormon and the Jesus of many early nineteenth-century American Protestants.

In March 1830, five thousand copies of the Book of Mormon emerged from E. B. Grandin's printer's shop in Palmyra. Early the next month, Joseph Smith and a small group of followers established what they at first simply called the Church of Christ. A few of Smith's family and friends tried to sell Smith's book, asking as much as $2.50, a steep sum for a book at the time. "The Books will not sell for no Body wants them," lamented Martin Harris, who had mortgaged his farm to finance the book's publication over his wife's opposition. Finding few takers, missionaries quickly resorted to giving them away. News of the "Gold Bible" spread quickly, though. Even if they had no interest in buying the Book of Mormon, many Americans found the book and its prophet author an irresistible curiosity.[46]

At the same time, some Protestant clergy quickly denounced the Book of Mormon as a naked fraud. Ironically, one argument raised against the book was its anachronistically Christian theology. The Christian reformer Alexander Campbell denounced the Book of Mormon precisely on that score. "[The prophet] Mormon was very orthodox," Campbell commented, because he affirmed that Jesus "was the very Christ and the very God." Campbell objected because the Book of Mormon "represents the christian institution as practiced among [ancient] Israelites." Campbell, an early Protestant critic of what he termed "imposture" and "delusion," observed that the "Nephites, like their father, for many generations were good christians, believers in the doctrines of the Calvinists and Methodists, and preaching baptism and other christian usages hundreds of years before Jesus Christ was born!" Many antebellum American Protestants read Christianity into the Old Testament, through typology and prophecy, but for Campbell, the explicit presence of Jesus Christ and Christian believers among ancient Israelites contravened biblical history. Campbell, moreover, criticized the Book of Mormon for taking sides in the intra-Protestant debates of the early nineteenth century. He mockingly observed that the Book of Mormon included "every error and almost every truth discussed in New York for the last ten years . . . [and] decides all the great controversies." Among them, Campbell continued, were "infant baptism, ordination, the trinity, regeneration, repentance, justification, the fall of man, the atonement, transubstantiation," and many more. For an opponent like Campbell, such apparent anachronisms served as proof of the Book of Mormon's fraudulency.[47]

For the small number of men and women that accepted the divine basis of the Book of Mormon, by contrast, the new scripture confirmed the truth of the Bible's message about Jesus Christ. Conversions to Mormonism did not closely resemble evangelical conversions, which typically began with an intense time of confession and repentance followed by an emotional assurance of Christ's saving love. Most converts to Mormonism already understood Jesus Christ as their savior. Thus, their embrace of Mormonism involved the acceptance of the Book of Mormon as a true, ancient record, of the Church of Christ as their savior's true church, and of the requirement of baptism by immersion. Converts had diverse religious backgrounds, including unchurched but pious Christian seekers and skeptics who felt that existing churches failed to meet their standards of rationality. Significant numbers came from two groups: radical Methodists who appreciated the expanded practice of spiritual gifts within early Mormonism, and the Reformed Baptists, a small group influenced by Alexander Campbell and Walter Scott's call for the restoration of a New Testament, or "primitive," Christianity in part through the rejection of creeds.[48]

Joseph Smith himself recounted that he had been "somewhat partial to the Methodist sect,"[49] and Brigham Young and his siblings participated in splinter Methodist churches prior to their 1832 baptisms into the Church of Christ. Many less prominent Latter-day Saints also traced their religious roots to various forms of Methodism. Mary Ann Brown converted to Mormonism in 1832. She grew up in a strict Methodist family, raised by parents who kept the Sabbath day, worked hard, and expected their daughter to adhere to a rigid code of morality. Her central New York community did not yet have a local Methodist minister; itinerant circuit riders visited every two weeks. At the age of thirteen, Brown expressed her desire to join the Methodist church, and after a six-month probationary trial, she was admitted into full fellowship. Presumably she had been baptized as an infant, but she felt that she needed to be baptized now that she was of age and had made a decision to join the church. She asked the itinerant preacher. He told her he did not consider baptism to be a "saving ordinance." She could be baptized to satisfy her conscience, but it would have no bearing on her salvation. Brown disagreed, and she thought that the Bible taught baptism by immersion. Some Methodist preachers would have acceded to a convert's wishes on this point, but hers did not. The itinerant insisted that Jesus himself had only kneeled in the water. At her baptism, Brown recalled, the minister "Stood on the bank" while she kneeled in the water. He "did not wet his feet." She left unsatisfied.[50]

A few years after Mary Brown's baptism, she married Zerah Pulsipher. In the early 1830s, she wrote, "We hapened to See the book of mormon we borowed it read and believed it but did not know anyt[h]ing more about it." When a "mormon preacher come," she recounted, "He told us how the book was found and translated he knew it to be a true r[e]cord we went to hear him preach he Sa[i]d, Baptism by immersion was the only right way it was for the remission of Sins." Mary Brown Pulsipher's response was simple: "that looks right." She was baptized by immersion on a very cold day, and she emerged from the water convinced that God in the process had cured her of a bout of rheumatism. "The Spirit of the lord was there," she recalled. "We Sung praid and

Zerah and Mary Ann Brown Pulsipher. (Photograph by George Edward Anderson.
Courtesy of the Church History Library, The Church of Jesus Christ of Latter-day Saints.)

praised God together." Her husband Zerah was also baptized. The
Book of Mormon had not introduced the Pulsiphers to Jesus Christ or
to Christianity. Instead, it had pointed them to a church whose practices they had long sought.[51]

Parley Parker Pratt was a Reformed Baptist prior to his Mormon conversion. Although revivalism characterized some branches of Christian
primitivism, Pratt had been more inclined toward rational reflection than
evangelical emotion. He had never had an experience of conversion, but
he had become convinced of the necessity of baptism for salvation, and
he believed that the millennium was imminent. When Pratt first obtained a copy of the Book of Mormon in 1830, he read it all day and into
the night. "The Spirit of the Lord came upon me," he recalled a quarter-
century later, "while I read, and enlightened my mind, convinced my
judgment, and riveted the truth upon my understanding, so that I knew
that the book was true." Pratt was thrilled with the new scripture's
teaching that the resurrected Jesus Christ had appeared "to the people
in America in ancient times." The Book of Mormon, he proclaimed,
"does contain the fulness of the Gospel as revealed to them by a cruci-

fied and risen Redeemer." Within days of laying eyes on the Book of Mormon, Pratt was baptized.[52]

Other converts came from religious backgrounds even further removed from antebellum revivalism. Eli Gilbert was an elderly Universalist, believing—as had Joseph Smith's paternal grandfather—that all men and women would be saved. When Gilbert's son sent him a copy of the Book of Mormon, the father found that it "bore hard upon . . . [his] favorite notions of universal salvation." The Book of Mormon foresaw damnation for those who rejected Jesus Christ. Still, Gilbert compared the new volume to the Bible "and found the two books mutually and reciprocally corroborate each other." "I felt if I let go the book of Mormon," Gilbert explained, "the bible might also go down by the same rule." In particular, Gilbert took comfort in the harmony between Jesus Christ's ministry in Jerusalem and in the New World. "[D]id he not truly do these things here," Gilbert asked, "as he did the same in Jerusalem before his resurrection?" For many early converts, the very familiarity of the Book of Mormon's depiction of Jesus Christ bolstered its claims.[53]

In July 1831, twenty-five-year-old schoolteacher William McLellin heard of the arrival of two "*quear* beings" near his home in eastern Illinois. They were missionaries. McLellin saddled his horse and hurried to a "beautiful sugartree grove" where the "strange preachers" were to speak. During his brief adulthood, McLellin had lived a peripatetic existence, traveling from state to state, teaching school. McLellin's wife had died recently, in labor with the couple's first child. The young widower mourned his wife's death and endured "many lonesome & sorrowful hours." McLellin's religious affiliation and beliefs to this point are unknown.

After McLellin reached the meeting at the grove, missionaries Harvey Whitlock and David Whitmer held up the Book of Mormon, which they claimed was a "Revelation from God." Whitlock spoke about the "Signs of the times" that suggested Jesus Christ's return was imminent, and Whitmer testified that a "Holy Angel" had made known to him the truth of the record. McLellin found their message unusual but captivating. Whitlock, he wrote in his journal, "expounded the Gospel the plainest I thot that I ever heard in my life."

The young schoolteacher invited the missionaries to preach in his town the next day and soon spent a night with them. He noted the solemnity of their manner and "the plainness of the truths which they declared." McLellin then decided to accompany the traveling elders to Jackson County, Missouri, in order to meet Joseph Smith, "the man who translated the book" and a man the missionaries spoke of as "a Prophet." Along the way, McLellin bought his own copy of the Book of Mormon and began to read it. When he reached the town of Independence, Missouri, the locals told him that the "Mormonites" were "generally a very honest people but very much deluded by Smith." McLellin ignored the warning.

On August 19, McLellin spent four hours in the woods talking with Joseph Smith's brother Hyrum about the origins of this new church. The next morning McLellin woke early and prayed that God would direct him to the truth. He soon concluded that he was "bound as an honest man to acknowledge the truth and Validity of the book of Mormon and also that I had found the people of the Lord—The Living Church of Jesus Christ." McLellin experienced spiritual euphoria at a prayer meeting the next evening. "I really felt happy," he wrote, "that I had seen the day that I could meet with such a people and worship God in the beauty of Holiness, For I saw more beauty in Christianity now than I ever had seen before." McLellin had found Christ's true church and another ancient history of humanity's savior. "I was bound to believe the book of Mormon to be a divine Revelation," he wrote in a letter the next year, "and the people to be christians." Hyrum Smith baptized McLellin after breakfast on August 20.

A few days later, McLellin learned that it was his duty to follow the example of those who had introduced him to the Book of Mormon. He was ordained an elder and went forth to share "the glorious Gospel of the great Redeemer." In 1835, McLellin became one of the original members of his new church's Quorum of the Twelve Apostles. His missionary work continued that spring; McLellin preached frequently on the "coming forth of '*the book*.'" The next year, McLellin became disaffected with Joseph Smith's leadership, and a church council excommunicated him in 1838. Despite McLellin's apostasy, he never lost his belief in the authenticity of the Book of Mormon as an ancient, inspired record.

"When a man goes at the Book of M[ormon]," he wrote in 1880, "he touches the apple of my eye."[54]

As the experiences of McLellin and others illustrate, from the church's earliest years the Book of Mormon was a key proselytizing tool, presented as miraculous evidence that God had restored Christ's church. Literate individuals often read the book, or at least parts of it, at the time of their conversion. The book itself served as the preeminent sign of restored revelation, that God the Father and Jesus Christ were again speaking as they had spoken to the ancients and to the earliest Christians, in this case through the prophetic figure of Joseph Smith.[55]

The book left an imprint on the church and its members in many other ways as well. Other Americans referred to church members as "Mormonites" and then "Mormons." Church members initially regarded such nicknames as pejorative, but the latter term stuck. Some church members named their sons after Book of Mormon prophets. Louisa Beaman, a plural widow of Joseph Smith and then wife of Brigham Young, named two of her infants Moroni and Alma. (The Book of Mormon has few female characters, none of them significant.) Following their 1846 exodus to the American West, Mormons used the scripture to name settlements, including Lehi, Nephi, Bountiful, and Manti. In 1849, Mormon leaders in the Salt Lake Valley established the independent state of Deseret, a Book of Mormon word for "a honey bee."[56] Even after the Compromise of 1850 replaced Deseret with the Utah Territory, Latter-day Saints named institutions and companies after Deseret. Thus, in very visible ways, the Book of Mormon shaped the identity of Joseph Smith's early followers.

On a deeper level, during the early 1830s in particular the Book of Mormon's predictions about the conversion of the Lamanites, the future establishment of Zion, and the imminent judgment preceding Christ's return directly shaped the church's activities. Even after the church's early millenarian fervor waned, the Mormon identification of American Indians as Lamanites persisted for generations.

Nevertheless, especially after the church's first several years, the scripture exercised relatively little direct influence on early Mormon thought and practice. Church leaders, including Joseph Smith, rarely quoted or alluded to the Book of Mormon, whereas their sermons overflowed with biblical language.[57] William McLellin, for instance, regularly preached about New Testament passages and used their congruence with the Book of Mormon to contend for the latter's truth. Nineteenth-century Mormon leaders spoke with some frequency about the Book of Mormon's significance, but they seldom discussed its contents.[58]

There are several reasons for the church's early relative neglect of its founding scripture. Latter-day Saints, like other Protestant Americans, grew up in a "Bible-drenched" culture, and their rhetoric and writing remained steeped in the language and ideas of the King James text.[59] The Book of Mormon is a long, complex volume, and early Latter-day Saint leaders did not encourage church members to read it devotionally. Also, while Joseph Smith never produced another scripture akin to the Book of Mormon in either length or complexity, he brought forth a torrent of further revelation and scripture during the several years following its publication. Especially during the very early years of the church, there was always new revelation that demanded church members' attention and adherence.

By the start of the twentieth century, the flood of formal revelation had slowed. Church leaders were no longer bringing forth new revelations with any frequency. At the same time, Latter-day Saints published illustrated versions of the Book of Mormon for young church members, and church periodicals began introducing members to its narratives and teachings on a more regular basis. Correspondingly, the Book of Mormon steadily grew in importance as an influence on Mormon thought and culture over the course of the twentieth century.

In 1982, the church appended "Another Testament of Jesus Christ" as a subtitle to the Book of Mormon. The church also arranged the publication of its own edition of the King James Bible through Cambridge University Press, replete with exhaustive cross-references to the Book of Mormon, Doctrine and Covenants (the revelations of Joseph Smith and subsequent church leaders), and Pearl of Great Price (a short volume containing five writings that are also scripture for Latter-day Saints). The church then published these four cross-referenced "Standard Works" within a single volume, now colloquially known as the "Quad," short for

"Quadruple Combination." In an October 1982 General Conference talk, Apostle Boyd Packer explained the new editions and the new subtitle as the fulfillment of Ezekiel's prophecy that the "stick of Judah" (per Mormon interpretation, the Old and New Testaments) and the "stick of Ephraim" (the Book of Mormon) would one day become "one stick." All of the scriptures, Packer explained, were "now woven together in such a way that as you pore over one you are drawn to the other." Packer further announced that the "entire curriculum of the Church" had been revised so studies for all age groups would "center on the scriptures, on Jesus Christ." Packer hoped that this massive preparation of Christ-centered resources would respond to those who refused to accept that Latter-day Saints are Christians.[60]

The new "Another Testament" subtitle was added in the midst of ongoing evangelical criticism of Mormonism as a non-Christian or anti-Christian cult. At the above-mentioned October 1982 General Conference, Robert E. Wells countered such accusations. "This is the Church of Jesus Christ of Latter-day Saints," Wells stated. "We are Christians." He argued that the Latter-day Saint Restoration had simply added more knowledge and light to the repository of faith shared by other Christians. "We have the Book of Mormon," he explained, "which is another testament of Jesus Christ. . . . Can anyone doubt that we are Christians in the full sense of the word?" In its blanket condemnation of other churches as "the church of the Devil," the Book of Mormon has symbolized the LDS Church's rejection of and separation from existing forms of Christianity. Wells and Packer, though, used the founding Mormon scripture precisely as evidence of their church's inherently Christian identity.[61]

Also in the 1980s, church leaders began placing a major ecclesiastical emphasis upon the regular reading and study of the Book of Mormon as a means whereby church members could obtain a deeper knowledge of and communion with their savior. Ezra Taft Benson, church president from 1985 to 1994, did much to advance this effort. An ardent Mormon Cold War-era anticommunist, Benson believed that the study of the Book of Mormon inoculated Latter-day Saints from the dangers of communism and other secular ideologies and foretold a grand divine destiny for the United States. Most of all, however, he maintained that the

Book of Mormon brought individuals to a knowledge of Jesus Christ. At the church's October 1987 General Conference, the eighty-eight-year-old church president delivered an emphatic discourse on the centrality of Jesus Christ in the Book of Mormon. Benson noted that more than half of all of the Book of Mormon's verses contain a reference to Jesus Christ. Benson taught that the Book of Mormon helped individuals become "committed to Him [Jesus Christ], centered in Him, and consumed in Him." Benson reminded church members that Joseph Smith had termed the Book of Mormon the "keystone of our religion," and he urged them to read from it every day. With the constant encouragement and prodding of their leaders, today's Latter-day Saints approach the Book of Mormon in roughly the same way that evangelical Protestants approach the Bible. Increasing numbers of Latter-day Saints use the scripture for private and family devotions, in marked contrast to their ancestors' more exclusive reliance upon the Bible for such exercises.[62]

Benson also called on Latter-day Saints to "flood the earth with the Book of Mormon." Church members have answered that call. Annually, nearly 100,000 Latter-day Saint missionaries volunteer their time to "further the work." The church's current missionary guide, *Preach My Gospel*, strongly affirms the centrality of the Book of Mormon as "the keystone of our religion." *Preach My Gospel* presents the Book of Mormon as "evidence of the divinity of Christ" and "proof of the Restoration through the Prophet Joseph Smith," although, for the most part, Latter-day Saint missionaries convert individuals already inclined to believe the former. *Preach My Gospel* carefully discusses the relationship between the Book of Mormon and the Bible. The guide observes that people hold many different beliefs about the Bible, some viewing it as inerrant in all respects and others understanding it as merely another piece of ancient literature. Quoting the church's 1842 Articles of Faith, the guide reminds missionaries that Latter-day Saints "believe the Bible to be the word of God as far as it is translated correctly," while the Book of Mormon is simply "the word of God." While *Preach My Gospel* asserts that missionaries "should use the Book of Mormon and the Bible to support one another," it emphasizes the superior reliability and utility of the scripture brought forth by Joseph Smith. "Give priority to Book of Mormon passages when you teach," it instructs, "but also show how the Book of Mormon and the Bible teach the same principles." Mormon missionaries indefatigably take the Book of Mormon—now translated into nearly one hundred languages—to prospective converts around the world.[63]

Benson reminded church members that while the Book of Mormon testifies to the divinity, atonement, and resurrection of Jesus Christ, it also witnesses to the truth of the 1830 restoration of Christ's true church. If "the Book of Mormon be true," Benson maintained, "then one must accept the claims of the Restoration and all that accompanies it." If the Book of Mormon really is an ancient record, he reasoned, using a standard Latter-day Saint missionary argument, Joseph Smith was a prophet. The Church of Jesus Christ of Latter-day Saints, then, is Christ's true church. The point of the Book of Mormon, per Benson and other Mormon leaders, is not merely to teach individuals about Jesus Christ or help them form a personal bond or relationship with the Christian savior. The point is to bring people into the LDS Church, the only place in which they can find the "fulness of the Gospel of Jesus Christ." For Latter-day Saints, therefore, the Book of Mormon simultaneously bears witness to Jesus Christ and to the truth of the LDS Church and the authority of its prophets. It affirms Mormon Christianity and Mormon distinction.[64]

During the nearly two centuries since the publication of the "Gold Bible," the main branches of Mormonism have at various times mirrored and departed from the Book of Mormon's almost single-minded focus on Jesus Christ. The figure of Jesus Christ was not as central to the theological ideas and rituals Joseph Smith introduced in the last several years of his life. Nor did Brigham Young's theological reflections revolve most intensely around the Son of God. Still, subsequent church leaders revived the christocentricity of Mormonism's earliest years. Young's immediate successor, John Taylor, published a book on Jesus Christ's atoning death, and by the early twentieth century Jesus Christ was at the forefront of Mormon thought and devotion. The church's overriding emphasis on Jesus Christ has continued to increase in recent decades. Indeed, the Book of Mormon has served as christocentric ballast for Mormon theology and devotion. Any church that gives sustained attention to the Book of Mormon as an inspired scripture would be hard pressed to drift away from the divinity of Jesus Christ and his centrality for human salvation.

Indeed, the Book of Mormon reveals much about the relationship between Mormonism and Christianity. Here is an appropriate place to return to the analogy between early Mormonism and early Christianity discussed in the introduction. Early Christians differentiated themselves from Judaism in part through the compilation of scriptures centered on the figure of Jesus. The Book of Mormon also sets Mormons apart from Protestants, Catholics, and all other Christians. Only the Book of Mormon, insists the LDS Church, contains the "fulness of the everlasting Gospel." Yet while Jewish motifs such as the temple remained significant themes in the New Testament, the early followers of Jesus did not compile scripture that revolved around Moses. Instead, they moved in decisive new directions. The Latter-day Saints, by contrast, have as the "keystone" of their religion a scripture that revolves around Jesus Christ, in which Jesus Christ repeats many of things he states in the New Testament gospels, and in which his role expands across time and place. Simply put, the Book of Mormon is a thoroughly Christian scripture. The Book of Mormon established a clear line of division between Mormons and other Christians, but at the same time it anchored the Latter-day Saints to the Christian savior.

CHAPTER TWO

✣

JESUS MEETS GENESIS

FEW IMAGES MORE APTLY illustrate Mormonism's complicated relationship to Christianity than that of a young prophet sitting down and marking corrections on the pages of a King James Bible.

Joseph Smith was a relentless organizer and innovator. Less than a year after the Book of Mormon's publication, Smith relocated from New York to northeastern Ohio, where scores of individuals had responded to the message of early Mormon missionaries. He traveled to the Missouri frontier, and he visited cities in the eastern United States. He directed missions, dictated revelations, introduced new ideas about priesthood, salvation, and the Second Coming. All the while, he presided over the growth of a Mormon community in Kirtland, Ohio.

Another project occupied him for three years after the church's founding. Smith "translated" the Bible. At the time, Smith did not know Greek or Hebrew. As with the Book of Mormon, however, Smith was not "translating" in any conventional sense. His was strictly an English-language project. Working his way through the King James Bible, he revised and expanded the text. He did so without scholarly resources. He did not own a stack of biblical commentaries. He did not consult learned theologians, ministers, or linguists. When he read the Bible, however, he believed some things were wrong and some things were missing. Thus, he produced his own text through revelation and inspiration.

Smith was not alone among his contemporaries in finding fault with the biblical text he inherited. Some Enlightenment-era thinkers, such as Thomas Paine in *The Age of Reason*, dismissed the Bible in its entirety as a collection of fables of dubious moral value (although he had not hesitated to employ biblical arguments against monarchy in his famed pamphlet *Common Sense*). Few Americans embraced Paine's wholesale rejection of the Bible, but during the first half of the nineteenth century a small number of American ministers and theologians embraced the first fruits of critical biblical scholarship in Europe, which questioned traditional beliefs such as the Mosaic authorship of the Pentateuch and the accuracy of biblical history.

For nearly all American Protestants, though, the Bible remained the trustworthy "word of God." It was a storehouse of facts, reliable in its history and credible in its report of miracles. Some Protestants specifically found fault with the King James Version, either because of its archaic language or because they found it insufficiently supportive of their own theologies. Several dozen nineteenth-century Americans published revisions of the King James text, for the most part to eliminate anachronisms of language. A few went a step further. For example, the Universalist Abner Kneeland published a parallel Greek-English New Testament in 1821 in which he refused to translate *aion* as "everlasting" or "eternal." He understood the Greek *aion* to mean "for an age" rather than forever in any infinite sense. Kneeland did not believe in God's eternal punishment of any human beings, so neither did his version of the New Testament.[1]

Joseph Smith was probably aware of Alexander Campbell's 1826 *The Sacred Writings of the Apostles and Evangelists of Jesus Christ, Commonly Styled The New Testament*, which used a new edition of the Greek New Testament in an attempt to get closer to the life-giving ideas expressed in the original Greek. The problem was that while the biblical languages were "dead," with only a superficial resemblance to contemporary Greek and Hebrew, languages such as English continued to change. Therefore, fresh biblical translations were needed to keep revelation accessible and alive.[2] At times, Campbell revised in accordance with his own theological positions. For example, Campbell rendered as "immersion" the Greek word typically translated as "baptism." John the Baptist became "John the Immerser."

Some Americans took offense at Campbell's translation, known among his followers as the "Living Oracles." One Virginia politician complained that "even the God of heaven cannot please this man, for he has a Bible all his own."[3]

Kneeland and Campbell were not the only Americans to want their own Bibles. For his private devotional use, Thomas Jefferson on two occasions created an account of Jesus's life and teachings out of the four canonical gospels. The second such attempt, *The Life and Morals of Jesus*, became known as the "Jefferson Bible." Employing a razor, scissors, and paste, Jefferson assembled his extractions in four parallel columns of Greek, Latin, French, and English. Ancient manuscripts and traditions of biblical scholarship were largely irrelevant to Jefferson, who proceeded on the basis of his own reason. Like other nineteenth-century biblical revisers, the Sage of Monticello did not hesitate to correct the linguistic infelicities of the King James, occasionally marking corrections on the pages themselves. More unusually, Jefferson extracted a set of passages shorn of most miracles, including the resurrection. Combining verses from the gospels of John and Matthew, Jefferson ended his *Life and Morals* abruptly: "There they laid Jesus, and rolled a great stone to the door of the sepulchre, and departed." Jefferson's intent was to separate "the gold from the dross," thereby preserving the content he found reasonable and edifying.[4]

Like Kneeland, Campbell, and Jefferson, Joseph Smith wanted to refine scripture's language and harmonize its contradictions. He too was comfortable with the idea of taking a pen and correcting the printed Bible. But instead of eliminating perceived theological additions like Jefferson, Smith envisioned a grand restoration of lost narratives and truths. In the Book of Mormon, an angel of the Lord asserts that through the "great and abominable church" (apostate Christians), "there are many plain and most precious things taken away from the Book, which is the Book of the Lamb of God."[5] Ancient narratives and truths were missing from the Bible. Thus, shortly after the Book of Mormon's publication, Smith began an attempt to restore those lost "plain and precious things." Whereas Jefferson subtracted according to the dictates of his reason, Smith inserted according to the fruits of his revelations. Smith added more gold instead of removing dross.

Portrait of Joseph Smith, by Sutcliffe Maudsley. (Courtesy of L. Tom Perry Special Collections, Harold B. Lee Library, Brigham Young University.)

Three months after the Book of Mormon's March 1830 publication, Smith dictated what his scribe Oliver Cowdery initially titled "A Revelation given to Joseph the Revelator."[6] In this text, Moses is taken upon a mountain, sees God "face to face," and is transfigured by God's glory. God explains that Moses is "in similitude to mine only begotten and mine only begotten is and shall be [the Savior] for he is full of grace and truth."[7]

After the vision passes, Moses encounters Satan, who asks to be worshipped. Moses is not deceived. "I am a Son of God," he rejoins, "in the similitude of his only begotten, and where is thy glory that I should worship thee?" Satan lingers, repeatedly attempting to entice Moses into worshipping him. Finally, Moses commands Satan to depart in "the name of Jesus Christ." Satan weeps, wails, gnashes his teeth, and leaves. Moses then again sees God's glory, and God shows him a multitude of earths. God informs Moses that "by the word of my power have I created them which is mine only begotten Son." God, through Jesus Christ, has created "worlds without number." Why? God explains that his "work" and "glory" are to bring about "the immortality and the eternal life of man."[8]

Several New Testament passages describe God's work of creation as proceeding through Jesus Christ. For example, the Gospel of John asserts that "all things were made by him, and without him was not any thing made that was made."[9] Smith made Moses privy to such ideas. Israel's lawgiver learns that God's "only begotten" was the agent of creation. He learns that he too is a son of God. This knowledge, moreover, enables him to resist Satan's wiles.

In the subsequent months, Smith proceeded with a redaction of the early chapters of Genesis. For instance, in a "Revelation concerning Adam after he had been driven out of the garden of Eden," an angel informs Adam that animal sacrifice "is a similitude of the sacrifice of the only begotten of the Father." God's "Son" then addresses the penitent first man and assures him that redemption is possible despite his sin. "[A]s thou hast fallen," he comforts Adam, "thou mayest be redeemed & all mankind."[10] The Son of God offers an opportunity for repentant human beings to find redemption.

Smith greatly expanded Genesis's brief reference to Enoch, a man who "walked with God: and he was not; for God took him."[11] Enoch figures prominently in rabbinical literature, and the New Testament makes several references to him. In a passage emphasizing the faith of the ancient patriarchs, the Epistle to the Hebrews explains that by "faith Enoch was translated that he should not see death; and was not found, because God had translated him: for before his translation he had this testimony, that he pleased God."[12] Here the word "translated" means transported or taken away. The epistle suggests that God rewarded Enoch's faith by immediately bringing him into God's presence in heaven, thus sparing him from having to experience death.

In Smith's expanded text, Enoch ascends a mountain, sees "the heavens open," and is "clothed upon with glory." "I saw the Lord," recounts Enoch, "he stood before my face and he talked with me, even as a man talketh one with another face to face." God sends Enoch to preach throughout the surrounding lands, baptizing those who repent in the name of the Father, Son, and Holy Ghost.[13]

While he travels and preaches, Enoch relates a dialogue between God and Adam after the latter's sin and expulsion from the Garden of Eden. God calls on Adam and instructs him that in order to be saved, men must "believe & repent of all their transgressions & be baptised even by water in the name of mine only begotten Son which is full of grace and truth which is Jesus Christ." God adds that the name of Jesus Christ is the "only name" that will bring salvation to human beings. Adam seeks to understand the need for repentance and baptism. "[Y]e must be born again of water & the spirit," God responds, "& cleansed by blood even the blood of mine only begotten into the mysteries of the kingdom of Heaven." The future death of Jesus has already "atoned for original guilt," the sin of Adam, and God's "only begotten" will cleanse all of those who repent of their sins. Adam learns that there is a single "plan of salvation unto all men the blood of mine only begotten which shall come in the maridian [meridian] of time." Adam obeys, is baptized, and becomes "a son of God." Smith's scribe wrote "the Plan of Salvation" on top of this manuscript page in order to denote its significance. In order to secure his salvation, Adam had to respond with faith, repentance, and baptism, just like individuals who lived in the time of Jesus, and like those living in the nineteenth-century United States.[14]

Enoch's preaching mission is successful, because God gives him great "power . . . of language." Enoch's converts fight battles against the wicked, and "the Lord" (here the title could mean either God the Father or Jesus Christ) comes and dwells with Enoch and his followers in a holy city. The Lord calls his people "Zion because they were of one heart and of one mind and dwelt in righteousness and there was no poor among them." Genesis records that God takes Enoch from the earth. In Smith's expanded text, the Lord takes the entire city of Zion into heaven and weeps over the remaining inhabitants of the earth, whom he plans to destroy in a flood save for the family of Noah.[15]

Finally, God shows Enoch a host of future events. He sees the "Son of man lifted up on the cross," which sets free the spirits of those righteous men and women who died prior to his incarnation. Enoch then sees a second gathering of God's elect at the time of the earth's final tribulation before Christ's return and millennial reign. He sees a wave of apocalyptic destruction but also the preparation of a second "holy City," a "New Jerusalem."[16] Enoch has seen the entire span of human history, from Adam to the Second Coming of Jesus Christ and his millennial reign on earth. He has witnessed the first city of Zion and the final New Jerusalem. And in all that Enoch sees, from Adam to the millennium, Jesus Christ plays a central role.

A "Prophecy of Enoch" appeared in several church publications between 1832 and 1835, and the figure of Enoch, the concept of Zion, and the millennial gathering of God's saints became important to the church's early development. Early Mormons believed that they were gathering to build the New Jerusalem to which Jesus Christ would return, and Mormon leaders called on church members to imitate the followers of Enoch in their holiness and unity. Other portions of the Genesis revisions appeared shortly before Smith's 1844 death, and his Utah-based ecclesiastical descendants published the Moses, Adam, Cain and Abel, and Enoch material in the 1851 Pearl of Great Price. Later editions of the Pearl of Great Price became a canonical volume of scripture for Latter-day Saints; in these, the revisions of the early chapters of Genesis appear together as "The Book of Moses."

The revision of Genesis evolved into a larger project. Soon Smith referred to his work as "translating the scriptures." In March 1831, Smith dictated a revelation in the words of Jesus Christ, who instructed him to "translate" the New Testament as well. For the next two years, he worked on the project intermittently, often directing his scribes to mark phrases requiring revision on the pages of a King James Bible he and Oliver Cowdery had purchased in 1829.[17] He undertook several significant expansions of the text, reordered other passages, and corrected still other verses for clarity, grammar, and theology. For the most part, the revisions were not as extensive as those to the early chapters of Genesis, but some books—such as the Gospel of John—received careful attention. In July 1833, Smith announced that he and his scribes had "finished the translation of the bible."[18]

In 1867, The Reorganized Church of Jesus Christ of Latter Day Saints (now Community of Christ) published *The Holy Scriptures, Translated and Corrected by the Spirit of Revelation*, later retitled the *Inspired Version*. The volume included the entirety of Smith's corrected King James text. At the time, the Reorganized Church was led by Smith's namesake son (Joseph Smith III), who was eleven years old at the time of his father's June 1844 murder. Along with Joseph Smith Jr.'s first wife Emma, those who eventually aligned themselves with the Reorganization rejected polygamy and, with it, Brigham Young's leadership. They maintained aspects of the founding Mormon prophet's legacy, shorn of many of his later innovations.

Other than what it included in the Pearl of Great Price, the Utah-based LDS Church paid little heed to Smith's translation, regarded with suspicion because of its publication by the Reorganized Church. Ironically, despite Smith's concerns about lost "plain and precious things" and his Bible revisions, the LDS Church has clung to the King James Bible. The church announced in 1992 that the King James would remain "the English language Bible used by The Church of Jesus Christ of Latter-day Saints."[19] Having been open to revision during Joseph Smith's lifetime, the Mormon Bible became fixed in the language and content of the King James. Nevertheless, Smith's Bible translation eventually gained a small foothold within his church. In 1979, when the church printed its own edition of the King James Bible, it included substantial excerpts from Smith's revisions as notes.

The LDS Church describes Joseph Smith as "a translator." As both the Book of Mormon and Bible translation project illustrate, however, Smith imbued "translation" with a meaning all his own. He translated not primarily through studying ancient languages. Instead, Smith revealed texts and restored their true meaning "by the gift and power of God." For him, translation meant revelation, and he understood his work as the restoration of lost or corrupted texts.

Smith did not limit himself to textual translation or revelation, though. The Mormon prophet found things to reveal almost everywhere he looked: in ancient burial mounds, on Egyptian papyri, in the ceremonies of Freemasonry, and—more than anywhere else—on the pages of the King James Bible. Smith rarely borrowed an insight or practice in its entirety. Instead, he appropriated and adapted what he valued. In this broad sense, Smith's entire prophetic career was one task of unending translation and revelation. Everything was always open to revision. And Smith tended to add rather than subtract.[20]

So it was with the King James Bible. Like Paine, Kneeland, and Jefferson, Joseph Smith concluded that the Bible as he had received it was flawed. The problem was not primarily anachronistic language, nor was it the accretion of superstition. Instead, what was missing from major portions of the Bible was Jesus Christ. Smith fused the Christian Old Testament with the New. Moses, Adam, and Enoch all learn about God's "only begotten" son. They hear his words. Adam is baptized. Enoch sees the Crucifixion and—millennia before Jesus's first advent—the Second Coming. In Smith's revised Bible, Jesus Christ is the fulcrum of creation and salvation throughout all scripture.

In one sense, Smith was doing what others had done in their readings of the Old Testament. From ancient bishops such as Irenaeus to American theologians like Jonathan Edwards, Christians had presumed that it was Jesus Christ who walked in the Garden of Eden or spoke to Moses from the burning bush. For Irenaeus and Edwards, though, such conclusions were matters of interpretation, not revelation.[21] They did not revise the texts to make explicit the presence of Jesus Christ in the Old Testament. Through his revelatory translations, by contrast, Joseph Smith directly inserted the preincarnate Jesus Christ into the narratives of the Christian Old Testament.

✣

CHAPTER THREE

SEEING THE SAVIOR'S FACE

THE MEN AND WOMEN who converted to Mormonism during the church's earliest years were not seeking a new or different Jesus. Many early Mormons, however, were seeking Jesus himself. They longed to see their Lord, not just in a future heaven, but on earth.

Joseph Smith promised that the saints of the "last days" would enjoy the same blessings as had the ancient patriarchs and the earliest Christians. Prophecy, speaking in tongues, miraculous healings, and visions were not confined to the pages of scripture. Instead, present-day believers could and should exercise such gifts. These expectations fostered expressions of ecstatic spirituality among Smith's first followers.

Newel Knight's conversion vividly illustrates early Mormonism's spiritual atmosphere. Almost thirty years of age at the time of the church's 1830 founding, Knight's adulthood had until that time been marred by setbacks. After marrying, he had moved out on his own and acquired a gristmill. Then he fell sick with consumption, sold out, and moved back home to Colesville, in south central New York State. There his father (Joseph Knight Sr.) became acquainted with Joseph Smith, hired Smith for occasional work on his farm, and provided the budding prophet with food and paper during his work on the Book of Mormon.[1]

The Knights had been Universalists, but they now contemplated a new scripture and Joseph Smith's prophetic leadership. In the weeks following the new church's founding, they spent long hours in conversation with Smith and attended church meetings. They believed, at least to a point, but they were hesitant to commit themselves. In particular, both Newel Knight and his father were loath to pray in front of others at meetings. Praying aloud served as a sign of faith and commitment; it signaled openness to divine intervention and instruction. It was a hurdle over which many hesitated to leap. The church's founding "Articles and Covenants" required elders to visit church members' homes and "exhort them to pray vocally and [as well as] in secret." Smith exhorted the Knights accordingly. Eventually, Newel Knight promised Smith that he would "try and take up his cross, and pray vocally." Yet his courage failed him again that evening.

The next morning, a dejected Newel Knight went into the woods to pray in solitude but found he could not. He realized "that he had not done his duty, but that he should have prayed in the presence of others." Feeling wretched and ill, he staggered home. His condition worsened: "His visage and limbs distorted and twisted in every shape and appearance possible to imagine; and finally he was caught up off the floor of the apartment and tossed about most fearfully." A small crowd gathered, and Joseph Smith came to his side. Knight begged the prophet "to cast the Devil out of him." Smith rebuked the devil in the name of Jesus Christ, and Knight reported seeing Satan leave him. Knight's afflictions ceased. The exorcism gained renown as the church's "first miracle."

Free of the devil, Knight now felt a divine spirit course through his body. "The visions of heaven were opened to my view," he related. After a short while, "I found that the Spirit of the Lord had actually caught me up off the floor . . . and that my shoulder and head were pressing against the beams." Knight was in a trance-like state. After he regained consciousness, he was so weak that those who were gathered in his home helped him to bed. Not surprisingly, after these dramatic spiritual experiences, Knight was baptized in late May. His father, his wife, and many other relatives followed suit.

Shortly after his baptism, the church (with about thirty members at the time) held a conference. Again, the heavens opened: "The Holy Ghost was poured out upon us in a miraculous manner, many of our number prophesied, others had the Heavens opened to their view, whilst several were so overcome that we had to lay them on beds." Newel Knight was again placed on a bed. It was a scene very much akin to evangelical camp meetings, at which new converts were sometimes placed on beds of straw to protect themselves during spiritual convulsions. While resting in a state of spiritual euphoria, Knight had "a vision of futurity" and "saw Heaven opened and beheld the Lord Jesus Christ, seated at the right hand of the majesty on high." Jesus assured Knight that he would one day spend eternity in his presence. When Knight and the others regained their bodily strength, they "rehearsed the glorious things which they had seen and felt, whilst yet in the Spirit."

About eight years later, Newel Knight narrated the above episodes to church clerks who were helping Joseph Smith compile a history. By then, the Latter-day Saints no longer reveled quite so much in ecstatic manifestations of the Spirit. Still, the history insisted that such visions were not tricks of overheated imaginations. Church members had "engaged in the very same order of things, as observed by the holy Apostles of old." To "witness and feel with our own natural senses," the history added, "the like glorious manifestations . . . combined to create within us, sensations of rapturous gratitude." Church members had heard and seen Jesus Christ with their ears and eyes.[2]

Mormonism remained a visionary faith throughout the nineteenth century. By the twentieth century, however, Mormon leaders urged church members to privilege their belief in Joseph Smith's earliest vision above a desire to see Jesus Christ for themselves.

Visions and dreams have a long pedigree within human religious experience, associated with mysticism, religious ecstasy, near-death experiences, healing, trances, hallucinations, and insanity. Some visions occur wholly unexpectedly, while others appear to be the fruit of spiritual disciplines (such as meditation, visualization, fasting, or the use of hallucinogens) designed to foster contact with supernatural beings or departed humans. Individuals sometimes interpret their dreams as visions, others experience visions while in a trance or state of semiconsciousness, while still others claim to have such experiences while fully awake.

There are many names and explanations for such experiences. Hallucinations. Delusions. Dissociation. Sensory overrides. The blessings of God or the wiles of the devil. The result of nutritional and sleep deprivation. Regardless of the source of visions, throughout human history, many people have seen and heard things that are not physically present.[3]

The Hebrew scriptures abound with dreams and visions. Abram (later Abraham) falls into a "deep sleep" and then experiences the fiery presence of the Lord. God appears to men such as Jacob and Solomon in their dreams. The prophet Ezekiel reports that while among the exiled Judeans in Babylon, "the heavens were opened, and I saw visions of God." Ezekiel sees a great cloud, full of light and fire, out of which come four living creatures with four faces each. The prophet then sees the "likeness of a throne," and upon the throne, "the likeness as the appearance of a man above upon it." All around the divine figure Ezekiel sees fire and brightness. The vision is intensely anthropomorphic, even mentioning "the appearance of his loins." Ezekiel, though, is careful to back away from the suggestion that he has seen God. He has seen "the appearance of the likeness of the glory of the LORD." Ezekiel falls upon his face in response.[4]

Visions and visionary dreams are also common in the New Testament. In the Book of Acts, a man named Saul dramatically converts to the faith of the Christians he had been persecuting. As he travels to Jerusalem, he is surrounded by "a light from heaven." He later describes its radiance as "above the brightness of the sun." A voice asks him, "Saul, Saul, why persecutest thou me?"[5] It is Jesus. Saul, soon known as Paul, became Christianity's most famous missionary. Although a vision had prompted his conversion, Paul was reticent about his own experience and wary about the visionary claims of others. His opponents and rivals in some churches used visions to bolster their own authority. In his second letter to the church at Corinth, Paul writes that he knew a Christian "caught up to the third heaven . . . and [who] heard unspeakable words, which it is not lawful for a man to utter." Most New Testament scholars believe that Paul is somewhat awkwardly writing about himself. Paul informs his readers that he does not know whether this vision of heaven occurred while he was "in the body" or "out of the body." While Paul allows that he gloried in this experience, he encourages Christians to not boast of private visions and revelations, but of being persecuted for Christ's sake. As Paul observed, it was not easy to sift the genuine from the counterfeit or demonic, not easy to separate fanciful illusions from edifying messages. Furthermore, dreams and visions could threaten ecclesiastical authority.[6]

The final book of the New Testament, the Book of Revelation, contains a series of visions. In it, a man named John on the island of Patmos repeatedly finds himself "in the Spirit" or carried "away in the Spirit."[7] In the first of many visions, John sees a majestic Jesus Christ with white wooly hair, brass feet, and a double-edged sword coming out of his mouth. The visions continue. John sees the Lord God Almighty on his throne surrounded by elders and angelic beings. He sees death-bringing horsemen, beasts, and a "mother of harlots." Eventually, he sees a holy city in which God and Jesus Christ ("the lamb") reign forever.

In the mid-second century, when a prophet Montanus appeared near the Asia Minor city of Philadelphia, he repeated John of Patmos's message with great urgency. Much like Ezekiel and John, Montanus explained that he spoke in God's name because he had been caught up "in the spirit." According to a later critic of the Montanists, another prophet named Quintilla (or Priscilla) related a vision in which Jesus Christ came to her in the form of a woman, clothed in a white robe. Most of the region's bishops, meanwhile, rejected the "new prophets." Farther away, Gaius, a Christian leader in Rome, opposed both the new prophets and the acceptance of John's Apocalypse. For Gaius, the age of prophecy had ended with the death of Jesus's apostles.[8]

Later generations of Christians repeated these debates about the validity of visions. While many church leaders still maintained that God or Jesus Christ on occasion appeared to human beings in visions, these experiences were reserved for persons of unusual spiritual merit, namely priests and ascetics. Nor would God reveal new teachings or knowledge about the end of the world through special visions. Instead, those few who could subdue their passions might receive a foretaste of the beatific vision—seeing the very essence of God—which the saints would enjoy in heaven. Despite the wariness of many European church leaders, visionary activity became common in medieval monastic settings. Monks cultivated visions through prayer, fasting, chanting, focusing upon visual objects (such as a crucifix or illuminated book), and by visualizing the life of Christ.[9] Many women in medieval religious orders reported visions of Jesus Christ, often stemming from practices of Eucharistic devotion.

The leading Protestant reformers of the sixteenth century looked askance at visions, partly because they associated them with the monastic religious culture they had rejected. Martin Luther, himself a former monk, believed that most visions originated with the devil rather than with God. The Genevan reformer John Calvin counseled that "oracles are not now sent from heaven, neither doth the Lord himself appear by visions."[10] Calvin and other Protestant leaders urged Christians to rely on the promises contained in the Bible instead of seeking personal encounters with God or Jesus Christ.

Some later Protestant leaders affirmed visionary claims, however. John Wesley reported that he knew "several persons in whom this great change [conversion] from the power of Satan unto God was wrought either in sleep, or during a strong representation to the eye of their minds of Christ, either on the cross or in glory." While others disputed the genuineness or value of such phenomena, Wesley insisted that visions of Jesus could turn sinners into Christians. Wesley knew that intra-Christian debates about visions stretched back to the earliest centuries of the church. In 1750, a few days after encountering a "poor old woman" who "having for several months . . . seen as it were the unclouded face of God," Wesley commented in his journal that the "Montanists in the second and third centuries were real, scriptural Christians."[11]

In the British colonies of North America, visionary activity accompanied the revivals that began in the mid-eighteenth century. Men and women saw Jesus Christ upon his throne, revealing to them that their names were written in the "book of life" described by John of Patmos. "Visions [are] the Main Subject of Conversation," commented one New England divine.[12] Jonathan Edwards, who presided over a religious awakening in Northampton and who defended the revivals despite their emotional excesses, cautiously advised that while visions could be the result of "overpowered" minds, they could also be the fruit of God's Holy Spirit.[13]

Many American ministers, however, regarded visions and revelations with intense suspicion. They were a sign of "enthusiasm" (at this time, the term meant fanaticism or delusion) and a potential challenge to established authority.[14] Influenced both by the Reformation's campaigns against many forms of popular Catholic spirituality and by the Enlightenment-era skepticism about supernatural claims, many Protestant leaders—akin to Gaius, the ancient Roman priest—believed that divine healings, prophecy, and other miracles had ended with the apostolic age. At the very least, ministers suggested that men and women should keep their dreams and visions to themselves. "No person is warranted from God," editorialized a writer in the 1805 *Connecticut Evangelical Magazine*, "to publish to the world the discoveries of heaven or hell which he supposes he has had in a dream, or trance, or vision." Individuals who have "remarkable views of the invisible world, in dreams or visions," should imitate Mary and "*keep all these things, and ponder them in their heart.*"[15] At the same time, ministers felt compelled to offer such admonitions because visions remained so prevalent.

During Joseph Smith's lifetime, visions of Jesus were common, especially in the nation's hinterlands and within the radical evangelical churches growing exponentially on the frontier. Charles G. Finney, who would become the nation's most renowned revivalist, had a series of visions surrounding his conversion. As of 1821, Finney was a twenty-nine-year-old aspiring lawyer living near the eastern shore of Lake Ontario in New York State. That October, troubled over the state of his soul, he resolved to pray in the woods until he had settled the matter. A biblical passage came to his mind while he prayed: "Then shall ye seek me and shall find me, when you search for me with all your heart." Finney believed that "it was God's Word, and God's voice, as it were, that spoke" to him. A host of biblical promises then came to him, which he "fastened upon . . . with the grasp of a drowning man." When he finally emerged from the woods hours later, his soul was filled with a "profound spiritual tranquility." He realized he had experienced conversion. He had heard God, and now he saw Jesus. That evening, Finney went into the back room of his office to pray. "There was no fire, and no light, in the room," he remembered, "nevertheless it appeared to me as if it was perfectly light." When Finney shut the door to the room, "it seemed as if I met the Lord

Jesus Christ *face to face.*" Jesus did not speak. The way he looked at Finney, though, prompted the lawyer to collapse, weep aloud like a child, and make confessions until the tears he shed bathed his savior's feet. Finney allowed that he was in "a most remarkable state of mind; for it seemed to me a reality that he stood before me." When the encounter ended, Finney returned to his front office, where he felt the Holy Spirit descend upon him "*like a wave of electricity.*" It was as if the "*breath of God*" baptized him, with waves of divine power rolling over his weeping and exulting body.[16]

Influenced by the account of Paul's conversion in the Book of Acts, many Protestants had visions of light "above the brightness of the sun" followed by visions of God the Father, Jesus, or both. A short time after his conversion, Finney found himself nearly knocked to the ground by a "light like the brightness of the sun." Those with Finney had not seen it. Finney could not bear to describe with words what he could only say was "the glory of God." "I *wept* it out," he later wrote. Many others employed the same metaphor. A Universalist minister named John Samuel Thompson, who in 1825 spent several months preaching at an academy in Palmyra, New York, once dreamed of Christ descending from heaven "in a glare of brightness, exceeding ten fold the brilliancy of the meridian Sun." Skepticism about visions reigned in some quarters, but many American Protestants claimed to have seen their savior.[17]

These biblical narratives, traditions of Christian spirituality, and debates helped shape the content of and reaction to Joseph Smith's visionary claims. After the visions that led to the Book of Mormon project, others followed. Smith saw biblical figures, such as John the Baptist, and heard the voices of Jesus's disciples Peter, James, and John. Sometimes, along with his followers, he saw God the Father and Jesus Christ. Of greatest significance for future generations of Latter-day Saints, Smith began telling church members and outsiders alike about an early vision, one that preceded the visit of the angel and the reception of the golden plates.[18]

In the summer of 1832, Smith wrote a brief account of his early life. In it, Smith's discussion of his early vision takes the shape of an evangelical coming-of-age narrative. The fifteen-year-old Smith is troubled by thoughts of sin and salvation. He mourns for his "own sins and for the sins of the world." There is nowhere for him to turn but to the Lord, because there is "no society or denomination that built upon the gospel of Jesus Christ as recorded in the new testament." Then, as in Paul's account of his conversion, Smith sees a light "above the brightness of the sun at noon day come down from above." As the heavens open, Smith sees "the Lord."

"Joseph my son thy sins are forgiven thee," the Lord announces. Then, the divine being identifies himself as Jesus Christ. "Behold I am the Lord of glory," he states, "I was crucifyed for the world that all those who believe on my name may have Eternal life." The Lord next expresses his dissatisfaction with his followers, complaining that "the world lieth in sin at this time." In words that echo those found in Isaiah and the gospels, Jesus laments that Christians draw near to him "with their lips while their hearts are far from" him.[19] The savior informs Smith that such hypocrites will soon suffer because of their sins. "Mine anger is kindling against the inhabitants of the earth to visit them according to their ungodliness," Jesus warns. Ancient prophecies will soon be fulfilled. "Lo I come quickly," he promises, "as it [is] written of me in the cloud clothed in the glory of my Father." In the brief message he has received, Smith has learned that Jesus Christ has forgiven his sins, will give eternal life to those who have faith in him, and will soon return to judge the wicked.

The vision thrills the young Smith, filling his "soul" with "love" and causing him to rejoice for many days. Then, though, his history departs from evangelical conventions. After this brief season of spiritual elation, Smith again falls into "transgressions." In Smith's 1832 history, a vision produces an unsuccessful conversion, followed by a deep spiritual despondency.[20]

In June 1832, shortly before he composed the above history, Smith, while traveling, wrote a letter to his wife Emma. "I have visited a grove which is Just back of the town almost every day," Joseph informed Emma, "where I can be secluded from the eyes of any mortal and there give vent to all the feelings of my heart." While praying in the woods, Smith contemplated his past shortcomings. He "shed tears of sorrow," he confided, "for my folly in Sufering the adversary of my Soul to have so much power over me as he has had in times past." Smith rejoiced, however, that God had forgiven his sins and sent the Holy Spirit to comfort him. Smith observed that because he had placed his life in God's hands he was "pre-pared to go at his Call." "I desire to be with Christ," he declared, "I count not my life dear to me only to do his will." In the summer of 1832, Smith had mourned over his sinfulness, prayed "in the wilderness," and received forgiveness for his sins. It is likely that Smith's times of prayer and his intense longing for Christ influenced the way he remembered and wrote about his youthful vision.[21]

In 1838, Smith began preparing a fuller and more polished history for publication. Again, he told the story of his early vision. This account begins rather differently. Smith prays not out of a concern over his own sinfulness but because he wants to know which church he should join. It then narrates an even more dramatic spiritual encounter. Similar to Newel Knight's struggle with Satan, when Smith begins to pray an evil power—an "actual being from an unseen world"—overcomes him and binds his tongue. As "thick darkness" gathers around Smith, he feels that he is "doomed to sudden destruction." Finally, as his desperation mounts, light appears. Two divine beings stand above him in the air.

"This is my beloved Son," says one being, pointing to the other. "Hear him." Smith, once he gets possession of himself, poses the ques-tion he intended to ask all along. Which church should he join? Jesus Christ's answer is that Smith should join none of them. There are sev-eral related reasons. Their creeds are an "abomination," and they are full of corrupt individuals who—as in the 1832 account—"draw near to me with their lips but their hearts are far from me." Echoing a passage in the New Testament Second Epistle of Timothy, Jesus adds that the churches "teach for doctrines the commandments of men, having a form of Godliness but they deny the power thereof." The churches do not teach true doctrines, and they lack spiritual power. Jesus forbids Smith from joining any of them. At the end of this narrative, Smith makes it clear that he was in a trancelike state during his vision. "When I came to myself again," the history concludes, "I found myself lying on my back looking up into Heaven." The encounter leaves him without any strength.[22]

The multiple and partly contradictory accounts raise many questions. Did Smith encounter only Jesus Christ, or Jesus and God the Father? Was Smith's chief concern his sinfulness or the churches' apostasy? Or

The First Vision, stained glass, ca. 1911–1912. Brigham City Third Ward Chapel, Brigham City, Utah. (© by Intellectual Reserve, Inc.)

did Smith from the start connect his personal quest for forgiveness with his search for a true church? Did Smith describe a discrete moment of spiritual transcendence seared into his consciousness, or did he imaginatively refashion his youthful spirituality to mesh more readily with his subsequent development?

Critics, faithful Mormons, and scholars have spent much time in re-cent decades parsing the various accounts of Smith's early vision, some using apparent contradictions to cast doubt on its validity and others finding consistencies to support the vision's authenticity. Answers to such questions remain speculative because of the sparse historical evidence. Visionaries, after all, claim to see things others cannot see. One does not have to accept their supernatural origin to acknowledge that, throughout human history, countless individuals have narrated such experiences, nor must one adhere to a methodological naturalism to acknowledge that Smith's memories of his earliest spiritual encounters evolved as his be-liefs and practices developed. The nexus between experience and memory is complicated.

In both accounts, much of Smith's visionary experience resembles that of his evangelical contemporaries. During revival meetings, some individuals received visions while tormented over the state of their souls, and in those visions Jesus often forgave their sins. Moreover, many American Protestants would have shared Christ's lament that "the world lieth in sin at this time and none doeth good no not one they have turned aside from the gospel."[23] The blanket condemnation of existing churches was not unusual. The early 1800s had given birth to a number of religious movements bent on restoring the teachings, practices, and ecclesiastical structure of the New Testament church in its primitive purity. These restorationist Christians regarded the Protestant denominations as, at best, corrupt and, at worst, in apos-tasy. Finally, the idea that a largely uneducated youth like Joseph Smith should ask God for help rather than seek clerical advice was thoroughly in keeping with popular attitudes in the early American republic.

Just as the tropes contained in Smith's visionary claims were familiar to many Americans, so the reactions to them continued longstanding debates over the place of dreams and visions within Christianity. "[I] could find none that would believe the hevnly vision," Smith wrote in 1832, later adding that a Methodist minister informed him that it "was all of the Devil." The minister stated that "there was no such thing as visions or revelations in these days, that all such things had ceased with the apostles."[24]

The careful way that Protestant revivalist Charles Finney described his visionary conversion suggests that he, too, was well aware of such skepticism. Finney wrote in his memoirs that at first "it seemed to me that I saw Him [Jesus Christ] as I would see any other man." He allowed, though, that his vision could have been "wholly a *mental* state," and he clarified that he "had no distinct impression that I *touched* him."[25] Finney perceived a need to qualify his claims. Smith, by contrast, became more insistent on the reality and materiality of his experience. Heavenly beings had visited him, he affirmed without any equivocation. "I had actualy seen a light," Joseph insisted, and divine beings "did in reality speak unto me."[26]

While critics of Mormonism found Smith's visionary claims preposterous, for many converts Smith's visions were a selling point rather than a stumbling block. In the fall of 1829, for example, a visionary seeker named Solomon Chamberlin heard rumors of a "Gold Bible" and stopped at the Smith farmstead. Chamberlin had experienced all sorts of dreams and visions: of Satan, of Jesus, of church meetings and church members. "Is there any one here that believes in visions or revelations?" he asked Joseph Smith's brother Hyrum. "Yes," replied Hyrum, "we are a visionary house." After giving them a pamphlet detailing his own visions, Chamberlin left with an advance sixty-four pages of the Book of Mormon. Chamberlin was thrilled to find in the Smith family a group of kindred spirits. Skeptics abounded in early nineteenth-century America, but so did visionaries.[27]

As he continued to tell his story, Smith made his visionary narratives more concrete. In his 1832 account, Smith merely said that he "saw the Lord." In the late 1830s, Smith stated that he saw "two personages . . . standing above" him in the air. Their "brightness and glory," the prophet informed, "defy all description." By the early 1840s, Smith hazarded some comments on the appearance of the divine beings. An 1842 statement on the history of the church observed that the "personages . . . exactly resembled each other in features, and likeness."[28]

By the end of his life, Smith shared still more. One month before Smith's murder, Alexander Neibaur visited the prophet's home. A native German speaker, Neibaur was born Jewish before converting first to Protestantism and then, after immigrating to England, to Mormonism. Smith told Neibaur that he "saw a fire towards heaven came near & nearer saw a personage in the fire light complexion blue eyes." Then another person appeared at the side of the first and told Smith that the Methodists were "not my People" and to listen to his "Beloved son."[29] The heavenly beings who had once defied description had become men similar in appearance, with fair skin and blue eyes. The added details may reflect the Latter-day Saint teaching—firm by the early 1840s—that God and Jesus Christ were two separate, embodied, material beings. Instead of backing down in the face of skeptics, Smith doubled down on the physical reality of his vision.

Visionary Mormonism crested in Kirtland, Ohio, to which Joseph and Emma Smith relocated in early 1831. The previous fall, Mormon missionaries had baptized Sidney Rigdon, a restorationist Baptist minister in a nearby town. Most of Rigdon's congregants were horrified when he aligned himself with Mormonism, but his preaching in the surrounding area inspired others to follow his lead. Two thousand five hundred church members correspondingly followed Smith's lead and gathered in northeastern Ohio. For the next seven years, Kirtland was Joseph Smith's home.[30]

In Kirtland, Smith presided over the organization of his elders into priesthood quorums, some in the order of Aaron and some in the higher order of Melchizedek (in the Book of Genesis, the "king of Salem" who is described as a "priest of the most high God" and who brings bread and wine to greet Abraham). For Smith and his followers, priesthood meant not only office holding and ecclesiastical authority, but the very power of God, and even direct access to Jesus Christ.

In late 1832, Smith dictated a revelation that established what became known as the "School of the Prophets," in which church elders washed each other's feet, shared spiritual experiences, and received instruction in theology and secular branches of knowledge. In a March 1833 meeting of the school, Smith met with "an assembly of the high Priests." Quoting the Sermon on the Mount, Smith reminded those present of the "promise that the pure in heart . . . should see a heavenly vision." The men prayed silently, and the "promise was verified." Smith distributed sacramental bread and wine, "after which many of the brethren saw a heavenly vision of the saviour and concourses of angels." The experience was a Mormon version of the medieval Christian longing for the beatific vision, a glimpse of heaven enjoyed on earth.[31]

In May 1833, Smith asserted that all church members could receive a vision of the savior. The prophet dictated a revelation, a divine message that came in the words of Jesus Christ: "Evry soul who forsaketh their sins and cometh unto me and calleth on my name and obeyeth my voice and keepeth all my commandments shall see my face and know that I am." Obedient and righteous church members could see their savior's face. They would know that Jesus Christ is the Lord ("I am"), as he had claimed to be in the Gospel of John. Visions would bring them spiritual assurance and power.[32]

How would church members see Jesus Christ, and where? An early 1831 revelation had asserted that the "elders" needed to gather in Kirtland and be "endowed with power from on high," evoking the resurrected Jesus's instructions to his disciples to "tarry ye in the city of Jerusalem, until ye be endued with power from on high." Then they would be prepared for effective missionary work. Many mid-to-late-nineteenth-century American evangelicals taught that an individual's complete surrender to God led to the indwelling or baptism of the Holy Spirit, a prerequisite for effective Christian service. In contrast to evangelicals such as Charles Finney or Phoebe Palmer, however, Smith and his followers aimed for a communal spiritual outpouring akin to that of Pentecost.[33]

Moreover, Smith increasingly thought of temples as the sacred spaces in which his followers could obtain this spiritual empowerment. At first, these thoughts centered on Independence, in Jackson County, Missouri, which Smith's revelations identified as Zion, the future site of the New Jerusalem to which the Saints (as church members increasingly referred to themselves) should gather prior to Jesus Christ's return. A summer 1831 revelation identified a site for the temple near the Independence courthouse, and Smith soon contemplated a second temple in Kirtland. According to further revelations, Jesus Christ promised that, as the divine presence in the form of a cloud had followed the ancient Israelites through the wilderness and eventually into Solomon's temple, so his glory would reside in the both the Zion and Kirtland temples. In 1833, anti-Mormon settlers in Missouri forced church members there to abandon their Jackson County properties, so Kirtland took on an even greater significance. Mormon elders would see Jesus Christ in the Kirtland

Temple, endowing them with the power they needed for missionary service.

In February 1835, when twelve men were ordained as the church's apostles, Smith and his associates explained that a personal vision of the divine should precede the apostles' planned overseas missionary service. Oliver Cowdery, Smith's foremost scribe during the translation of the Book of Mormon, told the newly ordained apostles not to rely on the testimony of others for their faith but instead to "receive a testimony from Heaven for yourselves . . . [that] you have seen God, face to face." "God is the same," Cowdery stated, "If the Saviour in former days laid his hands upon his disciples, why not in the latter days?"[34] Seeing God, or seeing God's Son, was an essential preparation for missionary service. By the end of 1835, Smith promised those same apostles that "[a]ll who are prepared, and are sufficiently pure to abide the presence of the Savior, will see him in the solemn assembly," the dedication of the temple anticipated by the spring. Smith connected visionary experience to a particular location, the planned Kirtland Temple, the House of the Lord in which the apostles would see Jesus Christ.[35]

In preparation for the temple's completion, church leaders began a series of rituals designed to prepare them for the occasion, beginning with foot washing and proceeding to ceremonial washing and anointing. In mid-January 1836, Smith, Oliver Cowdery, and John Corrill met at Smith's house. They washed each other's bodies, bathed each other with whiskey "perfumed with cinnamon," confessed their sins, and covenanted to be faithful to God. While engaged in the washings, wrote Cowdery, "our minds were filled with many reflections upon the propriety of the same, and how the priests anciently used to wash always before ministering before the Lord." A few evenings later, a larger group of elders met in one of the temple rooms. Joseph Smith anointed his father's head with consecrated oil and blessed him as the church's patriarch. Joseph Smith Sr. then laid his hands on his son, anointing his head and sealing upon his son "the blessings, of Moses."[36]

After the anointings, Smith and the others saw the heavens open. "I beheld the celestial kingdom of God," Smith wrote, and the throne of God "whereon was seated the Father and the Son." Alluding to Paul's vision of the "third paradise," Smith commented that whether he beheld these things "in the body or out I cannot tell." The prophet saw Adam, Abraham, and Michael, and he also saw his own brother Alvin, who had died in 1823. Next, Smith saw his church's twelve apostles, clad in rags and standing in a circle "and Jesus standing in their midst, and they did not behold him, the Saviour looked upon them and wept." Visions proceeded throughout the night, as Smith anointed other church leaders: "The vision of heaven was opened to these also, some of them saw the face of the Saviour, and others were ministered unto by holy angels." The veil between heaven and earth had parted.[37]

Over the next several weeks, other men were washed and anointed, and the outpourings of God's spirit continued. "[S]ome have seen the heavens opend & seen the savior," wrote church member Benjamin Brown to his wife, "others have seen angels on the four corners of the house of the Lord with drawn swords & also stood thick on the ridge Elisha with his chariot of Fire, Peter John & James, & the highway cast up the ten tribes returning in chariots as far as the eye could extend." In this "holy season" of spiritual abundance, the ancients, the angels, and God's own son were in the midst of the Kirtland Saints, and the Latter-day Saints could glimpse their future celestial communion.[38]

At the March 27, 1836, dedication of the Kirtland Temple, Sidney Rigdon preached a long sermon on a passage from Matthew's gospel: "The foxes have holes, and the birds of the air have nests; but the Son of Man hath not where to lay his head." Now, Jesus Christ had a fitting home, the temple of a church founded on the belief in "present revelation." The temple would be, Joseph Smith prayed, a place for Jesus Christ "to manifest himself to his people." Smith beseeched God to bless his people as he had done "on the day of Pentacost: let the gift of tongues be poured out upon his people, even cloven tongues as of fire." A choir then sang a recently composed hymn: "The Spirit of God like a fire is burning / The latter day glory begins to come forth / The visions and blessings of old are returning / The angels are coming to visit the earth." Next came the administration of the "Eucharist," the distribution of the bread and the wine. After the final prayer, the assembled Saints shouted in acclamation: "Hosanna! Hosanna! Hosanna to God and the Lamb, Amen, Amen and Amen!"[39] Some present reported seeing angels.

Several days later, hundreds of Mormon elders met in the temple, partook of generous quantities of bread and wine, prayed, prophesied, and spoke in tongues. Smith's scribe observed that the "Saviour made his appearance to some, while angels minestered unto others, and it was a penticost and enduement indeed." Through these rituals, visionary experiences, and the entire process of building and dedicating the temple, church members recapitulated the ancient events and practices they found in the Bible, from Levitical priestly rites to the day of Pentecost. They relived those experiences and made them their own. In the temple, moreover, the yearning to see Jesus became a ritualized quest. Some, though by no means all, saw the savior as promised.[40]

In early April 1836, at the end of an afternoon service that included the Lord's Supper, Joseph Smith and Oliver Cowdery retired behind one of the Kirtland Temple's pulpits, cut off from the rest of the congregation by a lowered, canvas curtain or veil. After they came out, one of Smith's scribes recorded what the pair had experienced while praying:

> They saw the Lord standing upon the breast work of the
> pulpit before them, and under his feet was a paved work
> of pure gold, in color like amber: his eyes were as a flame
> of fire; the hair of his head was like the pure snow, his
> countenance shone above the brightness of the sun, and his
> voice was as the sound of the rushing of great waters, even
> the Voice of Jehovah, saying, I am the first and the last. I am
> he who liveth. I am he who was slain. I am your Advocate
> with the Father. Behold your sins are forgiven you.

The vision drew together a pastiche of images from the Book of Revelation, emphasizing both the majesty and mercy of a glorified and mighty Christ. Jesus Christ assured the pair that he had "accepted this house," and he promised to further "manifest" himself to church members who would keep his commandments. Smith and Cowdery also reported seeing Moses, Elias, and Elijah, who told them that the "great and dreadful day of the Lord" was near and that therefore "the Keys of this dispensation are committed into your hands."[41]

Non-Mormons in Kirtland heard of the church's claims to visions and pentecostal gifts. Truman Coe, the Presbyterian minister of Kirtland's

Jesus Christ Appears to the Prophet Joseph Smith and Oliver Cowdery, by Walter Rane. (© by Intellectual Reserve, Inc.)

Old South Church, struggled to know what to make of the "Religious Fanatics" in his midst. Ordinary church members he found "industrious" and "possibly very sincere christians," who displayed their devotion through prayer and biblical knowledge. At the same time, he thought Mormon leaders were ecclesiastical tyrants taking advantage of their gullible followers. Coe puzzled over the temple, with its rows of pulpits reserved for the church's Melchizedek and Aaronic priesthood orders. He considered the edifice "a strange compound of Jewish antiquity and Roman Catholic mummery." The "fundamental principle of Mormonism," according to Coe, "is that God continues to hold intercourse with the saints on earth by visions and revelations, as freely and familiarly as he has done in any age of the world." Coe put his finger on some of the things that set the Latter-day Saints apart from their Protestant counterparts.[42]

Despite the spiritual fervor and ecstasy surrounding the temple's dedication, Mormon Kirtland soon collapsed, brought about by dissension among church members. The unrest stemmed from the spectacular failure of a bank established by Joseph Smith and other church leaders.

In early 1838, Smith fled to Missouri, where mobs and militia troops soon forced the Mormons to leave the state under the threat of "extermination." In the summer of 1839, downtrodden church members regrouped on the Iowa and Illinois banks of the Mississippi River.

During those months, as the Saints began to recover from their Missouri travails, Smith frequently met with the Quorum of the Twelve Apostles. The Mormon prophet spoke about Peter's exhortation that followers of Jesus Christ should "make [their] calling and election sure" and Paul's promise that they could be "sealed with that holy Spirit of promise." The concept of sealing was important to Smith and his followers. As it did for American Protestants, the image of a seal evoked the certainty that a believer belonged to God. Back in October 1831, when church leaders promised to "cleanse ourselves and covenant before God," Smith assured them that "our names are sealed in the Lamb's Book of life." Their names would not be erased or blotted out. Furthermore, those men ordained to the church's high priesthood would "have power given them to seal the Saints unto eternal life."[43]

Throughout Christianity's long history, believers have sought many forms of spiritual assurance. Ancient Christians desired burial near the tombs of saints and martyrs in the hope that such proximity would facilitate the ascent of their souls to heaven. For others, visions of themselves with Christ in heaven alleviated fears of hell. Evangelicals during the American awakenings longed to see their names written in the "book of life." Then they would know they had a future home in heaven. Likewise, the Latter-day Saints wanted to know that they would indeed receive the eternal glory they had been promised. Such anxieties were especially acute after the Missouri experiences of persecution, bloodshed, and exodus.

Smith sought to provide balms for such concerns. The prophet quoted the assertion in the New Testament Second Epistle of Peter that believers may become "partakers of the divine nature" through faith, virtue, knowledge, temperance, godliness, brotherly kindness, and charity. Smith encouraged his closest followers to, in like manner, humble themselves and to hunger and thirst after righteousness. Any church member who did so would obtain spiritual certainty. "The Lord will soon say to him,"

Smith explained, "Son thou shalt be exalted." Then a Saint's "calling and election [would be] made sure," and that believer would receive the "other Comforter" Jesus spoke of in the Gospel of John. That "other comforter," Smith explained, "is no more or less than the *Lord Jesus Christ.*" Smith promised that a faithful Saint could expect "the personage of Jesus Christ to attend him or appear unto him from time to time," and the savior would even "manifest the Father unto him." This would be more than a moment of spiritual ecstasy. Jesus Christ and his Father would "take up their abode with him." The "visions of the heavens" would "be opened." The Lord would teach such individuals "face to face," giving them a "perfect knowledge of the mysteries of the kingdom of God." Smith reminded them that the ancient prophets had received such blessings. Prophets like Isaiah, Ezekiel, and John of Patmos. God did not favor the ancients more than the Latter-day Saints, however. They all belonged to the "*church of the First Born,*" and they could all have the privilege of seeing Jesus Christ and receiving instruction directly from their savior, giving them assurance of their eternal glory.[44]

Once the Latter-day Saints had recovered from the Missouri tragedy sufficiently to turn their attention to building a new community in Illinois, Smith never again spoke so insistently on the need for church members to see Jesus Christ. In the early 1840s, Smith introduced a series of rituals or "ordinances," including the eternal sealing of couples in marriage; an endowment ceremony (consisting of washings, anointings, and a sacred drama during which initiates make a series of covenants with God); and the "second anointing," the highest ordinance, in which men and women receive "the fulness of the priesthood." Those who received this final ordinance would know for certain that they would one day reign in heaven alongside God the Father and Jesus Christ. Their "calling and election" was made "sure." Remembering Smith's promise about the "other Comforter" in connection with such concepts, some later church leaders connected the second anointing with the privilege to receive visitations from the savior. At the same time, ordinances came to overshadow visions as a source of spiritual assurance. At the end of the endowment ceremony, men and women pass through a veil into a room symbolizing the celestial kingdom, a foretaste of their eventual return to their Heavenly Father. Perhaps in part because of this reconfiguration of

Mormon spirituality, the church never again experienced an extended season of visionary manifestations as it had in Kirtland.

For the remainder of the nineteenth century, Mormon leaders were of two minds about visions and other forms of spiritual ecstasy. The Book of Mormon teaches that because God has not changed, the spiritual gifts described in the New Testament (such as prophecy, healing, and speaking in tongues) have not ceased, and the church could not easily defend Joseph Smith's visions while denying others the right to their own such experiences. In an 1853 sermon, apostle Parley Pratt observed that a man who had an "open vision" would be a "simpleton" if he did not write it down. By contrast, while Brigham Young affirmed that some individuals received divine visions, he echoed the concern of Martin Luther and Jonathan Edwards that it was difficult to differentiate between visions from God and deceptions of the devil. Young warned that although "a man might have visions . . . and see as many visions as you could count, he might have the heavens opened to him, and see the finger of the Lord . . . neither would it prove that he was even a Saint." Thus, it was far better for individuals to obey church teachings than to seek visions.[45]

Still, church members recorded visions and sought meaning in their dreams. "I have been as it were carried away in visions and dreams," wrote church member Azariah Smith (no relation to Mormonism's founding prophet) in his journal in 1853, "causing my heart to rejoice; hardly knowing whether I was in the body or out of it, feeling quite well; Holyness to the Lord." That spring, Brigham Young visited Azariah Smith's home in the San Pete Valley. "He layed hands on me," Smith recorded, "sealing me up unto eternal life, and exaltation in the Kingdom of God, praying that my heart might be comforted and that my Faith might increase so as to receave visions and dreams, and the administration of Angels."[46] Young himself saw Joseph Smith in his dreams, receiving the martyred prophet's advice from beyond the grave. Despite caution on the part of some leaders, visions and other "gifts of the Spirit" remained important parts of mid-to-late-nineteenth-century Mormonism.

English emigrant Patience Loader did not have visions with the regularity of Azariah Smith, but she saw Jesus Christ during a storm while crossing the Atlantic. Born in 1827 to the west of London, Loader as a young woman worked as a servant, maid, and seamstress. Mormon missionaries first came to the British Isles in 1837 and, over the next fifteen years, tens of thousands of English, Welsh, and Scots joined the church. Patience Loader was baptized shortly after her parents' conversion. She and her father both lost their jobs because of their employers' hostility toward their new faith, and in December 1855 the family boarded a Liverpool ship that would start their journey to Utah.

Loader wrote an autobiography about thirty years after her emigration. In it she discusses their tumultuous ocean crossing in broken language but with riveting detail. It began with "aterrable severe voiage." The Loaders endured a "avery rough cross" captain who complained about the Saints' "d[amned] preachen and praying," fierce storms, and endless days full of tedium and sickness below deck. Sixty-two people died, including Patience Loader's niece. There were also happy moments. The company included a contingent of Danish Mormon emigrants. The Danish men could not speak English, but they played "dance tunes" on their instruments, and the "English sisters" danced with them for hours.

One sleepless night, in the midst of a storm, Patience Loader clung to her berth for dear life. Her father had hung curtains to create a more private area for the women and girls of the family. In the midst of the ship's tossing and turning, the curtains opened. "[A] beautiful lovely figure stood there," Loader wrote in her autobiography. A bright light illumined the figure's brown eyes and hair. Jesus Christ spoke to her: "fear not You shall be taken there all safe." He left and the curtains closed again. She quickly woke her parents. As Joseph Smith's family had believed in his visions, so Loader's trusted hers. "We all fealt encouraged and fealt to relie on this promise," she wrote. They all reached New York safely.

Patience Loader is famous for what happened as her family crossed the plains. Because Brigham Young decided to economize on that year's emigration expenses, they and hundreds of other families pulled their belongings on handcarts. Her father died, along with one-quarter of her company's members. They wrapped her father in a quilt and laid him in a hastily dug grave. "I will never forget the sound of that dirt beign shoveld anto my poor fathers boday," she wrote. Her autobiography contains no other visions of Jesus. Patience Loader lived in Utah for over six decades, until her death at the age of ninety-four.[47]

The last canonized vision within the LDS Church came nearly a century after Joseph Smith's first. Church president Joseph F. Smith (1901–1918) was the son of Joseph Smith Jr.'s brother Hyrum. Shortly before his death, he had a vision of Jesus Christ between his crucifixion and resurrection preaching to the "spirits in prison," bringing a message of salvation to the righteous dead. Smith also saw his father and uncle, Brigham Young, and other past church leaders joining in this postmortal task. Born in 1838, Joseph F. Smith had been shaped by the visionary culture of Mormonism's founding era.[48]

By the time of his church presidency, however, that culture had already largely faded. Speaking in tongues became rare, as did public narrations of visionary claims. As part of a broader effort to burnish the church's public image, the Latter-day Saints distanced themselves from the ecstatic and visionary forms of spirituality that had characterized the church's early decades. Mormon leaders now stressed the reasonableness and rationality of Latter-day Saint doctrine and religious practice. John Widtsoe, a Norwegian-born agriculturist (and future apostle) with a Ph.D. from the University of Göttingen, contended that Joseph Smith "taught doctrines absolutely free from mysticism, and built a system of religion in which the invariable relation of cause and effect is the cornerstone." Widtsoe and other like-minded thinkers reinterpreted miracles as the result of natural laws currently inaccessible to current human understanding. In this framework, visions and dreams were of dubious value, perhaps of some use for private spiritual edification, but inappropriate for public consumption and teaching. Apostle Anthon Lund bluntly told one church member that his dream of the devil was likely caused "by an overloaded stomach."[49]

These trends mirrored the trajectories of other American churches. For instance, while some evangelical leaders still referenced visions from God and Jesus, they rarely described the sight of heavenly beings. More restrained claims were less likely to arouse the disdain that Pentecostal visionaries such as Aimee Semple McPherson generated.[50] Like many Protestant leaders of the time, Latter-day Saint hierarchs privileged respectability and ecclesiastical order. Mormons certainly retained their belief in miracles and the supernatural, but their supernatural claims became much less audacious. Mormon leaders encouraged members to encounter the divine as mediated through the institutions, meetings, and ordinances of the church. Correspondingly, it became far more common for Latter-day Saints to report the quiet promptings of God's Spirit rather than the sort of spectacular theophanies their predecessors had openly discussed.

By the late twentieth century, Mormon leaders strongly discouraged open talk of personal visions. In a 1971 General Conference talk, Apostle Boyd K. Packer observed that church members occasionally asked him, "Have you seen Him?" "There are some things just too sacred to discuss," Packer answered. The sacred temple ordinances were among such things, but so were any personal manifestations of the savior. Although he affirmed that he was "a witness of Jesus Christ," he cautioned church members not to inquire into the details of such moments.[51]

A rare exception to this trend came in a 1989 General Conference talk by Apostle David B. Haight, who described a dream vision he experienced while unconscious for several days during an acute illness. Haight explained that through spiritual "impressions," he received a "panoramic view" of Jesus Christ's life, crucifixion, and resurrection. Haight saw everything in vivid detail, including the Garden of Gethsemane, in which "the Savior took upon Himself the burden of the sins of mankind from Adam to the end of the world . . . [and] overcame all the power of Satan." Haight said that he had not learned anything he did not already know and believe, but he now "knew, because of the impressions of the Spirit upon my heart and soul, these divine truths in a most unusual way." As Haight's own words suggest, his experience was "unusual," and it was uncharacteristic for a Latter-day Saint apostle to share a vision or dream in such detail.[52]

On occasion, church members have used knowledge of the church's intensely visionary early history to question its contemporary approach toward visions. Denver Snuffer, a Salt Lake City attorney and church member, authored a book in 2006 (*The Second Comforter*) in which he not only claimed to have seen and conversed with Jesus Christ but also maintained that all righteous and believing church members should expect such blessings. "Christ lives and comforts his followers today, just as He promised and did anciently," Snuffer writes. "I know He lives, for I have seen Him." In a later publication, Snuffer clarified that Jesus Christ first appeared to him on February 13, 2003. He never elaborated on his visions in print, stating that to publicize them would profane them. He was clear, though, that visions had not ceased. God had opened the heavens in response to the teenage Joseph Smith's prayers, and God would likewise reward any faithful and obedient Latter-day Saint who desired a vision of deity.[53]

The title of Snuffer's book came from Joseph Smith's 1839 assurance that Jesus Christ, the "other" comforter, would appear to faithful church members. Other Mormon authors had also repeated Smith's promise, but Snuffer was more vigorous than most in his insistence that all faithful Latter-day Saints should expect an experience akin to Joseph Smith's. In a subsequent book, Snuffer contended that Smith's successors had apostatized from the church's original doctrine and teachings, in part because they lost regular communion with the Lord. Not surprisingly, current leaders took offense at Snuffer's sweeping condemnation of them, even more so because Snuffer continued to publicize his beliefs on a blog and through speaking engagements. In 2013, Snuffer's stake president (a regional church leader) ordered him to cease his book's publication and abandon his speaking tour. Snuffer refused to do so, and, for that disobedience, lost his church membership.[54]

For most contemporary Mormons, visions are private, not public. Church leaders have not adopted the stance of the ancient Roman priest Gaius. They still believe that Jesus Christ visits select human beings. Visions have not ceased. But the advice of Mormon leaders now echoes that of the above-quoted Protestant minister who in 1805 had warned that "[n]o person is warranted from God to publish to the world the discoveries of heaven or hell which he supposes he has had in a dream, or trance, or vision." Visions might still provide individuals with spiritual assurance, but those so blessed should keep such things to themselves.

While Mormon leaders gradually discouraged the public airing of contemporary visions, it became essential for faithful Latter-day Saints to believe in what Joseph Smith once termed his "first communication."[55]

In 1842, the church's Nauvoo and Liverpool periodicals began the serial publication of the "History of Joseph Smith," which familiarized church members with Smith's youthful vision of God the Father and Jesus Christ. In an 1849 essay, Orson Pratt introduced the term "first vision," which became a key part of the Latter-day Saint lexicon.[56] In 1851, the church published the Pearl of Great Price, a miscellaneous collection of revelations, revelatory expansions of biblical passages, a brief statement of core doctrines, and the 1838 account of Joseph Smith's early history. The Pearl of Great Price eventually became a fourth volume of scripture for Mormons, alongside the Bible, the Book of Mormon, and the Doctrine and Covenants. Thus, Smith's account of "two personages" who instruct him to join no existing church became scripture for Latter-day Saints.

In 1869, Danish-born Latter-day Saint painter C. C. A. Christensen began work on a series of twenty-two large paintings depicting the history of his church. About a decade later, he began using the paintings as illustrations for lectures he gave on the story of Mormonism's first half-century. Sewn together, the individual paintings were rolled out as Christensen spoke. The first was of Joseph Smith's First Vision. In 1878, English immigrant George Manwaring saw Christensen's painting and wrote a poem on the same theme. Adapted for publication and set to music, "Oh How Lovely Was the Morning" (later renamed "Joseph Smith's First Prayer") became a popular Mormon hymn. "Suddenly a light descended, Brighter far than noon-day sun.... While appeared two heav'nly beings, God the Father and the Son." Manwaring's poem attested that Joseph Smith had seen "the living God."[57] Christensen's scene of the First Vision was lost, but Mormons created a host of other paintings and stained-glass windows illustrating the visit of God the Father and Jesus Christ. Others wrote poems, novels, and inspirational literature dedicated to Smith's boyhood theophany.[58]

According to historian Kathleen Flake, the First Vision assumed even greater importance during the early twentieth-century church presidency of Joseph F. Smith, precisely at the time that the church definitively abandoned polygamy. For a church shaken by the shedding of a long-defended practice and principle, the First Vision provided a new marker of Mormon identity. Latter-day Saints, Joseph F. Smith argued, had suffered persecution because they had accepted divinely revealed truths about deity that offended their Protestant neighbors. "The greatest crime that Joseph Smith was guilty of," Joseph F. Smith once declared with considerable hyperbole, "was the crime of confessing... that he saw those heavenly beings." The church no longer followed Smith's final revelation, which justified plural marriage. Instead, it elevated his first encounter with the godhead, a founding myth that contains other principles that bridged early and later Mormonism: the restoration of Christ's church from centuries of apostasy, a belief in concrete forms of continuing revelation, and the authority of Joseph Smith and his successors.[59]

Given the importance church presidents attached to it, the First Vision became a key part of missionary lessons and church educational manuals. In 1952, the church for the first time published a set of seven missionary lesson plans designed for use around the world. *A Systematic Program for Teaching the Gospel* began with a lesson on "the Godhead" and identified "Joseph Smith's story" as the "source of our knowledge." The lessons used the First Vision as evidence that God the Father and Jesus Christ are two separate, embodied "personages" and as evidence that Joseph Smith was God's chosen prophet. The church's current missionary manual (*Preach My Gospel*) encourages missionaries to "Memorize Joseph Smith's description of the Father and the Son." Prospective converts hear about the "Great Apostasy" of Christian churches following the death of Jesus's original apostles and then learn about the "Restoration" that began in 1820.[60]

The First Vision continued to grow in importance as the twentieth century proceeded. "The appearing of the Father and the Son to Joseph Smith is the foundation of this Church," stated mid-twentieth-century church president David O. McKay. More recently, President Gordon B. Hinckley (1995–2008) proclaimed that his church's claims rested squarely on the veracity of Smith's visionary reports. "Our entire case as members of The Church of Jesus Christ of Latter-day Saints rests on the validity of this glorious First Vision," he maintained. Hinckley likewise contended that the fact that Smith saw "two personages" affirmed the distinctive Mormon understanding of the godhead, that God and Jesus have glorified, separate bodies "of flesh and bone." If Smith really talked with divine beings, moreover, individuals should accept his other claims. "It's either true or false," Hinkley explained in a 2007 interview. "If it's false, we're engaged in a great fraud. If it's true, it's the most important thing in the world. . . . That's our claim. That's where we stand, and that's where we fall, if we fall."[61]

The First Vision is the Mormon version of Moses and the burning bush, or Muhammad and the angel. Latter-day Saint historian James B. Allen explains that for Mormons, "belief in [Smith's] vision . . . is second only to belief in the divinity of Jesus of Nazareth."[62] Latter-day Saints testify that two divine beings appeared to the young Joseph Smith and inaugurated the "last dispensation" of time, the restoration of Jesus Christ's true church.

Each year, tens of thousands of Latter-day Saints visit the "Sacred Grove," a small wooded area near the old Smith farmstead. Especially on a sunny day, the well-spaced trees in the grove permit considerable light to reach the forest floor, summoning up a suggestion of the brightness the prophet-to-be encountered.

Each year, a similar number of Latter-day Saint visitors also tour the Kirtland Temple, owned by the Community of Christ (the former Reorganized Church of Jesus Christ of Latter Day Saints). For much of the twentieth century, Latter-day Saint pilgrims came to Kirtland primarily to "see where Elijah stood," referring to Joseph Smith and Oliver Cowdery's April 1836 vision. The LDS Church connects Smith's receipt of the "Keys of this dispensation" from Elijah with the authority to preside over the temple ordinances the prophet later introduced in Nauvoo. More recent visitors to the Kirtland Temple express a greater interest in seeing "where 'the Savior' stood." Of course, Latter-day Saint pilgrims need not choose between the vision of Jesus Christ and the vision of Elijah. It is a question of emphasis, and current Mormon thought and discourse are focused squarely on Jesus Christ.[63]

Early Mormonism proclaimed that God continues to reveal such visions to human beings, collapsing the distance between nineteenth-century believers and the world of ancient scripture. Like Moses and Enoch (according to Mormon scriptures), Joseph Smith and his followers could aspire to see Jesus Christ and his Father "face to face." By the twentieth century, however, some of that distance had reemerged. Mormon leaders placed a singular importance on Joseph Smith's First Vision, identifying it with the beginning of the restoration of Christ's true church. Like the Book of Mormon, the First Vision sets the Latter-day Saints apart from other Christians. In another sense, though, the First Vision's significance for contemporary Mormonism makes the LDS Church more closely resemble the religious culture from which Joseph Smith had sharply dissented. It is one thing to believe that ancient Christians—or even those who lived two hundred years ago—saw divine beings. It is another matter to claim to have seen them oneself or to accept the visionary claims of one's contemporaries. Similarly, it is one thing to anticipate seeing supernatural beings in heaven and something else to report seeing them in this lifetime. While contemporary Mormons expect their leaders to enjoy such privileges, most Latter-day Saints are now content to look forward to seeing their savior's face in heaven.

CHAPTER FOUR

✛

THE WORDS OF THE LORD

THE LORD SAID not to back down. "Let not my servants who are called
to the Presidency of my church," the divine voice instructed, "deny my
word or my law, which concerns the salvation of men."

It was November 1889. Lawyers had advised church president Wilford Woodruff to make a conciliatory gesture toward the U.S. government. Since 1882, thousands of Mormon polygamists had been convicted
and incarcerated under the Edmunds Anti-Polygamy Act. More recently,
courts had stripped the church of Salt Lake City's temple block (returned
to the church the next year), the church president's office, and other key
properties. Hundreds of Mormon polygamists remained in jail. Washington politicians made it clear that Utah would not obtain statehood
until the church abandoned polygamy. Now, federal judges had begun
denying naturalization to Mormon immigrants out of fear that they
could not be loyal U.S. citizens. The church was on a political precipice.[1]

Woodruff went home from his session with the lawyers and spent several hours alone. He prayed. "[B]y the voice of the spirit he was directed
to write," recorded his clerk L. John Nuttall.[2] "Thus saith the Lord," the
revelation began. The Lord reminded Woodruff and other church leaders
that he ultimately controlled "the destiny of the courts." Judges could not
overrule divine providence. The Lord instructed the lawyers to "make

their pleadings . . . without any further pledges from the Priesthood." No concessions. The Lord would deliver the Saints from their enemies. The law of plural marriage, moreover, was sacred. The "salvation of the children of men" hinged on it.

Whose words did Woodruff write? Who was "the Lord"? "I, Jesus Christ, the Savior of the world, am in your midst," stated the revelation, "I am your advocate with the Father." The revelation closed with a reminder from Jesus Christ that he would "come quickly."[3]

When Woodruff read his revelation to a gathering of high-ranking church leaders the next month, they understood it as a divine commandment to hold firm. "The word of the Lord was for us not to yield one particle of that which He had revealed and established," wrote apostle Abraham H. Cannon in his diary. "It sets all doubts at rest concerning the course to pursue."[4] Jesus Christ had settled the question.

The next year, however, Woodruff buckled to federal pressure. In February 1890, the Supreme Court upheld an Idaho statute that disenfranchised church members. Several months later, the Court upheld the church's disincorporation and government seizure of its assets. Federal officials prepared to seize the church's temples in St. George, Manti, and Logan. "We are like drowning men," Woodruff observed, "catching at any straw that may be floating by that offers any relief!"[5]

Woodruff decided to act "for the Temporal Salvation of the Church." He released an "Official Declaration" addressed "To whom it may concern," which advised church members to "refrain from contracting any marriage forbidden by the law of the land." The statement, which became known as "The Manifesto," added that the church had already begun reproving members whose statements could "be construed to inculcate or encourage polygamy." Woodruff did not reject polygamy as a principle, but he made it clear to American politicians that he intended to do what was required to avoid the church's dissolution.[6]

Woodruff announced his decision through his own words, not those of Jesus Christ. Among church members, this raised questions about the validity of his declaration. Woodruff publicly addressed these concerns one year later. "Read the life of Brigham Young," he reminded the Saints, "and you can hardly find a revelation where he had said, 'Thus saith the Lord.'" Woodruff explained that Young "taught by inspiration and by revelation; but with one exception he did not give those revelations in the form that Joseph did; for they were not written and given as revelations and commandments to the Church in the words and name of the Savior." By contrast, Woodruff continued, Joseph Smith had "said 'Thus saith the Lord' almost every day of his life." Regardless of the presence or absence of written revelations in the words of Jesus Christ, Woodruff assured church members, the church's leaders possessed the spirit of revelation. "The Lord showed me by vision and revelation exactly what would take place if we did not stop this practice," Woodruff explained. Furthermore, he had written "what the Lord told me to write."[7]

Woodruff's Manifesto was added to the Doctrine and Covenants in 1908 as an "Official Declaration." It came at the very back of the volume, after an index and concordance. Although contemporary Latter-day Saints regard the Manifesto as a revelation, its title and placement denote its distinctive form.

Woodruff's comments about his Manifesto and the respective leadership styles of Joseph Smith and Brigham Young, moreover, point to the changing meaning of revelation over the course of the LDS Church's history. More so than most American religious groups, early Mormons insisted that Jesus Christ was speaking to them. They heard and read his words, not only words in the New Testament and in the Book of Mormon, but the words he spoke to them through the mouth of their prophet.

Contemporary Mormon leaders seem to have little in common with Joseph Smith's style of leadership. As modern executives, they do not share visions, unveil new doctrines, or prophesy in the name of the Lord. Accordingly, many have used Mormonism as a classic example of what German sociologist Max Weber termed the "routinization of charisma."[8] In this vein, Rodney Stark observes that "religious movements founded on revelations will attempt to curtail revelations or to at least prevent novel (heretical) revelations."[9] The Mormon experience demonstrates the tumultuous and uneven nature of this process. The Latter-day Saints have maintained a firm belief in ongoing revelation, yet they have reformulated its form and function.

Prophets, seers, and oracles have long uttered the words of the gods. For centuries, people traveled from distant parts of the Mediterranean world to Delphi, seeking the words of Apollo from priestesses (known as the Pythias) who served as his mouthpiece and could be consulted on a handful of days each year. There are many theories, ancient and modern, about the Delphic oracle's process of inspiration. Regardless of the mechanics, a Pythia was understood to utter Apollo's words.[10]

Jewish and Christian scriptures record various means by which humans divined God's will. The Book of Samuel observes that if one consulted Ahithophel, one of King David's advisers, it "was as if a man had inquired at the oracle of God."[11] Seers and prophets sometimes transmitted their messages while in an altered state of consciousness, other priests and oracles consulted lots or employed other means of divination, while still others simply spoke with divine authority. Prophets served as intermediaries between God and the people. In the Book of Jeremiah, God touches the prophet's mouth with his hand. "Behold, I have put my words in thy mouth," the Lord tells Jeremiah.[12]

Since the development of written language, scribes have recorded the spoken words of lawmakers and prophets, investing them with the authority that comes from apparent permanence and immutability. So it has been with the Torah and the Talmud, the gospels, the Qur'an and the Hadith. While mystics and prophets did not disappear, within many traditions canonization discouraged the additional creation of scripture. Canonization also fostered a tension between the spoken and the written word. Jews, Christians, and Muslims have all at times privileged the recitation and hearing of scripture, while regarding the preservation of its written text as of utmost importance.

Political and religious leaders have often understood additional prophecy and revelation as threats to their authority. In the first decade of the Massachusetts Bay Colony, Anne Hutchinson stated in court that she received "immediate revelation . . . by the voice of his own spirit to my soul!" Hutchinson was on trial because of her role in a theological dispute about whether or not sanctification (i.e., righteousness and good works) provided evidence of one's membership among God's elect. Hutchinson's opponents asserted that she was deluded by the wiles of Satan, partly because the spirit told her things that clashed with the accepted orthodoxies of her church and partly because she did things not "comely in the sight of God nor fitting for [her] sex." John Cotton,

Hutchinson's own minister, countered that revelations "being under-stood in the scripture sense . . . are not only lawful but such as Christians may receive." Cotton prevaricated when asked if he believed Hutchin-son's revelations were true. John Winthrop, the colony's governor, had no doubts. "I am persuaded that the revelation she brings forth is delu-sion," he stated. The court banished Anne Hutchinson from the colony.[13]

At the time of the American Revolution, claims of divine commu-nication remained hotly contested. The Enlightenment nurtured sharp critiques of miracles and revelation. "I totally disbelieve," wrote the pamphleteer and religious skeptic Thomas Paine, "that the Almighty ever did communicate anything to man, by any mode of speech, in any language, or by any kind of vision."[14] He found it absurd that any man would trust the prophetic claims of another, which necessarily came without corroboration.

Those Protestant leaders determined to maintain respectability in an age of Enlightenment denied that humans—at least in modern as op-posed to ancient times—could hear God's voice. Individuals could and should speak to God, but they should not expect any audible voices or even mental impressions in response. Ralph Waldo Emerson, the Unitarian-turned-transcendentalist philosopher, defined most prayer—whether for supplication or confession—as "a disease of the will" and appropriate prayer as the "soliloquy of a beholding and jubilant soul."[15] Most Protestant ministers believed that God communicated with human beings, but not by speaking to them. God subtly answered prayers; God nudged people to action through their reason or intuition. It was dan-gerous for Christians to claim that they heard the voice of God or Jesus. It might lead them beyond ecclesiastical authority, creeds, or the suffi-ciency of the Bible. Instead of seeking to hear the words of God for themselves, congregants should read the written Word of God in scrip-ture and listen to its proclamation from church pulpits. For all of these reasons, many religious leaders felt it of great importance to discredit the aural experience of the divine. Those who claimed to hear divine voices opened themselves to charges of madness.[16]

Nevertheless, countless Americans believed that God and Jesus spoke to them. For example, the itinerant Methodist evangelist Nancy Towle wrote of being "accountable for my doings alone to the LORD JESUS

CHRIST." She tried "to listen to the voice of His spirit, in my own soul, as the only infallible guide."[17] Towle's language echoed Anne Hutchinson's. Neither reported an audible voice. Instead, they felt God's spirit speaking in their souls. Whereas Hutchinson's claims promptly led to her banishment, similar claims were commonplace among early nineteenth-century evangelicals. Unconvinced by Christianity's rationalist critics, Americans talked to God and Jesus and claimed to receive answers. The long-haired and independent-minded Methodist itinerant Lorenzo Dow sometimes understood himself in an "interior dialogue" with God. As a young man, he kneeled in prayer "alone in a solitary place." While he prayed, "words were suddenly impressed on my mind; 'Go ye into all the world and preach the gospel.'" Dow objected, "Lord! I am a child, I cannot go." More divine words came in response: "Arise and go, for I have sent you." It took months, but Dow eventually responded to his summons.[18]

Although Emerson scoffed at the idea of divine voices, he expressed a longing for new truths, new revelation. "Men have come to speak of revelation as somewhat long ago given and done, as if God were dead," he lamented in an 1838 address at Harvard Divinity School. Lifeless scriptures and creeds could not lead individuals to an encounter with the divine. "It is my duty to say to you, that the need was never greater of new revelation than now," Emerson proclaimed. The "Concord Sage" hoped to restore a lost mystical aspect to religion. Words had a permanence, but religion focused on those past words often declined into formalism. When he spoke of a need for fresh revelation, of course, Emerson did not have someone like Joseph Smith in mind. Divine beings did not speak to humans. Instead, according to Emerson, men and women should intuit the divinity in the world around them and within their own souls.[19]

Joseph Smith, by contrast, believed that God was again pouring out his spirit through dreams, visions, and prophecy. God was speaking as God had spoken to the ancient Israelites and the first Christians. Indeed, Smith argued that God would violate his own promise to not be a "respecter of persons"—to not show favoritism—should new generations of believers fail to receive what their ancient predecessors had been granted. After all, Smith wrote his uncle Silas, God had never "revealed that He had ceased to speak, forever, to his creatures." "Why should it be thought a thing incredible that he should be pleased to speak again, in these last days?" Why did God bless Abraham with his "direct voice" when Abraham could have relied upon God's words to Noah? Why did God speak to Isaac when the latter could have relied upon God's words to Abraham? Past revelations were of limited present value. Individuals must obtain "an assurance of salvation" for themselves. "And have I not an equal privilege with the ancient Saints?" the young prophet asked his uncle. "And will not the Lord hear my prayers, and listen to my cries, as soon as he ever did to theirs, if I come to him in the manner they did?" Why was it so easy for Christians to believe in ancient visions and prophecies, but then reject the possibility that they still occurred?[20]

Among early nineteenth-century Americans, Smith and his followers were not alone in hearing their savior's words in visions and dreams. What was unusual is that they believed that Jesus Christ was speaking to them through a prophet. Joseph Smith was Jesus Christ's latter-day oracle. In the words of Jesus Christ, Smith brought forth revelations that contained doctrinal instruction and immediate commandments. Early Mormons expected their Lord to lead them through his words, and those words from the mouth of Joseph Smith led them down paths none could have anticipated.

Beginning in 1828, "Joseph the Seer"—as his followers often called the budding prophet—dictated revelations. Scores of them are extant. Scribes wrote them down and copied them into bound volumes. Church members made copies and carried them between Ohio and Missouri. The church published them in newspapers and printed them in books, books that became scripture for Latter-day Saints.

In some cases, Smith claimed that Jesus Christ "spoke" to him. "He spake unto me," Smith recorded of the savior in the earliest account of his First Vision. "We heard the voice," Smith and Sidney Rigdon asserted when they dictated the fruits of another vision in February 1832. When Jesus Christ appeared to Smith and Oliver Cowdery in the Kirtland Temple four years later, Smith's clerk recorded that "his voice was as the sound of the rushing of great waters," alluding to the Book of Revelation. In none of these instances did anyone else report hearing the divine voice, nor do the accounts suggest that Smith believed that he heard Jesus Christ in the same way that he heard human voices. Instead, God granted Smith and his companions the ability to perceive divine speech.[21]

In most instances, Smith dictated revelations to a clerk. Parley Pratt recalled that "each sentence was uttered slowly and very distinctly, and with a pause between each, sufficiently long for it to be recorded, by an ordinary writer, in long hand."[22] Similarly, William McLellin informed that "the scribe seats himself at a desk or table, with pen, ink and paper. . . . The subject of enquiry being understood, the Prophet and Revelator enquires of God. He spiritually sees, hears and feels, and then speaks as he is moved upon by the Holy Ghost, the 'thus saith the Lord,' sentence after sentence, and waits for his amanuenses to write and then read aloud each sentence."[23] It was a dialogue. Smith asked and received an answer. Then, Smith calmly and deliberately spoke divine words.[24] In several of the early revelations, Smith used a seer stone as a conduit for revelation. Within a short time, however, he abandoned the use of such objects.

Smith's own voice is absent. Instead, he is a messenger, an oracle who relays God's commandments for his church or for certain individuals. It is not always entirely clear which divine being is speaking in Smith's revelations. "The Lord," for instance, is a malleable, multivalent term, used by Christians to signify either God the Father or Jesus Christ. The confusion stems from the New Testament's own dual use of the title.

In a relatively small number of revelations, it is clear that it is God the Father who is speaking. "Behold," God tells Smith and four others in an 1830 message about the Book of Mormon's copyright, "I am the father & it is through mine only begotten which is Jesus Christ your Redeemer."[25] In two 1829 revelations, God the Father ("behold I am God") apparently introduces the words of his Son ("Behold I am Jesus Christ, the Son of God").[26] When they read or listened to the words that Smith's scribes wrote down, the recipients of the prophet's revelations may have perceived the voices of both God the Father and Jesus Christ. The succession and conflation of divine voices emphasizes the unity between Jesus and God.

The dominant voice in Smith's revelations, however, is that of Jesus Christ. "I am Jesus Christ, the Son of God," proclaims the divine voice in one early message, which instructed Smith to not retranslate a section of the Book of Mormon lost by his financial backer Martin Harris.[27] Several revelations begin with an exhortation to listen to the voice of God's Son, as in this September 1830 message: "Listen to the voice of Jesus christ your Redeemer the great I am whose arm of mercy hath atoned for your sins."[28] These opening words stress Jesus Christ's divinity ("the great I am") and his work of redemption.

In some revelations, the divine speaker does not identify itself, but the context suggests that it is Jesus Christ. A string of 1829 and 1830 revelations foretold of a "great and marvelous work" and encouraged specific individuals (from Smith's own father to several recent converts) to devote themselves to it. In these messages, language that mirrors Jesus's from the New Testament ("the field is white unto harvest"; "knock, and it shall be opened unto you") indicates that it is Jesus speaking to his church. In one revelation, directed to Emma Smith, the divine speaker forgives her sins, terms her an "Elect Lady," warns her to "murmur not because of the things which thou hast not seen," encourages her to support her husband Joseph "in his afflictions," states that she will be ordained to "expound Scriptures," and gives her the task of preparing a hymnal for publication. The closing words—"where I am ye cannot come"—echo the words of Jesus to his disciples in the Gospel of John.[29]

At times, Smith dictated a revelation in response to an individual church member's entreaty. For example, about six weeks after first encountering the missionaries that had set him on the path toward his baptism, William McLellin traveled to northeastern Ohio to meet "Joseph the Seer." McLellin met the prophet about twenty miles outside Kirtland, and Smith promptly ordained him "to the High-Priesthood of the Holy order of God." The next day, McLellin badly hurt his ankle. Smith asked him if he believed that God would use him to heal his ankle. McLellin answered yes, and Smith "laid his hands on it and it was healed although It was swelled much." McLellin traveled with Smith to stay in the prophet's home.

Even after the healing, McLellin harbored doubts about his new church. Questions, he wrote in his diary, "had dwelt upon my mind." It is hardly surprising that McLellin faced such anxieties. Joseph Smith asked a great deal of the men and women who accepted the Book of Mormon and believed in him as a prophet. He asked them to leave their homes and gather together with other church members, directing many to Jackson County in western Missouri and others to the town of Kirtland in northeastern Ohio. He asked men to leave their families behind and preach "without purse or scrip," and he asked women to persevere in poverty and loneliness while their husbands served constant missions. It was a relatively simple matter for the recently widowed McLellin to leave behind his school teaching, but for all involved, much was at stake: livelihoods, kinship connections, and reputations. Throughout the early 1830s, many women and men left the church, disillusioned by the extreme spiritual enthusiasm of some church members, failed attempts at healing, and the direction of Smith's visions and revelations. Such matters often boiled down to a simple question: Was Joseph Smith really God's prophet, seer, and revelator?

McLellin devised a plan to test the prophet. He prayed to "the Lord." He later wrote that he "asked him to reveal the answer to five questions through his Prophet, and that too without his having any knowledge of my having made such request." McLellin never specified in writing what his questions were, but he hoped to receive a revelation that would answer them.

Per McLellin's diary, Jesus Christ responded to his prayer by giving him "a revelation of his will, through his prophet or seer (Joseph)." Smith dictated a message that he had received from "The Saviour of the World," which McLellin wrote down. In the revelation, Jesus Christ praised McLellin for having turned away from his sins and for having embraced "the fulness of my Gospel," though he warned him that he was "clean but not all." The savior added that adultery was a particularly troubling temptation for the schoolteacher. Jesus told McLellin to proclaim his "gospel from land to land, and from city to city," especially in places other missionaries had not stopped. Furthermore, McLellin should send as much money to Zion—to the Saints in Jackson County—as he could. Should he be faithful, McLellin would receive great blessings. He would be able to heal the sick. Eventually, he would "have a crown of Eternal life on the right hand of [the] Father."

William McLellin, ca. 1870. (Courtesy of the Church History Library, The Church of Jesus Christ of Latter-day Saints.)

The revelation demanded much from McLellin, but it came from someone he could not ignore: "Verily, thus saith the Lord your God, your Redeemer even Jesus Christ." Joseph Smith had passed McLellin's test. McLellin later stated that his five questions had been answered to his "full and entire satisfaction." Full of joy and determined to obey his savior and his prophet, McLellin soon left on a mission, taking a copy of the revelation with him.[30]

The power of the written word still exercised a strong sway over Joseph Smith's early followers. It was not enough for Smith to tell McLellin what he should do, just as it was not enough for Smith to tell his followers that "plain and precious" things were missing from the King James Bible. Instead, Smith created texts, commandments that his followers should obey, biblical narratives they could read and reread. He and his followers immediately transformed the divine words he spoke into scripture, a written record of Jesus Christ's commandments for his church.

The fact that Joseph Smith dictated revelations raised all sorts of questions and concerns, within and beyond his church. In 1834, Ohio newspaper editor Eber D. Howe published *Mormonism Unvailed*, a blistering exposé of what he termed a "singular imposition and delusion." Howe discussed Smith's revelations at length, relying in large part on a series of letters from former church member Ezra Booth. Howe asserted that "the prophet ever kept in view the finances of his devoted followers, and to filch from their pockets he had only to issue a revelation." There was some truth to Howe's claim, as some revelations called on church members to donate money or property to the church.[31] The fiery editor compared Smith to Muhammad and warned of the Mormon prophet's pretensions to military and political power. "They say that when they get the secular power into their hands," he warned, "every thing will be performed by immediate revelation. We shall then have Pope Joseph *the First.*"[32]

Such fears intensified as Mormons skirmished with mobs and militia troops in Missouri and then established a Latter-day Saint city in Illinois. In 1842, the abolitionist and educational reformer Jonathan Baldwin Turner published *Mormonism in All Ages.* Turner labeled the church's *Doctrine and Covenants* (an 1835 publication containing roughly one hundred revelations and some additional materials) the "BLACK BOOK of Mormonism." Turner warned that Smith's "voice is the voice of God, in all things, great and small, whenever he chooses to call it so."[33] Several critics, including Howe and John C. Bennett (who attained high leadership within the church prior to his 1842 excommunication), noticed that the revelations promised that the Saints would obtain land in Missouri "by purchase *or by blood.*" In this instance, the critics ignored the context of the phrase in question, which stated that if the Saints purchased lands, they would be blessed, but if they had to obtain land by bloodshed, they would "be scourged from city to city."[34] Also, some outsiders warned that even if Smith's revelations had been harmless to date, the very principle of ongoing revelation meant that he or future prophets might lead the church down darker paths. Such detractors understood immediate revelation as a grave danger to more than just Smith's deluded followers.[35]

Even among his followers, though, Smith's revelations sometimes generated doubts. How could imperfect human language convey divine speech? This concern was heightened by the rough and unrefined spelling and grammar found in many revelations. Smith once rebuked William Phelps and other Missouri Mormon leaders because they had the temerity to complain about "glaring errors" in one revelation. "We would say, by way of excuse," the prophet responded, "that we did not think so much of the orthography, or the manner, as we did of the subject matter." Even in imperfect language, the revelations were the "word of God, as much as Christ was God, although *he* was born in a stable."[36] What mattered were the ideas and commandments, not their precise wording. The explanation, however, cast doubt on whether the "word of God" contained the actual words of God. Church leaders prepared the early revelations for publication in an 1833 *Book of Commandments*, correcting errors and infelicities of language and occasionally making more substantive revisions. The 1835 *Doctrine and Covenants* contained a larger number of revelations, again revised for publication.

At the same time, many church members wondered whether Smith's gift of divine communication was his alone. Could other church members receive revelations? If so, could they obtain the same sort that Smith received? Elements of Mormonism were democratic and egalitarian. Baptized men were immediately ordained as elders and sent forth. All men in good standing held the priesthood. Most church decisions did not require written revelations but were made by church councils and conferences. Moreover, the gift of prophecy was for the church and its elders, not just for Joseph Smith. In November 1831, Smith dictated a message in which Jesus Christ promised that "whatsoever" the church's missionary elders "shall speak as they are moved upon by the Holy Ghost shall be Scripture shall be the will of the Lord shall be the voice of the Lord & shall be the power of God unto Salvation."[37] The church affirmed that others besides Joseph Smith were prophets. At the Kirtland Temple's 1836 dedication, Smith presented "the several Presidents of the church . . . as being equal with himself, acknowledging them to be Prophets and Seers." Church members rose to affirm them as such.[38] The assembly then affirmed that the members of the Quorum of the Twelve Apostles were also "Prophets and Seers."[39] God spoke to them as well, and they led the church with revelatory authority.

Moreover, all church members could approach God in prayer and expect answers. "It is the privilege of the children of God to come to God & get revelation," Smith taught in 1839. As Smith had told his uncle Silas, "God is not a respecter of persons." Everyone could exercise the "same privilege" and be blessed with revelation. At least in most instances, revelations would come through the "Spirit of God," not through an audible voice or a vision. Those so blessed would feel "pure Inteligence flowing unto" them, followed by "sudden strokes of ideas." All men and women could receive revelation.[40]

Not surprisingly, however, some church members wished to more fully imitate Smith. For example, during their work on the Book of Mormon, Smith's scribe Oliver Cowdery prayed that he also might have the gift of translation. In a revelation, Jesus Christ praised him for so inquiring and promised to "grant unto you a gift if you desire of me, to translate even as my servant Joseph." However, when Cowdery made an attempt to translate a portion of the Book of Mormon, he failed, apparently because he did not know the proper method. "You took no thought, save it was to ask me," Jesus Christ explained in a subsequent revelation. Cowdery needed to learn how to receive the revelations that were the basis for the "translation" of ancient texts. "You must study it out in your mind," Jesus Christ instructed, "then you must ask me if it be right, and if it is right, I will cause that your bosom shall burn within you." There would be no divine voice, but an inspiration confirmed by the Holy Ghost. The savior informed Cowdery that it would not be "expedient" for him to translate at this time. He should continue assisting Smith.[41]

Nor should others dictate divine commandments. In September 1830, church member Hiram Page challenged Smith's authority with a "roll of papers," revelations he had received while looking into a seer stone. Smith himself had used a seer stone during the Book of Mormon translation and as a conduit for some of his earliest revelations, but he had stopped using a stone by this time. Smith's change in method troubled some church members. David Whitmer, who alongside his father and brothers was one of Smith's earliest supporters, later concluded that once Smith set aside his seer stone, his subsequent revelations were "of the Devil."[42] Page's claims, meanwhile, raised the specter of prophetic chaos. What was the relationship between magical objects and prophetic authority? Did Smith need a seer stone? Did others with such artifacts receive valid revelations? In response to the challenge, Smith dictated a revelation that clarified that "no one shall be appointed to Receive commandments & Revelations in this Church excepting my Servent Joseph." Worried about Cowdery's possible jealousy, the revelation added that Cowdery would serve as Aaron to God's latter-day Moses but would himself "not write by way of Commandment." Hiram Page received a harsher rebuke. The "things which he hath written from that Stone," the Lord stated, "are not of me & . . . Satan deceiveth him." Smith affirmed that no objects were necessary as conduits for revelation and that his prophetic authority was unique.[43]

Jesus Christ had one supreme prophetic oracle. All church members might receive personal visions and revelations, but they should not presume that their revelations would bring forth new teachings or direct church affairs. Indeed, what most Saints should seek was spiritual confirmation that Joseph Smith's translations and revelations were of the Lord.

For a half-decade, Smith's revelations sent elders on missions, brought forth new doctrine, predicted Christ's imminent return, identified Independence, Missouri, as the "New Jerusalem," and commanded the construction of temples in Jackson County and Kirtland.

In the fall of 1833, some of those plans collapsed when mobs forced the Jackson County Saints to abandon their properties at the pain of death. Until Smith received the August 1833 report of the Jackson County persecutions, he had dictated revelations with great frequency over the previous four years. Indeed, of the 135 revelations during Joseph Smith's lifetime canonized by his church, he had dictated nearly one hundred by that August. The divine voice became more infrequent thereafter. Perhaps for a time Smith lost some prophetic confidence. In December

1833, Edward Partridge expressed his hope from Missouri that "ere this there may have been a comforting word from the Lord through you."[44] Smith soon provided the beleaguered Missouri Saints with a revelation, but the flow of divine instruction never reached its former tide. By the end of his life, Joseph Smith no longer functioned as Jesus Christ's oracle with any regularity. Going forward, Smith dictated no more than a handful of revelations each year.

When Smith introduced major theological and ritual innovations, he did so primarily through other means. For example, in 1840 Smith announced to church members in Nauvoo, Illinois, that they could be baptized on behalf of individuals who had died without access to Mormon baptism. He did not promulgate the doctrine through a revelation. Likewise, no known written revelation accompanied the 1842 introduction of the endowment ceremony, a ritual soon regarded as a requirement for human exaltation. In the early 1840s, Smith led the church differently than he had a decade earlier.

A revelation did confirm what became Smith's most controversial teaching. The catalyst for the formal revelation was Emma Hale Smith's growing opposition to her husband's plural marriages. In the early 1840s, Joseph Smith married ("was sealed to," in Mormon parlance) more than two dozen women, mostly without Emma's knowledge and consent. Joseph and Emma clashed repeatedly over polygamy. Then, in May 1843, Emma gave her approval to her husband's marriages to Eliza and Emily Partridge, who worked in the Smith household. Unbeknownst to Emma, however, Joseph had already been sealed to the Partridge sisters in March. Even with Emma's partial blessing, tension in the household grew as she realized the extent and meaning of Joseph's marriages. According to Joseph's confidante William Clayton, Emma wanted "to be revenged on him for some things she thought that if he would indulge himself she would too." Joseph once had expressed concern that Clayton had displayed too much "familiarity" with Emma. The Mormon prophet could afford the criticism of hostile newspaper editors and a few former church members, but Emma's opposition raised the stakes.[45]

Joseph's brother Hyrum, who had only recently become convinced of the doctrine of plural marriage, recommended that the prophet present

Emma with a written revelation. The proposal illustrates the spiritual power and authority such documents wielded within the church. For many of Joseph Smith's followers, a conversation or sermon sufficed as proof of a doctrine's divinity, but the written word of God still carried more weight. "Joseph dictated sentence by sentence and I wrote it as he dictated," recalled scribe William Clayton nearly three decades later.[46]

Like those of the late 1820s and early 1830s, the revelation came in the voice of Jesus Christ. The message refers to "my father" at several points. "I am Alpha and Omiga [Omega]," it closes, repeating Jesus Christ's words from the Book of Revelation. In the revelation, the savior cautions that only marriages "sealed by the Holy Spirit of promise, through him whom I have aniointed [anointed]" will persist for eternity. Those so sealed "shall . . . be Gods, because they have no end. Therefore shall they be from everlasting to everlasting, because they continue." Having established the principle of eternal marriage, the revelation turned to plurality and used the Old Testament patriarchs as exemplars. Finally, Jesus Christ had pointed warnings for Emma. The savior instructed her to "partake not of that Which I commanded you to offer unto her. For I did it, saith the Lord, to prove you all, as I did Abraham." Had Joseph offered Emma a plural husband? Regardless, the revelation warned her to "cleave unto my servant Joseph, and to none else." Otherwise, Jesus threatened, "she shall be destroyed." Although the revelation suggested that men should receive permission from their wives to enter into plural marriage, it added that if first wives "receive not this law," husbands were "exempt from the law of Sarah" and could proceed.[47] The revelation was an unsubtle attempt at persuasion, and it did not persuade Emma. According to Clayton, Emma "did not believe a word of it."[48] After Smith's June 1844 murder, Emma denied that her husband had ever practiced polygamy, a testimony to the depth of her opposition.

The gradual introduction of polygamy to other church members, by contrast, had proceeded in the absence of a written revelation. When he revealed the doctrine to prospective wives, Smith asked them to obtain by prayer their own revelation of its truth. Much as Moroni's words in the Book of Mormon encouraged readers to pray that God would reveal the book's truth to them, so individuals should pray that God would reveal the truth of this new commandment. Several of Smith's wives later recounted having done just that. For instance, Lucy Walker was fifteen or sixteen years of age when Smith proposed plural marriage to her in 1842. The prophet showed her no written revelation (he had not yet dictated it); he simply informed her of the following: "I have been commanded of God to take another wife, and you are the woman." She reacted with shock and indecision. The next year, when Smith told her to reach a decision within a day, she received a divine answer after a sleepless night spent in prayer. "My Soul was filled with a calm sweet peace that I never knew," she wrote many years later. She met Smith the next day, who blessed her "with every blessing my heart could possibly desire." It was not that Smith wanted church members to receive their own revelations on the nature of marriage. Instead, he wanted them to receive confirmation that his revelation was true.[49]

Lucy Walker did not need a written revelation to convince her of Joseph Smith's prophetic call or the divine origin of plural marriage. Still, Smith's early flurry of written revelations, published in the Doctrine and Covenants, set a precedent for prophetic leadership among his followers. After Smith's death, his grieving followers thirsted for new revelations. Several men quickly sought to claim the martyred prophet's prophetic mantle. Smith's former assistant Sidney Rigdon reported that Smith had appeared to him in a vision and asked him to serve as the church's guardian. In early August 1844, however, a majority of the Nauvoo Saints accepted the leadership of the Quorum of the Twelve Apostles, over which Brigham Young presided.

That did not end the struggle over succession. James J. Strang, a recent convert to Mormonism, produced a letter purportedly from Smith appointing him the prophet's successor. He also claimed that an angel had ordained him as the church's new leader. Strang baldly imitated Joseph Smith, dictating revelations and soon unearthing a set of plates from the ground in Voree, Wisconsin.[50]

While consolidating his leadership of the Saints in Nauvoo, Brigham Young sought to assuage concerns that Smith's death had sealed the heavens and stilled God's voice. "Do you suppose the mouth of God is

Closed to be opened no more unto us?" Young asked in a mid-August 1844 sermon. "If this was the Case I would not give the ashes of arie [a rye] straw for the salvation of the church. If God has Ceased to speak By the Holy Ghost or revelation their is no salvation but this is not the case."[51] Soon, word reached Nauvoo of Strang's claims, and it became clear that Rigdon had not accepted the apostles' authority either. "When men rise up with revelation and say they can lead this people," Young stated, "I know it comes from the devil." If others "have visions and revelations let us all have them," he jeered, probably with Rigdon and Strang in mind. At the same time, Young insisted that God had not stopped speaking to his church. "My mind is stored with many revelations," he promised.[52] Young instructed the Saints that his words were the fruit of revelation, and he did not need to dictate or write revelations. "I never read much scripture," he commented in 1845. "I have not time to read it. I am a perfect Bible myself."[53] Young urged his followers to value his sermons and instructions over any written revelation.

Young's words were not good enough for everyone, though. Indeed, Strang and his followers argued that Young's lack of written revelations and visions invalidated his leadership. How could the church continue without a prophet like Joseph Smith? The fact that Young produced no written revelations stoked doubts. In January 1846, Reuben Miller, a church member impressed by Strang's claims, informed Young that "the word of the Lord would be decidedly satisfactorily to him." Young commented that Miller was "considerably bewildered by Strang['s] new fangled Revelation." Knowing that nothing else would satisfy Miller, Young stated, "thus saith the Lord unto Reuben Miller through Brigham Young—that Strang is a wicked & corrupt man & that his revelations are as false as he is." Young was terse. His time, he wrote, was "to[o] precious to be spent in hearing and even talking about such trash." Young made plain his prophetic authority, but such statements were rare. Later that year, Miller lost faith in Strang and eventually joined the Saints in the West.[54]

Only twice did Young write out "the word and will of the Lord." In January 1847, he wrote a revelation that affirmed the apostles' authority and organized companies for the trek from the Missouri River to the West. The text provided an explanation for Joseph Smith's death. "Many have marvelled because of his death," the Lord allowed, "but it was needful that he should seal his testimony with his blood, that he might be honored, and the wicked might be condemned." Whether the divine voice in Young's revelation was God the Father or Jesus Christ is unclear. "So no more at present," it concluded, "Amen and Amen." When Young presented "the word and will of the Lord," many Saints were relieved. Heber Kimball noted that it "was the first one that has been penned since Joseph was killed." Over the next half year, it was read frequently at church meetings. Even so, one revelation did not ease all concerns. "Many have doubts [about] how we can get along without a Prophet," commented Willard Richards later that year.[55]

In April 1847, Young left the church's Winter Quarters on the Missouri River, leading a vanguard group of Saints toward the Valley of the Great Salt Lake. After one month, he grew frustrated with the men's increasing frivolity and lack of caution. The pioneers seemed more interested in dancing than in diligence. Young blamed the spirit on a few men who did not belong to the church and on several black slaves brought by southern converts to Mormonism. A steady rain added to the somber atmosphere.

At night, Young retreated to his wagon and prayed, called several of the Twelve together, and "wrote some of the word of the Lord Concerning the camp." Unusually, the revelation began in his own voice: "I, Brigham, am constrained by the spirit to say to you . . . except you repent, and humble yourselves before the Lord, you will not have power to accomplish your mission." Then, "the voice of the Spirit of the Lord" warned the people to prepare for the "coming of the Son of Man," in which Jesus Christ would take vengeance "on the ungodly." It closed with a promise from Jesus Christ, "your Advocate with the Father," to deliver the pioneers should they repent. Then, after writing sixteen lines, Young stopped. According to Willard Richards, he "did not care to write any more." He set the text aside.[56]

The next day, instead, Young harangued the camp at length. "I have let the brethren dance," he lamented, "and fiddle, and act the nigger night after night to see what they will do." He was angry about lounging, card playing, and profane talk. He warned the few non-Mormons traveling with the group that if they introduced "iniquity" into the camp, "they shall never go back to tell the tale." Anyone who did not wish to repent and covenant with God "to put away iniquity" should head back to Illinois, he added. Then, in conclusion, recorded William Clayton, Young "very tenderly blessed the brethren." Heber C. Kimball then stood up to say that he received Young's discourse "as the word of the Lord to this camp." There is no record that Young or anyone else read aloud the revelation he had written the previous night. There was no need for it.[57]

Brigham Young never wrote or dictated another revelation. Although he sometimes joked about being "profitable" or merely a "Yankee guesser," Young thought of himself as a prophet. His words, he insisted, were revelation. They came constantly. "As for revelation," Young observed in 1850, "they say it has ceased—no such thing." Should he choose, he could give the people revelation "as fast as a dog could trot. I'm in the midst of it." He observed that Joseph Smith had given the people enough revelation in his final two years to last them for twenty. Before seeking more, they should obey what they had already received.[58] Especially in the mid-to-late 1840s and early 1850s, Young frequently had one of Smith's revelations read at church meetings. For instance, when he publicly announced the church's practice of plural marriage in 1852, he did so by having Smith's 1843 revelation read aloud. Although the Saints had practiced polygamy openly since leaving Illinois, the controversial doctrine needed the imprimatur of written scripture.

Not all church members were of one mind about the relative importance of past revelation and current prophetic teaching. In a heated 1856 disagreement with Apostle Orson Pratt, an exasperated Young informed Pratt that "things were so and so *in the name of the Lord.*" Young and Pratt were at loggerheads over the former's identification of Adam as humanity's God and divine Father. Pratt observed that the account of Adam's creation in Genesis ("the LORD God formed man of the dust of the ground") and the Book of Moses contradicted Young's contention that Adam had come to the earth as a resurrected, exalted being. Pratt insisted "that the President's word in the name of the Lord was not the word of the Lord to him." Still unconvinced the next month, Pratt clarified that he "preferred to receive the written revelations of J[oseph] S[mith]." This attitude was unacceptable to Young. Though he cited both scripture and Joseph Smith's revelations as authoritative sources in his sermons, Young claimed that the "living oracles" were more valuable "than all that has ever been written from the days of Adam until now." For Young, ongoing revelation did not merely mean an expanding canon of scripture. It meant that the living oracles took precedence over all past words of the Lord. Well into the twentieth century, Mormon leaders would echo Young's privileging of the living oracles over all other sources of authority.[59]

In the several years before his 1877 death, Young encouraged church members to consecrate their property to the church and join cooperative economic enterprises known as the United Order. The people should work together as the saints of old had done in Enoch's city. In some Utah communities, the Saints enthusiastically embraced the plan, but elsewhere, many church members hesitated. In March 1874, Young spoke about the United Order while he wintered in the southern Utah settlement of St. George. Young observed that "if the people wanted the word of the Lord written, he could give it to them in this way." If he did so though, "the curse of God would the more directly and speedily come upon those who would not obey."[60] According to Young's line of reasoning, in light of their stubbornness the people were better off without a formal revelation.

Young grew frustrated with ongoing resistance to his initiative. Therefore, several months later he verbally granted the request for a revelation. "Thus saith the Lord unto my servant Brigham," Young intoned in the Salt Lake Tabernacle, "Call ye, call ye, upon the inhabitants of Zion, to organize themselves in the Order of Enoch." If the Saints wished to call this a new revelation, they could do so. For himself, though, Young knew "it is no new revelation, but it is the express word and will of God to this people."[61] The fact that Young felt obliged to accommodate church members' desire for new revelations indicates that even decades after Joseph Smith's murder, the founding prophet's early style of leadership remained normative for many Mormons. Church members read his revelations in the Doctrine and Covenants and longed for more. They wanted the word of the Lord, the words of Jesus Christ.

Young's immediate successors promptly returned to the former model of revelation. Because Young had held many church properties in his own name, after his death there were conflicts of interest between his family and the church. At the time, John Taylor was president of the Quorum of the Twelve Apostles; he was formally sustained as church president three years later. Taylor prayed repeatedly for guidance about the thorny legal conflicts over Young's estate, and he dictated a revelatory answer in November 1877. "Thus saith the Lord," the revelation began, "Be one, be united, be honest, act upon the principles of justice and righteousness to the living and to the dead and to my Church, and I, the Lord, will sustain you and will acknowledge your labors." Taylor wrote or dictated at least eight additional revelations over the next decade.[62]

Taylor's revelatory process resembled that of Joseph Smith. Clerk George Reynolds recalled that he sometimes found the church president working on a revelation at the Gardo House (the mansion Young had built for two of his wives). Taylor would then "continue the revelation he had commenced to write by dictating it to me." Reynolds next read it aloud several times. "On only one occasion do I remember that he made any alteration in that which was written."[63] Taylor published only two of his revelations, and the church did not add any of them to new English-language editions of the Doctrine and Covenants (two were included in certain European editions).[64] Church leaders circulated several of them, however, which were read aloud at local church meetings.

Taylor's revelations were explicitly dialogic. He brought questions to the Lord and received specific responses. The identity of the divine voice is not clear in some of Taylor's revelations, but others refer to "my father," making it clear that it is Jesus Christ who speaks. "As thou hast asked me concerning this Temple, thus saith the Lord," began a brief revelation about the just-dedicated Logan Temple, "I accept this house which thou hast built."[65] Taylor's revelations touched on a range of topics. Several encouraged the church to defend its principle of plural marriage. For example, an 1882 revelation clarified that men called to high offices should "conform to my law [of marriage]; for it is not meet that men who will not abide my law shall preside over my priesthood."[66] As Joseph Smith had done, Taylor led the church as Jesus Christ's oracle.

In keeping with the church's understanding of its apostles as prophets, seers, and revelators, longtime apostle Wilford Woodruff occasionally dictated revelations. In 1880, while tenting by himself in the snowy mountains of northwestern Arizona, Woodruff awoke at midnight, whereupon "the Lord poured out his spirit upon me and opened the vision of my mind." Woodruff wept, noting that his pillow became "wet with the dew of heaven." Then, Woodruff wrote a revelation. He had not heard a divine voice. Instead, he wrote, "my mind was open to comprehend the situation of our Nation." The words came "by the inspiration of the Holy Ghost." "The hour is at the door when my wrath and indignation shall be poured out upon the wicked of this Nation," warned the Lord. There would be earthquakes, plagues, famine, and wars. Anyone who obstructed the Saints from practicing polygamy would be damned. "I say again woe unto that Nation or House or people," threatened the Lord, "who seek to hinder my People from obeying the Patriarchal Law of Abraham which leadeth to a Celestial Glory which has been revealed unto my Saints through the mouth of my servant Joseph." As was customary in Joseph Smith and John Taylor's revelations, the divine voice was that of Jesus Christ. "I am in your midst," the savior comforted the Saints. "I am your Advocate with the Father." Jesus Christ promised that his coming was at hand.[67] Woodruff also acted as the savior's oracle.

Throughout the 1880s, Taylor, Woodruff (who succeeded Taylor as church president in 1889), and other church leaders insisted that the church would never abandon polygamy. It was a religious principle that could not be jettisoned for reasons of political expediency. Eventually, out of desperation, Woodruff declared that the church would conform to the laws of the land. When Woodruff presented his decision to the Quorum of the Twelve, it took a week to reach consensus. Unlike the response to Taylor and Woodruff's written revelations, some apostles objected. John W. Taylor, the former president's son, allowed that when he first heard of the Manifesto, he felt like saying, "Damn it." Eventually, though, Taylor and others who were hesitant swallowed their doubts and endorsed the Manifesto.[68]

The Manifesto did not settle the matter of polygamy, however. Over the next fifteen years, some high-ranking church leaders continued to seal men to plural wives with the tacit approval of Woodruff and his immediate successors. Many of these sealings took place in Mexico and Canada; the church had only promised to end additional plural marriages in the United States. Still, some plural sealings took place on American soil as well. The full extent of the practice's persistence is unknown, but a number of the church's apostles took new plural wives during these years. Utah had received statehood promptly after Woodruff's Manifesto, but by 1900, outside concern about the continuation of polygamy sparked a new round of political controversy.[69]

When the Utah state legislature elected Mormon apostle Reed Smoot—a monogamist—to the U.S. Senate in 1902, antipolygamy groups mobilized to prevent his seating.[70] They alleged that the church had neither abandoned polygamy nor its treasonous stance toward the U.S. government. Church president Joseph F. Smith took the witness stand before the Senate committee investigating whether or not Smoot should retain his seat. As best he could, Smith sought to deny any personal or church culpability for additional plural marriages while at the same time avoiding blatant dishonesty. For example, Smith testified that "there has not [been] any man, with the consent or knowledge of the church, [who] ever married a plural wife since the Manifesto."[71] Apostles who performed plural sealings did not obtain explicit approval from Smith, at least not in any way that would implicate the church president.

The Senate committee, however, did not confine itself to the issue of polygamy. Somewhat akin to the 1830s objections of Eber D. Howe and Jonathan Baldwin Turner, senators questioned whether the church's concept of revelation conflicted with loyalty to the nation's laws. "Which, as a matter of obligation, is the prevalent authority," inquired Senator George F. Hoar, "the law of the land or the revelation?" Smith hedged, "Well, perhaps the revelation would be paramount." Hoar pressed. If a revelation conflicted with civil law, which were church members obliged to obey? Smith answered meekly, "They would be at liberty to obey just which they pleased." Most Protestants would have affirmed that divine law trumped human law, but as of the early 1900s, few would have imagined that their understanding of the former would have conflicted with American statutes. Other Americans, though, worried that Latter-day Saint principles of revelation and priesthood authority fomented political disloyalty.

Joseph F. Smith found himself discussing the reality and mechanics of revelation with a group of hostile politicians. Earlier in his testimony, Smith had affirmed that church members were at liberty to decide for themselves whether to obey or reject any given revelation. When asked if he had revelations, Smith demurred. "I never said I had a revelation,"

FIRST PRESIDENCY of the MORMON CHURCH.
Taken on the 87th Birthday of President Wilford Woodruff, 1894.

Church President Wilford Woodruff with his two counselors in the First Presidency, George Q. Cannon (left) and Joseph F. Smith (right), 1894. (Photograph by Charles Roscoe Savage. Courtesy of the Church History Library, The Church of Jesus Christ of Latter-day Saints.)

the church president asserted, "except so far as God has shown to me that so-called Mormonism is God's divine truth."[72] Senator Hoar returned to the subject: "you have received no revelation yourself?" Smith answered, "No, sir." In fact, Smith testified that no church president had received a revelation since Woodruff's Manifesto. Smith talked of receiving divine inspiration, just as other church members did. Hoar wanted to know how church leaders received revelations. "By an inward light, by an audible voice, by a writing, or in what way?" he wondered. Smith replied that a revelation "might come by an audible voice or it might come by an inspiration known and heard only by myself." Other senators wondered whether Woodruff's Manifesto was really a revelation. "A revelation," observed Senator Joseph W. Bailey, "comes from on high. That manifesto seems to have been merely a way of reaching and denying a report made to the American Congress." Smith countered that it was "essentially religious" and affirmed by the church.[73]

After Smith and the church expelled two members of the Quorum of the Twelve and made a far firmer declaration that they would not tolerate additional plural marriages, Smoot retained his seat. Joseph F. Smith's testimony, however, reverberated in Utah for quite some time. The anti-Mormon *Salt Lake Tribune* reprinted his testimony in its entirety one year later and mercilessly skewered the church president both for his prevarication and for his claims to have received no revelations. "Joseph F. Smith has publicly denied that he receives revelations from God to guide the Mormon church," the paper editorialized. "Why should the Mormon people sustain him?" As the *Tribune* reported, Smith and several apostles made a point of defending his prophetic authority at the church's April 1905 General Conference. Smith had received many revelations from God, even if he had not presented written revelations for public acceptance or canonization. He received constant divine inspiration and guidance. Smith never budged from his insistence that such inspiration was a perfectly appropriate way for a prophet, seer, and revelator to lead the church.[74]

After Wilford Woodruff, no subsequent church leaders revived the practice of written revelations in the words of the Lord. The philosopher

William James printed a letter from a Mormon correspondent, in which he reported that Woodruff's immediate successor Lorenzo Snow "claims to have had a number of revelations very recently from heaven."[75] There is no evidence, however, that Snow committed any of them to writing. Joseph F. Smith wrote out the account of his vision of the spirit world a few weeks before he died in 1918, but Brigham Young's 1847 revelation at Winter Quarters is the last item in the church's Doctrine and Covenants that contains the "word of the Lord." After decades of uncertainty and contention, church members gradually accepted a new model of prophetic leadership.

Given Joseph Smith's insistence that Christians should not rely on the revelations found in the Bible but should hear the current words of the Lord, it is not surprising that over the course of Latter-day Saint history, some Mormons have rejected this shift in the form and function of revelation. Such critiques began during Joseph Smith's own lifetime. William McLellin, excommunicated in 1838, claimed that Smith himself had abandoned his prophetic calling after the very early years of the church. After 1834, he noted, Smith "professed to give but a few revelations, and in them I have no confidence."[76] McLellin expected a true prophet to lead through written revelations. Likewise, James Strang and his followers mocked Brigham Young for his lack of revelations.

In 1860, Joseph Smith III (the prophet's son) became the president of the Reorganized Church of Jesus Christ of Latter Day Saints, which denied that Joseph Smith Jr. had practiced polygamy. "Young Joseph," as he was sometimes called, promptly wrote a revelation in the voice of Jesus Christ, the "Alpha and Omega." Smith never approached the early revelatory output of his father, but his revelations directed the church, sometimes in the voice of Jesus Christ and sometimes in the "voice of the Spirit." The Reorganized Church, renamed the Community of Christ in 2001, has continued to add revelations to its own Doctrine and Covenants with some regularity. More recently, however, these have appeared not as the words of Jesus Christ but rather as the words of the church's current prophet, guided by inspiration and then debated at church conferences.

Those Mormons who persisted with polygamy and became known as fundamentalists also often adhered to earlier models of oracular revelation. They did so in part by rejecting Woodruff's 1890 Manifesto. Some understood the statement as a clever political dodge, designed to create political breathing space while enabling a revival of polygamy after Utah statehood had been achieved. Others, though, condemned it as the church's apostasy from an eternal principle. As evidence, such detractors pointed to a purported 1886 revelation from John Taylor in which "the Lord" insisted that "everlasting covenants cannot be abrogated or done away with." Those who want to enter into God's "glory" "must & shall obey my law . . . they must do the works of Abraham."[77] The revelation was not published, nor, apparently, presented to other church leaders for their approval. John W. Taylor, the church president's son, stated in 1892 that "among my father's papers I found a revelation given him of the Lord, and which is now in my possession, in which the Lord told him that the principle of plural marriage would never be overcome."[78] In 1911, while facing excommunication for his post-Manifesto plural marriages, John W. Taylor produced a copy of his father's 1886 revelation in his defense.[79] Church authorities rejected the revelation because it had not been approved, either by the Quorum of the Twelve or by the church as a whole. Subsequently, the LDS Church's First Presidency asserted—probably incorrectly—"that no such revelation exists."[80] Within some branches of Mormon fundamentalism, moreover, revelations continued to guide ecclesiastical decisions.[81]

Within the LDS Church, however, church members no longer expected their leaders to bring forth new revelations, at least not the written words of the Lord. In 1978, the church's First Presidency announced that by revelation God had lifted the church's withholding of the priesthood from black men. The members of the church's First Presidency (church president Spencer Kimball and his two counselors Eldon Tanner and Marion Romney) explained that that they had spent "many hours in the Upper Room of the Temple, supplicating the Lord for divine guidance." In response, they continued, God "by revelation has confirmed that the long-promised day has come when every faithful, worthy man in the Church may receive the holy priesthood." Apostle Bruce R. McConkie described the revelatory experience in greater detail. "From the midst of eternity," he wrote, "the voice of God, conveyed by the power of the Spirit, spoke to his prophet. . . . And we all heard the same voice, received the same message, and became personal witnesses that the word received was the mind and will and voice of the Lord." McConkie did not clarify whether it was an audible voice or a spiritual impression, but he described it as "akin to what happened on the day of Pentecost and at the dedication of the Kirtland Temple." The church's fall 1978 General Conference unanimously affirmed the revelation, appended to the Doctrine and Covenants as Official Declaration 2, after Woodruff's Manifesto. The declaration described a revelation, but it did not contain divine words. In affirming the 1978 revelation, church members renewed their faith in the "living oracles" and in their new model of divine communication.[82]

American Christianity today is not an Emersonian soliloquy. Instead, large numbers of women, men, and children engage in dialogues with God and with Jesus. They pray, and they believe that God listens and responds. They believe that God considers their requests, sometimes granting them and sometimes wisely rejecting them. Some Christians might occasionally hear an audible divine voice. More often, they report spiritual impressions or simply interpret the unfolding of events as answers to prayer.

Continuing revelation remains central to Latter-day Saints, but its meaning and forms have shifted. Through the early 1900s, Mormons spoke of their leaders as the "living oracles." Joseph Smith, John Taylor, and Wilford Woodruff dictated the words of Jesus Christ for church members to hear and read. Thereafter, the preferred phrase became "living prophets," a subtle revision that reflects this different form of revelatory output. Church leaders proceed primarily based on the "still small voice" of God's Spirit. With rare exceptions, they do not claim to have heard the words of God's Son, and they do not claim to transmit the savior's words. Nor should church members expect to hear Jesus Christ's voice, audibly or otherwise. "We hear the words of the Lord most often by a feeling," church president Ezra Taft Benson taught in 1988. "If we are humble and sensitive, the Lord will prompt us through our feelings." Similarly, Apostle Boyd Packer explained that the "Holy Ghost speaks with a voice that you *feel* more than you *hear*." The understanding of revelation is now primarily one of inspiration, for members and leaders alike. The voice of Jesus Christ has become hushed, muted.[83]

Along with the changed place of visions within the church, this evolution in revelatory and prophetic leadership points to the Latter-day Saint adjustment to the demystification or rationalization of the modern world, what sociologist Max Weber termed its "disenchantment" or "demagification."[84] For Weber, a key aspect of modernity was that science, coupled with rationalized approaches to philosophy and theology, eroded magical, mythical, or supernatural ways of understanding the world. Both early Mormons and their elite Protestant critics insisted that their systems of thought were rational and scientific, but the Latter-day Saints also wedded themselves to the persistence of apostolic-era supernatural gifts and accepted the use of objects such as seer stones and divining rods. In more recent generations, the Latter-day Saints have accommodated themselves to modernity. It is one thing to speak in unknown, heavenly tongues and another to believe that God helps missionaries learn foreign languages with unusual alacrity. It is one thing to expect immediate miraculous healing and another to pray for healing while placing oneself under the care of a physician. It is one thing to believe in discrete, heavenly communications in the words of Jesus Christ and another to believe in the "still small voice of the Spirit." The latter are more modern forms of spirituality and religion in which God mostly works through ordinary means. In the contemporary West, it is easier for individuals to believe in these sorts of miracles.

Early Mormonism rested upon an understanding of revelation distinctive in its cultural context. As the savior's oracle, Smith understood himself as reprising the roles of ancient prophets, bringing forth revelations and commandments. Those words guided Mormon gathering and settlement, reshaped the church's understanding of heaven, and ultimately transformed its practice of marriage. The early years of the church have become an exception rather than the normative standard. Today, Latter-day Saints regard Smith's own revelations in much the same way that other Christians understand those of Isaiah and Jeremiah. The authority of Mormon leaders rests on the authority of their office, not on their ability to bring forth the words of the Lord.

CHAPTER FIVE

I COME QUICKLY

"I COME QUICKLY," was Jesus Christ's constant message to Joseph
Smith and his earliest followers. The phrase appears a dozen times in revelations dictated by Smith between 1830 and 1837.

Early Mormons believed that Jesus Christ would soon return, and
they expected to reign with him on the earth. The wicked, meanwhile,
would suffer unless they repented. "Mine anger is kindling against the
inhabitants of the earth to visit them according to th[e]ir ungodliness,"
Jesus Christ warned, according to the history Joseph Smith wrote in
1832.When the Son of God came, he would slay the vast majority of
humankind, a wave of destruction that would cleanse the earth of all
wickedness. Then, proclaimed an 1842 summary of the church's beliefs,
"Christ will reign personally upon the earth, and . . . the earth will be
renewed and receive its paradasaic glory."[1]

The promise of the Second Coming provided early Mormonism with
much of its energy and purpose. In 1831, Joseph Smith identified Independence, in Jackson County, Missouri, as Zion, the site of the New Jerusalem to which Jesus Christ would return. Millenarian fervor, a belief
that Jesus Christ would soon return and inaugurate his thousand-year
reign on earth, sent missionaries across the United States, Canada, and
Europe.[2] In response, converts gathered to western Missouri, where they

expected to greet their returning savior. Expectations of the Second Coming even sent one high-ranking church leader on a mission to Jerusalem. It took only a few years, however, for events to contravene early Mormon millenarian expectations. After hundreds of church members had gathered to Zion, anti-Mormon mobs and politicians forced them to leave Jackson County in 1833 and then Missouri altogether five years later.

For the remainder of the nineteenth century, Mormon hopes for an imminent Second Coming ebbed and flowed, sometimes in connection with Joseph Smith's prophecies and sometimes because of the course of current events. Latter-day Saint millenarianism revived again in the mid-twentieth century, though without the radical implications of the church's earliest years. Although Latter-day Saints retained their own particular interpretations of the end times, their Cold War-era fears and politics resembled those of their American evangelical counterparts.

Although Mormon eschatology—the church's doctrine of the Second Coming and millennium—has changed little since the mid-nineteenth century, most Latter-day Saints no longer live as if Jesus Christ will soon appear. Certainly, Mormons hear references to the "last days" in relation to everything from serving missions to maintaining an emergency supply of food. Church members, however, are no longer gathering to a New Jerusalem to await their savior's return, nor does the idea of a wrathful Christ make much sense in the context of contemporary Mormonism. Instead, Latter-day Saints have become accustomed to the steady growth of God's kingdom, expressed in membership statistics and the construction of temples around the world. Church members still keep their lamps lit should their bridegroom return unexpectedly, but they do not expect him to come as quickly as they once predicted.

The idea that Jesus Christ will return soon is as ancient as Christianity itself. In the New Testament gospels of Mark, Matthew, and Luke, Jesus predicts that judgment and the establishment of God's kingdom are near. After wars, earthquakes, famine, persecution, and the desecration of the Jewish Temple, foretells Jesus in the Gospel of Mark, "then shall they see the Son of man coming in the clouds with great power and glory."

"Verily I say unto you," Jesus informs his disciples, "that this generation shall not pass, till all these things be done." He cautions them, however, that they will not be able to predict the exact time of his coming. "Take ye heed, watch and pray," he warns, "for ye know not when the time is."[3] Many of Palestine's Jews revolted against Roman rule in the year 66 CE, only to suffer a crushing defeat that included the Temple's desecration. And yet the "Son of man" did not descend from the clouds.

The delayed return of Jesus did not extinguish the expectations of his followers, as illustrated in the New Testament's final book. The Book of Revelation introduces itself as the "apocalypse of Jesus Christ," an unveiling of hidden mysteries delivered by an angel to a man named John, a prophet on the island of Patmos at the turn of the second century. Although some early Christian bishops as well as later leaders such as Protestant reformer Martin Luther questioned its value ("Christ is neither taught nor known in it," stated Luther),[4] the Book of Revelation has deeply shaped the imaginations of Christians, from Dante to Milton to popular American novels. It also exerted a strong influence on Joseph Smith and other early Latter-day Saints.

"While in the Spirit," John of Patmos saw Jesus Christ with hair white as snow, eyes aflame, with a countenance as "the sun shineth in his strength" and a voice that sounded like rushing waters. According to John's visions, four horsemen will unleash unimaginable horrors on the earth: warfare, famine, plagues, and natural disasters. The sun will turn black, the moon red as blood, and stars will fall to earth like figs dropping from a tree during a gale. Vast swaths of people will die. Others will wish they could. Eventually though, Jesus Christ and his armies will defeat Satan and his allies. For a thousand years, Satan will be imprisoned, and the living and resurrected saints will reign with their Lord. Then, Satan will emerge from prison only to suffer a final defeat, and a "holy city," a "new Jerusalem" will descend from heaven to earth. The saints will live forever in this city of God, through which the river of life flows. The concepts of a thousand-year reign and the descent of the heavenly New Jerusalem to earth do not appear elsewhere in the Bible. John emphasizes that what he has seen in visions will "shortly come to pass" and that the "time is at hand." Jesus Christ, moreover, repeatedly declares that he will soon come. "Surely I come quickly," Jesus says in his final words recorded by John.[5]

Apocalyptic texts and ideas were widespread by Christianity's second century. Irenaeus, a bishop in Gaul, believed that the Roman persecution of Christians signaled the advent of Antichrist's reign (the figure of Antichrist appears in two New Testament epistles, though not in the Book of Revelation). The Antichrist, Irenaeus taught, "will reign for three years and six months, and sit in the temple at Jerusalem; and then the Lord will come from heaven in the clouds, in the glory of the Father, sending this man [Antichrist] and those who follow him into the lake of fire; but bringing in for the righteous the times of the kingdom, that is, the rest, the hallowed seventh day." In an apocalyptic reversal, martyrs would reign with their savior, while their persecutors could only expect God's wrath. For Irenaeus, there was nothing allegorical about Christ's thousand-year reign, the physical resurrection of the dead, or the paradisiacal renewal of the earth.[6]

As the Roman persecution of Christians gave way to state-supported Christendom, though, the idea of a coming tribulation held less sway. Augustine, bishop of the North African city of Hippo in the early fifth century, rejected the application of biblical prophecy to present-day events and people. Instead, Augustine understood the apocalyptic sections of scripture as illustrating the struggle between good and evil within each human heart. That Jesus would eventually return remained Christian doctrine. In the year 381, a church council at Constantinople had affirmed that Jesus was "coming again with glory to judge the living and the dead."[7] Still, fewer Christians anticipated his imminent Second Coming or the literal thousand-year reign of their savior upon the earth. As Christians came to rule on earth, they displayed less interest in Jesus Christ's future reign.

If thoughts of the Second Coming and millennium became less widespread among Christians, the Book of Revelation and other apocalyptic passages in the Bible ensured their periodic reemergence. In particular, several groups came to believe that the New Jerusalem would descend, not in Palestine, but in their midst. For example, a fifteenth-century Bohemian group known as the Taborites believed that Jesus Christ would return to a mountain south of Prague (which they had renamed Mount Tabor, after the mountain in Palestine believed to be the site of Jesus's transfiguration, from which he had ascended, and to which he would return). Likewise, in 1534, a group of radical Anabaptists (the name means to baptize again, for the group's insistence on the rebaptism of those who had been baptized as infants) established their own city-state in Münster, in present-day northwestern Germany. They believed the Second Coming was imminent, and they called Münster their "Zion," the "New Jerusalem" predicted in the Book of Revelation. Along with other millenarian groups, the Taborites and the Münster Anabaptists understood themselves to be playing a key role in the unfolding of biblical apocalypse. Both groups prepared for war against what they perceived to be the armies of the Antichrist. Both movements suffered crushing military defeats. Meanwhile, the leading Protestant reformers largely kept apocalypticism at arm's length.[8]

The European discovery, conquest, and colonization of the Americas prompted Christians to ponder how new lands and new peoples fit into their understanding of sacred chronology, past and future. Many Puritans who immigrated to New England understood themselves as God's new Israelites, a chosen people rescued from their persecutors. The landscape and peoples they encountered carried what seemed to be hints of a distant, biblical past. Some New Englanders wondered whether the Garden of Eden had been on American soil, while others identified Indian tongues as lapsed versions of the language of heaven lost after the Tower of Babel. A few Puritans, such as Samuel Sewall, speculated that the city of New Jerusalem might be in the new world rather than the old, but that suggestion did not gain a foothold. Most eschatological theories among the Puritans hinged on the conversion of the Jews and their return to their ancient homeland. Some Puritans hypothesized that Native Americans were descendants of the Israelites, so they too would have to be converted "before the end can be."[9]

There were many other events to parse and many ways to parse them. The Massachusetts minister and theologian Jonathan Edwards, for instance, interpreted both the "awakenings" (later termed "revivals," these were times of unusually high numbers of conversions) of the 1730s and 1740s and British victories over Catholic France as harbingers of the approaching millennium, which Edwards understood as the gradual eclipse of Antichrist's power.[10]

A century later, American Protestants were nearly united in their belief that the millennium was near. In 1830, the revivals of the early nineteenth century were cresting. Methodists, Baptists, and others flocked to camp meetings in the American hinterlands, and that fall famed evangelist Charles Finney began a half-year-long campaign in Rochester (only a day's ride from Joseph Smith's Palmyra). Especially as the United States expanded to the West, it was easy for American evangelicals to imagine their brand of Christianity sweeping the nation and the world. Partway through the Rochester revival, a euphoric Finney told a rapt audience that if they "were united all over the world the millennium might be brought about in three months."[11] Finney and likeminded Protestants anticipated that evangelism, social reform, and the expansion of the United States would bring about God's kingdom upon the earth. Other Protestants scoffed at the idea that any program of evangelism and reform would bring about an earthly millennium. They foresaw doomsday rather than social progress. Such ideas gained force a few decades later, during the American Civil War. "Mine eyes have seen the glory of the coming of the Lord," sang Union soldiers, "he is trampling out the vintage where the grapes of wrath are stored." Protestants disagreed about the sequence of coming events. Finney and most of his contemporaries (termed postmillennialists by scholars) believed that Christ would return only after they had established his millennial kingdom upon the earth. By contrast, premillenialists expected catastrophic divine judgment, followed by Jesus Christ's return and millennial reign. The latter position gained support as the nineteenth century proceeded.[12]

For a select number of Americans, expectations of the Second Coming were even more consequential. This was especially true on the religious margins. For example, the United Society of Believers in Christ's Second Appearing, known as the Shakers, believed that Christ had returned in the person of Ann Lee. Her followers gathered themselves into communities, lived under a set of regulations—which included the strict separation of the sexes—named "Millennial Laws," and used a hymnal titled *Millennial Praises*. For the Shakers, the millennial order had already begun. A host of other small movements also organized themselves around apocalyptic expectations. George Rapp, a German Pietist, immigrated to Pennsylvania and gathered several hundred followers who practiced communal living and celibacy. Rapp expected to personally present his community, known as the Harmonists, to Jesus Christ upon his return, which Rapp thought might take place in 1829.[13]

In the early 1820s, a Baptist minister named William Miller became convinced that the Son of God would return to the earth by 1843. Miller's views were shaped by his reading of several commentaries on biblical prophecy and by his own examination of key apocalyptic books such as Ezekiel, Daniel, and Revelation. By the early 1830s, Miller began publicizing his views, as he wrote, "that the world might get ready to believe and get ready to meet the Judge and the Bridegroom at his coming."[14] In an 1831 letter, Miller predicted that when Jesus returned "in the year 1843 or before," the dead "Saints" would rise and the "children of God" then alive would be "changed" and rise up into the air to be married to Jesus. Meanwhile, "the World and all the wicked will be burnt up." After this outpouring of wrath, "Christ will descend and reign personally with his Saints." After a thousand years, God would resurrect the wicked and consign them to everlasting punishment. Miller's prophetic calculations proved alluring. By 1843, hundreds of thousands of "Millerites" eagerly expected the fulfillment of his predictions. In the early American republic, many different attempts to untangle the web of apocalyptic prophecies found an audience.[15]

Joseph Smith and his church's early missionaries also gained a hearing, partly by providing new answers to old Christian questions about the Second Coming. The Mormons tapped into a general Protestant anticipation of Christ's return, but Mormon scriptures and revelations provided distinctive guidance for believers on how to prepare themselves for this epochal event.

The Book of Mormon provided Joseph Smith's early followers with distinctive ways of thinking about what it termed the "latter days."[16] In the Book of Mormon, the prophet Ether predicts that "a New Jerusalem should be built up upon this land, unto the remnant of the seed of Joseph." Early Mormons understood the American Indians as the descendants of the Book of Mormon "Lamanites," themselves descendants of the biblical Joseph. Thus, church members expected converted and redeemed Indians to flock to a new city of Zion, an American New

Jerusalem. In the minds of some church members, the forced 1830s removal of Native Americans beyond the Mississippi seemed a step toward the fulfillment of these prophecies. The Book of Mormon also foretells the gathering and redemption of Jews. "[T]he Jews which are scattered, also shall begin to believe in Christ," prophesies Nephi, "and they shall begin to gather in upon the face of the land." The Book of Mormon predicts a glorious future for converted Jews, redeemed Indians, and a select few Gentiles who, through their repentance, demonstrate themselves to be members of Israel. Early Mormons and their detractors alike perceived this message as central to the Book of Mormon. Even before the scripture's publication, one resident of western New York reported that it "speaks of the Millenniam day and tells when it is a going to take place."[17]

Other early Mormon scriptures and revelations likewise spoke of Christ's millennial reign. In Joseph Smith's revision of Genesis, the "Son of Man" informs Enoch that he will come again, but only after "a veil of darkness shall cover the earth . . . and great tribulations shall be among the children of men." His elect will gather together in a "holy City," where Enoch and his ancient saints will meet them. "And there shall be mine abode," Jesus Christ promises, "and it shall be Zion . . . and for the space of a thousand years shall the earth rest." For nearly two millennia, Christians had debated whether the millennial reign of Christ would take place on earth or in heaven. The Enoch material made it clear that Christ would "dwell on the earth in righteousness for the space of a thousand years." The members of the Church of Christ, with the resurrected saints of old, would be in their savior's presence.[18]

The words of Jesus Christ in Joseph Smith's early revelations fired early Mormonism with a white-hot sense of urgency. Echoing a passage in the Book of Revelation, Jesus repeatedly told church members that "the field is white already unto harvest" and that they should "thrust" in their evangelistic sickles and rescue men and women from looming judgment. The day would not last long, and those who rejected the message would soon face a macabre demise. "Wherefore I will send forth flies upon the face of the Earth," Jesus Christ warned in a September 1830 revelation, "which shall take hold of the inhabitants thereof & shall eat their flesh & shall cause magots to come in upon them & their tongues shall be stayed . . . & their flesh shall fall from off their Bones & their eyes from their sockets." Therefore, it was time to get to work, time for a final pruning of the vineyard, time to rescue individuals from the looming judgment. Those called to preach, Jesus Christ repeatedly explained, should "declare my gospel as with the voice of a Trump both day & night." In October 1830, a revelation dispatched Oliver Cowdery, Parley Pratt, and three other men as missionaries to the Indian Territory west of the Missouri River, sending them to play a role in the fulfillment of prophecy.[19]

En route to the West, the missionaries stopped in northeastern Ohio, where they baptized the Baptist minister Sidney Rigdon and scores of other men and women. That winter, Joseph and Emma Smith moved to the Ohio town of Kirtland, and hundreds of church members flocked to a new place of gathering over the next several years. Kirtland, however, was not meant to be their last stop.

When the evangelical itinerant Nancy Towle visited Kirtland in 1831, she found a community fired with millenarian zeal. The "Mormonites," Towle wrote, believe that "a day of great wrath, is bursting upon all the kindred, of the earth." They planned to remove to western Missouri, build a temple, and hold all things in common. Soon "they should increase, and tread down all their enemies," and after this time of judgment, "Christ Jesus should descend, and reign with them, personally one thousand years upon the earth." As a skeptical and distressed Towle left Kirtland, a number of Mormon families set off for the "Promised-Land," which they told her would be their "dwelling-place, forever-more!"[20]

Grant Underwood, the foremost scholar of Mormon millenarianism, describes the early Latter-day Saints as "moderate millenarians." Unlike the Münster Anabaptists (to whom critical writers frequently compared the Mormons during the nineteenth century) or the Taborites, the Mormons never chose to fight their enemies on the battlefield. In their economic and sexual values, early Mormons resembled mainstream American Protestants rather than groups like the communitarian Harmonists, celibate Shakers, or Oneida Perfectionists, who practiced a form of free love. Like other new religious movements in the early nineteenth century, the Mormons were dogged by rumors of sexual impropriety, but Joseph Smith did not in fact teach polygamy until the early 1840s. Some early church members experimented with forms of communitarianism, but Mormon leaders could never persuade most church members to put economic consecration into practice. Finally, unlike William Miller, Smith never set a specific date for Jesus Christ's return.[21]

Nevertheless, in key respects, early Mormon millenarianism was thoroughly radical. Mormon missionaries warned prospective converts and church members alike that judgment was nigh. In response, mirroring an impulse of both the Shakers and the Oneidans, many Mormon converts sold their property and moved to one of the church's places of gathering. They expected to build the city of New Jerusalem and witness the second advent of their Lord and king. Most of those attracted to Millerism in the early 1840s, by contrast, stayed in their local communities and prior churches. Except for those who undertook missionary work, their lives outwardly changed little. Mormon millenarianism set a people in motion. New converts flocked to Ohio, Missouri, Illinois, and then Utah.[22]

In early 1831, Oliver Cowdery's group reached Jackson County, in far western Missouri. Cowdery and his fellow missionaries briefly preached to several tribes beyond the Missouri River before U.S. Indian agents threatened them with arrest for evangelizing on government land without permission.[23] There was no harvest of Indian converts, but the trip laid the groundwork for other developments.

In a June 1831 revelation, Jesus Christ commanded Smith, Sidney Rigdon, and other elders of the church to go to Missouri. "I the lord will hasten the city in its time," the revelation promised, "and will crown the faithfull with Joy & rejoicing Behold I am Jesus Christ the Son of God." After Smith arrived, a revelation outlined plans as grand as the surrounding landscape was unprepossessing. It identified the town of Independence as the "centre place," pinpointed a site for a temple as "westward upon a lot which is not far from the court-house," and instructed church members to buy up all the land they could in the area to the west. This was, the Lord said, the "land of promise." At the time, Independence amounted to only a few frontier log cabins. The Saints, however, took steps to obey the divine commandments. They bought land, and Smith laid the first stone at the temple site.[24]

Like countless other American Protestants, the early members of the Church of Christ believed in a Jesus who was God's divine son, who had atoned for their sins through his bloody death on a cross, and who would soon come again. No other group of American Christians, though, envisioned building a city of Zion on the frontier to which Indian converts and their Gentile coreligionists would gather in anticipation of their savior's imminent return and reign. Smith's followers would build New Jerusalem, not in Palestine or Bohemia or Münster, but in the New World, in Missouri.

The imminence of Christ's return was a key component of early Mormon missionary preaching, as exemplified by 1831 convert Orson Hyde. On the heels of his baptism, Hyde traveled around the northeastern United States, stoking controversy by asking for the opportunity to preach within Protestant congregations and then delivering a blunt and surprising message: Jesus Christ was returning soon. The righteous needed to separate themselves from the wicked and leave their apostate churches behind. "[I] had a great liberty in speaking upon the gathering and the second coming of Christ," Hyde wrote in his journal in September 1832, "gave them a loud call to arise and trim their lamps and go forth, many I saw were cut down and melted into tears." Those who answered his call should go to Missouri, Hyde counseled.

The Mormons were very distinctive in their belief that converted Indians would join them in a New World Zion. Like many Protestants, though, they expected Jews to return to Jerusalem prior to the Second Coming. "The Jews shall be delivered in Israel," Hyde noted in his journal, "and the Gentiles shall be delivered in Zion." Alongside the New Jerusalem of Jackson County, the old Jerusalem was of great significance to Mormons who were occupied with thoughts of the millennium. "They have made one of their young fanatics," reported the *Painesville Telegraph* in 1832, "believe that he is a descendant of, or belongs to the tribe of Judah, & that it is his duty to repair to Jerusalem, to preach Mormonism, or assist in restoring to Jews their ancient city." The "young fanatic" was Orson Hyde, who a decade later would indeed undertake a mission to Jerusalem.[25]

The preaching of Hyde and others drew church members to Missouri. Starting in the summer of 1831, hundreds of Mormons settled in Jackson County. *The Evening and the Morning Star*, the church's Missouri-published newspaper, announced itself in its prospectus as "the forerunner of the night of the end, and the messenger of the day of redemption." It was obvious, wrote editor William W. Phelps, that "not only the day but the hour is at hand for all to be fulfilled." He explained that the "gathering of the house of Israel hath commenced upon the land of Zion . . . the children of God are returning from their long dispersion, to possess the land of their inheritance, and reign with Christ a thousand years, while Satan is bound." Come to Zion, the *Star* implored from Independence.[26] Its issues included numerous millenarian hymns, some adapted from Protestant standards, others written by Phelps. Jesus Christ was coming soon, and he would rule over the kingdom foretold by Daniel.

> *A blessing, a blessing, the Savior is coming,*
> *As prophets and pilgrims of old have declar'd;*
> *. . . And thus is the vision of Daniel fulfilling;*
> *The Stone of the mountain will soon fill the earth.*[27]

Along with many Protestants, Phelps estimated that it had been nearly six thousand years since the world's creation. Influenced by a recent Joseph Smith revelation, Phelps believed that the seventh thousand-year period, the millennium, would soon commence. Using his own biblical chronology, Phelps predicted that the world was only "NINE years from the beginning of the seven thousandth year, or sabbath of creation [millennium]."[28] He admitted some uncertainty with the dates, but the message was clear. The Saints should rush to Zion.

The revelations foretold the Lord's destruction of humanity, but Zion's future was bright. Smith envisioned a series of temples in Independence, in which the presence of the Lord Jesus would reside. The city would teem with thousands of people, all living together in harmony and industry. Smith sketched a one-mile square city plat, complete with wide streets and twenty-four temples. Eventually, God's kingdom would spread throughout the earth. As the saints flooded into Zion, "when this square is thus laid off and supplied, lay off another in the same way and so fill up the world in these last days." Any righteous individual could take refuge in the "City of Zion." Thus, Smith introduced an optimistic note into his predictions of the catastrophic day of the Lord.[29]

As Smith unveiled his grand vision for Zion, the prophet learned that the Missouri Mormons had agreed to abandon their Jackson County properties. Although non-Mormons in Jackson County had many complaints about the influx of church members, the heart of the conflict stemmed from the simple fact that Mormon settlers would soon outnumber other citizens. "They declare openly that God hath given them this county of land . . . for an inheritance," stated a group of Jackson County citizens.[30] Motivated by fear and animus, non-Mormon mobs attacked Mormon houses, ransacked a church member's store, destroyed the church's Independence printing press, and tarred and feathered two Saints. In July 1833, Mormon leaders agreed that they would leave within six months but appealed to the governor of Missouri for redress.

In November 1833, the Saints in Kirtland witnessed a meteor shower one morning before dawn. "I arose," Smith recorded, "and beheld to my great Joy the stars fall from heaven they fell like hailstorms." With the plague of hail predicted by the Book of Revelation in mind, Smith interpreted the display as "a sure sign that the coming of Christ is clost at hand."[31] It was not to be. A spate of anti-Mormon vigilantism had already forced the Jackson County Mormons to flee their homes and take refuge in nearby counties.

The next spring, Smith led a ragtag Mormon army—known as Zion's Camp—from Kirtland to Missouri with the hope of "redeeming" Zion. Ultimately, the Mormon prophet chose not to fight, and after a cholera epidemic, the surviving members of the camp straggled back to Ohio. Zion had not proven a shelter from their enemies, let alone from the predicted apocalypse.

Undeterred by the loss of Zion, Mormon missionaries continued issuing apocalyptic warnings to prospective converts and encouraged church members to gather with the Saints. In 1837, Apostle Parley Pratt published A Voice of Warning. Its first half was a defense of the literal interpretation of the apocalyptic sections of the Old and New Testaments against what he considered "spiritualizing." Like Smith and Cowdery, Pratt had no patience with allegorical or figurative interpretations of the Bible. Pratt predicted the gathering of Judah and the lost "ten tribes,"

Saints Driven from Jackson County Missouri, by C. C. A. Christensen, ca. 1878. (Courtesy of Brigham Young University Museum of Art. Gift of the grandchildren of C. C. A. Christensen.)

their defeat of invading armies, and their recognition of Jesus of Nazareth as the Messiah upon his return. Pratt further discussed the "personal coming of Christ," the resurrection of the saints, and the coming judgments upon "the Gentiles," especially upon the "fallen church." Only in the latter half of his book did Pratt introduce prophecies from the Book of Mormon, explaining the redemption of the "red Men of the forest" and the construction of Zion. His "gospel" was simple: "Believe on the words of the Lord Jesus Christ, repent of all your ungodly deeds . . . and come forth and be baptized, by immersion in water, in the name of the Father, and of the Son, and of the Holy Ghost, in order that you may be filled with the Holy Ghost." Pratt and his fellow missionaries, he explained, were preaching this message "once more, for the last time." Many nineteenth-century Latter-day Saints esteemed *A Voice of Warning* next to only the Bible and Book of Mormon. Its popularity— some thirty editions of *A Voice of Warning* appeared by the end of the century—illustrates the ongoing appeal of millenarian thought among the Latter-day Saints.[32]

Expectations of the Second Coming found expression within the church in many other ways. Joseph Smith Sr., ordained in 1834 as the church's patriarch, pronounced blessings on many church members in the mid-to-late 1830s. Modeled on those given to their sons by ancient Israelite patriarchs, the blessings typically included statements of Israelite lineage and promises of long life, large families, and abundant spiritual gifts. In 1835, Smith Sr. assured Jonathan and Caroline Crosby that they would both stand upon the earth until Christ came, whereupon they would "rise and meet . . . God in the air."[33] The elder Smith did not make this promise to everyone. "Sister thou art aged," he informed sixty-one-year-old Lovina Wilson in April 1836, "and according to the course of nature must soon go down to the grave and not see the Savior come in 'the clouds of heaven.'"[34] Jesus Christ would return soon, but not immediately. In 1834, the patriarch blessed his family at a feast in the home of his namesake son. He promised Hyrum Smith (the prophet's brother) that he would see the "Redeemer come in the clouds of heaven." He then blessed Joseph with the promise that he would see the "tribes of Jacob come shouting from the north, and . . . thy Redeemer Come in the clouds of heaven, and with the just receive the hallowed throng with shouts of hallalujahs."[35] Given the flood of millenarian revelations, hymns, preaching, publications, and blessings, many church members believed that Christ would return during their lifetimes.

Still, sustained millenarian fervor was impossible without the "redemption" of Zion, a subject that occupied many Mormon thoughts and prayers in the mid-1830s. In 1838, hounded by creditors and Mormon dissidents, Joseph Smith fled Ohio and moved to Missouri. The prophet identified a valley in Daviess County as Adam-ondi-Ahman, the place to which Adam and Eve had traveled following their expulsion from Eden. An 1835 revelation had spoken of Adam-ondi-Ahman as the place where Adam had given his posterity his final blessing. In May 1838, Smith stated that here Adam would also return to "visit his people in the last days." The next year, the prophet elaborated on the nature of that meeting. At the time of "the coming of the Son of Man," there would be a "grand Council" presided over by Adam, at which "all that had the Keys [prophetic authority] must Stand before him [Jesus Christ]." Then, Adam would deliver "up his stewardship to Christ," who would reign as the earth's millennial king. Many nineteenth-century Mormons also reported that Smith had taught that the Garden of Eden had been in or near Jackson County.[36]

Smith's own Missouri experience, though, remained anything but Edenic. As of 1838, the Missouri Mormons were clustered in Caldwell County, but they were expanding into Daviess and other neighboring counties. Again, the growing presence of the Saints aroused opposition from non-Mormon settlers. In the summer and fall of 1838, mobs began forcing the Saints to abandon outlying settlements. Non-Mormons and church members skirmished on several occasions, and Missouri governor Lilburn Boggs eventually ordered the Mormons to leave Missouri entirely or face "extermination." Although church leaders organized the military defense of Mormon communities, Smith in the end again chose not to fight. The Mormons trudged east out of Missouri and regrouped on the Illinois banks of the Mississippi River in a community they renamed Nauvoo. The American Zion appeared irredeemably lost.[37]

Events elsewhere also remained important to Mormon beliefs about the Second Coming. In 1841, Orson Hyde made the journey to Jerusalem he had long envisioned. Joseph Smith appointed Hyde and John E. Page, both members of the church's Quorum of the Twelve Apostles, as missionaries to the Holy Land. Page turned back in New York, and Hyde continued alone.

Before departing the United States, Hyde experienced what he termed "a vision of the Lord," a message from Jesus Christ. He saw London, Amsterdam, Constantinople, and Jerusalem. Hyde reported that "the Spirit" told him that in these cities were "many of the children of Abraham whom I will gather to the land that I gave to their fathers." Once he reached London, Hyde shared the contents of his vision and his mission in a letter to Solomon Hirschell, the longtime Chief Rabbi of Great Britain. Hyde informed Hirschell that God had repeatedly punished the Jews for their sins. Jewish idolatry had led to the Babylonian captivity. Hyde also offered a customary Christian explanation for the Roman destruction of the Jewish Temple and the subsequent travails of the Jews. "If condemning and crucifying Jesus of Nazareth was not the cause of this great evil," Hyde asked, "what was the cause of it?" Now, the apostle warned the Jews to take refuge because a destroyer was coming to make the great cities of the world a wasteland. Once gathered at Jerusalem, they would see Jesus Christ—their Messiah—coming down "in fleecy clouds of light and glory." According to Hyde's understanding of biblical and Book of Mormon prophecies, if Jews hastened to Jerusalem, they would get their ancient kingdom back while God meted out judgment upon their Gentile enemies. There is no record of a response from the ailing Hirschell.[38]

After stops in Amsterdam and Constantinople, Hyde reached Jerusalem. He looked upon its surrounding mountains and hills, "where prophets were stoned, and the Savior of sinners slain." Buffeted by a "storm of commingled emotions," Hyde wept. He was the sole representative of his church in a land that was to him foreign yet familiar. After a frosty encounter with several Protestant missionaries, he had an equally disappointing interview with a Jewish convert to Anglicanism who did not appreciate Hyde's insistence that he "repent and be baptized [again] for the remission of his sins." Three days after his arrival in the city, Hyde arose before daybreak, ascended the Mount of Olives, and wrote out a prayer, informing God that he had "safely arrived in this place to dedicate and consecrate this land unto Thee, for the gathering together of Judah's scattered remnants." He prayed that God would raise up a modern-day Cyrus who would reestablish an independent Jewish nation. On both the Mount of Olives and on Mount Zion, he built a "pile of stones as a witness according to the ancient custom," akin to the altars made by biblical patriarchs. Hyde also "used the rod," probably his cane or walking staff, as a means of divination or as a conduit for revelation.[39]

Then he left. Hyde made no attempt to preach among or convert Jews, other than the convert to Anglicanism. He had come a long way to write out a formal prayer, build two makeshift altars, and employ a divining rod. Indeed, Hyde's actions were entirely impractical for a member of a fledgling church that had barely survived its recent travails in Ohio and Missouri. The Latter-day Saints, however, believed that they were living out the long-awaited fulfillment of ancient prophecies. They were in the last days before the return of Jesus Christ. Prayers such as Hyde's might help set critical events in motion. The Jews would return to Jerusalem and embrace a savior their ancestors had rejected.[40]

Back in Nauvoo, the Mormons enjoyed several years free from anti-Mormon persecution. By early 1843, William Miller had made the Second Coming a matter of intense national speculation. Miller's followers—whose numbers vastly exceeded those of the Latter-day Saints—anticipated Christ's return sometime between March 21, 1843, and March 21, 1844 (and when that second date failed, in October of 1844). In April 1843, the Mormon prophet stated before a Sunday congregation that he had prayed to know "the time of the coming of the son of man." Smith's prayers were answered: "Joseph my son, if thou livest until thou art 85 years old thou shalt see the face of the son of man, therefore let this suffice and trouble me no more on this matter." The response suggested that Smith had already asked repeatedly about "this matter."[41] In 1844, as Millerite hopes again intensified before the spring equinox, Smith explained that "the Lord gave me a sign & said in the days of Noah I set a bow in the heavens as a sign & token that in any year that the bow should be seen the Lord would not come." Smith had seen a rainbow that year, and he thus dismissed Miller's prophecy. "Christ will not come this year as Miller has prophecyed," Smith corrected, "for we have seen the bow."[42] In contrast to the early 1830s, the Mormon prophet now made it clear that the "last days" would last quite a bit longer.

By early 1844, the troubles that had beset Mormon Kirtland and Mormon Missouri were repeating themselves, as Nauvoo was wracked by internal dissension and mounting anti-Mormon political pressure. Smith contemplated moving the church elsewhere because of growing anti-Mormonism in Illinois. Wisconsin, Texas, and somewhere beyond the Rocky Mountains were all possibilities. In the spring of 1844, Smith created what became known as the Council of Fifty, tasked with investigating potential sanctuaries for the church and with advancing a quixotic bid for the White House Smith had launched earlier in the year. (The Mormon prophet was dismayed that none of the leading party figures would promise redress for the persecution the Saints had suffered in Missouri.) Moreover, the Council of Fifty was "the Kingdom of God and his Laws, with the Keys and power thereof, and judgment in the hands of his servants, Ahman Christ."[43] At an early council meeting, recorded William Clayton, Joseph Smith was voted "P[rophet] P[riest] & King with loud Hosannas."[44] Council members envisioned that as apocalyptic wrath destroyed other nations and governments, the Kingdom of God would gradually expand its theocratic authority. They would reclaim Jackson County, and the council's members would then greet and serve their returned king, Jesus Christ. For the next four decades, the Council of Fifty met episodically, never assuming the grand importance that Joseph Smith had envisioned for it.

Jackson County retained a preeminent significance as *the* Zion, but Smith and other church leaders spoke less frequently of its redemption. Also in the spring of 1844, Smith greatly expanded the geographic meaning of Zion in what he termed "another great and grand Revelation." The prophet observed that among the Saints there was "great discussion where Zion is." "The whole America is Zion," the prophet proclaimed, instructing his elders to "build churches where ever the people receive the gospel."[45] Smith hoped the expanded sense of Zion would generate additional zeal for missionary work.

Still, as was the case for many Americans, the millennium and the Second Coming continued to loom large in Smith's imagination. In mid-June 1844, an exhibitor brought what was probably a copy of Benjamin West's *Death on the Pale Horse* to Nauvoo, and it stood for several days on display at the Smith's store. The Pennsylvania-born West sketched and painted several versions of a terrifying scene from the sixth chapter of the Book of Revelation, in which John of Patmos sees four horses, with horsemen poised to unleash destruction on the earth. "And I looked," recorded John, "and behold a pale horse: and his name that sat on him was Death, and Hell followed with him."[46] Smith, by then besieged by Mormon dissidents, mobs, and hostile politicians, spent some time examining the painting, in which Death raises its sword while men, women, and children lie dead and dying. Smith may well have feared that he might not escape his own troubles. Resisting arrest for having ordered the destruction of a dissident newspaper, Smith raised the Nauvoo militia and contemplated fighting a war he could not have won. Then, he decided to submit to his arrest. Smith and his brother Hyrum were confined in the nearby Carthage, Illinois, jail while they awaited trial. On June 27, a mob, incited by anti-Mormon editors and politicians,

Death on the Pale Horse, by Benjamin West, 1817. (Courtesy of the Pennsylvania Academy of the Fine Arts, Philadelphia. Pennsylvania Academy purchase.)

stormed the jail and fatally shot Joseph and Hyrum. The Mormon prophet died at the age of thirty-eight.[47]

In the years that followed Joseph Smith's murder, the nearness of the Second Coming remained a standard part of Mormon missionary appeals. By the early 1840s, the church had a sizeable membership in England and Wales, and missionary work was expanding—albeit with more modest success—in other parts of Europe. "Oh! Babylon, oh! Babylon, we bid thee farewell," proclaimed a hymn written by Scottish-born Mormon Alexander Ross. "We're going to the mountains of Ephraim to dwell." Those who remained behind, Ross warned, would endure "the wrath of Jehovah." Similarly, the Welsh-language *Udgorn Seion* (or *Zion's Trumpet*) warned church members of long-prophesied "plagues and destructions." The paper reported on possible Jewish emigration to Palestine, earthquakes, Cholera epidemics, and wars—all developments that it pointed to as "signs of the times." One Welsh Mormon hymn imagined the regret of those who did not answer the call to Zion:

> *Those who went to Zion despite the wrath of the world*
> *Are singing and praising in secure salvation;*

But we who refused to go with them
Are in the midst of hunger, plagues, with no hope of deliverance.

When they reached Zion, they would soon have Jesus Christ in their midst. As a Welsh-language hymn anticipated, "we shall always Live all with our Lord / The Son of man, heaven's Heir, With no veil to separate us." Many other hymns foretold of the bounty the Saints would find in the American West, a peaceful land of fertile soil and material abundance, where the Saints would enjoy a foretaste of their future millennial reign. Ross's above-mentioned hymn included a vision of "the mountains sublime, Cover'd over with Saints, milk, honey, and wine." As such language hints, millenarian expectations were not the only reason European church members chose to emigrate. Many emigrants simply longed for a more abundant life in the United States or for the chance to gather with the Saints. Still, millenarian rhetoric was pervasive, as Latter-day Saint missionaries encouraged converts to sell their homes and flee to an earthly Zion. In this sense, Mormon millenarianism remained radical and concrete.[48]

Latter-day Saint preaching in the decades following Smith's death introduced new themes as well. "[K]now ye not that here is Zion?" Brigham Young asked the Latter-day Saints at the church's April 1845 conference in Nauvoo. "[K]now ye not that the millennium has commenced? We have had Zion upon the earth this fourteen years." In addition to Jackson County or any place of gathering, Zion also meant a people united in heart and mind, possible in the here and now. "We are not going to wait for angels," he instructed in 1862, "or for Enoch and his company to come and build up Zion, but we are going to build it." The Saints should busy themselves with the tasks at hand. The task of building up Zion communities in Deseret and Utah largely superseded the older goal of redeeming Zion in Jackson County.[49]

The temple theology and its related ordinances also reshaped the way that Mormons envisioned the millennium. While still predicting the destruction of the wicked at the time of Jesus Christ's return, Mormon leaders now explained that the living and resurrected Saints would spend the millennium in temples, performing divinely required rituals on behalf of the entire human family stretching back toward Adam. The Saints would be "saviors on Mount Zion," working together to redeem their ancestors. In the 1840s, Joseph Smith had introduced the idea that church members could perform proxy rituals for individuals who had died prior to the church's 1830 founding. The church taught that baptism was a strict requirement for salvation, and other ordinances—including being sealed in marriage—were needed in order for couples to attain celestial glory. The living could perform these ordinances on behalf of the dead, however, giving them an opportunity to embrace the gospel posthumously. During the millennium, such work would reach its consummation.[50]

Earthy realities disrupted irenic thoughts about the millennium. During the 1857–1858 Utah War, when President James Buchanan sent a U.S. Army expeditionary force to replace Brigham Young with a non-Mormon governor, Young speculated that the "winding up scene" was at hand. As Joseph Smith had done on several occasions, Young mobilized church members to fight but backed down when faced with certain defeat. Several years later, the Civil War sparked another resurgence of millenarian excitement. An 1832 revelation dictated by Joseph Smith had stated that "the wars that will shortly come to pass beginning at the rebellion of South Carolina . . . will eventually terminate in the death and misery of many souls."[51] Ten years later, Smith had prophesied that in South Carolina the "bloodshed . . . preparatory to the coming of the son of man will commence." Because South Carolina's secession and seizure of federal property had sparked the Civil War, Mormon leaders hoped that the carnage in the East might pave the way for the Saints' long-awaited return to Zion. In 1862, Young said that he expected to return to Jackson County in seven years. He did not want to complete the Salt Lake Temple because, he suggested, "there will not be any Temple finished until the One is finished in Jackson County Missouri."[52] The Union victory dampened such talk, and Young changed his mind about other temples.

Church members possessed many different ideas about when the millennium might come, what signs signaled its approach, and how they might hasten its coming. The Saints had expected that their exodus to the West would facilitate the redemption of the Lamanites, understood as a precondition for the Second Coming. Conquest and settlement took precedence over the evangelization of the Indians, but when such efforts met with occasional success, they excited millenarian expectations. Also, in the 1870s Young encouraged the residents of Mormon communities to consecrate their property and labor in cooperative efforts known as the United Order, reviving ideals introduced by Joseph Smith's 1830s revelations. Although many Latter-day Saints resisted ecclesiastical calls for economic consecration and unity, some church members connected the United Order with their millenarian timetable. "I have been looking for it [the Order] many years," stated Sarah Gibbons at an 1875 prayer meeting in Salt Lake City's Nineteenth Ward, "Joseph revealed it . . . when we go into it I think that will be the commencement of the Millenium."[53] The millennium and the Second Coming provided a lens through which mid-to-late-nineteenth-century Mormons interpreted a host of topics, from Indian conversions, to economic cooperation, to their conflicts with the U.S. government.

Mormon excitement about the Second Coming revived once again as the year 1890 approached. In its 1876 edition of the Doctrine and Covenants, the church published Joseph Smith's prophecy that he would see "the Son of Man" should he live to eighty-five years of age. "I believe the coming of the Son of Man will not be any sooner than that time," church members read. Although church leaders publicly cautioned that "the Prophet Joseph was not . . . definitely informed of the time of the stupendous occurrence," many Mormons fixated on 1890 or 1891 as the probable year of the Second Coming. Apostle Wilford Woodruff, for instance, informed an 1879 church conference in Arizona that "there will be no United States in the Year 1890." Woodruff also told church members that "thousands of the children of the latter day saints would not die but would live to see the Saviour come." As the U.S. government incarcerated polygamous men, seized church assets, and upheld the disenfranchisement of Mormon voters, millenarian expectations comforted a beleaguered church. Their enemies would not prevail in the end. Jesus Christ himself would avenge the Saints.[54]

In September 1890, Woodruff—now church president—called on church members to obey the law of the land on marriage. The change of course deflated millenarian expectations. Instead of Jesus Christ defeating their enemies, Woodruff had capitulated to them. One month later, Apostle George Q. Cannon sought to dampen millenarian zeal at the church's semiannual General Conference. "Concerning 1891," Cannon cautioned, "I will say the Savior will not then come in glory. Judah must rebuild Jerusalem, Zion must be redeemed and Jacob [the Indians] must be restored before this event occurs."[55] Other leaders maintained their hopes for 1891, but it became harder for most Latter-day Saints to believe that the United States would collapse and that their own kingdom would spread throughout the world.

The failure of millenarian predictions has brought about intense disillusionment within some religious movements, whereas other millenarian groups have persisted with their beliefs despite the apparent failure of prophecy. After their 1844 "Great Disappointment," the Millerites splintered into a host of factions, with most individuals drifting back into their prior congregational lives. (A remnant of those disappointed Millerites, under the leadership of the visionary prophetess Ellen White, founded the Seventh-day Adventist church.) The Jehovah's Witnesses, by contrast, have maintained millenarian expectations and a certain amount of organizational momentum despite the repeated failure of specific predictions about Christ's return.[56] Other Protestants have simply recalibrated their apocalyptic predictions when history moved in unexpected directions. "If the return of Christ was not around the next corner," explains historian Matthew Sutton, "it was always behind the corner after that."[57] For many Protestants, that past predictions have gone unfulfilled has not discredited the malleable framework of apocalyptic prophecy.

At the turn of the twentieth century, some Latter-day Saints still foresaw the return of Christ around the next corner. "Within ten, fifteen, or 20 years," promised church president Lorenzo Snow in 1899, "perhaps sooner, we are going to Jackson County." Only those who kept the law of tithing and the church's other commandments, moreover, would survive the judgments associated with the Second Coming. George Q. Cannon stated in 1897 that the payment of tithes would preserve church members "when the day of burning comes." At the time, the church was heavily indebted, and tithing receipts had declined during the depression of the 1890s. In order to preserve the church and ensure their place within the future millennial kingdom, church members needed to step up to the mark. The emphasis on tithing, though, rather than on the consecration of property as spoken of by Joseph Smith and as advanced by Brigham Young in the 1870s, suggested a backing away from the realization of the millennial order on earth.[58]

Nor did the LDS Church encourage its members to take it upon themselves to return to Jackson County. A small group of Mormons (known as the Hedrickites, for their leader Granville Hedrick) who did not join the exodus to the West eventually gained control of the exact spot dedicated by Joseph Smith and others in 1831 for Zion's temple. Along with the Reorganized Church, the LDS Church eventually bought adjacent land, but Mormon leaders never took any serious steps to "redeem" Zion.[59]

By the early twentieth century, predictions that Jesus Christ would soon return and that God's judgments would "cleanse" the world in a hailstorm of destruction were endemic among theologically conservative Protestants in America. Many of those who would become known as fundamentalists (and later, as evangelicals) embraced a prophetic framework termed dispensationalist premillennialism. Popularized by mid-nineteenth-century Plymouth Brethren leader John Nelson Darby, dispensationalism teaches that God relates to human beings in different ways in each of seven divisions—or "dispensations"—of human history. Darby believed that he was living near the end of the "church age." A seven-year period of trial was coming, but Jesus would return and "rapture" Christians from the earth prior to the great tribulations that precede the establishment of his millennial kingdom. The growth of Jewish Zionism and immigration to Palestine stoked the apocalyptic expectations of these Protestants.[60]

Yet while apocalyptic prophecy provided the lens through which many evangelicals made sense of their world and provided an additional rationale for evangelism, it generally exerted minimal influence over their everyday lives. For all but a few evangelicals, writes historian Timothy Gloege, prophetic speculations "were harmless parlor games that always ended with the reminder that no one knew God's inscrutable plan."[61] Few lived as if the world as they knew it would come to an end within their lifetimes.

In the several decades after 1890, the Latter-day Saints gradually moved into this sort of millenarianism. "STAY WHERE YOU ARE!"

ordered the church's Liverpool-based *Millennial Star* in 1921. "The counsel of the General Authorities to the yet ungathered Saints," informed the paper, "is not to flock Zionward under existing conditions."[62] There was no longer any need to take shelter from a coming storm.

Eventually, other storms arose, and if Mormon eschatology no longer led the Saints to gather to Zion, their leaders did call on them to prepare in other ways for Christ's return. In her memoir of a Cold War-era Mormon childhood, Joanna Brooks recalls that her Sunday school class studied long lists of "signs of the times," including the founding of the United Nations, the introduction of bar codes, and the teaching of evolution in public schools. Everything from the Equal Rights Amendment to un-savory music to the mere specter of homosexuality signaled both com-munist infiltration of American society and the Second Coming's approach.[63] Ultimately, though, righteousness would triumph. "All I knew," Brooks writes, "was that somehow, history was swinging our way, the way prophets had always predicted, toward the great destruction that would bring the opening of the skies and the return of a beautiful Jesus." Brooks recalled a reproduction of Harry Anderson's painting of the re-turning savior hanging on her refrigerator. The savior would come in the clouds to greet his faithful saints on earth. The destruction surrounding his coming, though, might temporarily make life on earth difficult for even the righteous, so Brooks and her family prepared both spiritually and practically for this great event. "Industrial-sized water barrels lined the back" of her home, and garage cupboards contained "giant tin drums" of wheat kernels, powdered milk, and dried pinto beans.

Among Mormons, Brooks's family was not unusual, either in its poli-tics or in its preparedness. In the 1860s and 1870s, Brigham Young had spoken of the need to store grain during times of plenty to prepare for famine, as the biblical Joseph had advised Pharaoh. By the mid-twentieth century, church leaders regularly reminded members that they should store a year's supply of food for all eventualities, including everything from natural disasters to possible unemployment. One such danger was the cataclysm that would accompany the Second Coming. Once

Christ established his reign, those righteous people still on the earth would live free from hunger, disease, and early death. There might be a time of famine during the establishment of the millennial kingdom, however. Especially under the leadership of church presidents Spencer W. Kimball and Ezra Taft Benson, the need to prepare was linked to "the last days." "The Lord wants us to be independent and self-reliant because these will be days of tribulation," preached Benson in 1980. "He has warned and forewarned us of the eventuality. . . . Those families will be fortunate who, in the last days, have an adequate supply of food because of their foresight and ability to produce their own."[64] Especially in the 1970s and 1980s, such messages were common. Church members should prepare themselves for natural disasters and times of economic dislocation, but also for apocalyptic tribulation.

With the end of the Second World War and the emergence of the Cold War, premillennial messages of doomsday became ubiquitous among conservative American Protestants, who fixated on enemy nations and dictators as the "beasts" and "Antichrist" of the New Testament. For these fundamentalists and evangelicals, Jesus was always coming soon, but the events of the Second World War's conclusion and aftermath generated renewed excitement. The August 1945 detonation of atomic bombs led many fundamentalists to believe they had witnessed the means of the coming divine destruction of the world. President Harry Truman himself interpreted an atomic bomb test in New Mexico as "the fire destruction prophesied" by the Bible. The 1948 establishment of the modern state of Israel, meanwhile, convinced many that the rapture was near. For many evangelicals, Israel's reestablishment meant that all of the preconditions for the Second Coming had now been fulfilled.[65]

In many respects, Mormon apocalypticism flowed on a parallel track. Latter-day Saints and evangelicals preached forms of premillennialism, connected their end-times speculations to conservative political concerns, and expected the world to hurtle toward a disastrous conclusion. "We are living in the Saturday Evening of Time," apostle Joseph Fielding Smith taught in 1936. Like his evangelical counterparts, he expected the world to grow in wickedness until the end. "*Do you think the world has improved?*" he asked. "If you do, you have not read [the scriptures] very carefully."[66] Numerous other Latter-day Saint leaders, including Ezra Taft Benson, Spencer W. Kimball, Cleon Skousen, and Smith's son-in-law Bruce R. McConkie, wove together apocalyptic speculation with fervent anticommunism in countless talks and publications.

While their rhetoric resembled that of their evangelical counterparts, Latter-day Saint leaders also retained many of the distinctive teachings introduced by their nineteenth-century predecessors. Christ would meet Adam and a council of exalted saints at Adam-ondi-Ahman, where he would "be received and acknowledged as the rightful ruler of the earth." Then he would destroy the wicked and usher in his reign of peace, which the Latter-day Saints would only enjoy if they maintained a high level of obedience and righteousness in the last days. Church leaders taught that at least some righteous non-Mormons would be present during the millennium. Missionary work would continue, and all men and women on the earth would eventually embrace the truth. Furthermore, as Joseph Fielding Smith explained, the chief work of mortal saints during the millennium would be "to labor for those who have passed beyond and who are waiting to have these ordinances performed for them."[67] In millennial temples, the Saints would perform rituals on behalf of the generations of the human family stretching back toward Adam.

Smith and McConkie were both keenly interested in the "signs of the times" that indicated Christ's imminent return. McConkie listed some fifty-one such signs in his influential 1958 *Mormon Doctrine*, most of which, such as the coming forth of the Book of Mormon, had already been fulfilled. Whereas many evangelicals interpreted the establishment of the modern nation of Israel as the final precondition, Mormons still looked ahead. As George Q. Cannon had articulated in the late nineteenth century, a few key prophetic conditions for the Second Coming remained unmet. For instance, McConkie believed the lost "ten tribes" of Israel would gather to Zion, that the Jackson County temple would be built, and that the Lamanites (Indians) would convert and become "white, delightsome, and desirable."[68]

McConkie also understood contemporary national and international politics as the "commotion" predicted by one of Joseph Smith's revelations.

Signs of this commotion are seen daily in the untempered
strikes and labor troubles that rock the economic world; in
the violence, compulsion, and destruction of property that
attend these strikes; in the unholy plots against our free-
doms and free institutions . . . Communism and every other
brutal and evil association or form of government are signs
of the times.

Other signs of wickedness included crime, "every form of sex immorality,"
juvenile delinquency, birth control, and unwholesome forms of entertainment. That McConkie and Joseph Fielding Smith included labor
strikes and communism among the "signs of the times" suggests that the
Cold War-era revival of Mormon apocalypticism was closely intertwined
with anticommunism and conservative politics, both of which deeply influenced Latter-day Saint culture during these years. As it did for conservative evangelicals, apocalypticism provided a means for the faithful
to make sense of a world apparently spiraling out of control. Doctrines
of the Second Coming and millennium provided the reassurance that,
despite moral decay or setbacks in Vietnam, Jesus Christ would ultimately take charge.[69]

Large numbers of Americans believe that Jesus is coming soon. A 2010
Pew survey found that 41 percent of all Americans affirmed that Jesus
would either "definitely" or "probably" return by 2050. Such expectations
remain especially common among evangelicals. More than half of white
American evangelicals believe Jesus will appear by the middle of the
twenty-first century, while a much lower percentage of Catholics and
mainline Protestants share this belief.[70]

The survey did not include enough Latter-day Saints to draw a firm
conclusion, but it is long-standing Mormon doctrine that Jesus Christ
will soon return. For most contemporary Latter-day Saints, though, the
Second Coming and the millennium are no longer even around the next
corner. Church members still encounter teachings about the Second
Coming and millennium in their scriptures and church educational
manuals. For example, a manual for the instruction of Latter-day Saint

collegians teaches that when Jesus Christ comes again, he will "come in power and glory with all the hosts of heaven," destroy "the wicked," "dwell on earth in the midst of His people," and "exercise political and ecclesiastical jurisdiction over all the earth."[71] As Grant Underwood has written, though, for "many Mormons these doctrines have a detached and textbookish quality."[72] Mormon leaders no longer discuss "the signs of the times" in any detail or speculate about the Saints' return to Jackson County. The subject of the Second Coming receives little attention in the church's semiannual conferences.[73] Educational manuals now suggest that the best preparation for the Second Coming is simply to be a faithful church member. "The best way we can prepare for the Savior's coming," explains *Gospel Principles*, a curriculum for the instruction of new members, "is to accept the teachings of the gospel and make them part of our lives. We should live each day the best we can, just as Jesus taught when he was on the earth." Instead of extraordinary measures and urgency, contemporary Latter-day Saints are encouraged to practice everyday faithfulness.[74] Rather than expecting the cataclysmic return of Christ and the spread of God's kingdom in the wake of desolation, Mormons today are accustomed to the steady, peaceful numerical expansion of their church.

There is no simple explanation for the current decline in Mormon apocalypticism. The Mormon belief that Jesus Christ will soon return and establish his kingdom has waxed and waned at different times over the church's history. The individual personalities and interests of Mormon leaders matter a great deal in terms of theological emphases. For instance, apocalypticism did not fit as well with the geniality inculcated by Gordon B. Hinckley, who led the church from 1995 to 2008. For a church that pays careful attention to its public image, moreover, some old beliefs are largely off limits. "I believe that the Garden of Eden was in Jackson County, Missouri," sings the lead character in *The Book of Mormon: The Musical* to guaranteed laughter. Nineteenth-century and some twentieth-century LDS leaders affirmed this idea. "Jackson County is the garden of Eden," Brigham Young once insisted. "Joseph has declaired this & I am as much bound to believe it as much as I am to believe Joseph is a prophet of God."[75] Today, such ideas no longer receive public affirmation.

The history of Latter-day teachings about the Second Coming helps position Mormonism within the broader stream of Christian eschatology, in which expectations of Jesus Christ's return and millennial reign have ebbed, flowed, sometimes disappeared, and then reemerged in new forms. The LDS Church's Doctrine and Covenants is full of promises from Jesus Christ that he will soon return. "I come quickly," Mormons read in their scriptures again and again. If those passages are currently of relatively little import, future Latter-day Saints might well revive them.

CHAPTER SIX

ELDER BROTHER

THE EARLY FOURTH-CENTURY Council of Nicaea defined Jesus Christ as "from the substance of the Father, God from God, light from light, true God from true God, begotten not made, consubstantial with the Father." Jesus Christ was God's eternally begotten son, not a creation, not something God made out of nothing. Theirs was an eternal father-son relationship. Jesus was God, as eternal and divine as his father. He was not just similar to God. He *was* God. According to Nicaea, the Father, Son, and Holy Spirit were three "persons" within one united "substance" or essence."

Jesus Christ was God, but also human. The fifth-century Council of Chalcedon defined Jesus Christ as "perfect in divinity and perfect in humanity, the same truly God and truly man." Echoing the language of Nicaea, the bishops at Chalcedon asserted that Jesus Christ was "consubstantial with the Father as regards his divinity." At the same time, he was "consubstantial with us as regards his humanity." Jesus Christ was fully God and fully human. Within one "person" were two natures, one divine and one human.[1]

During these centuries, bitter and sometimes violent debates served as the backdrop for these theological statements. Over time, though, these ancient creeds shaped a set of Christian beliefs regarded as orthodox. God was one and three. Jesus was divine and human. Jesus Christ was like human beings in ways God the Father was not. For example, the first of the Church of England's 1563 Thirty-Nine Articles affirmed that there is "but one living and true God, everlasting, without body, parts or passions" and that "in [the] unity of this Godhead there be three Persons, of one substance, power, and eternity." The next article identified the "Son" as "the very and eternal God" who after becoming flesh possessed "two whole and perfect Natures." These ideas also point to some of the basic paradoxes within Christian thought. God was not material, but Jesus Christ—one of three divine "persons"—had become flesh and had died a human death. Most Christians were not conversant with the formal language of their creeds, but these basic ideas exerted a deep influence on the way that Christians thought about God and Jesus Christ.[2]

Christology—literally the "study of Christ"—was not one of the points of contention between early Mormons and their many antagonists. When Joseph Smith and his few followers founded a church in 1830, they drafted a set of Articles and Covenants that explained the church's organization. In the tradition of creeds, they also listed a few core beliefs. The Articles and Covenants asserted that the "Father and the Son, and the Holy Ghost is one God, infinite and eternal, without end," a straightforward affirmation of the creedal Trinity.[3] The Book of Mormon's title page announced that the scripture's purpose was to persuade readers that Jesus is the "CHRIST" and "the ETERNAL GOD." The Book of Mormon states again and again that Jesus is God. "I am the Father and the Son," Jesus asserts. The Book of Mormon Jesus is also human. In fact, the Book of Mormon teaches that even prior to his mortal birth, Jesus Christ had a body. The Nephite king Benjamin prophesies that in the anguish before his death, Jesus will suffer pain, hunger, thirst, and fatigue. Blood will seep out of his pores. When Jesus appears in the New World, the Nephites come to feel his hands and feet. When Joseph Smith published the Book of Mormon and along with a handful of believers founded a church, they did not indicate any intention to question centuries-old Christian teachings about the relationships among God, Jesus Christ, and human beings.

Early Mormons also understood salvation in ways largely congruent with non-Calvinist branches of American Protestants. The "Almighty

God gave his only begotten Son," stated the founding Articles and Covenants, "that he was crucified and died and rose again the third day, and that he ascended into heaven to sit down on the right hand of the Father, to reign with almighty power according to the will of the Father, that as many as would believe and were baptized into his holy name and endured in faith to the end should be saved."[4] The language again echoes that of ancient Christian creeds. Elsewhere, Mormon scripture referred to these teachings as the "plan of salvation," a phrase common to American Protestants. Because of the shed blood of Jesus Christ, God forgave the sins of those who repented and were baptized in the name of his only begotten son. More distinctively, Joseph Smith and his followers taught that baptism was a strict requirement for salvation, and not just any baptism. Only those baptized into the true Church of Christ would be saved. Still, becoming a Mormon meant joining a new church, not embracing a new understanding of God or Jesus.

Over the next twenty-five years, however, Mormon leaders gradually embraced a different metaphysics and a new way of interpreting God's "plan of salvation." God, Jesus Christ, and humans were members of the same species. They were uncreated, eternal, and material beings. Jesus Christ was the Firstborn, the premortal son of a Father and a Mother in heaven, and also the mortal son of that same Father and Mary. In the premortal existence, men and women had the same parents. Jesus, then, was the "Elder Brother" of men and women, and mortal humans could become like him and like their heavenly parents.

Mormons came to realize that their understanding of Jesus Christ both connected them to and separated them from other Christians. "Do the Christian world believe in the Son of God—the Savior of the world?" asked Brigham Young. "They say they do, and we certainly do; and we also believe that he came and died for sinners—died to save the world." Were the beliefs the same? "Yes," Young replied. "They do not know how to define it, but we do."[5] Young recognized that Mormon and other Christian beliefs about Jesus Christ were alike but different, often employing the same terms, but defined in distinct ways. After the early Mormon reformulation of metaphysics and doctrine, the Latter-day Saints still understood Jesus Christ as fully divine and fully human, but they had redefined what it meant to be a god and what it meant to be human.[6]

Shortly after the church's founding, revelations introduced ideas about human salvation not present in the Book of Mormon or the church's founding Articles and Covenants. In February 1832, while contemplating the fifth chapter of the Gospel of John, Joseph Smith and Sidney Rigdon "beheld" Jesus Christ, God the Father, angels, and "satan that old serpent even the devel" (also called Lucifer and Perdition). Jesus Christ then instructed Smith and Rigdon to write what became known to church members simply as "The Vision." Elaborating on the imagery and language of Paul's First Letter to the Corinthians (which mentions "celestial bodies," "bodies terrestrial," and the respective glories of the sun, moon, and stars), the savior taught that the vast majority of humankind would receive at least some level of eternal blessing. Faithful members of "the church of the Firstborn" would become "gods, even the sons of God." In celestial glory, they would dwell in the presence of God and Jesus Christ forever. Other men and women would receive "terrestrial" or "telestial" glory. Only a few "sons of perdition" would suffer eternal punishment.[7] The Latter-day Saints came to speak of three kingdoms or degrees of glory.

The idea of different realms of heavenly glory has a long history within Christianity. Many early Christians expected martyrs, bishops, and especially righteous individuals to ascend into the presence of God more quickly or to attain higher positions within heaven. Jesus had said that his Father's house had "many mansions." The late-second-century Irenaeus, for example, expected the most worthy to be taken to heaven, a middle group to occupy a paradise between heaven and earth, and the least worthy to reside in the future New Jerusalem on earth. Protestants rejected such ideas, and they also denounced as unscriptural the Catholic teaching of purgatory as a state for those ultimately bound for heaven but requiring postmortal sanctification. For nearly all Protestants, the afterlife was strictly an up-or-down affair. European and American Protestants made a binary division between the faithful who would equally enjoy heaven and the wicked bound for hell.[8]

At the same time, there were some recent antecedents for the ideas Smith and Rigdon introduced. The eighteenth-century Swedish mystic Emmanuel Swedenborg had divided the heavens into realms, the highest being the "celestial." The 1832 vision's shrinkage of hell, moreover, reflected a trend within Protestant thought. While most American Protestants sharply rejected Universalism, they increasingly hoped that most people would be saved. Even before the American Revolution, Joseph Bellamy, a theological disciple of Jonathan Edwards, had speculated that "above 17,000 would be saved, to one lost" by the end of Jesus Christ's millennial reign. Evangelicals still incessantly preached about the dangers of hell (as did early Mormons), but they expressed a growing hope that hell would be less populous than most Christians had previously believed. Even so, more traditional Protestant ideas about heaven and hell held such sway that many early Mormons initially found Smith and Rigdon's February 1832 vision somewhat baffling. Brigham Young recalled that it was so "contrary and opposed" to his "former education" that he "could not understand it." In their preaching, early Mormon missionaries bluntly stated that those who rejected their message would be damned.[9]

One month after his joint vision with Rigdon, Smith outlined the common nature of God, Jesus Christ, and humans. In a revelation, Smith produced a "Sample of Pure Language," the language of heaven, the Garden of Eden, and human society prior to the Tower of Babel. Speculation about the Adamic tongue had intrigued generations of Protestants, especially after they encountered new peoples and languages in the New World. Smith identified "the name of God in pure language as "Awmen" (Ahman, in later transcripts), meaning "the being which made all things in all its parts." Jesus Christ, the Son of God, was the "Son Awmen . . . the greatest of all the parts of Awmen which is the Godhead the first born." Humans, or the "human family" were "Sons Awmen," occupying a status higher than that of the angels, whom God sent to minister to people on earth. The revelation stressed the similarity between Jesus Christ and humans as the sons of God. All were "Sons Ahman," with God's firstborn son preeminent among them.[10]

In May 1833, Smith dictated another revelation. Little is known about the context of this message. The prophet was in Kirtland, wrapping up his revision of the King James Bible. It was a time of relative peace and stability for the church. Construction would begin on the Kirtland Temple in a few weeks. The revelation came in the voice of Jesus Christ. It combined several themes, including chastisements of Frederick Williams, Sidney Rigdon, Newel Whitney, and Smith himself. The Lord warned the men to pay closer attention to their families and children. "Joseph you have not kept the commandments and must needs stand rebuked," stated the Lord, who also instructed the prophet to "hasten to translate my Scriptures."

The bulk of the revelation, though, concerned the eternity and glory of God the Father, Jesus Christ, and certain human beings. "I am in the father and the father in me and the father and I are one," Jesus Christ asserted. The language echoes the Gospel of John's repeated affirmations of the unity between the Father and Son. "I was in the beginning with the Father, and am the Firstborn," the revelation continued. Again, the words evoke New Testament passages. The Epistle to the Colossians describes "Christ Jesus" as "the image of the invisible God, the firstborn of every creature." The May 1833 revelation reaffirmed the long-held Christian doctrine that Jesus Christ is God's eternal son.

In the revelation, Jesus Christ announced that "the fulness of John's record is hereafter to be revealed." Accordingly, the revelation introduced the further testimony of John (either John the Baptist or John the Evangelist), who explained that Jesus had "received grace for grace" from his birth until he "received a fulness of the glory of the Father" at his baptism. Jesus Christ promised that those men and women who belong to "the church of the first born" could become "partakers of the glory of the same." Here the words recall a New Testament promise that those with faith in Jesus Christ will become "partakers of the divine nature."[11] Those who belonged to Christ's true church could follow their savior's example and obtain a full measure of divine glory.

The revelation clarified that just as Jesus Christ had been with God the Father in the beginning, so human beings had been as well. Men and women represented eternal "intelligence," "spirit," the "light and truth" of God. "Man was also in the beginning with God," Jesus Christ said. "Intelligence, or the Light of truth, was not created or made, neither indeed can be." Like God and Jesus Christ, human beings had always existed. Humans are spirit, the revelation taught, "inseparably connected" to eternal "Elements." The revelation identified eternity as a characteristic equally inherent to God, God's Firstborn, and those whom the "Sample of Pure Language" had named as God's other sons.[12]

By the early 1840s, Mormon leaders had more radically revised their ideas about God, Jesus Christ, and human salvation. Mormonism emerged at a time when certain strains of science and philosophy challenged traditional Christian concepts of God and the universe. Thinkers from the philosopher Baruch Spinoza to the astronomer William Herschel to the theologian Thomas Dick, themselves reviving and revising the ideas of ancient philosophers such as Democritus and Epicurus, understood the universe as eternal, expanding, and infinite. Spinoza rejected the idea that a deity fundamentally separate from the universe had created it out of nothing (ex nihilo).[13] God became a master creative organizer, rather than a conjurer of something fundamentally different from himself. Dick strongly affirmed the eternity of matter, its dynamism, and the infinite expansion of the universe. "There is no reason to believe," he asserted in 1829, "that, throughout all the worlds which are dispersed through the immensity of space, a single atom has ever yet been, or ever will be annihilated." Dick wrote that "the Creator is replenishing the voids of space with new worlds and new orders of intelligent beings . . . new systems will be continually emerging into existence while eternal ages are rolling on." Early Mormons found Dick's ideas attractive and printed excerpts from his work in church newspapers.[14]

Though such writings provided them with sources of inspiration and language, Mormon leaders did not simply borrow a ready-made metaphysics from Dick or any other early nineteenth-century philosopher.[15] The preeminent influence on Mormon thought during the church's early years remained the King James Bible, which church leaders often read in idiosyncratic ways. Moreover, Joseph Smith was not the church's only creative theological mind. William Phelps, brothers Parley and Orson Pratt, and Eliza Snow all contributed to the gradual emergence of new ideas. Given Mormonism's blanket rejection of all existing churches, Latter-day Saint leaders did not feel beholden to ancient creeds or long-held dogmas. Instead, they approached the Bible and other sources of inspiration with striking openness and creativity. The result was an understanding of God and the cosmos foreign to most other forms of nineteenth-century Christianity.

As it incorporated these new ideas, Mormon doctrine placed God, Jesus Christ, and human beings within an eternal and infinite universe, and the Latter-day Saints posited a correspondence between the order of heaven and human life on earth. The Mormon "plan of salvation" became a pathway for human progression toward divinity and the restoration of a heavenly family to which God, Jesus Christ, and men and women all belonged. Before their mortality, human spirits were, as Parley Pratt termed it, "men in embrio."[16] Many of those spirits progressed toward mortality on earth. Furthermore, as John Taylor later explained, each man on earth is a "god in embryo."[17] Within this framework, Jesus Christ's sacrificial death provided for the resurrection of all human beings. It also provided an opportunity for a more select number to progress toward exaltation, which meant a higher level of glory within the celestial kingdom. Those that on earth made and kept covenants with God—beginning with baptism, but also including other ordinances performed in temples—would be exalted back into the presence of God, become gods themselves, and reign alongside God and Jesus Christ.

Each progression—to mortality, and then toward exaltation—rested on the free choice of men and women to align themselves with Jesus Christ, to take the righteous side in a cosmic conflict between Jesus and Satan. On this point Mormon scriptures and doctrines intersected with long traditions of Christian thought. The Book of Revelation narrates that in the midst of a "war in heaven," a "great red dragon" (Satan) "was cast out into the earth, and his angels were cast out with him."[18] Building on such texts, the idea of Satan or Lucifer as a fallen angel became a staple in Western literature, figuring prominently in Milton's *Paradise Lost*, for example. In the Book of Moses (Smith's 1830–1831 revision and expansion of the early chapters of Genesis), Satan makes an offer to God after the earthly creation of the first man and woman: "send me I will be thy Son & and I will redeem all mankind that one soul shall not be lost." God's "beloved Son," by contrast, tells his father simply "thy will be done." God rejects Satan's rebellious attempt "to destroy the agency of man" and is "cast down," where he becomes "the Devil the father of all lies." The Mormon appropriation of Satan's fall was novel for its identification of "agency" as the issue at the heart of his rebellion. Later Latter-day Saint leaders described Satan as having offered to save individuals regardless of their actions, thus inviting disobedience and immorality.[19]

Joseph Smith returned to the conflict between Satan and Jesus Christ in a later scripture, published as the Book of Abraham. In a portion Smith dictated in 1842, God shows Abraham that he is one of many eternal beings that existed before the world's creation. The text identifies beings as "spirits," "intelligences," and "souls" without explaining the relationship among these terms. The Abraham material clearly describes uncreated beings and an uncreated universe, however. The Lord shows Abraham "the intelligences that were organized before the world was." They were not created out of nothing, but instead were organized. God chooses some of the spirits, including Abraham, to be his rulers. Another spirit, a being "like unto God" (Jesus Christ) proposes making an earth. "We will go down," Jesus says, "for there is space there, and we will take of these materials, and we will make an earth whereon these may dwell." Again, it is a question of organization, not creation out of nothing. God approves of the plan and asks who will take charge of the task. Two spirits—Jesus and Satan—volunteer. "I will send the first," answers the Lord. "And the second was angry, and kept not his first estate and forfeited his future glory." The text adds that "many followed after him." The devil's punishment, Smith stated elsewhere, was to never receive a body. In the Abraham narrative, "the Gods" then create the world and create mortal humans in their image. In a premortal existence, spirits choose whether to follow Christ in accepting God's plan or whether to follow Satan. Those who align themselves with Jesus Christ advance to mortality. In this framework, mortality is not a punishment or misfortune. Instead, life on earth is a reward for premortal obedience and righteousness.[20]

In the early 1840s, Smith expanded on what mortal men and women needed to do to progress from mortality to divinity. Exaltation hinged on the fulfillment of divine ordinances, and several of the ordinances Smith introduced in the early 1840s were for couples rather than individuals. Church members needed an eternal companion to attain exaltation, and the exaltation of eternally sealed (i.e., bound together for eternity) families rather than the salvation of individuals became the primary end of Mormon doctrine and ritual. As families, the Saints would return to the presence of their heavenly Father and savior, and they would participate in the creative work of the gods. Marriage and pro-creation were the heart of exaltation. Those who failed to marry "for eternity," Smith privately instructed a few trusted church members, would "cease to increase when they die" (i.e., would not have any children in the resurrection). By contrast, the Mormon prophet promised that those "who are married by the power and authority of the priesthood in this life . . . will continue to increase and have children in the celestial glory." To be exalted meant the eternal increase of progeny. Smith confirmed this meaning of exaltation when he dictated his revela-tion on eternal and plural marriage. "If a man marry a wife by my word," the revelation promised, "which is my law, and by the new and everlasting covenant. . . . Then shall they be gods, because they have no end. Therefore shall they be from everlasting to everlasting, because they continue." Only those whom Smith sealed for eternity would re-main married in heaven, and their families would continue to expand. Other human beings would be eternally single, without their earthly spouses and children.[21]

In the spring of 1844, Smith publicly proclaimed many of the ideas he and other Mormon leaders had developed since the church's founding. Smith did not preach on the eternity of marriage. Closely connected to the practice of polygamy, that subject remained largely private. Other-wise, though, the Mormon prophet taught boldly. In April 1844, Smith spoke in reference to church member King Follett's tragic death. About one month earlier, Follett had died while working in a well. As a group of men lowered a tub of rocks into the well, a rope broke. The rocks crushed Follett, who had belonged to the church since 1831 and was—according to an obituary in the *Nauvoo Neighbor*—"one of those who bore the burden . . . in the days when men's faith was put to the test." Follett had endured the church's persecutions in Missouri. He had lost his prop-erty and briefly been imprisoned. The *Nauvoo Neighbor* praised him as "ever ready to lay down his life, if necessary, for the cause and the 'wit-ness of Jesus.'" A procession a mile long accompanied his corpse to its burial. A month later, his death still troubled the Nauvoo Saints.[22]

How might an evangelical minister have responded to the tragedy? Given Follett's long church membership and known faith, a Methodist preacher would surely have comforted those who mourned with the solace that the deceased would be in the presence of God and Jesus. Smith, however, did not provide consolation through such ideas. One could not, after all, peer into Follett's heart and know for certain that he had faith. An evangelical preacher in the nineteenth century may have also moved from solace to exhortation, warning those that remained to prepare for their own deaths. Smith did not take that tack either. Instead, Smith discussed the eternity of matter. The prophet contended that something without a beginning would necessarily have no end. God had fashioned the universe out of eternal "elements," which could not be annihilated. He urged his listeners to savor this doctrine, whose sweetness the prophet compared to that of honey.

Earlier in his sermon, Smith had insisted that "in order to speak for the consolation of those who mourn for the loss of their friend it is necessary to understand the character and being of God." Smith revealed "the great secret," knowledge other churches had obscured or denied. "God himself who sits enthroned in yonder Heavens is a man like unto one of yourselves," Smith announced. God had once had a mortal existence similar to that of his son. "God himself the father of us all dwelt on an Earth same as Jesus Christ himself did." The prophet refuted the idea that "God was God from all eternity," immaterial and unchanging. Instead, Smith explained, he would discuss "how God came to be God." As Jesus Christ later did, God the Father at one point had chosen to "lay down his body and take it up." "Jesus treads in his tracks as he had gone before," Smith added. Smith used Jesus Christ as a means of understanding the nature of God. He worked from Jesus back to his Father, who necessarily had all the glories—including a body—that his son enjoyed. Having established that a time of mortality was common to God, Jesus Christ, and his listeners, Smith urged church members to "learn how to be a God yourself and be a King and Priest to God same as all have done by going from a small capacity to another." This potential for exaltation, the Mormon prophet explained, should comfort mourners. It was not just that King Follett's matter persisted but that, for faithful members of Christ's true church, "all Earthly tabernacle shall be dissolved that they shall be heirs of God and joint heirs of Jesus

Christ to inherit the same powers [and] exaltation." For its twin asser-
tions that God was an exalted man and that men could become gods, the
King Follett Discourse became Smith's most famous sermon.[23]

Two months later, in another sermon only eleven days before his
murder, Smith said he would "preach the doctrine [of] there being a God
above the Father of our Lord Jesus Christ." Fleshing out ideas introduced
in the Book of Abraham, the prophet suggested that "there are gods many
and Lords many . . . but to us there is but one God pertaining to us."
Smith reiterated his point: "if Jesus Christ was the Son of God and . . .
God the Father of Jesus Christ had a father you may suppose that he had
a Father also." Again, Smith explained that Jesus "laid down his life and
took it up same as his Father had done before." Smith's words hinted at
a chain of divine beings who had "laid down" their lives and taken them
up again: a possibly infinite regression of gods and saviors. Drawing on
an array of Old and New Testament passages, Smith also spoke of a single
"head of the gods" presiding over a divine council of heavenly beings, one
of whom became earth's god. The universe contained a plurality, perhaps
an infinitude of gods.[24]

By the time of Smith's 1844 death, Mormonism sharply challenged
several key tenets of Protestant belief. Nothing but matter existed in the
universe. "All spirit is matter," he taught, "but it is more fine or pure, and
can only be discerned by purer eyes; we cannot see it; but when our bodies
are purified we shall see that it is all matter."[25] Within an uncreated,
eternal universe, God and Jesus Christ were father and son, two resurrected and exalted men. Smith and other church leaders now skewered
creedal definitions of the Trinity. If "all are to be crammed into one
God," Smith joked, "it would make the biggest God in all the world . . .
he would be a Giant."[26] Creedal ideas about the Trinity, Smith asserted,
were an affront to reason. The Latter-day Saints came to revel in their
dissent from Protestant creeds in particular. Brigham Young, president
of the church's Quorum of the Twelve Apostles in the early 1840s, lam-
pooned the "sectarian God, without Body parts or pa[s]sion his center
everywhere and cacormfrance [circumference] no where."[27] Mormon
thought had become radically materialist and its doctrine of God un-
ashamedly anthropomorphic.

Parley Pratt summarized Jesus Christ's eternal materiality in 1845.

What is Jesus Christ? He is the Son of God, and is every
way like his father ... He is a material intelligence, with
body, parts, and passions; possessing immortal flesh, and
immortal bones. He can and does eat, drink, converse,
reason, love, move, go come, and in short, perform all
things even as the father—possessing the same power and
atributes. And he too, can traverse space, and go from world
to world, and from system to system, precisely like the
father; but cannot ocupy two places at once.

God the Father and Jesus Christ were two separate beings. They were
of the same species, of the same family. And so were humans. As Pratt
explained, men, angels, and God were "one great family, all of the same
species. . . . In short they are all Gods; or rather, men are the offspring or
children of the Gods, and destined to advance by degrees, and to make
their way by a progressive series of changes, till they become like their
father in heaven, and like Jesus Christ their elder brother."[28] Although
some biblical texts presented God in very human terms, both Catholic
and Protestant theologians maintained a stark ontological chasm
between creator and created. The Latter-day Saints dramatically narrowed this divide.

Shortly after Smith's murder, the Latter-day Saints introduced an
idea that brought the orders of heaven and earth more closely together.
"O Mormonism!" proclaimed William Phelps. "Thy father is God, thy
mother is the Queen of heaven." Phelps had worked as Smith's clerk and
ghostwriter; he traced the idea of a heavenly Queen and Mother to the
church's founding prophet.[29] Other church members also advanced this
idea. In 1845, Eliza R. Snow, a widow of Joseph Smith, wrote a poem
titled "My Father in Heaven," which gained popularity within the church
as a hymn. "In the heav'ns are parents single?" she asked. "No, the thought
makes reason stare! True is reason—truth eternal / Tells me I've a mother
there." She looked forward to her eventual reunion with her heavenly
parents in their royal courts.[30]

Also around the time of Smith's death, the title of "Elder Brother"
for Jesus Christ gained currency in Mormon rhetoric. Many nineteenth-
century American Protestants described Jesus as "elder brother" or as a

"brother." Unitarians and others skeptical of Jesus's divinity emphasized his humanity and brotherly fraternity with men and women. Mormons, by contrast, had no interest in stressing Jesus Christ's humanity to the point of diminishing his divine majesty. William Phelps wrote that, in the preexistence, Jesus Christ "was anointed with holy oil in heaven, and crowned in the midst of brothers and sisters, while his mother stood with approving virtue and smiled upon a Son that kept the faith as the heir of all things!"[31] It was not a relationship among equals. Instead, Jesus occupied a position of unquestioned preeminence.

Other Protestants used the phrase "elder brother" to explain that when God adopts believers as his sons and daughters, they become the brothers and sisters of their savior. "Pronounce me, gracious God, thy son," stated one hymn popular among Protestants in the early nineteenth century, "Own me an heir divine . . . Jesus, my Elder Brother, lives / With him I too shall reign." The language of adoption resonated strongly among the Latter-day Saints, though as was often the case, they imbued a Protestant term with new meaning. Through his death and resurrection, Jesus Christ, God's "Firstborn," had returned to his Father in royal glory. Men and women, who had been with God and Jesus Christ as eternal spirits, could aspire to share in their Elder Brother's glory. God would make them his children as well. If they molded their earthly lives according to the order of heaven, they could anticipate an exalted return to their heavenly family.[32]

Joseph Smith's 1844 murder left many of the ideas introduced during his lifetime unresolved or unclear. Was there a single head of the gods above the father of Jesus Christ? Or did that being also have a father? If there were worlds without end, were there gods and saviors without end as well? Also, Mormons taught that matter was eternal and that humans were eternal. They were also "sons Ahman," the children of God. Had they always been God's children? If not, how did they become his sons and daughters? What was the relationship between eternal "intelligence" and "spirit?" What did it mean for a man to become like god? To become a god?

In February 1849, Lorenzo Snow raised a question at a gathering of church leaders. It was the first winter in the Valley of the Great Salt Lake for many church members. Days earlier, Snow had been ordained as a member of the church's Quorum of the Twelve Apostles. During these years of doctrinal innovation and experimentation, church leaders often spent evenings chatting about matters of theology. Snow objected to the use of the title "Elder Brother" for Jesus Christ. For Snow, Jesus Christ was "of a different grade than prophets or more than our [brother] he is God the Father, and not our Elder Brother." Brigham Young rejected the idea of a strict divide between God and humanity. "As he [God] was, so are we now," Young explained. "As he is now, so we shall be."[33] Men could follow the example of their Elder Brother and become like God. Young said the idea had come to him almost a decade earlier while leading the church's mission to England. Snow apparently was persuaded. He articulated what became a well-known couplet within the church: "as man now is, God once was. As God now is, man may be."[34]

The Mormon idea that men could become divine has many Christian antecedents, usually revolving around the related Christian ideas of incarnation and resurrection. The Gospel of John taught that in Jesus Christ, the Word of God had become flesh and in so doing had shown human beings the fullness of divine glory. The same passage in John's gospel added that the Word of God gave those who received him the power to become "sons of God." Many early Christian bishops and theologians explained that, in the person of Jesus Christ, God had become like us, so that we correspondingly could become like him. Most famously, Athanasius summarized that "He was made man that we might be made God."[35] Such ideas retained their currency in Eastern Orthodoxy. In the West, however, Christians came to so strongly insist on the qualitative difference between God and human beings that the concept of human divinization seemed hubristic and blasphemous.[36] Still, the idea did not entirely disappear. Even the Protestant reformer Martin Luther sometimes echoed Athanasius's language. "God becomes man," he preached in a 1515 Christmas sermon, "in order that man should become God." A decade later, Luther explained that as Jesus Christ had become human (*vermenschet*), so human beings could become completely deified (*gantz und gar vergottet*).[37] Both in the East and in the West, Christians who found such ideas attractive generally meant that humans could partake or share in God's divine attributes, such as holiness and immortality. Or they spoke of believers eventually achieving complete union with the divine. Luther, for example, explained that Christ could dwell within human beings, giving them the ability to overflow with the love of God toward their neighbors. For Lutherans as well as Catholics, Christians who partook of the body and blood of Jesus Christ in the Eucharist also gradually became partakers of his divine nature.

The Latter-day Saints understood the nature of God and human potential very differently. What was most innovative about nineteenth-century Mormon doctrine was not the mere idea of divinization, but rather the meaning of divinization. In the Book of Moses, God tells Moses that it is his "work" and "glory" to bring about "the immortality and the eternal life of man." For mid-nineteenth-century Latter-day Saints, becoming like God or becoming gods meant that human beings could join in this work, and they understood that work in material, pro-creative ways that would have horrified ancient Christians such as Athanasius. For early Christians influenced by Greek philosophy, immortality was an escape from the material world of desire. Sexuality distinguished mortality from immortality.[38] For mid-nineteenth-century Mormons, by contrast, those obedient to God's commandments in this world would enjoy the eternal persistence of family relations and reproduction.

In the late 1840s and 1850s, Brigham Young fleshed out some of his predecessor's ideas precisely at the time that polygamy became a fiercely defended principle rather than a poorly guarded secret. The new order of marriage on earth almost certainly colored the way that Young described the divine work of creation. For Young, Adam was God the Father, a resurrected, exalted being whose privilege it had been to create a new world. "When our Father in Heaven came in the garden of Eden," he preached in 1852, "Father Adam came with a celestial body, brought one of his wives named Eve. They then stayed and ate of the fruits of the Earth until they produced seed from native element and were made mortal." Therefore, Young concluded, Adam "is Michael the Archangel, is the Ancient of Days, is our Father, our God, and the only God we have to do [with]." Adam was not the only god of the universe, but he was earth's god.[39]

According to Young, Adam and Eve left earth after beginning the process of peopling it, but the exalted Adam returned and produced a son with Mary. Young knew that his understanding of Jesus's celestial parentage would offend many, but he maintained that the traditional Christian doctrine of the Virgin Birth allowed infidels to infer that "God is a whoremaster and Jesus Christ a bastard." Young countered that his view of Jesus's earthly parentage shielded Mary and the savior from such blasphemy. For Brigham Young, Jesus was Adam's son.[40]

By the 1850s, Mormon leaders taught that God had fathered premortal spirit bodies in much the same way that earthly men fathered children. Parley Pratt taught that each "individual spirit body was begotten by the heavenly Father . . . by the laws of procreation. It was born and matured in the heavenly mansions." Pratt's understanding of spirit birth moved away from Joseph Smith's stricter rejection of creation ex nihilo. Smith taught that human beings were in the beginning with God. Now, church leaders taught that when spirit bodies were born, they looked exactly like mortal bodies, as Pratt explained, "the one being the exact similitude of the other."[41] Such reasoning suggested that prior to this premortal spirit birth, humans as individual persons did not exist. While the Latter-day Saints had previously considered God, Jesus Christ, and humans members of the same species, church leaders now introduced an idea that allowed for a critical difference between Jesus Christ and God's other spirit children. Unlike the rest, God's Firstborn was also God's physical child on earth. God (Adam, according to Brigham Young), not Joseph or the Holy Ghost, had fathered Jesus. Wilford Woodruff recorded Young as explaining that "when the VIRGIN MARY was begotten with Child, it was By the Father and in no other way ownly as we were begotten." God had sired Jesus twice, once in heaven and once on earth. "Jesus Christ Our Elder Brother was begotton by our Father in Heaven," Young reiterated.[42] As Young explained more than twenty years later, "Jesus the Savior" was "Father Adam's oldest son . . . his first begotten in the spirit world, who according to the flesh is the only begotten."[43] Here was a Mormon version of Jesus as fully divine and fully human. And by virtue of Jesus's parentage, there was a distinction between his divinity and the divine potential of God or Adam's other spirit children.

Not all Latter-day Saints accepted Young's identification of Adam as God the Father. Shortly after Young began introducing the idea publicly, one church member overheard Apostle Orson Pratt object that "Adam is not the God that he [Pratt] is praying unto."[44] Young did not tolerate challenges to his authority, and he corrected Pratt both privately and publicly. Even though Young browbeat Pratt into ecclesiastical submission, his conflict with the intellectually rebellious apostle helped bring about an end to what had been a quarter-century of theological innovation. Young never abandoned his belief that Adam was God, but he soon downplayed its importance. By 1857, Young conceded that "[w]hether Adam is the personage that we should consider our heavenly Father, or not, is considerable of a mystery to a good many." "I do not care for one moment how that is," he groused. In any event, he said, "we are of one species—of one family—and Jesus Christ is also of our species." However they named him, men and women needed to prepare to become like their divine father.[45]

In order to do so, men and women had to follow one fixed plan of salvation: "no man from the days of Adam, no woman from the days of Eve . . . will go into the kingdom of their father and God, to be crowned with Jesus Christ, without passing through the same ordinances of the house of God." In other words, the requirements for exaltation, which included temple rituals, had not changed over time. Eventually, Jesus Christ would bring the resurrected and exalted Saints back to their heavenly parents. "Jesus Christ our Elder Brother will take the whole Earth, with all the Saints and go with them to the Father even to Adam." "[W]hen you see your father in the heavens, you will see Adam," Young explained. "When you see your mother that bear [bore] your spirit, you will see mother Eve." The exalted Saints would then undertake Adam's work on new worlds with new saviors. "Every world has had an Adam," Young taught, "and an Eve . . . and the oldest son has always had the privilege of being ordained, appointed and called to be the heir of the family, if he does not rebel against the father, and he is the saviour of the family." The work of creation was endless and eternal. Adam had a father, and presumably so did that father. There was no beginning and no end. It was "one eternal round."[46] Mortal life was a spiritual school designed to prepare men for exaltation. "My spirit dwells in this earthly house," Young taught, "brought forth for glory, for [the] express purpose of becoming like him that brought it forth." The resurrected Saints would imitate Adam's work. Exalted men would "beget spirit," organize a world, "and begin to bring forth their progeny upon it."[47] For Young and many mid-to-late-nineteenth-century church leaders, achieving godhood meant participation in this work of creation, the creation of spirit children and the creation of worlds on which those children would assume bodies and themselves progress toward divinity.

As much as Young made Adam the central figure in the world's creation, Jesus Christ retained significance as the agent of redemption. Young insisted that Jesus's atoning death enabled human salvation, but he explained the atonement in distinctive and controversial ways. Although Christians through the centuries had articulated many different theories of exactly how Jesus's life and death saved human beings, it was a bedrock belief among American evangelicals that Jesus's blood paid the penalty for human sin and assuaged divine wrath. Evangelical hymns in the first half of the nineteenth century dripped with the bloody language of divine sacrifice. For Latter-day Saints as well, salvation was inseparable from Jesus's blood. Many church members understood the atonement in penal, substitutionary terms. "Behold the great Redeemer die," wrote Eliza R. Snow, the church's most significant nineteenth-century poet, "A broken law to satisfy; He dies a sacrifice for sin / That man may live and enter in."[48]

By the middle of the nineteenth century, however, some American Protestants—the forerunners of Protestant "modernists" or "liberals"—questioned whether divine justice required Christ's blood. Was it necessary for Jesus to die in order for God to save human beings? In the 1860s, Mormon apostle Amasa Lyman answered that question in the negative. Lyman denied "the necessity of an Infinite Sacrifice to appease an Infinite Wrath which has no existence in the God-Mind." Former church member Edward Tullidge praised the long-bearded and grizzled Lyman as Mormonism's "Theodore Parker." Tullidge explained that, like the Unitarian transcendentalist, Lyman claimed Christ had come as "the spotless example of purity" and the "great preacher of the Gospel." Jesus saved humans through his moral example, not through his bloody death. When Lyman's teachings gained the attention of Young and the other apostles, the church president rejected the notion that human beings could obtain salvation without a blood atonement. "When you do away with the blood of the Savior you do away with all the Gospel & plan of Salvation," he told the remainder of the church's apostles. "It is the worst herricy man can preach," added Lyman's fellow apostle Wilford Woodruff. In April 1867, Lyman was expelled from the Quorum of the Twelve and lost his priesthood, leaving him only a "lay member of the church." Within several years, Lyman left the church entirely.[49]

As much as Young defended the atonement, however, he did not believe that Christ's blood had atoned for all human sins. Instead, according to Young, there were sins for which men and women could atone only through the shedding of their own blood. Church leaders began teaching what became known as "blood atonement" in the late 1840s, arguing that certain sins placed individuals beyond the benefits of Christ's sacrifice. "There are transgressors," Young explained, "who, if they knew themselves, and the only condition upon which they can obtain forgiveness, would beg of their brethren to shed their blood, that the smoke thereof might ascend to God as an offering to appease the wrath that is kindled against them." Exactly what those sins were was unclear. Church leaders named murder, apostasy, adultery, and theft as reasons for individuals to have their blood shed, voluntarily or against their will. Young articulated the doctrine frequently in the mid-1850s, presenting such bloody logic as a form of spiritual charity. Some church members had committed sins that could not "be atoned for without the shedding of their blood." Were church members prepared to assist their coreligionists? "Will you love that man or woman well enough to shed their blood?" Young asked. He suggested that killing such sinners before they had the opportunity to forsake their salvation "is loving our neighbor as ourselves."[50]

Young's preaching about blood atonement terrified some of his listeners; a few church members even offered their heads as punishment for their past sins. Young declined such offers, telling the penitent to avoid future transgressions. It is possible that the doctrine inspired a small number of extralegal punishments in early Utah, although it would be a stretch to argue that any sort of spiritual charity motivated such actions. After Young's 1877 death, several church leaders repeated his argument that there were certain sins for which only the sinner's own blood could atone, using Young's logic to argue for the propriety of capital punishment. However, they contended that only civil courts possessed the authority to execute such judgment.

The temple theology of Nauvoo, the figure of the martyred prophet, and Young's interest in Adam all contributed to a partial eclipse of the intense christocentricity of Mormonism's earliest period. The nineteenth-century events of the restoration of Christ's church rivaled those of Jesus's lifetime. An edition of the church's Doctrine and Covenants published shortly after Joseph Smith's death maintained that "the prophet and seer of the Lord, has done more (save Jesus only,) for the salvation of men in this world, than any other man that ever lived in it." On the tenth anniversary of Smith's martyrdom, Young informed the crowd, "I am an apostle of Joseph Smith Jr. that brought forth life and salvation to the world." Young knew his words were provocative (he said they would make his listeners "marvel and some of you perhaps apostatize"), and he did not mean that Joseph had usurped the position of Jesus Christ as God the Father's Firstborn. Still, the significance of Joseph Smith for human exaltation was immense within Mormon thought, and parallels between the two martyrs proved irresistible. "I am a witness," Young testified, "that he was willing to die for his testimony and the people and he did lay down himself . . . he did go like a lamb to the slaughter and like a sheep to be shorn opening not his mouth . . . and was slain." Young and other nineteenth-century hierarchs taught that Smith would play a central role in human exaltation. At the time of Jesus Christ's Second Coming, Smith would preside over the raising up of the Saints. "No man or woman in this generation," Young cautioned, "will get a resurrection and be crowned without Joseph Smith says so." In the last days before the Second Coming, the prophet held the keys to the kingdom of heaven.[51]

Such teachings amounted to a Mormon version of the Catholic affirmation of "no salvation outside the church": the LDS Church and its prophets were the mediators of salvation. Only members of Christ's one church could reach the celestial kingdom, and an acceptance of Joseph

Smith as God's prophet was inseparable from a place in the highest of heavens.[52]

Moreover, the reformulation of doctrine coupled with the practice and defense of polygamy pushed Mormonism farther away from its more Protestant, Christian roots. For the early followers of Jesus, while the Jewish scriptures and figures such as Moses and Abraham remained important, the figure of Jesus Christ came to tower over everything else. Somewhat similarly, in the years following his murder, the figure of Joseph Smith assumed a cosmic significance for Latter-day Saints. "Praise to the man who communed with Jehovah," begins a hymn written by William Phelps a month after Smith's murder. For Phelps, Smith's "sacrifice," much like Jesus's, had brought forth "the blessings of heaven." Smith was now "mingling with Gods," where he could "plan for his brethren."[53] The hymn became and remains popular among Mormons. As the prophet whose visions inaugurated the events of the "Restoration," Joseph Smith receives a full measure of reverence and love from contemporary church members. Brigham Young also elevated the figure of Adam as an object for human imitation. Partly because Young's successors rejected his identification of Adam as God, however, they recentered Mormon doctrines more fully around the figure of Jesus Christ.

Both Joseph Smith and Brigham Young were charismatic and visionary leaders who did not hesitate to speak openly, to dismiss established truths, and to offer audacious new ideas, whether pertaining to theology, politics, or marriage. That audacity created both excitement and unrest within the church. Through the early 1850s, Young had innovated with the same bravado as Smith, though he pulled back when new ideas met with resistance. Still, even Young's close ecclesiastical ally George Q. Cannon observed shortly after his death that "in the promulgation of doctrine he [Young] took liberties beyond those to which he was legitimately entitled."[54] Thus, after Young's death, and especially after the full abandonment of additional plural marriages in the early 1900s, the church moved from an era of theological innovation into one of clarification and consolidation. Prudence and consensus became more highly valued than boldness. As Utah emerged from its cultural isolation, both modernist and fundamentalist Protestantism exercised more influence on Mormon thought, and many leaders became newly sensitive to the church's reputation outside of the Great Basin.

The foremost figure involved in creating a stable body of doctrinal consensus was James E. Talmage, a geologist who had studied at Lehigh and Johns Hopkins universities. Talmage joined several other rising scientists and intellectuals within the church who sought to demonstrate Mormonism's congruence with modern science and, indeed, with American society more broadly. Talmage, like many of his generation, had grown up in what were still rough, frontier circumstances in which Mormon leaders often went underground to avoid arrest. With the conflict over polygamy settled, though, men like Talmage looked more optimistically toward the church's future. Talmage felt that new scientific discoveries about the age of the earth and extent of the universe confirmed the truth of the church's understanding of the cosmos.

Talmage, along with agriculturalist and educator John A. Widtsoe and prolific Mormon author B. H. Roberts, strongly believed in the compatibility between modern science and Mormon doctrine. All three accepted at least some aspects of biological evolution. Roberts and Talmage both read and appreciated the works of modernist Protestants whose optimistic views of human nature and social progress agreed with certain elements of Mormon belief. Rather than an emphasis on individual salvation, Mormons and modernist Protestants both focused on the gradual building up of the kingdom of God, even if the two groups understood that kingdom rather differently. Modernist Protestants placed more emphasis on human potential than on human depravity, and Talmage, Roberts, and Widtsoe spoke of the eternal progress of human beings throughout the premortal, mortal, and postmortal segments of their existence. One should not overstate this congruence. Nearly all Latter-day Saints dissented from modernism's tendency to interpret biblical narratives and miracles as myth rather than history, preferring a literal understanding of scripture. Still, Widtsoe, Talmage, and Roberts evidenced a creativity and relative open-mindedness often absent from Mormon theology since the mid-nineteenth century.[55]

In 1899, Talmage published *The Articles of Faith*, an explication of doctrines Joseph Smith had identified as central to Mormonism in 1842. In

James E. Talmage, ca. 1910s. (Courtesy of the Church History Library, The Church of Jesus Christ of Latter-day Saints.)

his book, Talmage asserted that "both the Father and the Son are in form and stature perfect men; each of them possesses a tangible body, infinitely pure and perfect, and attended by a transcendent glory, yet a body of flesh and bone." Though he did not explicitly repudiate Brigham Young's teachings, Talmage observed that "Father Adam" was formed in the "image of his spiritual Father, God." In other words, Adam was not God. Talmage criticized "sectarian" (i.e., Protestant) falsehoods, but early in his career he expressed a striking optimism about the eternal potential of all people. Talmage suggested that "in accordance with God's plan of eternal progression, advancement from grade to grade within any kingdom, and from kingdom to kingdom, will be provided for." Higher-ranking leaders urged Talmage to express this idea more cautiously; some later Mormon leaders would reject it entirely. More often, church leaders have taught that whichever kingdom individuals attain at the time of the resurrection will be their eternal station.[56]

Although Talmage had quietly rejected it in his *Articles of Faith*, Brigham Young's identification of Adam as God continued to generate controversy. In 1900, the future apostle Charles W. Penrose wrote that "it should be understood that the views entertained by the great leader and inspired servant of the Lord, were not expressed as principles to be accepted by mankind as essential to salvation." It was a private letter, but after the Reorganized Church published the contents in its magazine, Penrose reprinted it in the church-owned *Deseret News*, for which he then served as editor-in-chief. Two years later, Penrose added—not very convincingly—that critics had made too much of a misunderstood "single sermon" of Young's and a few "isolated passages" about a doctrine never "formulated or adopted" by the church. Penrose stated more forcefully in 1916 that "Adam was neither the Father, nor the Son, nor the Holy Ghost . . . Jesus of Nazareth, born of the Virgin Mary, was literally and truly the Son of the Father, the Eternal God, not of Adam." Penrose observed that the stray teachings of church leaders "who entertain ideas of a more advanced nature . . . are not put forth as binding upon any person." Church members, Penrose insisted, ought to have enough sense to understand the difference.[57]

It was apparent to Latter-day Saint leaders that the church needed to clarify some key points of doctrine. In 1914, the church's First Presidency

gave Talmage, now an apostle, a room in the Salt Lake Temple to prepare a book about Jesus Christ, narrating the savior's life within the
structure of Mormon doctrine. Talmage stayed in the temple until late
at night, writing out the manuscript in long hand. The following spring,
on eighteen different occasions, Talmage read portions of the manuscript
to members of the First Presidency and the Twelve. In the summer of
1915, *Jesus the Christ* appeared with the stated approval of the First Presidency and the Quorum of the Twelve Apostles.⁵⁸

Talmage identified Jesus Christ as the "Jehovah" or "Lord" of the
Christian Old Testament, God's agent of creation and the divine being
who had appeared to Moses and other ancient biblical figures. He strongly
affirmed that God was the literal father of Jesus Christ, who was the
Father's "only begotten in the flesh." Talmage, though, discussed what
he termed "celestial Sireship" with more discretion than had Young. The
apostle then devoted most of his volume to a straightforward recounting
of the miracles Jesus performed during his lifetime as recorded in the
Bible. In what became very characteristic of Mormon thought, Talmage
discussed Christ's atonement for human sin not only in the context of
his death but also in the context of his suffering in the Garden of Gethsemane prior to his crucifixion. In discussing this "frightful struggle,"
Talmage wrote that in "some manner, actual and terribly real though to
man incomprehensible, the Savior took upon Himself the burden of the
sins of mankind from Adam to the end of the world." Referencing a
teaching from the Book of Mormon and an early Joseph Smith revelation, Talmage explained that Christ's "spiritual agony of soul" in Gethsemane "caused Him to suffer such torture as to produce an extrusion
of blood from every pore." Talmage's book helped magnify the meaning
of Gethsemane within future Mormon reflection on the atonement, but
he also discussed the crucifixion in detail. The spikes that nailed Jesus
to the cross did not kill him. The accumulations of physical torture and
spiritual anguish had taken their toll, and Talmage speculated that the
soldier's spear that pierced his side may have ruptured his heart. Rather
romantically, though, Talmage used the idea to conclude that "the Lord
Jesus died of a broken heart."⁵⁹

Jesus's postmortal activities were also important to Talmage. Touching
on a passage in I Peter, Talmage discussed Jesus's visit to the "spirits in

prison" (i.e., righteous spirits awaiting postmortal redemption). That mission to the "spirit world," Talmage explained, inaugurated the church's vicarious temple work, in which church members perform divinely required ordinances that bring the benefits of Christ's atonement to the dead. Talmage also described the resurrected Christ's visit to the western hemisphere and appearance to the Nephites. After discussing the postapostolic "great apostasy," Talmage turned to the 1820 appearance of the Father and the Son to Joseph Smith, which he explained had ushered "in the Dispensation of the Fulness of Times" and the restoration of Christ's true church. Talmage's *Jesus the Christ* remains among the influential Latter-day Saint books outside of the church's scriptures, one of a handful of books that missionaries are encouraged to read during their time of service.

One year after Talmage's book appeared, he helped author an official statement from the church's First Presidency and the Quorum of the Twelve Apostles clarifying the relationship between the "Father and the Son." "God the Eternal Father," the church's highest-ranking leaders asserted, "whom we designate by the exalted name-title 'Elohim,' is the literal Parent of our Lord and Savior Jesus Christ, and of the spirits of the human race." They explained that Elohim, God the Father, was "literally" the father of Jesus Christ's spirit in the heavens and of his body on earth. Thus, Jesus Christ is the "Son of God," the son of Elohim, not the son of Adam. Church leaders observed that in their scriptures and revelations, Jesus had identified himself as the "Father and the Son." Jesus Christ, they explained, is the Father of heaven and earth because of his role as creator and because he becomes the spiritual father of those who accept his gospel.[60] Jesus Christ and all human beings are the spirit children of Elohim; therefore, Jesus Christ is humanity's "Elder Brother." Only Jesus Christ, however, had also received his "body on earth" from the same Father, from an immortal, exalted God.

Since the death of Joseph Smith, the Mormons had endured considerable conflict over how to understand God the Father, Jesus Christ, and Adam. Through Talmage's formulations, the Latter-day Saints had in a sense arrived at their own Nicaea. Subsequent Mormon leaders would approach the same topics with differences in tone and detail, but Talmage had helped forge a durable doctrinal consensus.

Many of the ideas that Joseph Smith, the Pratt brothers, Eliza Snow, and Brigham Young introduced in the nineteenth century became central Mormon doctrines, such as the belief that humans are God's spirit children who have the potential to become like their Heavenly Father. Other ideas, however, did not become doctrinal or widely held, such as Joseph Smith's proposed regression of gods or council of gods. Functionally, at least, Mormonism is monotheistic because of its strict insistence that humans should worship only God the Father. The abiding popularity and influence of Talmage's *Jesus the Christ*, moreover, illustrates that for all of its mid-nineteenth-century innovations, by the early twentieth century the LDS Church had firmly retethered itself to the Christian savior.

James Talmage did not spend all of his time cloistered at his writing desk in the temple. The studious apostle became a vigorous apologist for Mormon teachings, to the point of sallying forth where his presence was not wanted. In November 1919, Talmage attended the weeklong World's Christian Citizenship Conference, organized by the National Reform Association. The NRA (no connection to the Second Amendment group) already had a long history, stretching back to the Civil War. Many northern Protestants had been piqued when the Confederate States of America invoked "the favor and guidance of Almighty God" in its constitution. In response, concerned northern Protestants formed the National Association for the Advancement of the Constitution. Advancement meant Christianization. The group lobbied for inserting a recognition of "the being and attributes of Almighty God, the Divine Authority of the Holy Scriptures, the law of God as the paramount rule, and Jesus, the Messiah, the Saviour and Lord of all" into the preamble of the U.S. Constitution.[61]

Having failed in their efforts to secure the Constitution's amendment, these Protestant reformers broadened their goals after the war and renamed their organization. The NRA was not large; for a while, its support was mostly confined to northeastern and midwestern Presbyterians. In the early twentieth century, the NRA hosted conferences, published newspaper articles, and lobbied politicians to combat social evils such as Bolshevism, alcoholism, Sabbath-breaking, and—even after the LDS Church's capitulation on polygamy—Mormonism.[62] NRA leaders despised Talmage, because he spoke and published newspaper articles around the country defending Mormon patriotism and unabashedly promoting Mormon theology. Talmage wrote on topics such as "Man Is a God in Embryo" and "Deity as Exalted Humanity."

At times, Talmage argued that Mormonism stood alone among religious systems because of its unique philosophies of god and humanity. "In the popular classification of religious bodies," he maintained, "the Church of Jesus Christ of Latter-day Saints . . . is generally given mention apart from churches and sectarian institutions in general. The segregation is eminently proper, for this Church is strictly unique."[63] When Protestants questioned Mormonism's Christianity, however, Talmage altered his approach, as his main goal was to defend his church's respectability and Christian bona fides. Like many Latter-day Saints, Talmage rejoiced in what he perceived to be his church's unique doctrines, but he also contended for the acceptance of Mormonism as Christian.

Talmage apparently enjoyed the first few days of the NRA's November 1919 conference, praising its "liberality, toleration, and freedom of speech." On November 12, though, the program consisted of a full-day Conference on Mormonism, featuring topics such as "The Mormon Menace" and "Defeating Mormon Proselyting." The conference's report on Mormonism denounced its "bald claim . . . that the Lord God Almighty repudiated the entire Christian church of the world in 1820." Even worse, the report alleged, the Mormons were growing by converting Protestants. "Mormonism makes its converts from evangelical churches," it asserted. Polygamy was suspended but not renounced as a principle. The conference's report on Mormonism maintained Mormon "priests teach that God and Jesus Christ are polygamists." According to Talmage, speakers even accused the church of bringing "great numbers of women and girls from other states and from foreign countries to Utah, and this for unlawful and immoral purposes." The conference called on the national government to expel Mormon members of Congress, ban the circulation of Mormon literature, and warn foreign governments about Mormon missionaries.[64]

Talmage wrote a note to James Martin, the NRA's presiding superintendent, asking for the chance to speak. Martin announced to the crowd that a Mormon apostle had requested the floor. According to Talmage, Martin reminded the delegates that "the Conference then in session was a *Christian* organization, and that *none but Christians* had the right to be heard therein." Out of fairness, though, he asked the crowd if a "non-Christian" Mormon should address the conference. After a mixture of vociferous opposition and a few calls for tolerance, the conference gave Talmage "five minutes *as a courtesy*." Talmage eventually received ten minutes of time.[65]

Talmage in print proclaimed Mormonism's distinctiveness and segregation from other religious systems. Nevertheless, Protestant criticism of Mormonism as non-Christian stung. "I used the time in affirming my status as a Christian in the strictest sense," he reported, "and in citing certain of the Articles of Faith in proof of the embodiment of Christianity in 'Mormonism.'" Talmage proclaimed his church's belief in Jesus Christ as God's divine son. Naturally, the delegates were not persuaded and greeted Talmage's arguments with a "torrent of hisses and scorn."

Later in the day, the organizers brought Talmage back to answer questions, including whether he believed in polygamy. A woman asked if he "was not wearing upon my under-garments devices typical and commemorative of treasonable oaths taken and obligations entered into in the 'Mormon' Temple." Talmage bitterly contested the connection between the garment—worn by Latter-day Saints underneath their clothing following their endowment—and disloyalty. Not assuaged, the woman then suggested that Talmage should "be taken and stripped by a committee of men who should report their findings." Talmage wrote that afterwards, Protestant ministers surrounded and menaced him. He feared they might actually strip off his clothes to reveal his temple garment, but was able to leave unscathed.[66]

For Talmage's NRA opponents, Mormon doctrines about Jesus Christ—or any other point of theology—were beside the point. Conservative Protestants were not interested in discussing the details of Mormon

doctrine, no more than Mormons were inclined to move beyond carica-
tures of the creedal Trinity. As long as other Americans equated the
Latter-day Saints with polygamy (or with temple ordinances, garments,
and an identification of Adam as God, depending on the context), Mormons ipso facto were something other than Christians.

CHAPTER SEVEN

THE JEHOVAH OF
THE TEMPLE

"THE DOCTRINE THAT UNDERLIES the work in the holy temple," longtime Apostle Boyd K. Packer stated in 1980, "more than any other thing, sets The Church of Jesus Christ of Latter-day Saints apart from and transcendent above every other religious organization."[1] Non-Mormons familiar with other forms of Christian worship would find much that is recognizable at the weekly Sunday services in Latter-day Saint chapels: hymns, talks, prayers, and the "sacrament" (the Eucharist or Lord's Supper). Mormon temples, by contrast, are not primarily houses of communal worship. Indeed, they are closed on Sundays. Instead, "temple Mormonism" is a different sort of religious culture, with sacred garments, a complex liturgy, and restricted access. It seems that there are two separate species of Mormonism within the same church.[2]

According to Latter-day Saint doctrine, Jesus Christ's atonement provides for the immortality of all human beings. Nearly all individuals will receive "salvation": resurrection to some level of eternal glory. The atonement also creates the possibility for men and women to attain the "fulness of salvation" or "exaltation." The blessings of exaltation include a return to the presence of God in the celestial kingdom, the eternal persistence of family relations, and godlike participation in the divine work of creation. It is for humans to become like God. Exaltation is not simply a matter of individual faith and good works. Instead, Latter-day Saint couples and families secure the full benefits of the atonement through rituals (Mormons prefer the term "ordinances") performed in temples under priesthood authority. Because these ordinances are eternal requirements for exaltation, God has also made provision for those who lived and died without access to Christ's church and temple ordinances. Therefore, Latter-day Saints perform the same ordinances on behalf of ancestors, thereby offering the same eternal blessings to both the living and the dead.

Latter-day Saints who grow up in the church customarily begin coming to the temple as teenagers in order to be baptized "for the dead." Most often, those "dead" are the ancestors of other church members, who assiduously conduct genealogical research and submit names for the rite. In keeping with its firm belief in human agency, the church teaches that "proxy baptism" does not compel conversion. Still, Latter-day Saints optimistically believe that their ancestors will respond positively to God's offer of posthumous salvation.

Then, ideally as young adults preparing themselves for missions or marriage, church members return to the temple to be "endowed." The endowment ceremony is a sacred drama, in which men and women reprise the roles of Adam and Eve, receive instruction in God's plan of salvation, and covenant to obey God and consecrate themselves to the church and kingdom of God. The endowment is a prerequisite for what is, for most church members, the crowning ritual of the temple, in which a couple is sealed in marriage for eternity. When Latter-day Saints have received their endowments and been sealed for eternity in marriage, they have performed the ordinances that will secure their exaltation should they continue to be faithful. Most active church members fulfill these requirements as young adults (though the sealing requirement creates a sore theological burden for those who, for whatever reason, do not marry), yet church leaders encourage them to return regularly to the temple. If they do, they perform the ordinances on behalf of those who could not or did not receive them during their lifetimes. Mormon leaders themselves speak at great length of the temple's sacred importance and encourage all church members to prepare themselves to conduct "temple work" on a regular basis.

The LDS Church has dedicated 150 temples around the world, in locations from Anchorage to Africa. Except for a short time before their dedication, only Latter-day Saints with "recommends" from their local leaders may enter temples. In order to obtain a recommend, church members must affirm core church doctrines, tithe 10 percent of their income, "keep" the "Word of Wisdom" (no coffee, tea, alcohol, tobacco, and illegal drugs), maintain standards of morality and righteousness, and obey ecclesiastical leaders. Outsiders or church members who do not qualify for a temple recommend may not enter the temple, even to witness the sealings (i.e., marriages) of their friends and loved ones.

When they are endowed, Latter-day Saints covenant not to reveal the ordinance's sacred "signs" and "tokens," and church leaders regularly remind members of the importance of sacred silence regarding temple ordinances. In 1990, future church president Gordon B. Hinckley instructed church members about their "absolute obligation to not discuss outside the temple that which occurs within the temple." Hinckley warned of the spiritual consequences that would result from a failure to uphold the "obligation, binding and serious, to not use temple language or speak of temple matters outside."³ Strictly speaking, Mormons promise not to reveal particular portions of the ordinance, but Latter-day Saint hierarchs instruct church members to maintain a more general silence about the temple. Nevertheless, given the temple's centrality within contemporary Mormonism, it is impossible to fully examine the place of Jesus Christ within Latter-day Saint thought and practice without discussing the temple in some detail.

Temples in the ancient Near East and other cultures housed the gods and brought human beings closer to their presence. They served as places for sacrifice and places of worship. Temples also drew lines of earthly power, between adherents and outsiders, and among different groups of adherents. They marked some spaces as "qualitatively different from others."⁴ At the Second Jewish Temple in Jerusalem, non-Jews could enter only the outermost court (known as the "Court of the Gentiles"). Jews had to meet standards for ritual cleanliness in order to enter the temple's inner courts and rooms, and women could not proceed beyond another square known as the "Court of Women." Only priests could enter another courtyard, and only once a year on Yom Kippur (the "Day of Atonement") did the High Priest pass through two curtains and enter the Holy of Holies. Reflecting these antecedents, Christian churches as early as the fourth century screened or even walled off the sanctuary or altar from the laity; the altar upon which the priest or bishop consecrated the Eucharist was too holy for ordinary church members. Most Protestants in the early United States, by contrast, preferred simple architecture or the wide-open spaces of camp meetings and market places. If they separated the sacred from the profane, they did so through their standards of admission to church membership and the Lord's Supper.[5]

Smith and his associates spoke of restoring "the ancient order of things," reestablishing priesthood offices, spiritual gifts, doctrines, and rituals they found in both the ancient Jewish scriptures and the New Testament.[6] Given this impulse, it was natural for Smith to become a temple builder. As was also the case for terms such as "salvation" and "endowment," the meaning of the temple evolved over Mormonism's first fifteen years. When Smith sketched the future of Zion in Jackson County, Missouri, he described temples as "houses of worship [and] schools."[7] When church members dedicated a temple in Kirtland, Ohio, they understood it as the "House of the Lord," a place for Jesus Christ to fill with his presence, a presence that would endow Mormon elders with spiritual power and blessings. Drawing on Old Testament passages about priestly consecration, Smith and close followers were washed with perfumed spirits and anointed with oil in preparation for the Kirtland Temple's dedication. Smith told his elders to anticipate an "endowment of power" in the temple, and in the early spring of 1836, Latter-day Saint men and women enjoyed several days full of rituals in the temple, including foot washing and the partaking of the Lord's Supper.

Joseph Smith's ritual innovation—or restoration, as he understood it—reached its peak in Nauvoo, Illinois, in the early 1840s. Drawing on a verse in the New Testament about believers "which are baptized for the dead," Smith encouraged the Latter-day Saints to be baptized on behalf of those who had died outside of membership in Christ's church. Baptism was a strict requirement for celestial glory, and no other form of baptism would do. "All old covenants have I caused to be done away with in this thing," stated a revelation dictated by Joseph Smith in April 1830, "and this is a new and everlasting covenant."[8] Mormons believed that after centuries of apostasy, God had restored Jesus Christ's one true church in 1830. Joined together, these beliefs about baptism and apostasy placed in question the salvation of church members' ancestors, not to mention that of all the others who had died without hearing the gospel as preached by the Latter-day Saints. Baptism for the dead provided a ritual solution for this problem. Church members began collecting genealogical information on their families, seeking to bring celestial blessings to their distant progenitors.

Just as Methodist or Catholic baptisms were invalid and of no eternal significance, so were other forms of marriage. In the early 1840s, Smith began teaching that only those couples sealed in marriage under his authority would remain together for eternity and gain their exaltation. Smith also introduced a ritual known as the "second anointing," a capstone ordinance that promised couples even more blessings and spiritual assurance than they had gained through the endowment.

Baptism for the dead and sealing in marriage adapted existing Christian rituals to new theological ends. Other Mormon ordinances, including the endowment, did not have obvious Christian antecedents. Instead, the prophet found inspiration elsewhere, including in the rites of Freemasonry. Originally rooted in medieval craft guilds, Masonic societies evolved in the eighteenth century into fraternal organizations with appeal to a broad range of affluent and upwardly mobile men. Most American men who joined the fraternity did so for reasons of social connection and economic advantage, though Freemasonry also represented access to ancient myths, rites, and symbols that blended biblical content with esoteric writings and legends. Freemasonry steadily grew in size and influence over the last two-thirds of the eighteenth century.[9] Due to local diversity and schisms, Freemasonry by the early nineteenth century was a world rich in rituals and legends.

Although initiates swore not to reveal the ceremonies on pain of a gruesome death, both active and former Masons published extensive descriptions of them. In Masonic orders, candidates ascend to higher "degrees" of knowledge through initiation rituals, rites in which they participate in sacred dramas. In order to achieve the rank of Master Mason (the third and highest degree of Craft Masonry), a blindfolded candidate played the role of Hiram Abiff, identified as the architect of Solomon's Temple and murdered for refusing to reveal the secret "Master's word" to three attackers. The master of the lodge assumed the role of King Solomon, who raised the "dead" candidate and whispered a "substitute for the Master's word" in his ear. Initiates learned that they "represented one of the greatest men that ever lived, in . . . his death, burial and resurrection." According to an 1826 exposé, Master Masons looked forward to the time that "the Son of righteousness shall descend, and send forth his angels to collect our ransomed dust; then, if we are found worthy, by his pass-word, we shall enter into the celestial Lodge above, where the Supreme Architect of the Universe presides." The ceremony, full of biblical excerpts and allusions, reformulated the Christian anticipation of resurrection and immortality by placing it within an ancient quest for sacred knowledge.[10]

Royal Arch lodges, which became prevalent in the United States during the early decades of the nineteenth century, took candidates through other, more elaborate sacred dramas. One version of the Royal Arch degree "exalted" its initiates "to the summit and perfection of ancient masonry." In this rite, God appears to Enoch and directs him to the top of a mountain, where he sees a "triangular plate of gold" inscribed with characters containing the sacred divine name. Enoch is then "lowered perpendicularly into the bowels of the earth, through nine arches," where he finds the plate and builds an underground temple. Enoch buries the plate in a vault, and Solomon's master architects eventually find it. The Royal Arch degrees were also suffused with biblical narrative and quotations, and they too taught that ancient, primordial knowledge and secret names held the key to mysteries, priesthood, power, and immortality.[11]

Most American members of the fraternity saw no obvious conflict between Masonic esotericism on the one hand and Christianity on the other. Many Americans saw Freemasonry as a complement to Christian churches, a handmaid of religion, an enlightened sacred fraternity that transcended the sometimes bitter divisions among churches. Many

Christian Freemasons understood the drama of Hiram Abiff as an allegory of Jesus Christ's death and resurrection. While Freemasonry attracted intense opposition from some evangelical Protestants (Charles Finney disassociated himself from Masonry after his conversion), others defended the fraternity. Then in 1826, William Morgan, a western New York member of the fraternity, disappeared while he was in the process of publishing an exposé of Masonry's rites. Freemasonry was immediately plunged into a maelstrom of political and religious opposition.[12]

Joseph Smith had grown up in an environment in which Masons and their opponents figured prominently. Smith's father and brother Hyrum were both active Masons prior to the church's founding, and the Mormon prophet shared the fraternity's fascination with Egyptian hieroglyphics, the figures of Enoch and Melchizedek, and the recovery of ancient ideas, practices, and treasure. At the same time, western New York was the center of political anti-Masonry after Morgan's presumed murder. The Book of Moses seems to reflect this anti-Masonic sentiment. In it, Cain makes a pact with Satan and becomes "master Mahon" prior to his murder of his brother Abel. Thus begins a "secret combination." Later, Lamech enters into the "covenant with satan," becomes "Master Mahon," and murders Irad, who—rather akin to William Morgan—had begun to reveal the order's secrets.[13] Morgan's widow Lucinda, along with her second husband, George Harris (another former Mason), converted to Mormonism in 1834. Smith stayed in the Harris home for two months in 1838. After Smith's death, Lucinda Harris was sealed to the Mormon prophet for eternity in the Nauvoo Temple; she may have become his plural wife during his lifetime. Thus, there were many occasions for contact between Mormonism and Masonry.[14]

In the early 1840s, Smith began a frenetic engagement with Masonry. In light of the expulsion of the Saints from Missouri, Smith probably hoped that Masonic affiliation would provide Nauvoo with political advantage and protection, and he saw potential value in Masonry's emphasis on strict secrecy, which was of growing importance to a prophet besieged by rumors of polygamy. "The secrets of masonry is to keep a secret," Smith explained in October 1843.[15]

In 1841, Smith welcomed as newly prominent associates two men (James Adams and John C. Bennett) who helped him establish relations with the Illinois Grand Lodge in Springfield. Smith founded a lodge in Nauvoo, and, over a period of just two days in March 1842, Illinois Grand Master Abraham Jonas raised Smith to the rank of Master Mason. Over the next few months, hundreds of Mormon men passed through Masonic initiation rites, performed in a room above the prophet's Red Brick Store. Eventually, nearly 1,000 Latter-day Saints in and around Nauvoo became Masons. However, the Nauvoo Lodge quickly fell out of favor with Illinois's non-Mormon Masonic leaders, who were alarmed by the rapid elevation of candidates and by stories of Mormon sexual impropriety.[16] In the end, Masonry failed Joseph Smith badly as a source of political and personal protection, but it proved a rich source of symbols and ideas as Smith introduced a new sacred ordinance for a select group of his followers.

Two months after he had initiated large numbers of Latter-day Saint men into Nauvoo's Masonic Lodge, Smith assembled a smaller group of trusted men in the same upper room. According to a diary kept by clerk Willard Richards, Smith gave "certain instructions concerning the priesthood."[17] Described in a history written by Richards a few years later, this new ordinance prepared individuals to "secure the fulness of those blessings which has been prepared for the church of the first-born and come up, and abide in the presence of Eloheim [God] in the eternal worlds."[18] Four decades later, Brigham Young described the day thus:

> When we got our washings and anointings under the hands of the Prophet Joseph at Nauvoo we had only one room to work in with the exception of a little side room or office where we were washed and anointed had our garments placed upon us and received our New Name, and after he had performed these ceremonies, he gave the Key Words signs, tokens, and penalties, then after we went into the large room over the store in Nauvoo. Joseph divided up the room the best that he could, hung up the veil, marked it, gave us our instructions as we passed along from one department to another giving us signs, tokens, penalties with the Key words pertaining to those signs.[19]

The idea was that after their death and resurrection, Mormon elders would repeat the signs, tokens, and key words in order to pass by the angels and gain entrance to the presence of God.

What Smith had introduced became known as the "the endowment," which was more an entirely new ordinance than an expansion of the washings and anointings that had preceded the "endowment of power" in Kirtland. In Nauvoo, people referred to the group of initiates as "the quorum," "the order of the Priesthood," the "Holy Order," the "Anointed Quorum," and as "J[oseph]'s lodge." Several years later, Heber Kimball wrote that he "was aniciated [initiated] into the ancient order was washed and annointed and Sealled and ordained a Preast." Although they did not hold priesthood offices in the church, women too became members of this priesthood quorum. In October 1843, for example, Brigham Young observed in his journal that three "sisters . . . was taken in to the order of the Priesthood." Several days later, he noted that his wife Mary Ann was "admited in to the hiest orderer Preasthood." By the time of Joseph Smith's death, thirty-two women had gained admittance into the new quorum, alongside thirty-seven men.[20]

Those who joined first the Nauvoo Masonic Lodge and then Smith's secret lodge knew that the two were intimately related. Heber Kimball informed fellow apostle Parley Pratt in June 1842 that "thare is a similarity of preast Hood in masonary"; Kimball quoted Smith's teaching that "masonary was taken from preasthood but has become degennated [degenerated,] but menny things are perfect." In the words of church member Joseph Fielding, Masonic ritual could serve the Saints as a "Stepping . . . Stone or Preparation for something else, the true Origin of Masonry." Smith and his associates openly discussed the connections between Masonry and "priesthood," the latter representing the true recovery of ancient Christian principles imperfectly preserved in Masonic rites. Not surprisingly, therefore, parallels between the Nauvoo endowment and Masonic rites were palpable. Masonry provided the immediate inspiration for the presence in the endowment of key words, oaths, penalties (including gestures that symbolized the gruesome punishments initiates would supposedly suffer should they reveal the ceremony's contents), robes, caps, and aprons.[21]

Other elements of the endowment, such as the significance of hand-clasps and the fascination with lost names and words, brought together Masonic themes, the longer-term interests of Smith and his associates, and biblical phrases and symbols. Smith had long been bent on recovering the lost, pre-Babel language of Eden, including its name for God in that heavenly tongue, and he had spoken of handshakes as a means of discerning whether a spirit was an angel or a satanic emissary (per Smith, angels with their resurrected bodies could shake hands, whereas demonic spirits could not). Increase Van Deusen, who with his wife Maria received the endowment in early 1846 and afterward published an exposé of Mormonism, reported that temple workers stated that the garment he received "represents the white stone in scripture, in which was a new name given," a reference to a passage in the Book of Revelation.[22] Smith's appropriation of Masonry almost certainly explains the presence of Masonic symbols such as the square and compass on Mormon temple garments. Along with the all-seeing eye, however, such symbols had become ubiquitous within American society and understandable within a Christian framework. Inspired both by Masonic aprons and by the Book of Genesis, Mormons came to wear green aprons over their temple robes, the aprons stitched with decorations resembling fig leaves, evoking the King James language that Adam and Eve "sewed fig leaves together, and made themselves aprons" to cover their nakedness.[23] The Latter-day Saints, like many other antebellum Americans, lived in a society in which biblical and esoteric ideas co-existed and intermingled with each other. The Bible was one of several sources of influence on the development of Masonic rites; the Bible and Masonic rites were both sources of inspiration for the Nauvoo endowment in ways that are not easy to untangle.

Despite his attraction to and appropriation of Masonry, Joseph Smith was after a very different sort of society. While Smith relished the pageantry and symbolism of Masonry, he and his successors adapted them for their own theological purposes. During these years, Smith's other rituals focused on sealing or binding together human families on earth in a way that would endure beyond the grave. Temple ordinances would bring about human exaltation, preparing a group of select men to rule as kings and priests for eternity, with their wives as queens and priestesses at their sides. Through baptisms, sealings, and the endowment, they

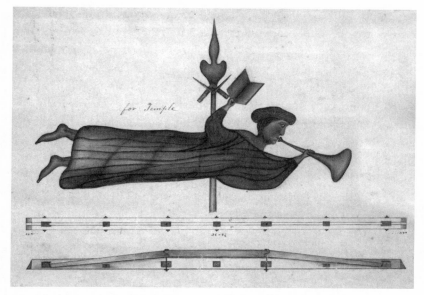

Drawing of the Nauvoo Temple weathervane, by William Weeks, ca. 1841–1846. Church member Perrigrine Sessions described the figure as "an Angel in his Priestley robes with the book of Mormon in one hand and a trumpet in the other." The Masonic square and compass are visible above the angel. (Courtesy of the Church History Library, The Church of Jesus Christ of Latter-day Saints.)

could also perform all of the ordinances their ancestors needed to join with them in an eternal familial kingdom. Thus, Smith did more than ape Masonic rites. In his attempt to create new forms of earthly and heavenly society, the prophet Mormonized what he found attractive in Freemasonry.[24]

The introduction of new ordinances confused some church members. "The question is frequently asked," Joseph Smith discussed in a January 1844 sermon, "can we not be saved without going through with all thes[e] ordinances?" His answer was "No not the fulness of Salvation."[25] One's degree of eternal glory depended in large part on one's participation in the newly introduced rituals. Men and women could not be exalted without sealing, without the endowment.

Joseph Smith and Sidney Rigdon's 1832 vision had introduced the idea that nearly all men and women would be saved, but to one of three possible levels of glory, with celestial glory being reserved for members of Christ's true church. Now, Smith introduced further distinctions by subdividing the celestial kingdom itself. William Clayton, one of Smith's confidants in matters of plural marriage, recorded the following instructions from the prophet in 1843: "He also said that in the celestial glory there was three heavens or degrees, and in order to obtain the highest a man must enter into this order of the priesthood." By "this order of the priesthood," Smith seems to have meant plural marriage.[26] Not all Latter-day Saints would achieve the highest heaven. Those baptized but not endowed would perhaps reach the lowest degree of the celestial kingdom, those endowed but not sealed in marriage would reach a higher realm, those sealed in eternal marriages would reach the highest realm. Presumably, those who entered plural marriage and received the second anointing would attain even higher levels of glory. Smith's heaven, if nearly universalist, was not at all egalitarian.

Although baptisms for the dead, sealings, and endowments initially took place elsewhere, Smith soon taught that a new "holy house" (that is, a temple) was the proper place for such rituals. "Let this house be built unto my name," the Lord commanded, "that I may reveal mine ordinances . . . for I deign to reveal unto my church things which have been kept hid from before the foundation of the world, things that pertain to the dispensation of the fulness of times." Several years later, Smith added that temples were required so that "men may receive endowment to make [them] Kings and Priests unto the Most High God." In April 1841, church leaders laid the Nauvoo Temple's cornerstone, and missionaries raised funds for the temple's construction.[27]

After Smith's June 1844 murder, Brigham Young made the need to complete the Nauvoo Temple his primary rationale for why the Saints should remain in Illinois despite mobs and political pressure. In fending off other potential successors to the martyred prophet, Young (then the president of the church's Quorum of the Twelve Apostles) argued that Smith had given the apostles the "keys" to bring church members through the ordinances they needed to secure their exaltation. They alone could give church members the knowledge they needed to gain entrance to the

Sketch of Nauvoo Temple, by Elvira Stevens, ca. 1846–1848. (Courtesy of the Church History Library, The Church of Jesus Christ of Latter-day Saints.)

highest heaven. "We have all the signs and the tokens to give to the Porter [of heaven] and he will let us in," Young assured the Saints.[28] By the winter of 1845–1846, construction on the temple was nearly finished. Renewed mob activity and political pressure forced Young to agree that the Mormons would leave Illinois in the spring of 1846, but before a hasty departure, thousands of Latter-day Saints received their endowments. Joseph Smith had Mormonized Masonic rites; Brigham Young democratized Smith's endowment.

In the Nauvoo Temple, Young expanded and revised what he had learned from Smith, who had never written down the ceremony or dictated its words to a scribe. After participants were washed and anointed, they passed through the various rooms of the temple's second story, progressing from a premortal existence, into the paradise of Eden (workers adorned this room with cedar trees and shrubs), through the Fall (grapevines with raisins provided a visible reminder of the forbidden fruit) and the corresponding trials of earthly life, and ultimately into celestial glory gained through obedience to divinely appointed authorities and ordinances. Participants made covenants with God and their priesthood leaders, and they swore an oath to avenge the deaths of Joseph and Hyrum Smith.

William Clayton sketched the basic contours of the ceremony's sacred drama:

> It is the province of Eloheem, Jehovah and Michael to
> create the world, plant the Garden and create the man and
> give his help meet [Eve]. Eloheem gives the charge to Adam
> in the Garden and thrusts them into the telestial kingdom or
> the world. Then Peter assisted by James and john conducts
> them through the Telestial and Terrestrial kingdom
> administering the charges and tokens in each and conducts
> them to the vail where they are received by the Eloheem
> and after taking with him by words and tokens are admitted
> by him into the Celestial Kingdom.[29]

As couples, initiates relived the experience of Adam and Eve, while church leaders acted out the drama's other roles. Mormon editor and

The Garden Room, Salt Lake City Temple, ca. 1911. According to early-twentieth-century apostle James E. Talmage, this room represents "the Garden of Eden depicted in minia- ture." The Bible rests upon the altar on the left of the photograph. (© by Intellectual Reserve, Inc.)

hymnist William Phelps frequently played the role of the serpent (Satan), reportedly "*admirably*."[30] Subsequently, other characters were in- troduced, including Protestant ministers who attempted to lead initiates astray.

According to Young, the endowment was an ancient ritual, known to Adam. "With regard to the ordinances of God's house to save the people in the Celestial kingdom of our God," Young explained, "there is no change from the days of Adam to the present time, neither will there be until the last of his posterity is gathered into the kingdom of God." Mor- mons understood their rituals not as innovation, but as a restoration of rituals required for human salvation. As the organizer of this world, Adam served as the archetype for men who after their exaltation would organize their own kingdoms on future worlds.[31] Likewise, Latter-day

Saint leaders such as Zina D. Young and Hannah Tapfield King broke from traditional Christian disparagement of Eve as the agent of sin's introduction to praise her as a majestic queen or even as humanity's divine Mother. King, renowned among the Saints for her poetry, regarded Eve as the "sovereign mother of all living [who] stands in close proximity to God the Father." Young understood Adam as humanity's Father God. Some Latter-day Saints likewise understood Eve as a mother goddess in heaven, though the latter idea received far less discussion.[32]

The Nauvoo Temple endowment attached significance to Jesus Christ. In December 1845, church member George Miller termed the symbolic cuts on the temple garment as the "marks of the Lord Jesus Christ"; he suggested that the Apostle Paul had worn garments with the same marks, "which was as plainly as he dare allude to these things in writing." According to Catherine Lewis, who left the church in disgust over the issue of polygamy and denounced the endowment as a farce, Elohim reassures Adam and Eve that because he knew they would transgress he had "prepared a Saviour" who would come "in due time." While explaining the meaning of the endowment ceremony in the St. George Temple, Brigham Young commented that the sacrifices instituted by God after the Fall showed "that Jesus would come and shed his blood." Latter-day Saints regarded Jesus Christ and his death as of such importance that they could not help describing the temple ordinances with reference to the atonement. "Nephi and his successors," taught Young's successor John Taylor, "were particularly careful in explaining that these ordinances, like all other rites of the Church of God, had their value in their association with . . . the great, infinite sacrifice to be offered up by the Lamb of God in His own person."[33]

In a broader sense, the endowment drama's narration of creation would have connected it with Jesus Christ in the minds of most initiates. Both the Book of Moses and the Book of Abraham (the latter completed shortly before Smith's introduction of the endowment in Nauvoo) revise the Genesis creation narrative, making textually explicit the Christian belief in Jesus Christ as the agent of God's creation. "We will go down," states Jesus Christ in the Book of Abraham, " . . . and we will make an earth." Smith and his associates used the Book of Abraham text to shape the endowment's dramatization of creation.[34]

Despite such connections, there was no obvious acted role for Jesus Christ in the Nauvoo or early Utah endowment. In the ordinance, Elohim, Jehovah, and Michael (whom Smith had identified as Adam) create the world. In the mid-1840s, and for many years, church members did not associate Jesus Christ with any of these three divine figures.

Elohim and Jehovah are Anglicized renderings of two different Hebrew names for the God of Israel. *Elohim* is a plural Hebrew word meaning gods; however, in the Jewish scriptures it usually refers to a single god, the God of Israel. Jehovah is derived from יהוה (*yhwh*), the answer that Moses receives when he asks God for his name. Sometime during the several centuries surrounding the birth of Jesus, Jews began considering it blasphemous to vocalize this sacred name, and they substituted *Adonai*, meaning "my Lord." In medieval Europe, though, some Christian scholars began utilizing the Latin form *Iehouah* as the vocalization for these four Hebrew letters (perhaps combining the consonants from *yhwh* and the vowels from *Adonai*).[35] Beginning in the 1500s, translators of the Bible into English sometimes used "Jehovah," and the term Jehovah became a common part of the Protestant lexicon, finding its way into commentaries, sermons, hymns, and literature such as Milton's *Paradise Lost*. Most Protestants on either side of the Atlantic understood Jehovah as synonymous with God, with Elohim if they were familiar with the Hebrew terms.

Early Latter-day Saints also had this understanding of Jehovah, which they understood as one of God's many ancient names. Early Mormon hymnist William W. Phelps adapted the popular "Guide Me, O Thou Great Jehovah / Pilgrim through this barren land" to Latter-day Saint themes, beginning with "Guide us, O thou great Jehovah / Saints upon the promis'd land." An 1845 proclamation of the Twelve Apostles, written by Parley Pratt, referred to the "Great Jehovah Eloheem," perhaps mixing biblical language for "the Lord God." And Jehovah was not Jesus Christ. "Jehovah saw his darling son," narrated an early nineteenth-century Protestant text included in the church's 1835 hymnal. As for most Protestant Americans, Jehovah was for Mormons one of many names for the God of ancient Israel, the father of Jesus Christ.[36]

The endowment, however, portrayed Elohim and Jehovah as separate beings. Brigham Young obliquely referred to the endowment in an 1852 sermon in which he stated that "the earth was organized by three distinct characters, viz.: Eloheim, Yahovah and Michael . . . in organizing elements perfectly represented in the Deity, as Father, Son, and Holy Ghost."³⁷ However, for Young, Michael (Adam) was Jesus Christ's father. Young later suggested that Elohim and Jehovah were Michael's grandfather and father, respectively.³⁸ When he recognized that many church members were unsettled by his identification of Adam as God, Young backpedaled and commented that "it is no matter whether we are to consider Him [Adam] our God, or whether His Father, or His Grandfather."³⁹ For some years, Young spoke less frequently and forcefully about Adam as God, but he reintroduced the teaching in the 1870s, including at the dedication of the St. George Temple.

In the last several decades of the nineteenth century, Latter-day Saints began associating Jehovah with Jesus, identifying the savior as the "Lord" of the Christian Old Testament.⁴⁰ "It was He who spoke to Moses in the wilderness," asserted Apostle George Q. Cannon in an 1871 talk to Mormon children, "and it was He who revealed Himself to the brother of Jared and came to him before He was in the flesh." As reflected in Cannon's talk, the Book of Mormon's teaching that Jesus had a spiritual body prior to his incarnation and had appeared to the brother of Jared before his incarnation encouraged Latter-day Saints to imagine a prominent role for Jesus Christ in the Old Testament. Apostle Franklin Richards, in an 1885 General Conference talk, reasoned similarly. "His name when He [Jesus Christ] was a spiritual being," Richards explained, "during the first half of the existence of the earth, before He was made flesh and blood, was Jehovah." Richards added that Jesus as Jehovah had given the law to Moses on Mount Sinai and had appeared to the brother of Jared.⁴¹

Christians had long assigned the leading role in the creation and governance of the world to a preincarnate messiah or Word of God. This idea is a significant motif in several New Testament books. "For by him were all things created," asserts the epistle to the church at Colossae, "that are in heaven, and that are in earth, visible and invisible." The Gospel of John presents Jesus Christ as the fleshly incarnation of the eternal Word of God. "Before Abraham was," Jesus tells "the Jews" in John's gospel,

"I am." That statement caused Jesus's opponents to prepare to stone him, perhaps because it echoed God's self-identification to Moses.[42]

It is unclear whether any early Christians consistently understood Jesus as *yhwh*, but many presumed that it was Jesus Christ who had communicated with the patriarchs in their scriptures. Irenaeus, a late-second-century bishop in Gaul, explained that "the Son of God is as seed scattered everywhere in His Scriptures, at one time speaking with Abraham, at another with Noah, giving them his measures: at another time seeking out Adam; at another again bringing judgement upon the Sodomites: as also when He appears and guides Jacob in the way, and speaks out of the Bush with Moses."[43] Such christological understandings of the Jewish scriptures were common. They shielded God the Father from anthropomorphism, and they affirmed Christ's divinity, majesty, and preincarnate role in creation and sacred history. Justin, a mid-second-century theologian and martyr, explained that "neither Abraham, nor Isaac, nor Jacob, nor any other man, ever saw the Father and Ineffable Lord of all things ... but Him, who according to His will, is both God His Son, and his Angel." Justin added that Christ "once even became fire when He conversed with Moses from the bush."[44] Many early Christians also believed that the patriarchs of ancient Israel knew that the Word or Son of God that they encountered would one day become incarnate. "So Abraham was a prophet," Irenaeus explained, "and saw things to come, which were to take place in human form: even the Son of God, that He should speak with men and eat with them." For many ancient Christian theologians, the Jewish scriptures contained accounts of the premortal, preincarnate Jesus Christ.[45]

The Protestant reformers likewise believed that the Old Testament chronicles the activities of Jesus Christ. In Genesis, Jacob wrestles with "a man," whom he defeats but who injures Jacob by putting his thigh out of joint. Jacob, given the new name of Israel for his victory, comments afterward, "I have seen God face to face, and my life is preserved." Martin Luther believed that Jacob had wrestled with the preincarnate Jesus Christ. "He was very familiar to the holy fathers and often appeared to them and spoke with them," Luther explained. "He exhibited Himself to the fathers in such a form that He might testify that He would at some time dwell with us in the form of human flesh."[46] The Swiss reformer John Calvin agreed that "the orthodox doctors of the Church have correctly and wisely expounded, that the Word of God was the supreme angel . . . [who] descended as in an intermediate form, that he might have more familiar access to the faithful."[47] Such ideas remained common among the ecclesiastical and theological descendants of the New England Puritans. The American theologian Jonathan Edwards, firmly committed to the theological unity of the Bible, wrote that it "was Christ, the second person of the Trinity, that was wont to appear of old in that effulgence of glory that was commonly called 'the glory of the Lord.'" Jesus Christ, in form, foreshadowing, or prophecy, could be found most anywhere within both testaments of scripture. The written Word of God in its entirety proclaimed the Word of God that eventually became flesh.[48]

However, the exact idea that *yhwh* or Jehovah always referred to Jesus Christ was uncommon. Calvin, for instance, applied the name Jehovah (using the Latin *Iehouah*) to the Father, Son, and Holy Spirit. Ethan Smith, a Congregationalist minister in New England (who also penned a book claiming that the American Indians were descended from the "long lost tribes" of Israel), asserted in his 1814 *Treatise on the Character of Jesus Christ, and on the Trinity* that biblical passages about Jehovah referred to Jesus Christ. Ethan Smith's main purpose in writing was to assert that, despite scriptural distinctions between the Father and the Son, they were thoroughly united in the Trinity. He wrote to affirm the oneness of God, who through his divine son had revealed himself as Jehovah to the ancient Israelites and later as Jesus Christ. In an 1833 book, Smith repeated his contention that "Jesus Christ is the Jehovah," but his argument gained little notice. In this respect, he was an outlier among his Protestant contemporaries.[49]

Over the course of the nineteenth and twentieth centuries, the Old Testament Jesus Christ largely faded from the American Protestant imagination. The historical-critical method, which achieved gradual dominance in mainline Protestant seminaries, demanded greater fidelity to scripture's original historical context. It became uncommon for mainline Protestants to view passages of ancient Jewish scripture as straightforward depictions of or prophecies about Jesus Christ. Although conservative American evangelicals resisted the methodology of their more liberal counterparts, they too gradually gave more attention to scripture's historical setting. Mormons went in the opposite hermeneutical direction. Jesus Christ dominated the Book of Mormon's narratives, and other Latter-day Saint scriptures made explicit that it was Jesus Christ who appeared to Adam, Abraham, Jacob, and other ancient patriarchs. For Latter-day Saints, who kept the historical-critical method of biblical interpretation at arm's length, all scriptures pointed to Jesus Christ as the divine agent of creation and redemption.

It took some time for the Jehovah-Jesus identification to gain traction within the church. For more than seven decades, from the end of Joseph Smith's lifetime to the early twentieth century, Mormon statements about the relationships among Elohim, Jehovah, Adam, and Jesus Christ were a jumble and welter of confusion and contradiction. In particular, Brigham Young's identification of Adam as humanity's God, adhered to by some but not all Latter-day Saint leaders in this time period, sowed uncertainty and dissension. In 1895, church president Wilford Woodruff instructed the Saints to "cease troubling yourselves about who God is; who Adam is, who Christ is, who Jehovah is."[50] Woodruff's caution, however, did not put an end to Mormon questions about the hierarchy of heavenly beings.

James Talmage's 1915 *Jesus the Christ* provided a definitive answer to such questions. In his preface, Talmage noted that he would examine not only the earthly life of Jesus Christ but would begin with "the antemortal existence and activities of the world's redeemer." Although Talmage conceded that Old Testament scriptures "are less specific in information concerning his antemortal existence," he asserted that New Testament passages and "the revelations given in the present dispensation leave us without dearth of scriptural proof." Talmage pointed to the prologue to John's gospel and several other New Testament books that affirm a premortal, cosmic existence and role for the Word of God. Talmage began his narrative of Jesus Christ with the "war in heaven" referenced by John of Patmos, which he linked to Satan's offer to save all of humanity as described in the Book of Moses. After Satan's rebellion, Jesus, the first-born spirit child of God the Father in heaven, was "ordained" by his Father as "the Savior of mankind," as the Christ, the Messiah.[51]

Many Christian writers presumed that anthropomorphic descriptions of God in the Old Testament referred to Jesus Christ. Given the Mormon identification of God as an exalted, resurrected man, Talmage felt no repulsion at the idea that God the Father himself could have appeared in human form. Still, he arrived at conclusions that in many respects paralleled earlier Christian interpretations of the Hebrew scriptures. For Talmage, the matter was "simple, precise, and unambiguous." "Jesus of Nazareth," he argued, "who in solemn testimony to the Jews declared himself the *I Am* or *Jehovah* . . . was the same Being who is repeatedly proclaimed as the God who made covenant with Abraham, Isaac, and Jacob." Just as Jesus did in the New Testament, the Lord in the burning bush identified himself as "I Am." "We affirm that Jesus Christ was and is Jehovah, the Eternal One," Talmage wrote. Jesus Christ was the creator who revealed himself to Adam, Enoch, Noah, Abraham, and Moses. He was the god of the ancient Israelites and the god of the Nephites. It was important to Talmage that the Old Testament described the work of two separate divine personages, the postmortal, immortal, and exalted Father and the antemortal Jesus Christ. The "former," Talmage explained, "had already passed through the experiences of mortal life, including death and resurrection, and was therefore a Being possessed of a perfect, immortalized body of flesh and bones, while the Son was yet unembodied." Subsequently, Jesus Christ had achieved essentially the same level of godhood as his Father through his mortal obedience, death, and resurrection. In the context of Mormon scriptures and temple ordinances, Talmage's conclusions made a great deal of sense.[52]

By this point, church leaders were taking clear, public stances against Young's Adam-God doctrine. In an April 1916 General Conference talk, Apostle Charles Penrose referred to the Book of Abraham's account of creation, incorporated into the endowment ceremony: "Jehovah, commanded by Elohim, went down to where there was space, saying to Michael, 'Let us go down.'" According to Penrose, the "Temple of God" illustrated that "Michael, became Adam, and that Adam was not the son Jehovah, and he was not Elohim the Father . . . Jesus of Nazareth was the Jehovah who was engaged with the Father in the beginning." The church's 1916 statement "The Father and the Son" again identified Jesus Christ as Jehovah. Going forward, Jesus-as-Jehovah became a clear point of Mormon doctrine.[53]

Still, it was not easy to put confusion and dissent to rest. Church members continued to express questions about the divine roles of Michael/Adam and other figures. Mormon leaders repeatedly felt the need to denounce Brigham Young's contention that Adam was humanity's God and the literal father of Jesus Christ. In a 1980 speech at Brigham Young University, Apostle Bruce R. McConkie identified the belief "that Adam is our father and our god" as one of "Seven Deadly Heresies." "The devil keeps this heresy alive as a means of obtaining converts to cultism," McConkie stated, referencing the belief's popularity among polygamist Mormon fundamentalists. "[A]nyone who has received the temple endowment," he continued, "has no excuse whatever for being led astray by it." Young's identification of Adam as God remains a fundamentalist Latter-day Saint tenet, but it is off limits for members of the LDS Church.[54]

Especially after publication of Talmage's *Jesus the Christ* and the 1916 First Presidency statement, Latter-day Saints passing through the endowment ceremony recognized Jehovah as the premortal Jesus Christ, thus giving the Savior a clear and prominent role in the ordinance. Jesus Christ, along with Michael, organizes the world and creates life upon it. Eventually, his death redeems human beings from the effects of the Fall and enables their resurrection and immortality. After more than a half-century of confusion, Jesus Christ now had a clear role in the endowment ceremony. In the process, the Son of God had acquired a distinctive Latter-day Saint title: the Jehovah of the Old Testament.

In the twentieth and twenty-first centuries, church leaders continued to revise the endowment ceremony, largely in ways that reduced its obvious connections to nineteenth-century Freemasonry and emphasized the centrality of Jesus Christ within temple theology and ordinances. Latter-day Saint leaders did not openly discuss the revisions; instead, they quietly responded to cultural sensitivities and to changing theological emphases.

The preparatory washings and anointings (which became known as the "initiatory") became more symbolic, less visceral. In the Nauvoo Temple, in the Salt Lake City Council House, in an Endowment House, and in early Utah temples, church members undressed entirely for the initiatory, with men and women in separate rooms. Officiators blessed them while applying oil near their eyes, ears, arms, legs, and loins. Ritual nudity was not unheard of during the early history of Christianity. Reflecting the biblical claim that Adam and Eve before the Fall were "naked . . . [and] not ashamed," at least some Christian communities asked catechumens to stand naked in water during their baptisms.[55] From the outset, however, Mormon ritual nakedness clashed with nineteenth-century American expectations of decorum and modesty. Thus, church leaders gradually introduced accommodations to such concerns. Instead of bathing in tubs, initiates received their washing (and anointing) while wearing a garment with certain openings that enabled the temple workers to apply water and oil. In 2005, the church made further changes. Individuals now clothe themselves in their sacred garments prior to the initiatory, and officiators pronounce the blessings on various body parts while touching initiates only on their heads.[56]

Other elements of the ceremony were modified, then discarded. In 1927, the church removed the oath in which participants promised to pray that God would "avenge the blood of the prophets upon this nation."[57] Well into the twentieth century, participants dramatized the throat-slitting and disembowelment they would purportedly suffer as the penalty for transgressing their vow of secrecy. These acts were symbolic. Dating to the mid-1840s, a number of church members broke their oaths of secrecy without suffering such macabre consequences. The "penalties"—the oaths and the gestures—became less detailed over time, then disappeared entirely in 1990. That year, the church also eliminated the depiction of Protestant ministers as Satan's minions, present since the Nauvoo Temple endowment. Finally, although the ceremony retains strongly patriarchal elements, the 1990 revisions softened language about the duty of wives to obey their husbands.[58]

The requirements for being admitted to the temple also changed.[59] In Nauvoo, church leaders simply invited members to come to the temple on a particular day. All members presumed faithful received such summonses. In early Utah, individuals received their endowments both by invitation and by request. In the 1850s, Young and other high-ranking leaders began articulating requirements for those seeking the privilege of ordinances. "Men and women, boys and girls over 16 years of age," church leaders instructed in 1856, "who are living the lives of saints, believe in the plurality [of wives], do not speak evil of the authorities of the Church, and possess true integrity towards their friends, can come up after their spring crops are sown, and their case shall be attended to." The payment of tithes also became a prerequisite. Probably with Old Testament standards of ritual purity in mind, Brigham Young counseled women not to come for their endowments for one week after the commencement of menses, and he told men to abstain from sexual intercourse for up to ten days prior to seeking their endowments.[60]

Over the years, church leaders dropped certain requirements (such as the necessity of believing in polygamy or abstaining from intercourse prior to temple attendance) and added others, including keeping the Word of Wisdom. For much of the twentieth century, a church handbook instructed bishops that applicants for temple recommends "should not join nor be a member of any secret oath-bound organization," thereby discouraging Mormons from becoming Freemasons, an ironic injunction in light of the church's Nauvoo-era history. Mormon leaders feared that active involvement in such groups would draw men in particular away from church activities and commitment. As of the mid-1970s, bishops asked members if they were "morally clean," sustained their leaders, paid their full tithe, dealt honestly with others, and kept the Word of Wisdom. They also asked if members had any sympathy for "apostate groups or individuals," if they had ever been divorced, and if they had committed any major unconfessed transgressions.[61]

In the late twentieth century, church leaders gradually placed a greater emphasis on matters of belief in temple recommend questions. In a 1990 General Conference address, Apostle Gordon B. Hinckley stressed that spousal abuse and the failure to pay child support are the sorts of moral failings that require repentance prior to a man's admittance into the "House of the Lord." However, Hinckley added that moral uprightness and obedience to church leaders were not the preeminent requirements. "Most important," he stated, "and above all other requirements, is the certain knowledge on the part of a recommend holder that God our Eternal Father lives, that Jesus Christ is the living Son of the living God, and that this is their sacred and divine work." Temple recommend questions reflected this change in emphasis. By 2000, the questions began with belief rather than behavior. "Do you have faith in and a testimony of God the Eternal Father, His Son Jesus Christ, and the Holy Ghost? Do you have a testimony of the Atonement of Christ and of His role as Savior and Redeemer? Do you have a testimony of the restoration of the gospel in these latter days?" Tithing, righteousness, and obedience remain firm requirements, but the first questions now revolve around the Godhead, Christ's atonement, and the restoration.[62]

Recent Latter-day Saint leaders have emphasized the centrality of Jesus Christ to the temple and its ordinances. "Central to the message about temples," wrote Apostle Boyd Packer in 1980, "is the fact that Jesus is the Christ, the Son of God, the Only Begotten of the Father; that He lives; that He directs His servants upon this earth." A 1998 church handbook stated that the "endowment ordinance explains the purpose of life, the mission and Atonement of Jesus Christ, and Heavenly Father's plan for the exaltation of His children."[63]

The temple provides a means for church members to participate in their savior's ongoing work of redemption. Joseph Smith explained baptism for the dead "as the only way that men can appear as saviors on mount Zion," referring to a vision of the Jewish prophet Obadiah, who foresaw that, at the time of Judah's deliverance, "saviours shall come up on mount Zion to judge the mount of Esau." Smith probably also had in mind the vision of John of Patmos, in which "a Lamb stood on the mount Sion, and with him a hundred forty and four thousand." Protestants had generally understood the former passage as referring to preachers of the true gospel who rescue the church from judgment. By the 1840s, the Latter-day Saints were no longer building the city of New Jerusalem. They had lost Zion. But they envisioned a millennial future in which they were "saviors on Mount Zion," carrying out the sacred task of saving and exalting the entire human family. This would involve more than proxy baptisms. "But how are they to become Saviors on Mount Zion?" Smith asked in 1843. "By building their temples erecting their Baptismal fonts & going forth & receiving all the ordinances, Baptisms, confirmations, washings anointings ordinations, & sealing powers upon our heads in behalf of all our Progenitors." Later that same year, Brigham Young explained that once the temple was finished, this expanded set of rites for the dead would commence.[64]

After they hurried to finish the temple before mobs forced them out of Illinois, the Saints went to the temple to secure their exaltation and that of their families. More than 5,000 Latter-day Saints passed through the endowment ceremony at that time, and around 1,000 were sealed in marriage. In some cases, church members were sealed in marriage to deceased individuals, with living Saints serving as proxies for the dead. A more select group of church members received the second anointing. Once the Mormons reached Utah, the church had no temple for several decades. Church members received endowments and sealings in other locations, but Mormon ritual activity as a whole slowed. There were few baptisms for the dead and posthumous sealings. Ordinances in these years focused on the exaltation of the living rather than the dead.[65]

In 1877, the church dedicated the St. George Temple in southern Utah, its first since Nauvoo. By the end of the century, Mormons also dedicated temples in Logan, Manti, and Salt Lake City. Ritual activity as a whole accelerated, and the task of redeeming and sealing together the dead now rose to the fore. "We've been baptiz'd for them, and now, as agents, in their stead," Eliza R. Snow wrote in a hymn composed for the St. George Temple's dedication. "We're wash'd and we're anointed too—the living for the dead."[66] Everything that the living could do for themselves they could and should do for their ancestors. Therefore, church members passed through the endowment ceremony on behalf of their deceased siblings, parents, and grandparents, and then, as proxies for them, were sealed in marriage and received the second anointing.

In 1918, church president Joseph F. Smith had a vision of the "Son of God" in the "spirit world," preaching to the spirits of the righteous who had died without a full knowledge of the gospel. Smith saw former

Sealing Room for the Dead, Salt Lake City Temple, ca. 1911. According to Apostle James E. Talmage, this room is "reserved for the sacred ordinances of sealing in behalf of the dead, which ordinances comprise the sealing of husbands and wives and of parents and children." Behind the altar is a stained-glass window depicting Joseph Smith receiving the golden plates from the angel Moroni. (© by Intellectual Reserve, Inc.)

church leaders such as Joseph Smith Jr., Brigham Young, and Wilford Woodruff joining in the task of postmortal missionary work. Smith's vision also referenced the "building of temples and the performance of ordinances therein for the redemption of the dead." The dead could be redeemed "through obedience to the ordinances of the house of God," but they needed the living to perform those ordinances on their behalf. Today, such "temple work" is the main activity within Mormon temples, as the Latter-day Saints busy themselves with the task of redeeming the entire human family. It is an immense ritual undertaking. Indeed, it is impossible given the limitations of genealogy, but the church teaches that temple activity will accelerate during the millennium, when God's saints across time complete the work of redeeming all who will accept the gospel.[67]

For Latter-day Saints, the temple provides an opportunity not only to secure the fullness of celestial glory for themselves and their immediate family but also to participate in the larger ritual task of connecting and exalting as many living and dead individuals as possible, creating a chain of redeemed humanity stretching back to Adam and Eve. "Just as our Redeemer gave His life as a vicarious sacrifice for all men," taught church president Gordon B. Hinckley in 2004, "and in so doing became our Savior, even so we, in a small measure, when we engage in proxy work in the temple, become as saviors to those on the other side who have no means of advancing unless something is done in their behalf by those on earth." Participants in the endowment drama assume the roles of Adam and Eve in the ordinance, but the temple as a whole provides Mormons with an opportunity to mirror their savior's concern for the dead, to work in his stead as "saviors on Mount Zion." Temple work, thus, is a distinctively Mormon imitation of Christ.[68]

Those church members who rejected Joseph Smith's theological and ritual innovations and then rejected Brigham Young's leadership—many of whom joined the Reorganized Church—saw the Nauvoo Temple as a symbol of apostasy from the original truth of the 1830-founded Church of Christ.[69] The Reorganized Church maintained a variety of Mormonism shorn of its Nauvoo developments, such as the ordinances of sealing and endowment. The Community of Christ (as the RLDS renamed itself in 2001) owns two temples, the historic Kirtland Temple and a temple in Independence, Missouri, completed in 1994. The former attracts tens of thousands of visitors each year, the majority of them members of the LDS Church. The latter doubles as the Community of Christ's headquarters; the temple rooms themselves serve as a place for meetings, worship, and meditation. Most Protestant and Catholic Christians would probably find the Independence temple a bit of an oddity, if only for its nautilus-shaped spire. And within its walls they would see a rather abstract artistic rendering of Joseph Smith's first vision. They would not, however, encounter any sacred boundaries that clearly separate them from the Community of Christ. The Independence temple is open to all, members and nonmembers alike. It is a place for rituals such as the Lord's Supper, but not for the rituals introduced by Joseph Smith Jr. in the 1840s.

It is those rituals that in large part maintain the ecclesiastical and even physical boundaries between Latter-day Saints and other Christians. For Mormons, sealings and the endowment represent the promises and blessings individuals can find only in Christ's true church. For outsiders and some insiders, though, the Mormon temple has long been a lightning rod. In the nineteenth century, many Americans understood temple secrecy as a cover for licentiousness and treason. Once those concerns faded in the early twentieth century, Protestants denounced the temple as a symbol of Mormon heresy, occultism, or "Romanism" (Catholicism). "The Christian," wrote prominent evangelical countercult author Walter Martin, "does not need temples, secret services, rituals, and mysteries." Mormon temples still generate plenty of nontheological criticism as well, for example, when those without temple recommends cannot witness the marriages of their relatives and friends. As the Latter-day Saint sociologist Armand Mauss commented in 1987, "the temple and its ceremonies remain as one of the very few aspects of Mormonism still able to evoke suspicion about how 'normal' Mormons really are." Active Mormons as well as the church's critics recognize the significance of the temple for the maintenance of the LDS Church's distinctive claims.[70]

Many of the defining aspects of early Mormonism, such as the principle of gathering, the expectation of the savior's imminent return, the earthly tasks of kingdom building, and polygamy, have been abandoned or have faded in importance. The temple, by contrast, has grown in importance, a symbol of the distinctive theology, rituals, and community of Latter-day Saint Christianity. "I love to see the temple," young children sing, "I'm going there someday." Latter-day Saints from an early age learn to love Jesus Christ and prepare themselves to come to the temple. For active Mormons, these are not separate endeavors, but inextricably connected. Mormons affirm that Jesus Christ died for all of humanity and that they can further his work of redemption and exaltation through temple work. In its theology and in the significance placed upon sacred ordinances, Mormonism is temple Christianity.

✥

CHAPTER EIGHT

THE GREAT BRIDEGROOM

EARLY IN THE GOSPEL of John, Jesus and his mother attend a wedding in Cana. During the festivities, Jesus's mother (never introduced by name in John's gospel) informs him that the household's supply of wine has run out. After some initial reluctance, Jesus tells the servants to fill large jars with water, draw out a sample, and take it to the "governor of the feast." The latter tastes it and then takes the bridegroom aside. "Every man at the beginning doth set forth good wine," he compliments the bridegroom, "and when men have well drunk, then that which is worse: but thou hast kept the good wine until now." The Gospel of John informs its readers that the water's transformation was the "beginning of miracles."[1]

Many early Christian writers interpreted the miracle as a demonstration of Jesus's divine power and unity with his Father. Others believed that it symbolized a progression from Judaism's water to Christian wine. Medieval and later Catholic theologians perceived allusions to the Eucharist, to the transubstantiation of wine into the life-giving blood of Jesus. Martin Luther believed that the passage teaches that Christ saves human beings in their moment of desperation, when they recognize no other means of salvation.[2]

For mid-nineteenth-century Mormon apostle Orson Hyde, the passage had a much different lesson. Although he confessed that he had not read the Bible "for some time, but looked more to him who rules on high, and to those who hold the words of life in the inspiration of the Holy Ghost," the apostle boasted that he had once memorized the entire Bible in English, Hebrew, and German. According to Hyde, Jesus was the bridegroom at Cana. "We say it was Jesus that was married," Hyde explained, "that he might have seed [children] before he died." Hyde added that "he who has not the blood of Abraham flowing in his veins; who has not one particle of the Savior's in him, I am afraid is a stereotyped Gentile, who will be left out, and not be gathered in the last days." For Hyde, the Latter-day Saints were the descendants of Jesus Christ.[3] Hyde was not alone in these opinions. Many high-ranking Mormon leaders during the second half of the nineteenth century described Jesus as married, with wives and children.

"Because Christ also suffered for us," instructs the author of the New Testament's First Epistle of Peter, "leaving us an example, that ye should follow his steps." Christians should seek to live as their savior lived, without sin and guile and "unto righteousness."[4] Building on this New Testament idea, the fifth-century Council of Chalcedon affirmed that Jesus was "in all things like unto us, [but] without sin."[5] Jesus's humanity provides Christians with a model for imitation, but his divinity makes perfect imitation difficult. At the same time, that goal of imitating Christ has often led Christians to imagine and refashion Jesus's life in ways that correspond with their own ideals and practices. Accordingly, nineteenth-century Mormons believed that Jesus had practiced the same principle of marriage they cherished and fiercely defended. He became, in terms of marriage, more like them.

The Mormon Jesus did not remain married, however. Once the church abandoned polygamy, Latter-day Saint leaders publicly distanced themselves from the idea of a married savior. For Mormons, Jesus Christ remained the preeminent exemplar of compassion and obedience, but in terms of marriage and sexuality, he became less "like unto us." Instead, the Mormon savior came to more closely resemble the masculine but celibate Jesus of other American Christians.

Most Christians throughout the last 2,000 years have assumed that Jesus did not marry. Clement of Alexandria, writing in the late second century,

Orson Hyde, ca. 1850s. (Courtesy of the Church History Library, The Church of Jesus Christ of Latter-day Saints. Daguerreotype collection.)

observed that some Christians "proudly say that they are imitating the Lord who neither married nor had any possession in this world." According to Clement, such Christians believed that "marriage is fornication." The apostle Paul's allowance that "it is better to marry than to burn" hardly seemed a ringing endorsement of matrimony, and Paul

observed that a man who "is unmarried careth for the things that belong to the Lord." Clement, though, believed that Paul himself was
married and warned Christians only against a polygamous "second
marriage." For Clement, the gospel had abrogated polygamy, not monogamous marriage. Other New Testament writings, including the
Gospel of John's narration of the wedding feast at Cana, made an easy
case for the permissibility and even desirability of Christian marriage.
Clement, however, did not believe that Jesus had set an example in this
respect.[6]

Tertullian of Carthage, Clement's contemporary, agreed that the
gospel had done "away with excesses or controlled irregularities" such as
polygamy and concubinage. While he affirmed marriage as a "good," he
believed Paul had instituted celibacy as a Christian ideal. Moreover,
Christ also had been "wholly disengaged from marriage," except in the
sense that he was the church's bridegroom. Only in that spiritual sense
did Christ provide a model of monogamous marriage. As the examples
of Clement and Tertullian illustrate, early Christian writers who mention the subject stated that Jesus did not marry.[7]

One possible exception is found in the noncanonical Gospel of Philip,
which scholars date to somewhere between the second and fourth centuries. This collection of Gnostic teachings states that the "Father of the
All united with the virgin who came down ... in the great bridal
chamber," leading to the birth of Jesus. Another passage in the Gospel
of Philip refers to Mary Magdalene as Jesus's "companion"; the Coptic
word in question could also mean "wife" or "lover." Yet another passage,
filled with confusing lacunae that make any clear interpretation even
more difficult, informs that Jesus's other disciples grew jealous of his love
for Mary Magdalene, whom he kissed many times. Because of its relatively late date, the Gospel of Philip does not serve as useful historical
evidence that Jesus was married. At most, it provides clues that some
groups of early Christians believed that Mary Magdalene had been his
wife.[8]

The idea of a marriage or sexual relationship between Jesus and
Mary Magdalene occasionally surfaced in medieval Europe. In 1367,
a man named John Hartmann was tried in Erfurt in connection with
a diffuse movement known as the Free Spirits. The church con-

demned these mystics for their claim that, through a union with the divine, men and women could attain a spiritual state in which sin became an impossibility. Hartmann explained that a free spirit simply could not sin, even if he had incestuous sex, and he asserted that Christ through his crucifixion and resurrection had become truly free. Hartmann was so recklessly loquacious that his inquisitor, Walter Kerlinger, offered him a chance to claim insanity. He declined the offer. On one topic, though, Hartmann became coy. Kerlinger asked Hartmann whether Christ had had postresurrection sex with Mary Magdalene. Hartmann claimed to know the answer but preferred not to say. The record is silent, but presumably Hartmann was executed.[9]

Few Christians were so free with their speculations. Indeed, many Christian thinkers concluded that sexual desire and pleasure were inherently sinful, making a celibate Jesus the model for human devotion. Origen discouraged married Christians from praying in their beds. Sexuality and holiness could not mix. Gregory of Nyssa, an influential late-fourth-century defender of the Nicene understanding of the Trinity, contended that the mysterious incarnation of the divine Word within flesh did not corrupt Jesus's divine nature with passion and desire. For Gregory, the incarnate Jesus was apathetic, free from human passion in the same way that God was free from passion. Only the human soul, not the human body, reflected the image of God. Marriage and sexual intercourse were baneful results of the Fall; they illustrated mortality's distance from divinity. In the resurrection, Gregory explained, repeating what had become a widely held Christian teaching, men and women would remain sexually differentiated but be free from both marriage and sexual desire. Such dim views of passion and sexual intercourse were common among Christian theologians. They excluded any possibility of a Jesus who had married on earth.[10]

At the same time, many Christians—especially monks and nuns who themselves eschewed earthly marriage—thought of themselves as the "bride of Christ." In several New Testament passages, Jesus uses a metaphor to describe himself as the "bridegroom" of his disciples. His followers are like virgins, who should remain vigilant lest the expected bridegroom return unexpectedly. "Blessed are they which are called unto the marriage supper of the Lamb," proclaims the Book of Revelation, which identifies the church as "the bride, the Lamb's wife."[11] These verses exerted a deep influence on Christian piety, as did the Christian interpretation of the Song of Songs as an allegory about the love between Christ and his church.

Many medieval monastics applied these verses to the union between devoted souls and Christ. For example, Hadewijch, a Dutch beguine (a member of a lay religious order), had a series of visions in which she learned that Christ was her bridegroom and she was his beloved. Once, she saw Christ "in the form and clothing of a Man" while partaking of the Eucharist:

> Then he gave himself to me in the shape of the Sacrament,
> in its outward form, as the custom is; and then he gave me
> to drink from the chalice. . . . After that he came himself to
> me, took me entirely in his arms, and pressed me to him;
> and all my members felt his in full felicity, in accordance
> with the desire of my heart and my humanity. So I was
> outwardly satisfied and fully transported. And then . . .
> after a short time . . . I saw him so fade and all at once
> dissolve that I could no longer recognize or perceive him
> outside me, and I could no longer distinguish him within
> me. Then it was to me as if we were one without
> difference.[12]

Hers was a mystical union with Christ described in openly erotic terms of consummation. Hers was a Christ full of passion and love, far removed from Gregory of Nyssa's passionless divinity.

Many other medieval and early modern Christians similarly imagined their union with Christ in a mystical bridal chamber. "He it is," wrote the twelfth-century Bernard of Clairvaux in reference to a passage in the Song of Songs, "whose speech, living and powerful, is to me a kiss . . . the imparting of joys, the revelation of secrets." Such ideas persisted within certain strains of Protestantism. "Jesus, lover of my soul," wrote the Methodist hymnist Charles Wesley, "let me to Thy bosom fly." In rather erotic terms, some Moravian hymns imagined the believer's entrance into the bloody "side hole" of the crucified "bridegroom of the soul." Certain evangelical hymns and popular books (such as Brent Curtis and John Eldredge's *The Sacred Romance*) still hearken back to such ideas in their understanding of human beings as objects of their bridegroom and lover's desire.[13]

Nevertheless, whether Protestant, Orthodox, or Catholic, whether celibate or married, whether inclined toward mysticism or not, few Christians questioned longstanding presumptions about Jesus having not married on earth. Why then did many nineteenth-century Mormons? The conclusion that Jesus was married—and to more than one woman—was quite logical within the contours of nineteenth-century Mormon theology. What did men and women need to do in order to obtain exaltation? "If a man gets the fulness of God," Joseph Smith taught in June 1843, "he has to get [it] in the same way that Jesus Christ obtain[ed] it & that was by keeping all the ordinances of the house of the Lord." In that sermon, Smith specified baptism and the "endowment washings & anointings" as among the required ordinances. Jesus Christ had kept all of the ordinances that members of Christ's true church still practiced. In other contexts, Smith identified eternal marriage as the heart of exaltation, the fullness of salvation. "Those sealed in marriage "by the new and everlasting covenant," Smith taught, "shall be gods, because they have no end." Why would Jesus not have kept that ordinance as well?[14]

In keeping with this positive and sacramental understanding of marriage, the Latter-day Saints—while strictly prohibiting sexual relations outside of marriage—sometimes expressed very positive attitudes about marriage and intercourse. "If the Lord did put not the desire into both men and women," Brigham Young reasoned pragmatically, "the world would soon be depopulated." "It is perfectly right that you enjoy a woman all you can to overflowing," he added.[15] Many church members would have been far less explicit and exuberant, but Mormon theology created no reasons for the Latter-day Saints to praise celibacy or the absence of passion. Moreover, Joseph Smith and some of his top associates had rejected the immaterialist, Platonic metaphysics of most of Christian history in exchange for a materialist, corporeal view of God. Rather than the God of Gregory of Nyssa, Mormons worshiped a God of body, parts, and passion. Mormon theology, as reformulated over the course of the 1830s and 1840s, gave church members no reason to recoil from the idea that Jesus was married.

"My self and wife Vilate was announted [anointed] Preast and Preastest unto our God under the Hands of B[righam]. Young and by the voys [voice] of the Holy Order," wrote Mormon apostle Heber C. Kimball in a diary entry dated February 1, 1844. At that ceremony, Young poured oil upon Kimball's head, anointing him as a priest and king "unto the most High God in & over the Church." Young promised his friend long life and that he would have the power to redeem his "progenitors . . . & bring them into thy Kingdom." He also anointed Vilate Kimball "a Queen & Priestess unto her husband . . . & pronounced blessings upon her head in common with her husband."

Two months later, Vilate Kimball privately prepared her husband for his eventual burial. She washed his feet, then anointed his feet, head, and stomach. The ritual ensured their readiness to rise together when Christ returned, presuming they died before that event. Vilate Kimball wrote that she had anointed her husband so that she might "have a claim upon" her "dear companion" in the resurrection. Death would not separate them from each other or from the promises and blessings conferred upon them by the priesthood.[16]

Joseph Smith continually introduced new rituals to assure his followers of their future salvation and exaltation, new ordinances designed to make sure the promises of which he spoke. The "second anointing" or "Last Anointing,"[17] described by Heber and Vilate Kimball, is the highest of those ritual ordinances. According to Brigham Young, this final ordinance conferred "the fulness of the Priesthood, all that can be given on earth," a promise that the recipients' exaltation was certain rather than contingent.[18] Anointed and ordained as kings and priests in anticipation of their future kingdoms, men now possessed the authority—the "keys"—to perform "all the ordinances belonging to the kingdom of God."[19] A wife in turn was priestess and queen "unto her

Husband," participating at his side in the governance of an eternal familial kingdom. Over the next century, tens of thousands of Latter-day Saints (in their lifetimes or posthumously) received their second anointings. Since the early twentieth century, only very high-ranking leaders and their wives have received the ordinance, which church leaders seldom discuss.[20]

The Kimballs connected the second stage of the ordinance, in which Vilate Kimball washed her husband's feet and anointed his body, with the anointing of Jesus shortly before his crucifixion. "Even as Mary did Jesus," Heber Kimball wrote, "that she mite have a claim on Him in the Reserrection." Likewise, Vilate Kimball wanted to have a "claim upon him [Heber] in the morning of the first Reserrection." Heber and Vilate Kimball were now husband and wife for eternity. So, apparently, were Jesus and Mary.[21]

All four New Testament gospels contain a story of a woman anointing Jesus with perfumed oil or ointment.[22] In the gospels of Mark and Matthew, as Jesus travels to Jerusalem prior to his arrest and crucifixion, a woman in the town of Bethany pours an expensive spikenard oil over his head. Some of the men present complain that the jar could have been sold and the money given to the poor. Jesus, however, responds that the woman quite properly has "come aforehand to anoint my body to the burying." Luke's gospel diverges from the accounts in Mark and Matthew, as the anointing takes place long before Jesus's crucifixion at an unnamed location. A woman identified as a "sinner"—or, according to some translations, a "prostitute"—bathes Jesus's feet with her tears, dries them with her hair, kisses them, and then rubs them with oil. Jesus's host, a Pharisee, objects that his guest, if a prophet, should have known about the woman's sinful life, whereupon Jesus lambasts his host for his self-righteousness and lack of hospitality and forgives the woman's sins. Only the Gospel of John identifies the woman as Mary, sister to Martha and Lazarus in the town of Bethany. Some Christians would later equate Mary of Bethany with Mary Magdalene, present at Jesus's crucifixion, and, according to two of the gospels, the first to see him following his resurrection.

The first stage of the second anointing reflected the ancient Isra-elite practice of pouring oil on the head of a newly chosen king. The

The anointing of Jesus, mural painted by Felix Lieftuchter, 1918. (Photograph by Deacon Lynn Johnson. Courtesy of the Cathedral of the Madeleine.)

ordinance's second stage recalled the anointing of Jesus. When Vilate Kimball washed her husband's feet, she imitated the woman at Bethany. Other couples made this association even more explicit. Julia Pack anointed her husband's feet and head with oil, dried them, then "wiped his feet with the hair of my head and Sealed upon him my claim that he Should bring me fourth in the reserection."[23]

Several decades later, Ruth Page Rogers also recapitulated the anointing of Jesus. In 1853, she became the plural wife of Samuel H. Rogers, who ten years earlier, while a missionary in New Jersey, had confirmed Ruth following her baptism. Shortly after Ruth's marriage, church leaders asked Samuel to move to the southern Utah settlement of Parowan. He initially brought his first wife and left Ruth behind with her parents; Ruth joined the family a year later. Several years later, Samuel married Ruth's sister Lorana. For the Rogers family, polygamy was a strain, but they persevered. Samuel, Ruth, and Lorana Rogers received their second anointings in February 1878. In 1879, Samuel was preparing to move to a Mormon settlement in Arizona. He asked Ruth if she would consent to remain behind in Parowan. She answered that she "was willing if he would return the next fall and we could go to the Temple." Before the move, Ruth and Samuel completed the church's most sacred ordinance. Samuel noted in his diary that this took place on the fifty-second anniversary of Joseph Smith receiving the plates of the Book of Mormon from the angel Moroni. "I dedicated the house and

Ruth Page Rogers, date unknown. (Courtesy of International Society Daughters of Utah Pioneers.)

room," Samuel wrote, "also blest the Oil after which my Ruth Anointed my feet and wiped them with the hair of her head, then kissed them after the patern as written in the Testament of the Lord Jesus Christ." At times, Ruth may have felt that her earthly claim on Samuel was tenuous, but he would bring her forth as his wife in the resurrection.[24]

Church leaders passed down the connection between the second anointing and that of Jesus at Bethany. In 1889, apostle and future church president Joseph F. Smith wrote the following to Susa Young Gates:

> Under certain conditions women have been ordained
> Priestesses unto their husbands, and set apart to rule and
> reign with them &c. Then comes the holy ordinance of
> "*washing of feet*" and anointing with holy ointment, as Mary
> administered to Jesus. The wife to the husband. This is a
> law of the Priesthood which Mary understood, having
> learned it of the Lord. And she received his blessing and
> approval for it. It was not confined to *her* nor to the Lord,
> but so much was given out for a key to the truth.[25]

Mary, in this formulation, administered to Jesus in the manner of a "wife to the husband." Through the second anointing, Mormon ritual quietly introduced the idea of a married savior. Couples such as Ruth and Samuel Rogers reprised the biblical roles of Jesus and Mary, husband and wife.

For nineteenth-century Latter-day Saints, it was hardly a leap to presume that a married Jesus Christ would have had more wives than one. When Latter-day Saints spoke of living "in the dispensation of the fulness of time," they meant a restoration of eternal laws and practices after a long period of apostasy. Church members might add to their knowledge "line upon line, precept upon precept," but the end goal was continuity of religious practice across the chasm of time. The Mormons understood baptism for the dead, sealing in marriage, the endowment, and other ordinances as the restoration of ancient practices. Whereas some Christians have understood the New Testament as an abrogation or supersession of the Old Testament law, the Latter-day Saints aimed for harmonization. Joseph Smith restored a priesthood, built temples, and introduced rituals of washing and anointing. A few nineteenth-century Mormons even contemplated the future reintroduction of animal sacrifice. It is hardly surprising, therefore, that Smith considered the marital practices of the ancient Israelite patriarchs of the Bible and sought to restore them as well.

In the Book of Mormon, the Lord God commands the Nephites that "there shall not be any man among you have save it be one wife; and concubines he shall have none." However, God adds a caveat: "For if I will . . . raise up seed unto me, I will command my people: otherwise they shall hearken unto these things."[26] In the early 1840s, Smith told his most trusted followers that God had commanded him and them to take additional wives. For the most part, however, Latter-day Saints did not specify that the command was for the purpose of "rais[ing] up seed." Instead, they were simply doing the "works of Abraham," following the example of the ancient patriarchs. Indeed, most nineteenth-century church members who accepted plural marriage understood it as an eternal principle, not as a temporary expedient. When Smith dictated a revelation on marriage in 1843, the words presented themselves as the instructions of Jesus Christ, who identified himself as "Alpha & Omega."[27] It was the Mormon savior who revealed to many astonished Latter-day Saints that his "father" commanded them to enter into plural marriages.

Some church leaders and members believed that the extent of a couple's glory hinged on the status of the husband. In accordance with his stated belief that women should have the prerogative to choose their husbands, Brigham Young taught that "a woman can find a man holding the keys of the priesthood and higher in power than her husband, and he is disposed to take her he can do so."[28] In other words, a woman could divorce her current husband to marry a higher-ranking man.

In the late 1840s, one church member took this idea further than Young envisioned. Dissatisfied after becoming one of Young's several dozen plural wives, Augusta Adams asked her husband if she could be sealed for eternity to Jesus Christ instead. If he assented, Young would stand as a proxy for Jesus in the sealing ceremony, which would make Jesus Augusta's eternal husband. On earth, she would remain as Young's "proxy wife," a nineteenth-century Mormon term for a woman sealed to one man for "time" and another for "eternity." Young responded coolly to the proposal. Augusta then suggested another alternative. "[I]f I cannot be Sealed to him whom my soul loves and longs after," she wrote Young, "I will take the next step and go to Joseph."[29] Two years later, she again expressed her desire to be sealed to Joseph, though she added that if a sealing to Jesus Christ should ever become possible, she would "prefer Him [Jesus] to any other." Young granted her second choice. In April 1848, he stood as a proxy in an unusual sealing, expressing his willingness "to give up Augusta Adams to Joseph Smith in the morn of the first resurrection."[30] Augusta Adams pluckily took Mormon ritual theology to one logical conclusion. Why not obtain the most desirable eternal companion?

Even had Brigham Young granted her wish to be married to Jesus, Augusta Adams—according to the statements of many church leaders—would still have found herself one wife among many. In the late 1840s and early 1850s, Mormon leaders occasionally referenced a married Jesus. In 1847, at the church's Winter Quarters community on the banks of the Missouri River, Brigham Young obliquely referred to a marriage between Jesus and Mary. When Mary came to Jesus's tomb and instead encountered the risen Lord, Young explained, "she fell right down at his feet—every woman will come right to her husband's feet same as Mary."[31] Young's understanding of this resurrection scene paralleled the conclusions that church members drew from the story of Jesus's anointing.

John W. Gunnison, part of an 1849 U.S. Army expedition that explored the Valley of the Great Salt Lake and wintered in Salt Lake City, wrote about Mormon polygamy prior to the church's 1852 acknowledgment of the doctrine and practice. "They go so far as to say," informed Gunnison, "that our Savior had three wives, Mary and Martha and the other Mary whom Jesus loved, all married at the wedding in Cana of Galilee." As Gunnison noted, Mormon apostle Orson Hyde had advanced the idea in a newspaper he published in Kanesville, Iowa. "If at the marriage of Cana of Galilee," Hyde speculated, "Jesus was the bridegroom, and took unto him Mary, Martha, and the other Mary whom Jesus loved, it shocks not our nerves." Otherwise, Hyde observed, Jesus's "familiarity" with these women would have been "highly improper." Jesus must have had children, Hyde continued, in order to fulfill Isaiah's promise that "he shall see his seed." The apostle conceded that the marriages of Jesus comprise "a new and strange feature in christianity." Gunnison, a rather dispassionate observer of Mormonism, was the first of many nineteenth-century American writers to report that the Saints believed in a polygamous savior.[32]

Within several years, other church leaders publicly taught that Jesus was married to multiple women. The timing is probably not coincidental.

In 1852, the church openly acknowledged its practice of polygamy, reversing years of implausible denials. Brigham Young now instructed missionaries and writers to publicly defend plural marriage, prompting Latter-day Saints to extol it as biblical, salvific, healthful (especially for male vitality), and socially beneficial as an antidote for prostitution and adultery.[33] Also at this time, Young revealed his understanding that Adam was humanity's God, an exalted being who had come to earth with one of his many wives (Eve) and had begun to provide bodies for the spiritual children he had fathered in heaven. Young speculated that Adam had later returned to earth and had physically sired Jesus with Mary, who was no longer a virgin after her conception. In the process, Young opened the door to new ideas about divine sexuality and marriage.

In 1853, Jedediah Grant, the mayor of Salt Lake City, commented at a Sunday meeting that Jesus and his apostles suffered persecution because they had many wives. Jesus's opponents, Grant reasoned, were outraged when they saw a host of women following the popular rabbi. "The grand reasons of the burst of public sentiment in anathemas upon Christ and his disciples, causing his crucifixion was evidently based upon polygamy," the mayor concluded. "We might almost think they were Mormon." Thus, in practicing polygamy and suffering persecution for it, the Latter-day Saints were imitating their savior. Grant's larger point in his sermon was the pervasiveness of human rebellion and sinfulness across the centuries. His comments about Jesus's polygamy were a digression, an offhand remark he regarded as uncontroversial. Grant's sermon, published in London the following year, attracted little notice in the United States outside of Utah.[34]

That same year, apostle Orson Pratt began a vigorous and full-throated defense of Mormon beliefs and practices, including polygamy. Pratt's advocacy was ironic. In 1842, he was horrified when his wife Sarah alleged that Joseph Smith had proposed marriage to her. The apostle may have contemplated suicide. He was expelled from the Quorum of the Twelve, though he reconciled with Smith half a year later.[35] Pratt himself married plurally in 1844, and in August 1852, Brigham Young tapped the apostle to make the first extended public defense of polygamy in the Salt Lake City Tabernacle (built in 1851, a small and plain structure used for Sunday meetings and other large gatherings, replaced in 1867 by the current, more commodious tabernacle).[36] When he rose to speak, Pratt

mentioned that the honor was "unexpected," but he did not disappoint
the church president with his argument that plural marriage was "necessary for . . . our exaltation to the fulness of the Lord's glory in the
eternal world." Pratt explained that plural marriage would enable the
Latter-day Saints to more quickly provide bodies for righteous spirits
in heaven long awaiting fitting vessels for their mortality.[37] A church
clerk followed Pratt's sermon by reading aloud Joseph Smith's 1843
revelation on marriage.

Shortly after his August 1852 speech, Pratt moved to the nation's capital and began publishing *The Seer*, a newspaper amounting to little more
than his own long treatises on the topics of "celestial marriage" and "the
preexistence of man." Pratt disagreed with Young's identification of
Adam as God, but he agreed wholeheartedly with the church president's
contention that God the Father had many wives and had added a "choice
virgin" named Mary to that number. Jesus was not, as in the language of
the Apostles' Creed, "conceived by the Holy Ghost." Instead, "the Father
and Mother of Jesus, according to the flesh, must have been associated
together in the capacity of Husband and Wife." Pratt commented that
"the Virgin Mary must have been, for the time being, the *lawful* wife of
God the Father," and he speculated that God the Father then "only gave
her to be the wife of Joseph while in this mortal state." Mary, in short,
was Joseph's proxy wife. Eventually, God the Father would "after the resurrection take her as one of his own wives to raise up immortal spirits in
eternity."[38]

Pratt then turned his attention to Jesus, suggesting that "the Son followed the example of his Father, and became the great Bridegroom to
whom kings' daughters and many honorable Wives were to be married."
As Joseph Smith had taught, Jesus had done everything required for his
exaltation. Both God the Father and Jesus Christ have their wives in
eternity and therefore enjoy eternal increase through their children. Pratt
noted the lack of explicit biblical support for Jesus's marriages, but he
argued that Jesus's marriages and children fulfilled ancient prophecies.
Also, Pratt found it otherwise inexplicable that Jesus maintained such
close friendships with Mary Magdalene and other women. Pratt knew
his intended audience would recoil from his conclusions, that "it would
be so shocking to the modesty of the very pious ladies of Christendom

to see Abraham and his wives, Jacob and his wives, Jesus and his honorable wives, all eating occasionally at the same table, and visiting one another, and conversing about their numerous children and their kingdoms." The highest realms of heaven, in Pratt's mind, resembled certain households in Salt Lake City. For Pratt, it was important not just that Jesus was married and a polygamist, but that he had children, especially spiritual children in heaven following his exaltation. The fact that Jesus was a polygamous descendant of polygamists had ramifications for his followers, including the Latter-day Saints. By "marrying many honorable wives himself," Pratt reasoned, Jesus intended to "show to all future generations that he approbated the plurality of wives under the Christian dispensation."[39] Church members should follow the example of their savior.

Before the publication of the above essays, Brigham Young had already informed Pratt by letter that "many points" in *The Seer* were "not *sound* doctrine."[40] Young objected to Pratt's conclusion that human beings, God the Father, and any exalted beings might eventually share equally in divine attributes. However, Young did not object to Pratt's speculations about Jesus's marriages.

The Mormon identification of Jesus as a polygamist soon attracted more public notoriety, once again because of the rhetoric of Orson Hyde. The apostle defended the idea of a polygamous savior at length in an address published in the *Deseret News*. "If the Savior found it his duty to fulfil all righteousness," Hyde reasoned, "a command of far less importance than that of multiplying his race . . . would he not find it his duty to join in with the rest of the faithful ones in replenishing the earth?" Building upon a common Mormon belief in church members' Israelite descent, Hyde contended that the Latter-day Saints were the descendants of Jesus Christ. He added that had Jesus lived in nineteenth-century America, he would have been tarred and feathered because of his large family, which included his wives Mary, Martha, and other women who followed him.[41]

Brigham Young never hesitated to correct other church leaders—and Orson Hyde in particular—if he objected to ideas in their sermons. Young, who attended Hyde's address, stood up after Hyde finished speaking. The church president observed that Hyde had barely touched

on the important subject of the "marriage relation." Indeed, Young commented, "it is the thread which runs from the beginning to the end of
the holy gospel of salvation—of the gospel of the Son of God." Still, he
was pleased with Hyde's "splendid address" and stated that he did not
wish to "eradicate" anything from it.[42]

Distant readers of the *Deseret News* were less enamored. Washington's
Globe published extended excerpts of Hyde's talk, and other eastern
newspapers took note as well. The *New York Times* proclaimed it "disgust-
ingly obscene and blasphemous," observing that Hyde "argues the right
of the plurality of wives, from the patriarchal habit and *example of Christ*."[43]
Hyde probably relished the attention, which he mentioned in a tabernacle
sermon in March 1855. "All I have to say in reply to that charge is this,"
he retorted. "They worship a Savior that is too pure and holy to fulfil the
commands of his Father." Hyde added that "if Jesus begat children, he
only did that which he saw his Father do."[44] Hyde continued to repeat
such claims for the next few years. Many nineteenth-century exposés of
Mormonism cited Hyde's discussion of a polygamous Jesus. The Utah
journalist John Hanson Beadle, a bitter critic of the church, described
Mormonism as a strange amalgamation of every world religion and
Christian sect. "But it is in regard to the personality and life of Christ
that their ideas seem most strange and blasphemous," Beadle alleged,
using Hyde as his source. "They hold that He was literally begotten, that
he had five wives upon earth."[45]

Despite non-Mormon condemnations, Latter-day Saint leaders continued to publicly reference the marriages of Jesus and God. In the midst
of a long sermon, Brigham Young observed that other Americans—
including Freemasons, who because of their "founder" Solomon ought
to have known better—denounced polygamy as one of the twin "relics
of barbarism." "Yes," Young responded, "one of the relics of Adam, of
Enoch, of Noah, of Abraham, of Isaac, of Jacob, of Moses, David, Solomon, the Prophets, and Jesus and his Apostles."[46] Young's comment
was an aside, not an extended argument or exposition of scripture.
Young also continued to express his belief in a married and polygamous
God the Father. Several years later, Young observed that a passage in
Isaiah "says that He, the Lord, came walking in the Temple, with His
train; I do not know who they were, unless His wives and children." By

the ambiguous title "Lord," Young in this instance meant God the Father. Young commented that God's wives and children "filled the Temple, and how many there were who could not get into the Temple I cannot say."[47] Future church president Joseph F. Smith noted in his diary that Young spoke of the Saints' obligation to remember the poor, that he would not hold fellowship with church members who neglected their debts, and "very many other very excellent things." The idea of a married God the Father did not attract Smith's notice. It was unremarkable.[48]

A dozen years later, as a counselor in the First Presidency under Young's successor John Taylor, Joseph F. Smith delivered an evening sermon upon the marriage in Cana, positing that "Jesus was the Bridegroom and Mary & Martha the brides." Referencing several other biblical passages, Smith reasoned that "Mary & Martha manifested much Closer relationship than Merely A Believer which looks Consistent." For Smith, it simply made sense that Jesus would have obeyed the same divine commandments that God had given other mortal men. "He [Smith] did not think," recorded apostle Wilford Woodruff in his journal, "that Jesus who decended through Poligamous families from Abraham down & who fulfilled all the Law even baptism by immersion would have lived and died without being married." In 1899, Smith reasoned that "Jesus Christ never omitted the fulfillment of a single law that God has made known for the salvation of the children of men." He performed everything that was required. "It would not have done," Smith continued, "to have come and obeyed one law and neglected or rejected another." Obedient to all of his father's commands, Jesus had married women during his mortal life.[49]

Indeed, the idea that Jesus had married and fathered children seems to have gained some traction within the church by the turn of the twentieth century. In 1894, George Q. Cannon informed his son Abraham that Heber Kimball "once told him he [George Q. Cannon] was a direct descendant of the Savior of the world."[50] Several years later, the elder Cannon affirmed at a "solemn assembly" of male church leaders inside the Salt Lake City Temple that "there are men in this congregation who are descendants of the ancient Twelve Apostles, and shall I say it, of the Son of God himself, for he had seed, and in time they shall be known."[51]

Josiah E. Hickman was thrilled by Cannon's public declaration that there were "those in that room who were literal discendants of the flesh and blood of Jesus Christ." Hickman wrote in his diary that "a wonderful feeling" overcame him. "O God, am I one of those?" he asked, though he dared not mention the sensation to anyone. Two years later, Hickman received a patriarchal blessing from Jesse B. Martin. As was then common, Hickman had received several such blessings, identifying his lineage as that of Ephraim and promising that he would receive an accumulation of wives and posterity. When Jesse Martin blessed Hickman in 1900, he promised that Hickman would "reign as a king thru out the endless ages of eternity and . . . sit in legislative halls at the center stake of Zion and shall help to make laws to govern the whole world during the 1000 years reign of Christ on earth." He would marry "many of the daughters of Ephraim" and have offspring as "numerous as the leaves upon the trees." When Martin finished, he added that he had also seen "things he dared not tell." Two days later, though, Martin returned and informed Hickman that he was "a literal descendant of the flesh and blood of Jesus Christ," adding that he "should not die, but be translated and live thru the millennium."[52] Hickman treasured this knowledge. "I am a literal descendant of the flesh & blood of Jesus Christ," he wrote in his journal twenty years later, "and I wish to transmit that same lineage to everyone of my children & I want them to build upon that lineage." He encouraged his future descendants to "be valiant for Him who is your ancestor."[53] Hickman would surely not have contemplated his own descent from Jesus Christ had he not heard leaders such as Cannon espouse the idea that at least some church members carried the blood of the savior in their veins.

During the second half of the nineteenth century, numerous high-ranking and influential church leaders had asserted that Jesus had married multiple women and had fathered children. A married or polygamous Jesus was never a key Mormon belief, never worthy of a formal statement by the church's First Presidency. More often, the topic arose as an aside or observation. Unlike other new ideas, such as Brigham Young's identification of Adam as humanity's God, the suggestion of a married and polygamous Savior never generated any known opposition. Within the contours of Mormon theology and current social practice, the idea was hardly outrageous. Being sealed in marriage was a requirement for exaltation. Jesus had done everything required to obtain the fullness of the priesthood. Therefore, Jesus had married.

Despite these nineteenth-century precedents, the idea of a married, polygamous Jesus disappeared from public Mormon discourse in the early twentieth century. During these years, church leaders codified their teachings about Jesus Christ, represented by James Talmage's *Jesus the Christ* (1915) and the 1916 First Presidency statement on the "Father and the Son." Talmage, who discussed Jesus's friendship with Mary Magdalene and other women at some length, did not raise the possibility that Jesus had married such women. He described Mary Magdalene's "feeling of personal yet holy affection" toward Jesus.[54] In light of past statements by Brigham Young, Joseph F. Smith, and many others, Talmage's lack of attention to the question of whether Jesus and Mary Magdalene were married is striking.

While discontinuing earthly polygamy, Mormons still made eternal marriage central to their religious thought and culture. Along with baptism and the endowment ceremony, being sealed in marriage for eternity remained an ordinance considered essential for human exaltation. The church also formalized its belief in a Heavenly Mother. "All men and women," observed a 1909 statement of the First Presidency, "are in the similitude of the universal Father and Mother and are literally the sons and daughters of Deity."[55] There was indeed a Heavenly Mother, even if she was seldom and very delicately discussed. In the twentieth century, church leaders were far more circumspect in their language and speculation than their mid-nineteenth-century predecessors. They no longer referred to God the Father being "married" or having a "wife," but the existence of a Mother in heaven was church doctrine.

Especially in the first half of the twentieth century, the idea of eternal increase remained central to Mormon teachings about exaltation, and it was often joined to the belief that polygamy would be the order of celestial marriage. James Talmage, in an essay for the church's *Young Women's Journal* titled "The Eternity of Sex," explained that just as humans existed as male and female in their premortal state and on earth, so sexual differentiation would persist for eternity. Those individuals sealed in marriage by the "Holy Priesthood" who stayed faithful to their covenants would eventually become like their heavenly parents in all respects. They would, taught Talmage, "enjoy the glory of endless increase" and "become the parents of generations of spirit-offspring," whose development through mortality they would then direct. Future Latter-day Saint hierarchs repeated and developed these ideas as the twentieth century progressed. Apostle and future church president Joseph F. Smith taught that resurrected humans in the terrestrial and telestial kingdoms would not retain their sexual organs. "Some of the functions in the celestial kingdom will not appear in the terrestrial body," he explained, "neither in the telestial, and the power of procreation will be removed." According to Joseph F. Smith, terrestrial and telestial men would become eternal eunuchs rather than eternal husbands. In keeping with founding prophet Joseph Smith's 1843 revelation on plural marriage, Bruce R. McConkie defined human exaltation in large part through eternal marriage and procreation. "Exaltation is eternal life," McConkie wrote in his 1958 *Mormon Doctrine*, "the kind of life God lives.... [Those men and women] have spirit children in the resurrection." McConkie asserted in the same volume that it was obvious that the "holy practice" of plural marriage would resume "after the Second Coming of the Son of Man and the ushering in of the millennium," but he stated that polygamy was "not essential to salvation or exaltation."[56]

Despite these ideas about a Heavenly Mother, exaltation, and marriage, the idea of a married Jesus entirely vanished from public Mormonism. On the rare occasion that church leaders publicly addressed Jesus's marital status, they declined to state any official position on the subject. In 1912, Charles W. Penrose, a member of the First Presidency, answered a series of "Peculiar Questions" in the church periodical *Improvement Era*. In response to a query about whether Jesus was married, Penrose replied that "we do not know anything about Jesus Christ being married." In the same article, Penrose upheld the divinity of Joseph Smith's revelation on celestial marriage and affirmed that a man who married again after his wife's death would spend eternity with both women. Penrose did not object to the idea of a married savior. Instead, he simply stated that there had never been an "authoritative declaration on the subject." The church had no doctrinal stance on Jesus's marital status, which had become a "peculiar question."[57]

One motivation was public relations. As the church sought to improve its image among other Americans, leaders distanced themselves from potentially embarrassing ideas. Responding to a Presbyterian pamphlet that alleged that Mormons "believe and teach that Jesus Christ was a polygamist," B. H. Roberts answered that the "'Mormon Church' . . . is absolutely silent upon that subject." Roberts acknowledged that there were "individual men who have advanced that idea," but he countered that "it is not a doctrine of the church." Roberts would not repudiate the notion, but he did not think it correct for outsiders to criticize the church on that score.[58]

Despite its public disappearance, there are clues that the idea of a married Jesus retained currency within the church. In 1963, a California church member named J. Ricks Smith wrote a letter to Joseph Fielding Smith, son of Joseph F. Smith. As of 1963, Joseph Fielding Smith was president of the Quorum of the Twelve Apostles. In his inquiry, J. Ricks Smith referenced the same promise in Isaiah ("he shall see his seed") that Orson Hyde and others had used as evidence that Jesus Christ had fathered children. "Does this mean that Christ had children?" J. Ricks Smith inquired. Joseph Fielding Smith had an emphatic response: "Please read your Book of Mormon!" He directed his inquirer to a passage in Mosiah, which echoes Isaiah's language ("he shall see his seed") but makes plain that the prophecy pertains to God's "Son." On the topic of Jesus's marital state, the apostle was even more emphatic: "Yes! But do not preach it! The Lord advised us not to cast pearls before swine!" Joseph Fielding Smith's response affirmed his belief that Jesus Christ had married and fathered children, but he warned that the idea was not for public consumption.[59]

Bruce R. McConkie (Joseph Fielding Smith's son-in-law) obliquely hinted that Jesus was the Cana bridegroom. In his 1965 *New Testament Doctrinal Commentary*, he observed that Mary seemed to "be the one in charge" at the wedding. "Considering the customs of the day," McConkie stated, "it is a virtual certainty that one of Mary's children was being married." Moreover, Jesus acted as if he had "some personal responsibility for entertaining the guests." Thus, the bridegroom was one of Mary's sons, possibly Jesus.[60]

In 1997, the *Ensign*, the church's flagship periodical, listed "Was Jesus married?" among "sensational or questionable gospel subjects" that might arise in church classrooms. Wayne Lynn, a former official in the church's Curriculum Department, did not explain whether the answer to this particular question was among the "mysteries" or whether it was simply a "gospel subject" that "should be spoken of not only with care but under proper conditions, in proper places, and, in some cases, by proper priesthood authorities."[61] Regardless, the question was not considered proper for discussion in Sunday school or other classes. Church members were advised to leave the subject alone.

Other Americans, however, were not leaving it alone. Indeed, interest in the sexuality and possible marriages of Jesus steadily increased over the second half of the twentieth century. In 1951, Greek author Nikos Kazantzakis published *The Last Temptation of Christ*. Kazantzakis's Jesus is consumed with doubts and guilt, partly because his cousin Mary Magdalene becomes a prostitute after he chooses to follow his sense of divine call instead of marrying her. On the threshold of his death on the cross, Jesus's final temptation is to imagine marriage and domestic tranquility with the Magdalene, and then, after her death, with both Mary and Martha of Bethany. "It seemed to Christ that he had taken the smooth, easy road of men," Kazantzakis explained in a preface. "He had married and fathered children."[62] The marriages, however, were only Satan's final temptation of Jesus, who ultimately chooses not to escape his suffering. Martin Scorsese's 1988 film adaptation of Kazantzakis's novel more clearly depicted Jesus's fulfilled desire for Mary Magdalene. The movie outraged American evangelical and Catholic leaders, who called on governments and movie theaters to censor its allegedly blasphemous and obscene portrait of the Son of God. Bill Bright, president of the evangelical organization Campus Crusade for Christ, offered to pay the film's production costs if Universal Pictures would turn over all copies of the film to him for destruction.[63]

On a more scholarly note, in 1968 Presbyterian minister and seminary professor William Phipps announced his belief in a married Jesus, a claim he repeated in a 1970 book. Several years later, Phipps went so far as to praise and echo nineteenth-century Mormon apostle Orson Hyde's biblical exegesis in a contribution to *Dialogue: A Journal of Mormon Thought*. "It would be contrary to both ancient and modern notions of virtuous behavior," wrote Phipps, "if Jesus were closely associated day after day with a group of unattached women." According to Phipps, Augustine and other early Christian thinkers had mistakenly associated sexual desire and intercourse with sin, thus creating celibacy as a model for moral behavior and applying it to Jesus in the absence of solid evidence. It was not exactly a common thing for a Protestant minister to commend a sermon by a polygamous, nineteenth-century Latter-day Saint, especially on the matter of marriage. Nevertheless, Phipps urged modern Christians to follow Orson Hyde's recognition "that a married Savior need not be regarded as less pure than one who was a lifelong celibate." Phipps sidestepped the issue of whether Jesus had married more than one woman. He referenced other "women-wives who are occasionally mentioned in the Gospels as traveling with Jesus and his male disciples," implying they may have been the disciples' wives. Unlike *The Last Temptation of Christ* or even *Jesus Christ Superstar* (in which Mary Magdalene, a repentant prostitute, is consumed with her passionate love for Jesus), Phipps's treatment of Jesus's sexuality was circumspect.[64]

Only rarely did Latter-day Saints demonstrate interest in such ideas. One who did was Ogden Kraut, who in 1969 published *Jesus Was Married*, in which he argued that a married and polygamous Jesus was far more "logical" and "reasonable" than a celibate savior. Kraut's book repeated many of the arguments made by Hyde, Orson Pratt, and other nineteenth-century Mormon leaders. Jesus was the bridegroom at Cana. He would not have associated with women in such a friendly and intimate manner had he not been married to them. As did Phipps, Kraut argued that a celibate Jesus would have struggled to gain a respectful hearing for his teachings because "it was against the traditional and scriptural law for a Rabbi to remain single." Unlike Phipps but like Hyde, Kraut imagined a polygamous Jesus. "We may determine that plural marriage was one of the reasons that caused the persecution and oppression of Jesus," Kraut asserted, "for if plural marriage was a part of the Gospel, then Jesus would have taught it and practiced it Himself." Kraut continued that since the "law of procreation [is] just as binding" as that of baptism or marriage, Jesus must have had children, which helps explain his agony in Gethsemane.[65]

Fundamentalist Latter-day Saints adhered to several nineteenth-century teachings subsequently abandoned by most Mormons, such as the legitimacy and centrality of plural marriage and Brigham Young's identification of Adam as God. A married Jesus remained part of this framework. Kraut, indeed, had been sympathetic to fundamentalism for quite some time. In 1948, he had been ordained as a "Seventy" by Joseph W. Musser, a leader in the "Council of Friends." Musser had been excommunicated by the LDS Church in 1921 when he attempted to marry an additional plural wife. Musser argued that Jesus had followed his Father's example in marriage and procreation. "Like Father like son," he wrote. Jesus was the bridegroom at Cana, married sisters Mary and Martha, and took as his wife the Magdalene and many more, daughters of kings and humble maidens. Jesus, Musser concluded, has prepared a place in the celestial kingdom of God for those who accept "the fulness of the Gospel plan, including the eternal principle of marriage in the Patriarchal order." The LDS Church excommunicated Ogden Kraut in 1972. Kraut, whose gravestone describes him as a "Joseph Smith Mormon," followed his prophet, his savior, and his Heavenly Father's example by marrying additional wives.[66]

Kraut and Musser were not the only ones paying attention to nineteenth-century Mormon depictions of Jesus as a polygamist. Many evangelical denunciations of Mormonism as a heresy or cult included as evidence the church's alleged belief in a polygamous savior. Evangelical countercult writers such as Anthony A. Hoekema, J. Oswald Sanders, and Jan van Baalen quoted Orson Hyde, Orson Pratt, and other mid-nineteenth-century Mormon leaders on the subject. Evangelicals implied that contemporary Mormon leaders accepted such past statements as current doctrine.[67]

Even more pointedly, Ed Decker's 1982 film *The God Makers* referenced Orson Pratt's teaching that Jesus had married "at least three wives, Mary, Martha, and Mary Magdalene." "Through these wives," the film narrates, "the Mormon Jesus, from whom Joseph Smith claimed direct descent, supposedly fathered a number of children before he was crucified." In one of his many publications critical of Mormon theology and practice, Decker identified the "LDS Jesus" as "a polygamist who fathered many children." He cited most of the above nineteenth-century statements on the subject and Joseph Fielding Smith's caution not to "preach" the idea that Jesus had married and fathered children. For Decker, such secret teachings provided shocking evidence that Mormonism was not Christian. "The Jesus of Mormonism," he wrote, "is no Jesus at all."[68]

Despite evangelical and Catholic objections to *The Last Temptation of Christ*, many Americans clearly enjoyed speculations about Jesus's sexuality. *The Da Vinci Code*, a best-selling novel by Dan Brown and a 2006 film, asserted that Jesus had married and fathered children with Mary Magdalene and that the Vatican ruthlessly covered up this and other secrets that threatened its patriarchal power. In certain respects, Brown's claims were rather less shocking than those of Orson Hyde and Orson Pratt. *The Da Vinci Code*'s Jesus, after all, had married only one woman. Still, American Catholic and evangelical leaders vigorously critiqued the book and movie, if with somewhat less hysteria than in response to *The Last Temptation of Christ*. Many evangelical authors and publishing houses rushed rebuttals into print, and they sought to use the film in particular as an opportunity to engage interested parties in evangelistic discussions. While liberal Christian leaders did not echo the vituperative comments of their conservative counterparts, they, as well as biblical scholars of all theological stripes, considered the film's historical claims to be groundless. Despite the sentiment of scholars, the book and film sparked heightened interest in the question of Jesus's alleged marriage to Mary Magdalene.

In response to *The Da Vinci Code* film, Latter-day Saint spokesperson Dale Bills distanced the church from the idea of a married Jesus. "The belief that Christ was married has never been official church doctrine," he stated. "It is neither sanctioned nor taught by the church." The Mormon case was unusual, however, because unlike their Protestant and Catholic counterparts, many nineteenth-century Mormon leaders had believed in a Jesus who married and fathered children. Thus, Bills felt compelled to address the Mormon past as well as the present film. While Bills conceded that "it is true that a few church leaders in the mid-1800s expressed their opinions on the matter," he insisted that "it was not then, and is not now, church doctrine."[69] While Bills's comments suggested

that the church viewed the concept of a married savior negatively, unlike his Protestant and Catholic counterparts, he did not reject the idea
outright.

Even before *The Da Vinci Code* further popularized the subject, several
Mormon writers took issue with Protestant and Catholic revulsion at the
idea of a married savior. Prominent Latter-day Saint apologists Daniel
Peterson and Stephen Ricks briefly discussed the topic in the midst of
defending the church from allegations that it understands Jesus's divine
sonship in an overly literal sense. They noted that anti-Mormon critics
often point to nineteenth-century statements about the wives of Jesus
or that God the Father had returned to earth to conceive a child with
Mary. Those who take "the Incarnation seriously," Peterson and Ricks
suggested, "must allow for some pretty gritty physiological attributes—
at least as much so as sexuality—to be predicated of Jesus." According to
Peterson and Ricks, Christians who shrink back in horror from a married Jesus are guilty of Docetism, the belief—deemed heretical by those
who prevailed in early Christian battles over theological orthodoxy—that
Jesus only seemed to be human. Peterson and Ricks did not argue that
Jesus was a married savior themselves. Instead, they suggested that Christians who believe in a fully human savior should not find the idea of-
fensive or dismiss it out of hand.[70]

Similarly, but at greater length, several Brigham Young University
scholars discussed Jesus's possible marriage in the context of debunking
The Da Vinci Code film. Richard Holzapfel, Andrew Skinner, and Thomas
Wayment contended that conversations about Jesus's marital status detract from more significant theological topics, such as Jesus's atoning
death. At the same time, they note that "many LDS Church leaders, beginning with the prophet Joseph Smith, have inferred or believed that
Jesus was married." While they affirmed the wisdom of contemporary
church leaders to avoid speculation on matters without clear scriptural
guidance, they asserted that "it would not bother modern disciples who
are firmly rooted in the doctrines and ordinances of the kingdom to find
out one day that Jesus was married while on earth."[71] While Peterson
and Ricks defended the Christianness of nineteenth-century Mormon
polygamists, neither they nor Holzapfel, Skinner, and Wayment offered
any support for the observation that Jesus might have married more than

one woman. A monogamously married Jesus, however, was not at all absurd.

Since the appearance of the "Gold Bible" in 1830, Americans have evidenced a persistent fascination with Mormonism, a curiosity that has often veered into cultural voyeurism. Temple rituals, garments, and polygamy, for example, have marked the Latter-day Saints as oddities in the eyes of other Americans and as cultists or heretics from the vantage point of many Christians. In turn, Mormons themselves have often appropriated the biblical appellation of "a peculiar people" as a badge of honor.[72]

The idea of a married, polygamous Jesus plays into this narrative of peculiarity. In the context of nineteenth-century Protestant or Catholic opinion about Jesus's marital status, the Latter-day Saints were certainly outliers. Even in the broader sweep of Christianity's long and diverse history, few followers of Jesus have believed that he had a wife, let alone wives. In another sense, however, the Latter-day Saints wrote new chapters in long histories, in which Christians have remade their savior in their image and have constructed ideal forms of sexuality and marriage for life on earth and in heaven. Depending on one's theological or intellectual vantage point, however, the Mormon answers to these questions were no more "peculiar" than those of medieval monastics or twenty-first century evangelicals.

Their theology of exaltation and practices of marriage led many nineteenth-century Latter-day Saints to conclude that Jesus had married on earth and fathered children. Some church members retain that belief today, having encountered it as folklore passed down from prior generations or having read the statements of nineteenth-century church leaders on the subject. For other church members, however, the idea of a married savior is nearly as foreign as it would be to Catholics or Protestants. Latter-day Saints read nothing about a married Son of God in their scriptures, do not see a married savior in the paintings and statues that adorn their churches and temples, and certainly do not learn about a married Jesus in the talks they hear during sacrament meetings, Sunday school, or General Conferences.

Despite a theological framework that makes marital sealing a requirement for exaltation, the Mormon Jesus today is a single savior. The unmarried Mormon Jesus more closely resembles the savior of other American Christians, who similarly promote monogamous marriage while striving to imitate a celibate and apparently asexual Christ.

✢

THE GREAT WHITE GOD

IN CONTEMPORARY MORMON CULTURE, Jesus Christ is every-where. Unlike in the 1830s, church members do not expect to see their savior in visions, nor do they expect that he will soon return to the earth. At the same time, today's Latter-day Saints see the Son of God all the time. When they walk into their meetinghouses, they see one or more paintings of Jesus Christ in the entryway. They see their savior's face and perhaps a scene from the New Testament or Book of Mormon, such as Jesus teaching the Nephites. Paintings of Jesus Christ illustrate church publications. Deseret Book and other businesses that cater to Mormon consumers feature paintings, statue replicas, and other forms of Jesus-centered artwork, items that often adorn Mormon homes.

Jesus Christ is an artistic presence in most Christian churches. Cath-olics see the Son of God as a baby in Mary's arms, in the Stations of the Cross, and as the dying savior on the cross. Most American Catholics of European descent no longer have much religious art in their homes, though statues of Mary remain somewhat common. Among newly arrived Catholics from the Americas and the Philippines, images of Mary abound, and one sees Jesus as well. Orthodox Christians are probably the most stalwart consumers of religious art in the United States, with iconography of Jesus Christ and the saints present in both churches and homes.

Images of Jesus were once common among American Protestants. For instance, prints of Warner Sallman's *Head of Christ* were ubiquitous in Protestant churches and homes for a generation after the Second World War. However, although Jesus Christ remains central to evangelical rhetoric, practice, and imagination, Protestants no longer display prints and paintings of their savior with any frequency.

Mormons, by contrast, make their savior a visible presence in their meetinghouses, visitor centers, homes, and temples. Such artwork reflects and proclaims contemporary Latter-day Saint devotion to Jesus Christ. Several decades ago, Latter-day Saint leaders decided to remove most artwork from within Mormon chapels (the sanctuary within meetinghouses), adhering to a plain style of worship. In other Mormon spaces, though, there is an abundance of artwork depicting Jesus Christ.

The LDS Church exercises considerable control and influence over the content of these images. In 2009, the church introduced an updated *Gospel Art Book*, containing 137 approved images for use in church and home lessons. Fifty of those selections depict Jesus Christ. Similarly, the *Church Facilities Artwork Catalog* offers local leaders a choice of paintings for purchase, including roughly seventy images of Jesus Christ. These guidelines reflect the church's process of "correlation," the systematic review and standardization of everything from Sunday school curricula to volumes of the Joseph Smith Papers. Correlation explains why there is a uniformity of architecture, worship, and publications in Mormon meetinghouses across the United States and around the world. Visitors and worshippers see the same artwork, the same Jesus.

In the approved paintings, the Mormon Jesus looks a lot like nineteenth- and twentieth-century Protestant versions of the Son of God: strong and triumphant, also tender and caring. And white. Over the past several decades, many other American Christians have expressed qualms about the ahistorical appearance of Jesus Christ as a long-haired, muscular white man, but Latter-day Saint leaders largely have not. Only very recently have a few racially diverse images of Jesus Christ appeared in church media.

In terms of understanding the evolution of Mormonism, however, what is most striking about Latter-day Saint depictions of Jesus is their ubiquity. Artwork among Latter-day Saints fosters devotion to Jesus

Christ, makes a quiet evangelistic appeal to prospective members, and demands that outsiders concede that Mormons are Christians. The culture and business of Mormon art also shows a certain weakening of the boundaries between Mormons and other Christians. Around the turn of the twentieth century, Latter-day Saint publications began featuring the paintings of Protestant artists such as Heinrich Hofmann. Although the church has promoted Latter-day Saint artists, it has also employed painters such as Seventh-day Adventist Harry Anderson, whose series of canvasses created for the 1964–1965 New York World's Fair became widely used within the church. Now, popular Mormon painters such as Simon Dewey, Greg Olsen, and Liz Lemon Swindle sell reproductions of their paintings to non-Mormon consumers. Jesus, at least in artwork, has transcended theological and ecclesiastical divisions.

In the mid-1870s, George Reynolds gained notoriety for appealing his conviction under the 1862 Morrill Anti-Bigamy Act to the Supreme Court, before which he—and his church—lost the argument that anti-polygamy legislation violated the constitutional right to the free exercise of religion. Nearly five years in penitentiaries did not reform Reynolds's view of marriage. After his release, while under indictment for continuing to cohabit with his plural wife, Reynolds married for the third time. Altogether, he fathered thirty-two children. Reynolds was prolific as a writer as well; he contributed countless essays to church periodicals and penned several books about Mormon scriptures.[1]

In 1868, Reynolds wrote a long essay for the *Juvenile Instructor*, a quasi-official church periodical geared toward young Mormons. In the serially published "Man and His Varieties," Reynolds informed Latter-day Saints that of "the many causes that have contributed to change the appearance of the human family and make mankind appear to be of different races, we must consider the blessing or curse of God the greatest of all." Reynolds rejected as contrary to divine revelation the theory that human beings had evolved from other species through a process of natural selection. Also rejecting the belief in the separate divine creation of various races, Reynolds asserted that the world's five races (the Caucasian, the Mongolian, the Negro, the Malayan, and the American) had all descended from Adam and Eve. The original human couple was white, like their Heavenly Father and their savior. "We understand that when God made man in his own image and pronounced him very good, that he made him white" Reynolds stated. He added that all of God's "favored servants," prophets, and apostles have been white, as were angels. Jesus was "very lovely" and "in the express image of his Father's person." Like his Father, then, Jesus was gloriously white.[2]

For Reynolds, divine curses explained the variety of human appearance. American Indians from "Patagonia to Alaska," all descended from the "house of Israel," bore the mark of their ancestors' sin, namely diminished intelligence and "a skin of darkness." Reynolds shared the common white American and European beliefs that God had punished the descendants of Cain with "black skin" and that the "pure Negro" was a descendant of Ham. Citing the Book of Abraham, Reynolds observed that "Egypt was discovered by a woman, who was a daughter of Ham, the son of Noah," whose descendants spread westward and southward across Africa. However, Reynolds affirmed that "the day will come, when all men capable of receiving the priesthood . . . will lose their extravagances of character and appearance, and become 'a white and delightsome people' physically as well as morally." Even dark-skinned Africans would eventually become white.[3]

Reynolds's conclusions incorporated the particular teachings of Mormon scriptures; however, his broader association of whiteness with God's blessing and blackness with God's curse was unoriginal. The belief that dark skin reflects God's curse was deep-rooted in Western Christianity during Joseph Smith's lifetime. Despite its rhetorical connection of whiteness with purity ("wash me, and I shall be whiter than snow"), the Bible does not posit a connection between skin color and God's favor or displeasure. Indeed, the Bible is rather unconcerned with skin color and racial difference, focusing instead on the conflicts between the Israelites and their immediate neighbors. Nevertheless, white American Protestants deployed their interpretations of several biblical passages to support their ideas about race and society.

In the Book of Genesis, God places an unspecified "mark" on Cain after he murders his brother Abel. Later, Noah's son Ham sees "the nakedness" of his drunken father and tells "his brothers without." Noah in response curses Ham's son Canaan, prophesying that "a servant of servants shall he be unto his brethren."[4] Jewish rabbis and Christian theologians alike speculated about the nature of Ham's offense, the nature of the curse, the reason why Canaan received the punishment, and the appearance of Canaan's descendants. As growing numbers of Africans came to live as slaves in the Eastern Mediterranean and on the Arabian Peninsula, Jews, Christians, and Muslims came to interpret the curses of Cain and Canaan as involving a punishment of dark skin, inherited by their descendants.[5]

At the time of the founding of the United States, it was common for white Protestants to connect dark skin with God's primordial curse. Even the African American poet Phyllis Wheatley referred to "Negroes black as Cain." Some African Americans vigorously contested these conclusions, and a few white American Christians agreed that there was no intrabiblical evidence for the link between the Genesis curses and dark skin. Still, if not uncontested, the belief was widespread that black Africans were the cursed descendants of Ham or Cain. For example, the Methodist Adam Clarke's influential early nineteenth-century commentary on the Bible, well known to several early Latter-day Saint writers, identified a portion of Canaan's descendants with Africa and with "perpetual servitude." At the same time, some European and white American Protestants speculated that the offspring of African converts to Christianity would grow progressively whiter, physically as well as morally.[6]

The Book of Mormon reinforced some of these existing white American ideas about race. According to the church's founding scripture, Lehi's family, which travels from Jerusalem to the New World, was "white, and exceedingly delightsome." When Lehi's descendants separate into a righteous people and an unrighteous people, God curses the wicked Lamanites. "That they might not be enticing unto my people," writes Nephi, "the Lord God did cause a skin of blackness to come upon them." At several points, the scripture warns against miscegenation. "And cursed shall be the seed of him that mixeth with their seed," warns God, suggesting that the offspring of Nephite-Lamanite interracial unions will be cursed with the same skin of blackness. The Lamanites, meanwhile, will remain "loathsome unto my people" until they repent. The Book of

Mormon, however, also predicts the eventual restoration of the Lamanites, promising that "their scales of darkness shall begin to fall from their
eyes; and many generations shall not pass away among them, save they
shall be a white and a delightsome people." When Joseph Smith made a
series of minor revisions for an 1840 edition of the Book of Mormon, he
changed "a white and a delightsome" to "a pure and a delightsome." However, another edition of the scripture published the next year in England
did not incorporate the revisions. Finally, in 1981, the church reintroduced Smith's alteration. The Book of Mormon does contain some
egalitarian statements on race. Lehi's son Nephi teaches that God "de-
nieth none that come unto him, black and white . . . all are alike unto
God." Still, readers who already believed that dark skin reflected God's
curse found much support for their presuppositions in the Book of
Mormon.7

The Book of Mormon Jesus is radiantly white. When the resurrected
savior ministers unto his New World disciples, "they did pray unto
him . . . and behold they were as white as the countenance and also
the garments of Jesus; and behold the whiteness thereof did exceed all
the whiteness, yea, even there could be nothing upon earth so white as the
whiteness thereof." A short while later, Nephi repeats that as the disciples steadfastly prayed to Jesus Christ, "they were white, even as Jesus."
This account evokes the transfiguration of Jesus in the gospels of Mark,
Matthew, and Luke, in which Jesus's garments become "exceeding white
as snow; so as no fuller on earth can white them." (A "fuller" whitened
cloth by washing and drying it in the sun.) The Book of Mormon identifies his mother Mary as a virgin "exceeding fair and white," certainly a
description of Mary's virtuous character, which may also refer to her
appearance. Likewise, Jesus's "whiteness" represents his glory and may
also describe his complexion.8

Other Latter-day Saint scriptures reinforced these links between
virtue, spiritual fidelity, and skin color. Smith pondered over the narratives
of Cain and Ham during his early 1830s "translation" of the scriptures,
and the prophet's revision of the early chapters of Genesis (eventually
published as the Book of Moses) made explicit what many white Europeans and Americans had presumed about the narratives of Cain and
Ham. Genesis, for example, states that Cain was cursed with a "mark" but

does not explain its meaning. The Book of Moses clarifies that "the seed of Cain were black" and "had not place among" the offspring of Adam. Similarly, in Smith's revision, Noah curses Canaan with both servitude and "a vail of darkness." Smith returned to these ideas in a portion of the Book of Abraham he dictated in 1835. This text identifies an Egyptian pharaoh as a descendant of Cain and Canaan, making him "of that lineage by which he could not have the right of Priesthood." The descendants of Cain and Canaan were cursed with blackness and stripped of spiritual privileges.[9]

The ideas present in Mormon scriptures influenced Latter-day Saint approaches to nonwhite peoples. Church members anticipated the conversion of Native Americans, whom they identified as descendants of the Lamanites, cursed with dark skin but with the potential for redemption and restoration. Into the mid-twentieth century, church leaders spoke of the whitening of converted Indians. "The day of the Lamanite is nigh," asserted apostle Spencer Kimball in 1960. Kimball commented that Navajo children placed in Mormon homes had become visibly whiter. He referenced the story of a "doctor in a Utah city who for two years had had an Indian boy in his home who stated that he was some shades lighter than the younger brother just coming into the program from the reservation." The prophecies of the Book of Mormon were being fulfilled. "These young members of the Church are changing to whiteness and to delightsomeness," Kimball stated. "One white elder jokingly said that he and his companion were donating blood regularly to the hospital in the hope that the process might be accelerated." Such ideas are no longer common among the Latter-day Saints, as reflected in the 1981 change of "white and delightsome" to "pure and delightsome." For more than a century, however, many Latter-day Saints anticipated the whitening of Native Americans. Redemption was physical as well as spiritual.[10]

Over time, Latter-day Saint scriptures also shaped the way that Mormon leaders understood the position of African American church members. During Joseph Smith's lifetime, a small number of black men were ordained as elders and thus "held the priesthood." By the early 1850s, however, Brigham Young had concluded that men of African descent could not hold the priesthood because of their inheritance of Cain's curse. In 1852, Young, as "a prophet" and "apostle of Jesus Christ," pronounced that "this people that are commonly called Negroes are the children of old Cain" and declared that "a man who has the African blood in him cannot hold one jot nor tittle of priesthood."[11] It does not seem, however, that Mormon scriptures directly influenced Young's conclusions about the place of African Americans within the church. Instead, Young responded with horror to the fact that a black church member had fathered a child with a white woman. Young's repulsion toward miscegenation was common among white Americans, including antislavery northerners. Moreover, the church's movement from relative egalitarianism toward racial discrimination and exclusion mirrored the trajectory of several other American religious movements, including early nineteenth-century Methodism and early twentieth-century Pentecostalism. From the mid-nineteenth century until 1978, the small number of black Mormons occupied distinctly second-tier status within the church. Black men could not hold the priesthood (and thus could not fill positions of church leadership), and black women and men could not obtain the temple ordinances church leaders taught were necessary for their eternal exaltation.[12]

During these years, church leaders used their scriptures to support their policies toward black members. The Book of Abraham suggested that human actions in a premortal existence affected their subsequent "second [mortal] estate." As the church's First Presidency explained in a 1949 statement, "the conduct of spirits in the premortal existence has some determining effect upon the conditions and circumstances under which these spirits take on mortality."[13] Specifically, when a conflict arose between Jesus Christ and Satan over the nature of salvation, spirits chose sides. "There were no neutrals in the war in heaven," taught then-apostle and future church president Joseph Fielding Smith in 1954. "All took sides either with Christ or with Satan. . . . The Negro, evidently, is receiving the reward he merits."[14] In other words, black people got what they deserved. Other church leaders described their premortal behavior and choices as "less valiant." In any event, some spirits merited the mark of Cain and the withholding of priesthood blessings.

George Reynolds used Mormon scriptures to support his contention that God's blessings and curses explained the varieties of human skin color. And yet Mormons did not need their own scriptures in order to construct links among whiteness, virtue, and God's blessing. Nor did they need the Book of Mormon or other scriptures to imagine Jesus as white. For centuries, European artists—especially those in northern Europe—had nearly always depicted him as radiantly white.

One influence on such depictions was a fraudulent description of Jesus's appearance, in circulation since at least its fifteenth-century publication in Europe. Known as the "Publius Lentulus Letter," it presents itself as the letter of a Judean governor and contemporary of Jesus Christ, whom it describes as a "man of stature somewhat tall, and comely, with a very reverend countenance." The letter adds that his brown, wavy, shoulder-length hair was parted "in the midst of his head" and that Jesus had a "thickish" beard, "in colour like his hair, not very long, but forked." After labeling his physique as "most excellent," the letter praises him "for his singular beauty, surpassing the children of men." The letter was a fake, probably composed sometime between the tenth and fourteenth centuries. By the nineteenth century, scholars had long since recognized that the letter did not provide an authentic description of Jesus. Despite questions about its provenance, though, the Lentulus Letter both reflected and shaped the way that late medieval and early modern Europeans imagined and depicted Jesus Christ. Several nineteenth-century Americans published the letter's text, sometimes with accompanying illustrations. Although the text itself did not identify Jesus's skin color, those illustrations depicted a white man. For most white Americans, "comely" evidently meant white.[15]

Latter-day Saint writers and leaders referenced the Lentulus Letter on many occasions in the late nineteenth and early twentieth centuries. Not all references were uncritical. In 1898, the church's *Improvement Era* excerpted Swiss-born Protestant church historian Philip Schaff's judgment that the Lentulus Letter was "not authentic, and certainly not older than the fourth century."[16] Still, despite such doubts, church publications and high-ranking church leaders quoted the Lentulus Letter approvingly. In 1882, the *Juvenile Instructor* termed the letter—which it identified as an "ancient manuscript"—a "fair and honest description, no doubt, so far as it goes, of the Savior of the world."[17] Most tellingly, apostle (and future

William S. Pendleton, *Letter from Publius Lentulus, to the Senate of Rome Concerning Jesus Christ*, 1834. (Courtesy of the American Antiquarian Society.)

church president) Spencer W. Kimball shared that church president David O. McKay had read the Lentulus Letter in a meeting within the Salt Lake City Temple prior to the April 1956 General Conference. "Whether authentic or not I do not know," Kimball added. "But it may stir our imaginations."[18]

Indeed, the question of the letter's authenticity or fraudulency was beside the point. This description of Jesus had stirred the imaginations of many Americans—Protestant, Catholic, and Mormon—as it had stirred those of medieval Europeans. As many white Christians presumed that the mark of Cain was blackness and that Canaan's descendants lived in Egypt, and as Mormons presumed that the premortal spirits of black people had been less "valiant" or had sided with Satan, so many European and American Christians presumed that everything from the Bible to the Lentulus Letter described Jesus as a white man. Given that nearly all Americans—including the growing number of African American Christians and a significant number of Native American Christians—envisioned Jesus as white by the mid-nineteenth century, it is hardly surprising that Mormons followed suit. Deep-rooted traditions shaped how the Latter-day Saints imagined Jesus, and the images of Jesus Mormons borrowed and created reinforced those ideas.

Joseph Smith came of age and founded a church just as Protestant suspicion of religious art was fading. During the Reformation, many Protestants removed—in an orderly or violent manner, depending on the location—artwork and adornments from churches. Many of the early English emigrants to the United States were Protestants who considered such items idolatrous violations of the Second Commandment and signs of "Popery." Thus, the early New England primers included pictures of Adam, Job, and Zacchaeus, but not Jesus. Most congregations placed no crosses on their church buildings because they associated the symbol with "Popish idolatry." There were Protestant exceptions to this iconoclasm. The Moravians cherished paintings of the crucifixion, with Jesus's blood pouring out of his wounds. Most Protestants, however, were content to read of Jesus Christ in their scriptures and hear the Word of God preached in their churches. They did not want to see his likeness.[19]

Over the first half of the nineteenth century, though, Protestants gradually became comfortable with depictions of their savior. Aided by the rise of inexpensive printing methods, Protestant missionary societies and publishing houses soon flooded the country with illustrated tracts and Bibles. For example, the Bible Joseph Smith used during his "translation of the scriptures" contained rudimentary woodcut pictures of Jesus Christ. The goals of evangelism and children's religious education overrode iconoclastic objections.[20]

Still, outside of their visions and dreams, early Mormons did not see the likeness of Jesus with any regularity. Unlike Protestants who printed millions of Jesus-suffused pamphlets and Bibles, unlike Catholics who treasured crucifixes or prints of the suffering savior, and even unlike Millerites who circulated charts predicting the Son of God's imminent return, most early Mormons were far too poor for art. Nineteenth-century editions of the Book of Mormon contained no illustrations. Early Latter-day Saint tracts, pamphlets, and histories were sparse publications with unadorned text. Some church leaders warned against the use of Protestant materials, moreover. Apostle Parley Pratt discouraged the consumption of popular Protestant religious literature, instructing members to "remove sectarian books, tracts, pictures, and paintings from their homes replacing them with maps, charts, works of science and religious information." Pratt feared that Mormon children might learn false doctrine from illustrated Protestant Bibles. Because of such attitudes, and then because of their geographic isolation in early Utah, the Saints were at least partly removed from the proliferation of Jesus images in mid-nineteenth-century American culture.[21]

A few Latter-day Saints began developing their own church-themed artwork as early as the 1840s. Portraits of church leaders and affluent church members decorated the walls of the Nauvoo Temple's celestial room, and, prior to the exodus, a few Mormon artists worked on a large canvas of Joseph and Hyrum Smith's martyrdom. Philo Dibble, a Mormon artist and collector, assembled several vast canvasses stitched together in a scroll as a moving panorama that he unrolled and displayed in Utah communities. Other Mormon artists followed suit, creating paintings and panoramas with scenes from the church's dramatic early history, bringing the church's persecution and persistence into sharp relief while mirroring the larger American fondness for majestic Western landscapes. Artists such as C. C. A. Christensen, George Ottinger, and Danquart Weggeland painted handcart pioneers, Indians, church leaders, and the rugged landscape of their new home amid the mountains.

Only occasionally did they paint scenes from their scriptures. The Norwegian-born Weggeland painted the crucifixion in the mid-1870s, a subject future Mormon artists would mostly eschew. Ottinger painted an occasional scene from the Book of Mormon but more frequently imagined the tragic end of the Aztec empire at the hands of the Spanish. Christensen's *Mormon Panorama* stitched together twenty-three large paintings, beginning with the First Vision and ending with the 1847 pioneer trek. During these decades, Latter-day Saint artists rarely created paintings or other artwork depicting Jesus Christ, and, compared to many other Americans, church members rarely saw mass-produced images of the Son of God.[22]

Mormon juvenile literature formed a small but significant exception to this lack of illustration. The recognition that pictures of Jesus could nurture children's faith had nudged American Protestants to abandon their prior opposition to artistic depictions of their savior. Mormons again followed suit. In 1866, the quasi-official *Juvenile Instructor*, published by Apostle George Q. Cannon and purchased several decades later by the church's Deseret Sunday School Union, printed a small image of the crucified messiah, possibly the first Mormon printed image of Jesus Christ. In keeping with the longstanding wariness of crosses, the magazine observed that too many so-called Christians pay more reverence "to the symbol or sign of the manner in which Christ died than to doing what He told them to do."[23] In 1888, George Reynolds published *The Story of the Book of Mormon*, the first illustrated volume of Mormonism's founding scripture. In order to capture the interest of younger readers, Reynolds combined thirteen commissioned paintings by Latter-day Saint artists, other stock images, and an abridged paraphrase of the scripture itself. The resulting book included the first published paintings of Book of Mormon scenes and quite probably the first published depictions of Jesus Christ created by Mormon artists. For instance, a painting by John Held Sr. depicted the premortal messiah's appearance to the brother of Jared; Held's apparitional Jesus Christ featured a thick beard, unparted hair, a halo, and no legs.[24]

Similar to their Protestant and Catholic counterparts, Latter-day Saint religious educators believed that illustrations made religious truths more real to children. Apostle Moses Thatcher praised Reynolds's

The Story of the Book of Mormon as "well calculated to inspire faith in the hearts of the young."[25] By the early decades of the twentieth century, illustrations of Jesus Christ were staples of Latter-day Saint religious education. The painter and sculptor J. Leo Fairbanks explained the necessity of illustrations for Sunday school instruction, arguing that "art causes us to feel that Christ was a man, that He lived a physical existence, that He was mortal, sympathized with sinners, moved among beggars, helped the infirm, ate with publicans and counseled with human beings for their immediate as well as their future spiritual welfare."[26] Mormon children increasingly saw Jesus in children's periodicals, Sunday school literature, and flannel-board cutouts.

Still lacking a significant body of their own artwork, Mormons utilized engravings and paintings of Jesus produced by non-Mormons. They favored straightforward, realistic portraits of the life of Jesus as narrated by the New Testament gospels, such as Heinrich Hofmann's *Christ in Gethsemane* and his fellow German Bernhard Plockhorst's *Good Shepherd*. Rather than reflecting any particular Latter-day Saint artistic tastes, these paintings (and others by the same artists) were beloved by American Protestants and widely purchased as prints. Oil magnate John D. Rockefeller bought and donated Hofmann's *Gethsemane* (and two other of his canvases) to New York City's Riverside Church. In addition to their broad popularity, such images were inexpensive for the church to use, and they appeared in LDS periodicals such as *The Children's Friend*. Their usage reflected a congruence between Mormon tastes and the broader culture of American Protestantism.[27]

Some Latter-day Saint leaders felt that even Hofmann and Plockhorst missed the mark in their depictions of Jesus Christ. In 1904, George Reynolds complained in the *Juvenile Instructor* that in the works of the European masters, Christ "is almost universally represented as a somewhat effeminate and sentimental young man with long flowing [red] locks, a weakling in body with few traces on his face of the strength of character within." Reynolds found this all wrong: "the Christ was not red-haired, nor effeminate, neither was he a dyspeptic, nor a dreamy sentimentalist." Instead, Reynolds asserted that Jesus was a "vigorous, deep chested,

Christ in Gethsemane, by Heinrich Hofmann, 1890. Peter, James, and John are visible in the background behind Jesus. From Henry E. Jackson, *Great Pictures as Moral Teachers* (Philadelphia: John C. Winston, 1910).

broad shouldered man, with well cut features and above the medium height." As evidence for his conclusions, Reynolds pointed to Jesus's divine lineage and the fact that those "in this generation" who had seen him in visions "state that he appeared to them to be not less than six feet in height."[28] Somewhat similarly, Janne Sjodahl, editor of the *Deseret News*, favored those pictures with an "expression of serenity and infinite dignity," as opposed to those depicting an anguished, suffering, downtrodden Messiah.[29]

These concerns about Jesus's appearance were not specific to Mormonism. American Protestants worried that churches needed a more muscular Christianity—a "Christian commitment to health and manliness"—to attract and retain the interest of men. Nearly all Protestant denominations were disproportionately female in their membership, with many of their activities centered around the need for congregants to develop a relationship with Jesus Christ as their savior and friend. By the latter decades of the nineteenth century, many male (and some female) Protestant leaders identified the need for a new generation of muscular and manly men to save both the church and the nation from effeminate decline. Christian concerns about the participation of men within the church coalesced with broader social fears that the end of the frontier and the advent of urban living and desk jobs had emasculated American men, who needed everything from imperial adventures to athletic clubs to rediscover their toughness and character. In response, Protestant denominations founded the Young Men's Christian Association and supported the establishment of Boy Scout troops. Through an emphasis on health and athletics, Protestant leaders would raise up a strong and noble generation of Christian men.[30]

Correspondingly, many Protestant leaders wanted to behold a tougher savior. R. Warren Conant, a physician turned teacher at the Chicago Latin School, sharply criticized "the Feminizing of Christianity," which he blamed for the fact that women overwhelmingly outnumbered men at Protestant churches. Conant argued that the "men of a strenuous age demand a strenuous Christ." "*Christ stands*," he emphasized, "for the highest type of a strong, virile man, and there was nothing effeminate about him." Conant found most artistic depictions of Jesus repulsively feminine and sentimental, as he "looks down upon us, 'meek and lowly,' with an expression of sweetness and resignation . . . long curling hair brushed smoothly from a central parting—all feminine, passive, negative." "Why not hold up to the world a portrait drawn to the life of the Manly Christ in place of the womanish?" he asked. Conant wanted paintings of a brave, commanding, and athletic Christ.[31]

Although some Protestants balanced ideals of tender friendship and rugged manhood in their descriptions of Jesus, the insistence upon a muscular Christ and Christianity spanned the Protestant theological spectrum. Harry Emerson Fosdick, then a rising proponent of the Social Gospel and later the country's most renowned modernist minister, joined the chorus of complaint over "medieval" depictions of a mournful and pale man of sorrows. In his 1913 *The Manhood of the Master*, Fosdick urged Christians to consider how Jesus "appeals to all that is strongest and most military in you."[32] Fundamentalist revivalist Billy Sunday, whose popularity crested during the First World War, lamented that there were often more "feathers than whiskers" in the pews. Sunday prayed that God would save Americans from "off-handed, flabby-cheeked, brittle-boned, weak-kneed, thin-skinned, pliable, plastic, spineless, effeminate, ossified, three-carat Christianity."[33] Such emphases increased during the war, as American soldiers (and their civilian supporters) imagined a strong, fearless savior marching at their sides.

While "muscular Christianity" died down or became subdued in some liberal Protestant quarters after the war's unsatisfactory aftermath, many Protestant male leaders still contended that American men needed a manly Christ as their model. Bruce Barton, a theologically liberal advertising executive whose *The Man Nobody Knows* sold a quarter-million copies in 1925 and 1926, extolled both Jesus's organizational efficiency and his manly bearing. Most artists, he lamented, have "misled" Christians. "They have shown us a frail man, under-muscled, with a soft face—a woman's face covered by a beard," Barton alleged. Christians, therefore, misunderstood their savior. "You . . . have let yourself picture him," Barton asserted, "as weak, as a man of sorrows, uninspiring, glad to die." Instead, Jesus was an "outdoor man" whose manly bearing commanded respect. Christian art should display *that* Jesus.[34]

Mormons were latecomers to the muscular Christianity movement, as their lives were already plenty strenuous during the first half-century of Utah settlement and conquest. During the mid-to-late-nineteenth century, Latter-day Saint hierarchs frequently asserted that polygamy produced virile men. "I have noticed that a man who has but one wife, and is inclined to that doctrine," preached Heber C. Kimball in 1857, "soon begins to wither and dry up, while a man who goes into plurality looks fresh, young, and sprightly."[35] Although the fifty-five-year-old Kimball had been sealed to more than forty women, he was rarely accused of sprightliness or an especially youthful appearance. In any event, many Mormon leaders were confident that their men stacked up well compared to dissolute Gentiles.

Even so, especially after the church capitulated to U.S. government demands on the issue of polygamy, the Latter-day Saints also turned toward athletics and Boy Scout troops in order to simultaneously "re-masculinize Mormon men" and "'Americanize' Mormons."[36] The concerns about masculinity Mormons shared with many other American Christians shaped the way that Latter-day Saints envisioned the savior. For example, Orson Whitney's later recollection of an 1877 vision reflects a growing emphasis on Jesus Christ's strength and masculinity. While serving a mission in the eastern United States, Whitney dreamed of Jesus Christ in the Garden of Gethsemane. Half a century later, Whitney wrote an account of his "dream, or a vision in a dream" in an autobiography. Jesus kneeled in agony and torment while the disciples slept; later in the dream, Whitney saw the resurrected Jesus before his ascension to heaven. Whitney fell at his savior's feet and begged to go with him. "He gazed upon me with inexpressible tenderness," he wrote, "then stooped and lifted me up into his arms and embraced me with all the affection of a father or an elder brother." Jesus spoke with "a voice full of sweetness and compassion," instructing Whitney to remain on earth to complete his work. The dream's lesson, Whitney concluded, "was stamped upon my mind eternally." After Whitney had drafted his autobiography, he added this comment in its published version: "He was of noble stature and majestic mien—not at all the weak, effeminate being that some painters have portrayed; but the very God that He was and is, as meek and humble as a little child." The comment reflects the early twentieth-century Protestant and Mormon effort to portray a more masculine and muscular Jesus, enhancing a tender and affectionate savior with added nobility and majesty.[37]

During the middle decades of the 1900s, the Latter-day Saints embraced Warner Sallman's *Head of Christ*, the most iconic American twentieth-century image of Jesus Christ. In Sallman's painting, the savior's long, flowing hair and short beard evoke the Lentulus Letter's description. Like their Protestant and Catholic counterparts, Mormons hung Sallman's head of Christ in their homes and in their Sunday school classrooms. Latter-day Saints placed the image on their missionary calling cards.

Sallman intended his *Head of Christ* to convey handsome manliness and virtue. Still, it was hard to satisfy everyone on that score. Some admirers of Sallman's painting praised it in contrast to Hofmann's allegedly too "feminine" Jesus, while other Protestants made the very same complaint against Sallman. Lutheran art critic Richard Muhlberger criticized both Hofmann and Sallman for turning Jesus Christ into a "bearded woman."[38] Over and over again, Americans—especially Protestants and Mormons—criticized paintings of Jesus Christ as insufficiently masculine. In the early 1980s, Latter-day Saint leaders commissioned Utah artist Del Parson to paint a head of Christ. When Parson submitted a series of sketches for feedback, church leaders recommended a more masculine rendering of the savior. Parson obliged, and his rugged, serene, and red-robed *Lord Jesus Christ* became the quasi-official Mormon "head of Christ."[39]

No one would have accused Latter-day Saint Arnold Friberg of painting an insufficiently masculine Christ. In the early 1950s, Friberg painted scenes of the Book of Mormon, first published in an LDS children's periodical and later included in the scripture itself. Most famous outside of Mormon circles for a painting of George Washington at prayer and because of his consulting work for Cecil B. DeMille's *The Ten Commandments*, Friberg filled his canvases with what art historian Vern Swanson calls "wide-shouldered Aryan men," tall and brawny figures such as Captain Moroni, who raises a banner of liberty against a group of Nephite dissenters who want to transform their society into a monarchy.[40] Friberg's depiction of Book of Mormon heroes perfectly matched the Cold War Mormon mood, where apocalypticism, patriotism, and anticommunism fed the celebration of brave and powerful men fighting for freedom and righteousness. Friberg understood his canvases as testimonies of human worth. "This idea that mankind is wretched and little is wrong," Friberg defended his style. "The muscularity in my paintings is only an expression of the spirit within."⁴¹

For his Book of Mormon series, however, church president David O. McKay urged Friberg not to "paint Christ into the Book of Mormon." McKay pointed to a lack of human ability to "conceive of the infinite."⁴² Friberg accordingly skirted a physical depiction of Jesus. He painted a canvas of the brother of Jared seeing "the finger of the Lord" from behind, creating a sense of blinding light that obscures any glimpse of Jesus Christ's body. Several years later, though, Friberg painted *The Risen Lord*, of Jesus among the Nephites. As the resurrected and exalted Jesus shows the people his wounded hands, his white robes reveal a bare chest with well-defined pectorals and abdomen. "Jesus is neither a weakling nor a victim," Friberg explained, "but a commanding presence; one look at His eyes and men sacrificed everything to follow Him."⁴³ The church briefly promoted *The Risen Lord* as part of its Gospel-in-Art series, but the painting was soon removed from the list. Church leaders had long wanted artists to show Jesus Christ as strong, commanding, and noble, concerns that stretched back nearly a hundred years and still persist. Friberg's hypermuscular risen Christ, however, apparently went too far. The physical body of Jesus Christ should not look like that of a body builder.

Friberg's career also marked a turning point in the history of Mormon art. Latter-day Saints had embraced the Protestant art of Hofmann and Sallman. Now a Mormon artist found immense popularity for the first time, as customers purchased reproductions of his *Ten Commandments*, George Washington, Canadian Mounties, and American West canvases. Meanwhile, his Book of Mormon illustrations made indelible impressions on two generations of church members.

Not all Mormon artists depicted chiseled and muscular saviors. Like Friberg, Minerva Teichert completed a series of commissioned Book of Mormon illustrations for a church publication, and she also painted a set of murals for the Manti Temple. Born in 1888 to a rancher whose family had disowned him when he was baptized as a Latter-day Saint, she studied art in New York and Chicago. Then, she married a rancher herself. For many years, Teichert painted at night after cooking for the ranch hands and caring for her children during the day. She favored large, dramatic canvases, and, like many of her predecessors, she painted scenes of Mormon pioneers. Teichert never achieved a broad non-Mormon audience akin to Friberg's, but her many Book of Mormon paintings earned her a devoted following among church members.

Teichert departed from the strict realism characteristic of many Latter-day Saint artists. Among her best-known paintings of Jesus Christ is *Christ in a Red Robe* (inspired by Isaiah 63), in which a scarlet-robed Jesus presides over the resurrection of the righteous and the dead. Teichert also painted multiple canvases of the risen savior superimposed on a map of the Western Hemisphere. On occasion, she placed biblical episodes in a New World context. For instance, in *Touch Me Not*, it is a Nephite woman who kneels at Jesus's feet following his resurrection, looking up at his pierced hands. In this and certain other paintings, Teichert's Jesus resembles the Jesus found in earlier woodcuts, with a halo surrounding his head. His hair is long and brown, parted in the middle, and he wears a neatly trimmed beard. In Teichert's paintings, Jesus is a strong but tender savior, not the brawny warrior of Arnold Friberg.[44]

Indeed, a more moderately muscled Mormon Jesus reflects the nature of contemporary Mormon masculinity. As Noel Carmack explains, Latter-day Saint leaders increasingly spoke of "consecrated manliness," emphasizing virtue and companionship.[45] Certainly, the church celebrates athletic achievement, but it places an even higher value on men's fidelity and devotion to their church and families. In 2014, Apostle Quentin L. Cook cautioned young Latter-day Saint men not to become involved in athletics to the detriment of more important life goals.[46] Being physically fit is important, but not an end in and of itself. Latter-day Saint missionaries receive a short amount of time each morning for exercise, but physical health and strength are only preparations for more sacred tasks. Similarly, the church today favors images of Jesus by both Mormon and non-Mormon artists that balance noble strength with tender concern and contemplativeness. Indeed, the Mormon savior is the Good Shepherd, the one who welcomes children, the one who reclines on a hillside in prayer. The Mormon Jesus is like the

Christ Blessing the Nephite Children, by Ted Henninger. (© by Intellectual Reserve, Inc.)

contemporary Mormon man, strong and fit, busy serving his family and community, cherishing a brief moment alone with his Heavenly Father.

One sees this image of Jesus Christ in the paintings of contemporary Mormon artists such as Greg Olsen, Simon Dewey, Liz Lemon Swindle, and Ted Henninger. Jesus is a tender shepherd, the savior who welcomes children of all races, and the risen Lord. Moreover, many contemporary Latter-day Saint artists first and foremost market themselves and their art as "Christian" rather than "Mormon." Their scenes come from the New Testament, more rarely from the Book of Mormon. On his website, Simon Dewey informs customers that his "paintings center around the life of the Savior Jesus Christ . . . [and] the stories of the New Testament and Christ's Ministry."[47] Greg Olsen's website allows visitors to select from his "Western," "Impressionistic," "Landscape," and "Christian" art.[48] As is true of Swindle's website, Dewey's online catalog begins with paintings that would appeal to Christians in general, such as *The Good Shepherd* and *Living Water*. It takes more time to discover paintings on the website such as those of Joseph Smith translating the Book of Mormon or as "Prophet and Seer."[49] This is not to say that the "Christian" paintings are not in some ways distinctively Mormon. In some of Olsen and Dewey's paintings, Jesus's radiantly white robes evoke thoughts of Latter-day Saint temples rather than the dusty roads of Galilee.[50] For contemporary Latter-day Saints, paintings of Jesus Christ evoke their shared Mormon and Christian identities.

Arnold Friberg's work is known beyond Mormon circles, and, within the church, the paintings of Greg Olsen, Minerva Teichert, and many others are recognizable. Even if they could not name the artists, Latter-day Saints know these paintings; they see them with regularity in their buildings and publications. The most famous Mormon image of Jesus Christ, however, is a statue rather than a painting.

Americans of many theological persuasions have long admired Danish sculptor Bertel Thorvaldsen's *Christus Consolator*, a statue of white marble showing the resurrected Christ with open arms. Despite his own unbelief, Thorvaldsen—baptized as a Lutheran—accepted numerous artistic assignments for the Vatican and for Copenhagen's Church of Our Lady, where the *Christus* has stood since 1833.[51] Many Americans saw Thorvaldsen's *Christus* during the 1853 Crystal Palace exhibition in New York City, and the Johns Hopkins Hospital received a donated replica in 1896. By this time, Latter-day Saints also admired *Christus*. George Reynolds praised it as "a very dignified example of the conventional idea of the appearance of the Redeemer when He tabernacled in the flesh."[52] By referring to the "appearance of the Redeemer" in *Christus* as "conventional," Reynolds signaled that Mormons, like other Americans, saw in the statue a Jesus they recognized. In Thorvaldsen's *Christus*, the savior has long, flowing locks parted in the middle, a short, parted beard, and flowing robes that open to reveal his muscular chest. Arnold Friberg must have wondered how Latter-day Saint leaders could have objected to his bare-chested *The Risen Lord*.

In the mid-1950s, church architect George Cannon Young began designing a new Bureau of Information on Temple Square. At the same time, Young and the Temple Square Presidency (Richard L. Evans, Marion D. Hanks, and church president David O. McKay's son Robert) wanted to ensure that visitors to Temple Square received a clearer and more inspiring introduction to the LDS Church. According to George Young's recollection, Evans complained in one planning meeting that "the world thinks we're not Christian . . . they see no evidence of Christ on this square." Young suggested placing a prominent statue of Christ on Temple Square. Robert McKay worried that "Catholics will come through and genuflect" before the statue. "What better place can they genuflect than right here?" Young responded. At first, the Temple Square Presidency considered placing a statue of Christ on the southeast side of the square, but George Cannon Young instead recommended the rotunda of the planned information center. Those curious about Mormonism would enter a space dominated by a large, imposing statue of Jesus Christ, making unmistakable the Christianness of Mormonism.[53]

Another high-ranking leader, counselor Stephen L. Richards of the church's First Presidency, played the most significant role in filling that space. Richards had seen a replica of the *Christus* at California's Forest Lawn Memorial Park; he probably also viewed the original during a 1950 trip to Europe. When church leaders considered obtaining a statue of Jesus Christ for Temple Square, Richards consulted Forest Lawn's director Hubert Eaton. Richards recalled "the lovely statue you have in Forest Lawn." "I suggest first that you get a replica of Thorvaldsen's 'The Christus,'" responded Eaton. "It is by far the finest one in existence." Eaton then facilitated Richards's acquisition of a replica produced in Italy, at a total cost of $6,485. Richards informed Eaton that he hoped the statue would become "one of the outstanding points of interest on our Temple Square." Richards's hopes were well founded. In terms of burnishing its Christian image, the church has rarely gotten such a positive return on a modest investment.[54]

Richards died just before the statue's June 1959 arrival in Salt Lake City, but his estate gave the statue to the church. Two years later, workers at the Deseret News Job Printing Plant opened a large crate that they believed had "been there for some years." Inside, they discovered the *Christus* replica, which they correctly identified because "the little toe on the right foot is turned under." "It is so Catholic in its appearance," Apostle Mark E. Petersen informed the First Presidency, "that I don't imagine we would have any use for it as Latter-day Saints. I do not know whether you are aware of the fact that it is even in our building."[55] Apostle Petersen did not explain why the statue struck him as Catholic. Elements of iconoclasm and anti-Catholicism still shaped the sensibility of some Latter-day Saints toward artwork and also toward the symbol of the cross. For instance, David O. McKay had discouraged Arnold Friberg from painting Jesus Christ, and he also instructed Mormon women not to wear crosses on necklaces because it reflected "a Catholic form of worship."[56] Despite such concerns, though, McKay and other top leaders gave their blessing to the *Christus*.

The next year, the church moved the statue into the center of a rotunda in its new Bureau of Information building (now the North Visitors Center). At roughly the same time, church leaders decided to create a pavilion for the 1964–1965 New York World's Fair. Mormons had not always been welcome at such venues. The conveners of the World's Parliament of Religions connected with the 1893 Columbian Exposition had pointedly excluded the Latter-day Saints, concluding that Mormonism was not a "religion." An earlier world's fair in New York City, held in 1939–1940, organized a "Temple of Religion" with only three faiths: Protestantism, Catholicism, and Judaism. In the mid-1960s, however, the Latter-day Saints were welcome, although fair officials at first encouraged Mormons to share space within a broader Protestant building. Rejecting the idea of shared Protestant identity, church leaders persuaded the officials that Mormons, just like Catholics, needed their own space.

Visitors to the Mormon Pavilion saw abundant artwork, including two vast murals of the life of Jesus Christ (painted by Seventh-Day Adventist Harry Anderson) and the history of the church, respectively. There were also statues of Adam and Eve, Joseph Smith, and the restoration of the priesthood. Towering over everything else, however, was the eleven-foot-tall *Christus*. Church leaders had at first contemplated moving the replica acquired by Stephen Richards to New York City. Realizing the difficulty and expense in repacking and transporting the statue, however, they decided to purchase a second replica from the same casting. Missionaries who guided visitors around the exhibit began by emphasizing that the "pavilion is centered around Jesus Christ and the Holy Scriptures" and that Latter-day Saints "believe that Jesus Christ, the

Mormon Pavilion, New York World's Fair, 1964. (© by Intellectual Reserve, Inc.)

Messiah, lives today, and that he had the same resurrected body of flesh and bones that he had when he ascended into heaven." A film, *Man's Search for Happiness*, introduced visitors to more distinctive Latter-day Saint beliefs, such as human preexistence and the possibility of eternal family connections. Visitors may or may not have listened carefully to the missionary presentations or film, but it was impossible to ignore the *Christus*. "The statue of Christ overwhelmed me!" wrote one guest in the exhibit's register. The fair was a remarkable public-relations success for the church, whose pavilion outdrew Billy Graham's. The fair had also introduced millions of visitors to a new symbol of Mormon Christianity in the *Christus*.[57]

Afterward, the World's Fair *Christus* went to the church's Los Angeles Visitors Center. In the years ahead, Mormon copies of the *Christus* multiplied exponentially. Other temple visitor centers acquired replicas, and Latter-day Saint families bought miniatures for their homes. A lightweight fiberglass "traveling *Christus*"[58] graced temple open houses, during which nonmembers may tour the buildings prior to their dedication.

Millions of visitors to Temple Square and other Mormon sites each year gaze up at the statue and associate it with the Church of Jesus Christ of Latter-day Saints and therefore more closely associate the church with Christianity. At the church's October 1987 General Conference, Apostle Dallin Oaks told of taking a non-Mormon friend to the Temple Square North Visitors Center. Afterward, Oaks's friend informed the apostle that he now better understood the Mormon faith. "I hope that every person who has ever had doubts about whether we are Christians can achieve that same understanding," commented Oaks.[59]

The *Christus* combined many of the traits that characterized other Mormon depictions of Jesus Christ. In Thorvaldsen's statue, the savior is a strong and muscular man. He has risen in triumph from the cross and the grave, and he tenderly calls to people, "Come unto me." The statue's marble is brilliantly white. For Latter-day Saints, this was how their Savior looked when he appeared to the Nephites, and it is how he might look when he returns in glory. Although the original remains in a Catholic cathedral, the *Christus* has become an icon of Mormon Christianity.

What does it mean for the Latter-day Saints to have a savior who is male and white? Even if they use male pronouns for God and call God their Father, most other Christians, if pressed, will say that God is beyond human traits such as gender and sex. Protestant and Catholic theologians, at least, would claim that God transcends such human matters. The Latter-day Saints, by contrast, assert that God is a material being and has a body of flesh and bones. The Mormon God *is* male, as is Jesus Christ, who possessed a male body before his mortality. The Latter-day Saints also believe in a Heavenly Mother, but Mormon leaders rarely speak of her and discourage church members from praying to or worshiping her. Heavenly Father and Jesus Christ are the most important divine figures for Latter-day Saints. Two white men. A white savior.

In their study of how American depictions of Jesus Christ have both reflected and reinforced racial privilege and oppression, historians Paul Harvey and Edward Blum note that when American Protestants abandoned iconoclasm, they created "a cultural icon of white power." The fact that Americans depicted Jesus as white reinforced the idea of white superiority. Blacks, Indians, and Asian Americans sometimes questioned or ridiculed the idea of a lily-white Jesus Christ that looked little like a man from Palestine. White Americans, though, often recoiled in horror at any suggestion that their savior may have had dark skin.[60] The fact that American Christians have consistently criticized paintings of Jesus as overly feminine suggests their belief in the superiority of male traits and the corresponding undesirability of female traits.[61] Likewise, an insistence that Jesus Christ was or is white implies the relative undesirability of darker skin. American Protestants have moved away from depictions of Jesus in recent decades, at least implicitly recognizing the hazards of associating the Son of God with any single skin color. (Children's bibles remain an exception; in their pages Jesus typically remains white). Until recently, by contrast, Mormons have shown no discomfort with their customarily white depictions of the savior.

"The Great White God of ancient America still lives!" proclaimed Apostle Mark E. Petersen in an article published in the church's flagship periodical in 1969. Building upon a theory advanced by late-nineteenth-century Latter-day Saints, Petersen claimed that Native American traditions of a "White God"—often identified with the Mesoamerican deity Quetzalcoatl (a feathered serpent, sometimes depicted in human form)—were evidence that Jesus Christ had appeared in the Americas. Quetzalcoatl was Jesus.

White Europeans and Americans had long embellished and appropriated native myths about Quetzalcoatl and similar Mesoamerican figures. In his 1820s *View of the Hebrews*, the American Congregationalist minister Ethan Smith identified Quetzalcoatl (*"a white man and bearded"*) as Moses, a "type of Christ." By the mid-nineteenth century, Europeans and Americans had linked Quetzalcoatl to several other biblical figures, including Noah and the Apostle Thomas. In the late 1800s, church president John Taylor asserted that "we can come to no other conclusion than that Quetzalcoatl and Christ are the same being." Quetzalcoatl was more than a type of Christ. He was Christ. Taylor cited the research of Irish antiquarian Lord Edward Kingsborough, who had scoured Spanish sources for evidence that Mesoamericans were descendants of the ten lost tribes of Israel.[62]

For many Latter-day Saints, the Christianized Quetzalcoatl became a piece of evidence to support the Book of Mormon's authenticity as a history of ancient peoples. Minerva Teichert, who had traveled to Mexico to visit what she considered Nephite and Lamanites ruins, adorned many of her Book of Mormon paintings with Quetzalcoatl birds. The Quetzalcoatl-as-Jesus identification and the idea that there might be parallels between the Book of Mormon and the Quiché Mayan *Popol Vuh* were attractive not only to white American Mormons but also to Central American Latter-day Saints. Anthropologist John Murphy conducted interviews with Guatemalan converts, many of whom "conflated the Sovereign Plumed Serpent . . . with the internationally recognized Jesus Christ" and believed that the *Popol Vuh* and Book of Mormon both describe a visit of Jesus Christ to the Americas.[63]

Apostle Petersen repeated the Quetzalcoatl-as-Jesus Christ argument on numerous occasions in the mid-twentieth century. "That he was a Christian divinity none can successfully deny," the apostle declared. "That his teachings were akin to the Bible is now readily admitted by many." Even more remarkably, he looked like the American and European Jesus. "He was described as a tall, white man, bearded, and with blue eyes," Petersen informed. "He wore loose, flowing robes." Petersen then concluded by asserting that the "Book of Mormon tells the facts about the coming of the Great White God." At a time when African Americans and some white Protestants were questioning the depiction of Jesus as white, Petersen demonstrated a complete obliviousness or indifference to such concerns.[64]

By this time, African Americans were contesting church restrictions on black members. As the *Christus* found its permanent home on Temple Square, Salt Lake City's central landmark was becoming a flash point in the Western civil rights movement. Supporters of racial equality pressured church leaders to endorse civil rights legislation and end the restrictions that barred black church members from the priesthood and from temple ordinances.[65] Many LDS leaders were very wary of the civil rights movement, sharing the paranoid suspicions of many political

Christ in America, by Minerva Teichert, 1949–1951. (Courtesy of Brigham Young University Museum of Art.)

conservatives that the movement was infiltrated and controlled by communists. In 1969, facing mounting pressure from civil rights leaders, the church's First Presidency released a statement that explained why "Negroes, while spirit children of a common Father . . . were not yet to receive the priesthood." According to church president David O. McKay, the church's practice of discrimination "is not something which originated with man; but goes back into the beginning with God." In that vein, most high-ranking Mormon leaders believed that the priesthood ban and associated policies could not be lifted without a divine revelation.[66]

Finally, in 1978, the church announced a revelation that lifted the racial restrictions on priesthood and temple ordinances. Contemporary church leaders are far more sensitive than their predecessors in terms of race and public relations. In 2012, they condemned the statements of Randy Bott, a Brigham Young University professor of religious education who, in an interview with the *Washington Post*, pointed to Mormon scriptures and God's will as reasons for the church's past racial policies. The LDS Church public affairs department promptly responded that "the Church disavows the theories advanced in the past that black skin is a sign of divine disfavor or curse, or that it reflects actions in a premortal life."[67]

Over the past several decades, most of the church's membership growth has occurred outside of the United States, most significantly in Central and South America, but also in Africa and on the islands of the South Pacific. While the church's membership has become markedly more diverse, its approved images of Jesus largely have not. In 1998, the church's Curriculum Department assessed nearly 350 images of Jesus Christ for use in publications. A six-man team, including apostles Dallin Oaks, Jeffrey Holland, and Robert Hales then appraised each image. The committee rejected several paintings as overly effeminate, found some overly Catholic, and believed some strayed too far from scriptural narrative. The committee's assessments helped shape the approved list of images available for use in church publications and on the walls of church meetinghouses around the world.[68] As of 2010, ward leaders could select from around sixty-five paintings of Jesus approved for display in Mormon meetinghouses. Therefore, whether one enters a Mormon ward building in Guatemala, Ghana, or the Kingdom of Tonga, one mostly sees the same paintings, including images of Jesus by Harry Anderson, Del Parson, and John Scott. Like the church's architecture and publications, paintings of the savior are correlated and standardized. In the paintings, one sees a strong and noble Jesus, but also the tender shepherd who welcomes children and converses with women. And the Jesus in these paintings is white.

The church's international growth and changing demographics have begun to alter the Mormon image of Jesus. Whether or not they understand Quetzalcoatl as a manifestation of Jesus Christ, no Latter-day Saint General Authority today would call Jesus the "Great White God," let alone repeat George Reynolds's contention that God, Jesus, and Adam are all white men. Especially as the church grows in Latin American and Africa, it is attracting members more accustomed to racially malleable

Christ Praying in Gethsemane, by Emile Wilson. (© by Intellectual Reserve, Inc.)

depictions of Jesus Christ. In the past several years, the church has introduced racially diverse images of the savior into its videos and online art exhibitions. For instance, an online church exhibit of artwork about Christ's atonement featured two paintings of a black Jesus by Emile Wilson, a Latter-day Saint artist from Sierra Leone.[69] Also, in the church's 2015 international art competition (with selected entries displayed at Temple Square's Church History Museum), Sopheap Nhem depicted a Cambodian Jesus surrounded by children.[70] These small steps suggest a growing willingness on the part of Mormon leaders to adapt their message and materials for local cultures. The Mormon Jesus may not remain white much longer.

In many Mormon homes, several things hang on the walls: family pictures, perhaps a plaque of the church's 1995 "Proclamation on the Family," a photograph or painting of a temple, and a painting of Jesus Christ. Why do Latter-day Saints, unlike American Protestants and many contemporary American Catholics, purchase and display so much religious art?

Latter-day Saint leaders encourage members to display such items. "Keep a picture of a temple in your home so that your children may see it," instructed Howard W. Hunter, who served as church president for nine months in the mid-1990s. "Have them plan from their earliest years to go there and to remain worthy of that blessing."[71] In its magazines, the church has repeated Hunter's advice on several occasions. Church leaders also encourage members to display paintings of the savior. "Recently I attended a Primary [the church's children's auxiliary] and was holding a 14-month-old child on my lap when she looked up and saw a picture of the Savior on the wall," recounted Primary general president Coleen Menlove during the church's April 2000 General Conference. "Her little face beamed as she said with her newly acquired language skills, 'Jesus.'"[72] Several years later, Anne Pingree, a counselor in the church's Relief Society (women's auxiliary) Presidency, described a satisfying visit to a young family's home. "Evidences of the Lord were all around," she recalled, "pictures of the Savior on the wall, a family photograph and picture of the temple in a prominent place, copies of well-used scriptures and Church videos neatly stacked on a

Illustration for "Choose the Right Way," by Beth Whittaker. From *Children's Songbook* (1989). (© by Intellectual Reserve, Inc.)

nearby shelf." Thus, when church members hang paintings of a temple or of Jesus Christ, they are following the counsel of their leaders.[73]

In 1999, church president Gordon B. Hinckley expressed his hope that paintings of Jesus Christ would change non-Mormon opinions of the church and its members. Observing that nonmembers are invited to tour Latter-day Saint temples before their dedication, he commented that such visitors "are most impressed with pictures of the Savior they see in these holy houses." Hinckley believed that such artwork would enhance the church's reputation as Christian. "They will no longer regard us as a non-Christian people," he predicted. "They must know that the central figure in all of our worship is the Lord Jesus Christ." Church leaders hope that the *Christus* statues in its visitor centers and the artwork in Mormon homes produces the same effect.[74]

Displaying a reproduction of Del Parson's *Head of Christ* or a replica *Christus* signals a family's relative affluence, its devotion to Jesus Christ, and its desire to testify to that devotion. In their sameness in terms of their depiction of Jesus's skin color, hair color, and physique, Mormon artworks reinforce the way that Latter-day Saints understand their savior. When they see a painting of Jesus Christ in a temple, meetinghouse, or home, Mormons see someone they already know and recognize, because they—at least the younger generations of Latter-day Saints—have seen such images with regularity all their lives. Mormons admire and purchase replica paintings and statues because the savior is real to them and because those images make him more tangible, especially to their children. The church's mass distribution of Jesus imagery and church members' purchase of those images have reshaped both the appearance and substance of Mormon religious culture, one of many steps in making that culture resolutely and unmistakably Christian.

CONCLUSION

THE AILING APOSTLE CAREFULLY made his way to the podium. For the past two decades, he had spoken frequently at his church's semiannual General Conferences. His many books had deeply shaped Mormon thought.

Now, in April 1985, Elder Bruce R. McConkie would speak to the church one final time. Fifteen months earlier, he had been diagnosed with liver cancer and given weeks or a few months to live. He had lived longer, but the end was now very near. The week before the early April conference, his doctors told him they could do nothing more for him. They advised that he would not have the strength to speak at the conference. McConkie spoke anyway.

In a talk titled "The Purifying Power of Gethsemane," McConkie began by asserting that the "atoning sacrifice of the Lord Jesus Christ" is the pivotal event in human history. "Through it," he continued, "all of the terms and conditions of the Father's eternal plan of salvation became operative." First, through Christ's atonement for human sin, all human beings experience "immortality and eternal life." All are saved from death. Furthermore, because of the atonement, the plan of salvation—human exaltation—becomes a possibility. Those who are obedient to the gospel "become as their Maker." Jesus Christ enabled men to become like him, like God.

The dying apostle then described the suffering of Jesus Christ in Gethsemane prior to his arrest. "We know he sweat great gouts of blood from every pore," McConkie said, "as he drained the dregs of that bitter cup his Father had given him." In the early twentieth century, James

Talmage had also dwelt on this scene. Gethsemane became the characteristic focus of Mormon reflections about the atonement. The Gospel of Luke teaches that in Gethsemane, Jesus's "sweat became like drops of blood." In the Book of Mormon, the Nephite king Benjamin predicts that when Jesus suffers, "blood [would] cometh from every pore, so great shall be his anguish." In one of Joseph Smith's early revelations, Jesus Christ himself recalled that "suffering caused myself, even God, the greatest of all, to tremble because of pain, and to bleed at every pore."[1] By the 1980s, the Mormon consensus was that the principal scene of Christ's suffering and, thus, his atonement, was at Gethsemane rather than on the cross. According to McConkie, "this holy ground is where the Sinless Son of the Everlasting Father took upon himself the sins of all men on condition of repentance." Prior to dying on the cross, Jesus's blood and suffering had already atoned for human sin.

If some Latter-day Saints preferred to move quickly from Gethsemane to the resurrection, though, McConkie also lingered on the savior's arrest, walk to Golgotha, and crucifixion. Indeed, McConkie stressed that the plan of salvation encompassed the gardens of Eden, Gethsemane, and the empty tomb from which Christ had arisen.

In the twentieth century, it became customary for Mormon leaders and church members to "testify" of their knowledge of core doctrines. "I testify," McConkie stated, "that he is the Son of the Living God and was crucified for the sins of the world." Less characteristically for Mormon leaders, he added that he had received a sure knowledge of these matters, and he would soon receive even more. He knew these things were true not because of the testimony of scripture or the testimony of others. He knew for himself. "The Holy Spirit of God has borne witness to me that they are true," he explained, "and it is now as though the Lord had revealed them to me in the first instance. I have thereby heard his voice and know his word." At the very end of his talk, he choked back an urge to weep. "I am one of his witnesses," McConkie proclaimed, "and in a coming day I shall feel the nail marks in his hands and in his feet and shall wet his feet with my tears. But I shall not know better then than I know now that he is God's Almighty Son, that he is our Savior and Redeemer, and that salvation comes in and through his atoning blood and in no other way." McConkie died two weeks later.[2]

Bruce R. McConkie, 1985. (Courtesy of Deseret News Publishing Company.)

By the time of his death, Bruce McConkie had been a powerful, beloved, and controversial figure within the LDS Church for several decades. The son-in-law of longtime apostle and eventual church president Joseph Fielding Smith, McConkie worked briefly for the *Deseret News* after several years in the army during the Second World War. Church leaders then appointed him to the First Council of the Seventy (the third-highest body of church leaders, under the First Presidency and Quorum of the Twelve Apostles).

In 1958, McConkie published *Mormon Doctrine*, a theological glossary containing hundreds of entries, from Aaron to Zoramites, the latter a breakaway group of Nephites in the Book of Mormon who believed "that there shall be no Christ."[3] McConkie stated that he designed *Mormon Doctrine* "to help persons seeking salvation to gain that knowledge of God and his laws without which they cannot hope for an inheritance in the celestial city."[4] In his entries, McConkie generously cited Mormon scriptures and the statements of prior leaders. He then added a small amount of forceful and often belligerent commentary.

McConkie drew sharp contrasts between Mormon teachings and those of "apostate" or "so-called" Christians. For McConkie, "*true doctrines* are of God and are found in The Church of Jesus Christ of Latter-day Saints. All other doctrines are false, except to the partial extent that they may chance on some points to harmonize with the Lord's revelations." McConkie asserted that "all who belong to the great apostate churches of the day are antichrist." On Catholicism, McConkie simply referred readers to his entry on the "Church of the Devil."[5] Despite the church's growth, some mid-twentieth-century Latter-day Saint leaders sounded embattled and defensive rather than optimistic and confident. If earlier leaders such as James Talmage and B. H. Roberts had been somewhat attracted to the modernist wing of American Protestantism, Joseph Fielding Smith, Ezra Taft Benson, and McConkie were more influenced by those Protestants who were conservative in their theology and politics.

As his attitude toward other churches illustrates, McConkie's was a strident and sectarian Mormonism, symbolic of what sociologist Armand Mauss terms Mormon "retrenchment."[6] His concerns were for Latter-day distinction and doctrinal clarity, not public relations. McConkie tire-lessly asserted the centrality of Jesus Christ for human salvation, yet he had no interest in using a shared devotion to Jesus Christ as a means of establishing common ground with other churches. Protestants rankled McConkie, not just in their criticisms of Mormonism but in their fa-miliar manner of talking about Jesus Christ. McConkie criticized the "repetitious use" of Jesus's given name, terming it "not in keeping with the true spirit of reverence and worship."[7] That Mormons usually speak of "Christ" and "the Savior" subtly distinguishes their piety from that of evangelicals, who often think of the Son of God in in terms of friend-ship and familiarity.

Higher-ranking church leaders were surprised and displeased by *Mormon Doctrine*. The church's First Presidency privately concluded that the book contained "errors and misstatements" and therefore should not be republished. The book's tone was harsh, and in some cases it reached unambiguous conclusions about teachings church leaders deemed am-biguous. Of the latter, Apostle Marion Romney identified matters such as the possible existence of "Pre-Adamite" humans (which McConkie rejected in his sweeping condemnation of evolution) and the "manner in which Jesus was begotten" (which McConkie described quite literally).[8] Not as many things, apparently, were Mormon doctrine as McConkie supposed. Or perhaps it was unwise for McConkie to assert doctrine in the manner in which he did. Nevertheless, McConkie persuaded the aging church president David O. McKay to permit the publication of a revised second edition. McConkie softened his tone toward Catholic and Protestant Christians; he excised his comment that "all who belong to the great apostate churches of the day are antichrist." His volume, though, remained a stalwart defense of the particularities of Mormon belief.

McConkie became one of the church's apostles in 1972. Even before his elevation, McConkie had seen it as his mission to articulate and defend church doctrine. As an apostle, however, he held the authority to correct things he regarded as false. In 1982 McConkie went to Brigham Young University and delivered a blistering critique of Professor George W. Pace's recently published *What It Means to Know Christ*. Pace identified "a dynamic personal relationship with Christ" as "the pearl of *greatest* price." He specifically placed a higher value on a "personal friendship" with Jesus Christ than on "having a testimony of the divinity of the restored Church." Pace further maintained that "redemption is not in the principles, ordinances, or programs of the Church but rather in Christ." Pace wrote at a time when evangelical Protestants were very publicly and forcefully denying Mormonism's Christianity; he commented that most non-Mormons did not believe that Latter-day Saints "know Christ." His book's argument suggested there was some truth to that claim. His foil, moreover, was not evangelicals but mainline Protestants, whom he repeatedly criticized for their failure to defend the fundamental truths of Christianity, such as the Virgin Birth and the bodily resurrection of Jesus Christ. McConkie may also have been concerned over reports that Pace encouraged BYU students to worship Jesus Christ and to pray to Jesus Christ, instead of directing their prayers and worship to God the Father.[9]

McConkie did not shirk from his responsibility to correct what he perceived as false doctrine in Pace's teaching. "We do not worship the Son," he stated, adding that "our relationship with the Father is supreme, paramount." McConkie rejected as "plain sectarian nonsense" the idea of a "special friendship" with Christ. It was an evangelical heresy. Those Mormons who "feel they have a special and personal relationship with Christ...[resemble] fanatical sectarians who with glassy eyes and fiery tongues assure us they have been saved by grace and are assured of a place with the Lord in a heavenly abode, when in fact they have never even received the fullness of the gospel." McConkie instructed the Latter-day Saints to cultivate a relationship "with the Lord [Jesus Christ]" that balanced intimacy with "the required reserve between us and him." Mormonism's "Elder Brother" was more than a best friend. He was humanity's Lord, the savior of humankind. In a subsequent book about Jesus Christ, Pace was more restrained in his language.[10]

It was not that McConkie disagreed with Pace about the central significance of Jesus Christ or his atonement for human sin. McConkie wrote more about Jesus Christ than about any other subject, including a six-volume work on the premortal, mortal, and millennial Jesus Christ. McConkie wrote the text for a hymn ("I Believe in Christ") that was added to the church's 1985 hymnal. McConkie's Jesus Christ, however, was first and foremost a thoroughly Mormon savior, a regal and royal Lord whom Protestants did not know and respect.

Over the several decades since McConkie's death, Mormon leaders have advanced his christocentricity, but shorn of his pugnacity. By the early 1980s, the church felt the need to respond to a torrent of evangelical countercult literature and *The God Makers* film. Evangelical churches across the country showed the film, teaching their congregants that Mormonism was a dangerous "cult." Even though many other religious groups condemned the film as bigoted, it was a public relations nightmare for the church. Mormons responded vigorously to evangelical criticism, sometimes directly and sometimes obliquely. "Do not mistake," Boyd Packer explained in 1982, just before the release of *The God Makers*, "our reverent hesitation to speak glibly or too frequently of Him to mean that we do not know Him."[11] From that point forward, however, Mormon leaders did not hesitate to speak frequently of Jesus Christ.

The "cult" label created additional obstacles for Mormon missionaries, especially in portions of the country with large evangelical populations. While the church worried about a downward trend in missionary baptisms, a mid-1980s draft for a revised strategy for missions observed that it was "most troubling" that non-Mormons perceived the church as "non-Christian."[12] In 1992, the church released a new handbook designed to increase "public understanding that members of The Church of Jesus Christ of Latter-day Saints revere Jesus Christ as the Son of God, the Savior and Redeemer of mankind."[13] Talks and publications about Jesus Christ proliferated. Mormon leaders regularly spoke about Jesus Christ, the atonement, and divine grace. Those were not new themes within Mormonism, but church leaders gave them more emphasis. In what is partly a rebuttal to evangelical criticism but also true to the church's own history, the recent proliferation of Mormon sermons, paintings, hymns, and public relations materials revolving around Jesus Christ signals the determination of Mormon leaders that no other church or group of Christians will "out-Jesus" them.

When the church updated its hymnal in 1985, many of the new selections focused on Jesus Christ. One such hymn, "Where Can I Turn for Peace?," has achieved great popularity within the church in recent years. Emma Lou Thayne, an author and poet, wrote the lyrics while her daughter struggled with a serious mental illness. The hymn describes the savior as a constant support through any of the struggles that inevitably accompany mortal existence:

> He answers privately,
> Reaches my reaching
> In my Gethsemane, Savior and Friend.
> Gentle the peace he finds for my beseeching.
> Constant he is and kind,
> Love without end.

This understanding of the Christian savior is representative of contemporary Mormonism. Any Latter-day Saint reasonably informed about church doctrine knows that Jesus Christ and God the Father are separate beings, that the savior's death provides all people with eternal life, and that how one lives on earth has consequences for the extent of one's eternal glory. Still, when Mormons think about Jesus Christ, they think of a shepherd, a comforter, an example for how to live their lives. The reference to Gethsemane in "Where Can I Turn for Peace?," moreover, is probably the only clue that it is a Mormon hymn.

Another sign of these developments is the runaway success of Brigham Young University professor Stephen Robinson's 1992 book *Believing Christ*. Robinson framed his book around what he termed the "parable of the bicycle." When his daughter begged him for a new bicycle, he off-handedly told her to save her pennies. After a few weeks, his daughter Sarah eagerly appeared with a jar of pennies. They went to the store. She fell in love with a bicycle but became crestfallen when she found that it cost over one hundred dollars. Sarah had only sixty-one pennies. "You give me everything you've got," Robinson told her, "the whole sixty-one cents, and a hug and a kiss, and this bike is yours." For Robinson, this is a parable of salvation through the grace of Jesus Christ.

Robinson's book engaged old debates within Christianity about the relative importance of faith and works for human salvation. In the Book of Mormon, Nephi (Lehi's son) teaches that "it is by grace that we are saved, after all we can do." *Believing Christ* reassured church members that they would be saved because of Christ's atonement, if they only responded affirmatively to God's offer of salvation and did their best to "keep the commandments." McConkie maintained a clear distinction between the meanings of salvation and exaltation, which he defined as human participation in "the kind of life which God lives," including having "spirit children in the resurrection." Just as baptism started an individual's journey toward the celestial kingdom, he analogized, so celestial, temple marriage started a couple's journey toward exaltation.[14] Unlike McConkie, Robinson eschewed discussions about levels of eternal glory or the exact nature of exaltation. He presumed his readers simply aimed for the celestial kingdom.

Believing Christ served as a gentle Mormon response to evangelical critics of Mormonism. Robinson observed that "other Christians" (a very different label than McConkie's "so-called Christians" or "apostate Christians") "accuse us of believing in salvation by works." He observed that "certain non-LDS interpretations of grace" have "turned off" Latter-day Saints, probably because those interpretations stressed divine grace to the point of making human agency meaningless. Robinson offered gentle correctives to what he considered misconceptions. As he noted, Latter-day Saints disagree with "salvation by grace *alone*" and—as the

Book of Mormon and the earliest Mormons taught—with Calvinist doctrines of predestination and irresistible grace.

Robinson argued that because of Jesus Christ's atonement, human beings can reach the celestial kingdom if they only respond to God's plan of salvation. And that response need not be perfect, because, in the Garden of Gethsemane and on the cross, Jesus Christ—the Son of God, born of an "infinite" Father and a "finite" mother—took upon himself all human sin and imperfection. In Gethsemane, Robinson wrote, "Jesus took upon himself the infinite weight of the world and was pressed with that tremendous load until the blood flowed through his skin." Since Jesus has borne the entirety of human sin, humans need only to enter his covenant and respond to his offer of salvation. That response includes faith, repentance, baptism, and the "laying on of hands for the gift of the Holy Ghost." *Believing Christ* had little talk of tiers within the celestial kingdom, exaltation, or temple ordinances. Robinson warned against evangelical-style "easy grace," but in *Believing Christ* he indicated that celestial glory was more readily attainable than past Mormon leaders had sometimes suggested.[15]

Over the past two decades, Mormon hierarchs have repeated Robinson's message in countless General Conference talks. "Salvation cannot be bought with the currency of obedience," explained Dieter Uchtdorf of the church's First Presidency in 2015.[16] Robinson's *Believing Christ*, Thayne's hymn, and talks such as Uchtdorf's reflect the way that many contemporary Mormons understand Jesus Christ. They also reflect the way that the church wishes to present itself. For different generations of Mormons, Bruce McConkie and Stephen Robinson did much to shape the way that Latter-day Saints understand Jesus Christ and their church. In both instances, they describe a distinctly Mormon Jesus, with, for instance, a focus on Gethsemane and an identification of Jesus as Jehovah. But not the exact same Mormon Jesus. McConkie's presentation of Jesus Christ was distinctly sectarian, a savior that only Latter-day Saints would accept. Robinson's savior was less exacting, more ecumenical, a Mormon Jesus that other Christians would readily recognize.

Mormonism separated itself from the religious context in which it emerged in part by answering questions that concerned many American

Christians but that Protestant ministers and theologians had set aside. For example, how can families ensure that they will be together forever, and, relatedly, what can the living do to bring about the salvation of the dead? For ancient and medieval Christians, this was a vital matter. Baptism for the dead, prayers, the intercession of saints, and the giving of wealth are among the answers earlier generations of Christians gave to such questions. Mormon leaders proposed that a series of rituals—baptism, the endowment, sealing in marriage—would enable the exaltation of living couples and create the potential for ancestors to enjoy the same glory. These ordinances represent Mormonism at its most innovative and distinctive, but they also connect the LDS Church to ancient Christian concerns.

In many other instances, Mormonism's basic questions and answers flow even more obviously within the broad stream of Christianity. What is the nature of the relationship between God the Father and Jesus Christ? Between divine and human beings? What is the meaning of Christ's sacrifice for humankind? Who will be saved, and how? What is the meaning of salvation? When will Jesus Christ return? Which is Christ's true church? What is the relationship between the two testaments of the Christian Bible? Should human beings depict God and Jesus Christ in artwork, and, if so, how? Jesus Christ is central to these questions and the Mormon answers to them. The figure of Jesus Christ both inextricably connects the Latter-day Saints to broader and longer currents of Christian thought and practice and carves out a distinctively Mormon place within them.

Contemporary Mormonism carefully navigates a dual Mormon and Christian identity. Beginning in 2013, the church released a series of essays on controversial subjects—such as "Race and the Priesthood"—on its "Gospel Topics" website. Among those essays was one titled "Are Mormons Christians?" Its inclusion signals the weight the contemporary church places on the issue. The essay observed that Latter-day Saints "unequivocally affirm themselves to be Christians." At the same time, it reminded church members and inquirers alike that converts join the church "in part because of its doctrinal and spiritual distinctiveness." Church leaders (this and other statements were carefully vetted by the highest-ranking Brethren) observed that while they "have no desire to compromise the distinctiveness of the restored Church of Jesus Christ, they wish to work together with other Christians—and people of all faiths—to recognize and remedy many of the moral and family issues faced by society." Furthermore, it concluded that there "is no good reason for Christian faiths to ostracize each other when there has never been more urgent need for unity in proclaiming the divinity and teachings of Jesus Christ." Far more than in previous decades, church leaders emphasize what they hold in common with other Christian churches through the figure of Jesus Christ.[17]

In a far less dramatic way than during the events of the 1840s or those surrounding the abandonment of polygamy, the church has changed a great deal over the past half-century. Some of those changes are at first glance merely cosmetic or matters of public relations. Subtitling the Book of Mormon "Another Testament of Jesus Christ" did not make the scripture more about Jesus Christ than it already was. It already revolved around the figure of Jesus. Enlarging the words "JESUS CHRIST" in the church's logo did not give the savior a greater prominence within the church. For that matter, putting an enormous statue of Jesus Christ in temple visitor centers changed no church teachings, nor did adding hymns about Jesus Christ to the church's most recent edition of its hymnal. Collectively, though, these changes represent Mormonism's christocentric turn over the past several decades and have shifted Latter-day Saint identity and the position of the LDS Church within the landscape of both American and international religion.

In her reflections on Mormonism's nineteenth-century development, Jan Shipps identifies "the Church of Jesus Christ as the essential core of the Mormon movement" and presents "the gathering of Israel and the 'restoration of all things' as subsequent theological and historical 'layers,' layers that sometimes so enveloped Mormonism's essential core that the Latter-day Saints' Christian understanding of themselves virtually disappeared from view."[18] Many of those layers, such as polygamy, theocracy, and the Latter-day Saint self-understanding as God's new Israel, have since fallen by the wayside. As Douglas Davies has put it, Christian Mormonism has largely superseded "Mormon-Israel."[19]

Given this trajectory, it no longer makes sense to consider Mormonism a "new religion," a "new world religion," or even a "new religious tradition," if that implies a supersession of or definitive break with Christianity. Instead, Mormonism is a vibrant new branch of Christianity, one in which temples, ordinances, and prophets have taken their place alongside a Jesus who is both utterly Christian and distinctively Mormon.

NOTES

ACKNOWLEDGMENTS

INDEX

NOTES

LIST OF ABBREVIATIONS

BYP   Brigham Young Papers (CR 1234 1), CHL.

CHL   Church History Library (Church Archives), Church of Jesus Christ
           of Latter-day Saints, Salt Lake City, Utah.

D&C   *Doctrine and Covenants* (available at http://lds.org/scriptures/dc
           -testament?lang=eng).

EMD   Dan Vogel, ed., *Early Mormon Documents*, 5 vols. (Salt Lake City:
           Signature, 1996–2003).

GCM   General Church Minutes, CR 100 318, CHL.

HBLL   Special Collections, Harold B. Lee Library, Brigham Young
           University, Provo, Utah.

JD   *Journal of Discourses by Brigham Young, His Two Counsellors, the Twelve
           Apostles and Others*, 26 vols. (Liverpool and London: various pub-
           lishers, 1854–1886).

JSP D1   Michael Hubbard MacKay, Gerrit J. Dirkmaat, Grant Underwood,
           Robert J. Woodford, and William G. Hartley, eds., *The Joseph Smith
           Papers, Documents*, vol. 1, *July 1828–June 1831* (Salt Lake City: Church
           Historian's Press, 2013).

JSP D2   Matthew C. Godfrey, Mark Ashurst-McGee, Grant Underwood,
           Robert J. Woodford, and William G. Hartley, eds., *The Joseph Smith
           Papers, Documents*, vol. 2, *July 1831–January 1833* (Salt Lake City:
           Church Historian's Press, 2013).

JSP D3   Gerrit J. Dirkmaat, Brent M. Rogers, Grant Underwood, Robert J.
           Woodford, William G. Hartley, eds., *The Joseph Smith Papers,
           Documents*, vol. 3, *February 1833–March 1834* (Salt Lake City: Church
           Historian's Press, 2014).

JSP H1   Karen Lynn Davidson, David J. Whittaker, Mark Ashurst-McGee, and Richard L. Jensen, eds., *The Joseph Smith Papers, Histories*, vol.1, *Joseph Smith Histories, 1832–1844* (Salt Lake City: Church Historian's Press, 2012).

JSP J1   Dean C. Jessee, Mark Ashurst-McGee, and Richard L. Jensen, eds., *The Joseph Smith Papers, Journals*, vol. 1, *1832–1839* (Salt Lake City: Church Historian's Press, 2008).

JSP J2   Andrew H. Hedges, Alex D. Smith, and Richard Lloyd Anderson, eds., *The Joseph Smith Papers, Journals*, vol. 2, *December 1841–April 1843* (Salt Lake City: Church Historian's Press, 2011).

JSP J3   Andrew H. Hedges, Alex D. Smith, and Brent M. Rogers, eds., *The Joseph Smith Papers, Journals*, vol. 3, *May 1843–June 1844* (Salt Lake City: Church Historian's Press, 2015).

JSP MRB   Robin Scott Jensen, Robert J. Woodford, and Steven C. Harper, eds., *The Joseph Smith Papers, Revelations and Translations, Manuscript Revelation Books* (Salt Lake City: Church Historian's Press, 2009).

LW   Jaroslav Pelikan, et al., *Luther's Works* (Saint Louis, Mo.: Concordia Publishing House, 1955).

WWJ   Scott G. Kenney, ed., *Wilford Woodruff's Journal, 1833–1898: Typescript*, 9 vols. (Midvale, Utah: Signature Books, 1983–1984).

INTRODUCTION

1   The description of the Hill Cumorah Pageant is based on two trips by the author to the pageant, one in 2002 and one in 2012. See also Gerald S. Argetsinger, "The Hill Cumorah Pageant: A Historical Perspective," *Journal of Book of Mormon Studies* 13 (2004): 58–69, 71; and Max Perry Mueller, "'A Spirit of Persecution,'" *Slate*, 19 July 2012, accessed 21 August 2015, http://www.slate.com/articles/life/faithbased /2012/07/the_hill_cumorah_pageant_helps_explain_mormon_identity _photos_.html.

2   Owing to its official status within the LDS Church, the King James Version is the source of quotations from the Bible.

3   Creed of Nicaea and Chalcedonian definition in Jaroslav Pelikan and Valerie Hotchkiss, eds., *Creeds and Confessions of Faith in the Christian Tradition*, vol. 1 (New Haven, Conn.: Yale University Press, 2003), 159, 181.

4   See Malcolm Lambert, *The Cathars* (Malden, Mass.: Blackwell, 1999), 84; Malcolm Barber, *The Cathars: Dualist Heretics in Languedoc in the High Middle Ages* (New York: Longman, 2000), 92.

5   On the recent growth of Christianity and Christian diversity outside of the West, see Philip Jenkins, *The Next Christendom: The Coming of Global Christianity* (New York: Oxford University Press, 2002), esp. chaps. 3, 5, and 6.

6   Jaroslav Pelikan, *Jesus through the Centuries: His Place in the History of Culture* (New Haven, Conn.: Yale University Press, 1985), 2.

7   "The Living Christ: The Testimony of the Apostles," 1 Jan. 2000, accessed 25 August 2015, https://www.lds.org/bc/content/shared/content/images/gospel -library/manual/34591/34591_000_APP_04-livingChrist.pdf.

8   Oral interview with McGray Magleby and Adrian Pulfer, 15 Dec. 1995, AV 1955, CHL.

9   Robert Orsi, *Between Heaven and Earth: The Religious Worlds People Make and the Scholars Who Study Them* (Princeton, N.J.: Princeton University Press, 2005), 2.

10   *The Friend* [Salt Lake City], Jan. 2015, 31.

11   Sydney Ahlstrom, *A Religious History of the American People* (New Haven, Conn.: Yale University Press, 1972), 508.

12   See J. Spencer Fluhman, *"A Peculiar People": Anti-Mormonism and the Making of Religion in Nineteenth-Century America* (Chapel Hill: University of North Carolina Press, 2012).

13   Thomas Nelson report of 14 March 1860, House Report No. 82, in *Reports of Committees of the House of Representatives*, 36th Cong., 1st Sess. (Washington, D.C.: Thomas H. Ford, 1860), 2.

14   *Late Corporation of the Church of Jesus Christ of Latter-day Saints et al. v. United States* (1890). See Sarah Barringer Gordon, *The Mormon Question: Polygamy and Constitutional Conflict in Nineteenth-Century America* (Chapel Hill: University of North Carolina Press, 2002), 211–219; W. Paul Reeve, *Religion of a Different Color: Race and the Mormon Struggle for Whiteness* (New York: Oxford University Press, 2015), esp. chap. 8.

15   Charles Carroll Bonney, *World's Congress Addresses* (Chicago: Open Court Publishing Company, 1900), 81. See Reid L. Neilson, *Exhibiting Mormonism: The Latter-day Saints and the 1893 Chicago World's Fair* (New York: Oxford University Press, 2011), chap. 5.

16   James Talmage Journal, 15 July 1915, vol. 18, MSS 229, HBLL.

17   *The Fundamentals: A Testimony to the Truth* (Chicago: Testimony Publishing Company, 1910–1915), 8:113 ("anti-American"), 114 ("anti-Christian"), and 127 ("heathenism" and "Satanic").

18   Walter Martin, *The Rise of the Cults* (Grand Rapids, Mich.: Zondervan, 1955), 46, 52.

19   On Decker and his ministry, see Sara M. Patterson, "The Ex Factor: Constructing a Religious Mission in the Ex-Mormons for Jesus / Saints Alive in Jesus,

1975–1990," in Quincy D. Newell and Eric F. Mason, eds., *New Perspectives in Mormon Studies: Creating and Crossing Boundaries* (Norman: University of Oklahoma Press, 2013), chap. 6.

20 *The God Makers* (Jeremiah Films, 1982). See J. B. Haws, *The Mormon Image in the American Mind: Fifty Years of Public Perception* (New York: Oxford University Press, 2014), chap. 5.

21 "Growth of the Church," accessed 3 July 2015, http://www.mormonnewsroom .org/topic/church-growth.

22 Jan Shipps, *Mormonism: The Story of a New Religious Tradition* (Urbana: University of Illinois Press, 1985), 169, n. 2, 68–69, 148–149; Shipps, "Is Mormonism Christian? Reflections on a Complicated Question," *BYU Studies* 33 (1993): 439–465. See Fawn Brodie, *No Man Knows My History: The Life of Joseph Smith* (New York: Knopf, 1945), viii.

23 Rodney Stark, "The Rise of a New World Faith," *Review of Religious Research* 26 (September 1984): 18–27; Stark (with Reid Neilson), *The Rise of Mormonism* (New York: Columbia University Press, 2005), 145–146.

24 Jonathan Z. Smith, "Religion, Religions, Religious," in Mark C. Taylor, ed., *Critical Terms for Religious Studies* (Chicago: University of Chicago Press, 1998), 280.

25 1 Nephi 14:10, 17.

26 Joseph Smith Journal, 9 July 1843, JSP J3, 56. Spelling and punctuation corrected.

27 William McLellin Journal, 14 December 1834, in Jan Shipps and John W. Welch, eds., *The Journals of William E. McLellin, 1831–1836* (Provo, Utah, and Urbana: BYU Studies and University of Illinois Press, 1994), 152.

28 Shipps, *Mormonism*, chap. 4.

29 Undated Smith teachings, ca. summer 1839, recorded by Willard Richards, "Pocket Companion Written in England," MS 1490, CHL.

30 Thomas O'Dea, *The Mormons* (Chicago: University of Chicago Press, 1957), 115.

31 "We'll Welcome Baptists, Pres. Hinckley Says," *Deseret News*, 15 September 1997.

32 Gordon B. Hinckley, "We Look to Christ," *Ensign*, May 2002, 90–91.

33 Terryl Givens, *People of Paradox: A History of Mormon Culture* (New York: Oxford University Press, 2007), xvi.

34 I am adopting this term from Jan Shipps.

35 The argument here concurs with Stephen H. Webb, *Mormon Christianity: What Other Christians Can Learn from the Latter-day Saints* (New York: Oxford University Press, 2013).

36 The same might be said of many other new religious movements, such as the Jehovah's Witnesses and the largely Filipino Iglesia ni Cristo.

I. ANOTHER TESTAMENT OF JESUS CHRIST

1 WWJ, 28 Nov. 1841, 2:139.

2 Mark Twain, *Roughing It* (Hartford, Conn.: American Publishing Company, 1872), 127.

3 Ether, chaps. 1–3, 8. I am quoting from the 1830 Book of Mormon, which is how the earliest converts to Mormonism encountered the scripture. See Joseph Smith Jr., *The Book of Mormon: An Account Written by the Hand of Mormon, upon Plates Taken from the Plates of Nephi* (Palmyra, N.Y.: E. B. Grandin, 1830). There is also a very incomplete scribal manuscript, as well as a printer's manuscript used to set the type for the 1830 publication. The 1830 edition of the Book of Mormon divided · its fifteen books into long chapters without verses. For the convenience of readers, I provide the chapters and verses from the current LDS edition of the Book of Mormon.

4 Grant Hardy suggests that Moroni "Christianize[d] the Jaredite record" in order to better integrate it with the records edited by his father, Mormon. See Hardy, *Understanding the Book of Mormon: A Reader's Guide* (New York: Oxford University Press, 2010), 235.

5 Ether 12:7, 39, 41.

6 Joseph Smith, "Church History," *Times and Seasons*, 1 March 1842, 77. See Eran Shalev, *American Zion: The Old Testament as a Political Text from the Revolution to the Civil War* (New Haven, Conn.: Yale University Press, 2013), chap. 4; Dan Vogel, *Indian Origins and the Book of Mormon: Religious Solutions from Columbus to Joseph Smith* (Salt Lake City: Signature Books, 1986).

7 On the religious culture of the early nineteenth century, see Richard Wightman Fox, *Jesus in America: Personal Savior, Cultural Hero, National Obsession* (San Francisco: HarperSanFrancisco, 2004), chaps. 4 and 5; Stephen Prothero, *American Jesus: How the Son of God Became a National Icon* (New York: Farrar, Straus, and Giroux, 2003), chap. 2.

8 Lucy Mack Smith history, 1844–1845 draft dictated to Martha Jane Coray and Howard Coray, in Lavina Fielding Anderson, *Lucy's Book: A Critical Edition of Lucy Mack Smith's Family Memoir* (Salt Lake City: Signature Books, 2001), 324–325.

9 Lucy Mack Smith history, 1844–1845 draft, in Anderson, *Lucy's Book*, 277.

10 On Joseph Smith's family, see Richard Lyman Bushman, *Joseph Smith: Rough Stone Rolling* (New York: Knopf, 2005), chap. 1.

11 *Doctrine and Covenants* [1835], 50:2 [D&C 27:5]. In what became the canonical "History of Joseph Smith," included in the LDS Church's Pearl of Great Price, Smith or a scribe identified the angel as Nephi. Another scribe later corrected the name to Moroni. See Joseph Smith History, [1838–], A-1, page 5, CR 100 102, CHL.

12 Joseph Smith History, [1838–], A-1, page 5. On Smith's trance, see Jan Shipps, *Mormonism: The Story of a New Religious Tradition* (Urbana: University of Illinois Press, 1985), 10.

13 "Saught" on Joseph Smith, 1832 History, in JSP H1, 14; Lucy Mack Smith History, 1844–1845 draft, in Anderson, *Lucy's Book*, 344.

14 Bainbridge (N.Y.) Court Record (1826), in EMD, 4:249–250. See Bushman, *Rough Stone Rolling*, 52.

15 Josiah Stowell Jr. to John S. Fullmer, 17 February 1843, in Mark Ashurst-McGee, ed., "The Josiah Stowell Jr.–John S. Fullmer correspondence," *BYU Studies* 38 (1999): 113.

16 Lucy Mack Smith History, 1844–1845 draft, in Anderson, *Lucy's Book*, 379, 414. Spelling and punctuation corrected. See the discussion in Samuel Morris Brown, *In Heaven as It Is on Earth: Joseph Smith and the Early Mormon Conquest of Death* (New York: Oxford University Press, 2012), chap. 3.

17 Book of Mormon, preface, page iii in the 1830 edition.

18 Joseph Knight Sr., "Reminiscences," in Dean Jessee, ed., "Joseph Knight's Recollection of Early Mormon History," *BYU Studies* 17 (Fall 1976): 35.

19 "Joseph Smith Documents Dating through June 1831," JSP D1, xxviii.

20 1 Nephi 1:9, 19.

21 1 Nephi 11:13, 18, 27, 33; 12:18.

22 Mosiah 3:7.

23 2 Nephi 2:25.

24 See Terryl Givens, *By the Hand of Mormon: The American Scripture that Launched a New World Religion* (New York: Oxford University Press, 2002), esp. 46–47, 199.

25 3 Nephi 9:12, 15.

26 3 Nephi 11:23, 26, 28, 33–34; Moroni 8:22.

27 3 Nephi 17:6–7, 14.

28 3 Nephi 18:7. The next day, Jesus again celebrates the sacrament. This time, his language does make a more direct connection between the bread and his body: "He that eateth this bread eateth of my body" (3 Nephi 20:8).

29 3 Nephi 19:12; 27:3, 8.

30 3 Nephi 28:7.

31 4 Nephi 1:2, 17.

32 3 Nephi 20:14–15, 17; 16:15; Jill M. Derr and Karen L. Davidson, eds., *Eliza R. Snow: The Complete Poetry* (Provo, Utah: Brigham Young University Press, 2009), 694. See Jared Hickman, "*The Book of Mormon* as Amerindian Apocalypse," *American*

Literature 86 (September 2014): 429–461; Ronald Walker, "Seeking the 'Remnant': The Native American during the Joseph Smith Period," *Journal of Mormon History* 19 (Spring 1993): 1–33.

33 This idea was not entirely without Christian precedents. See Stephen H. Webb, *Jesus Christ, Eternal God: Heavenly Flesh and the Metaphysics of Matter* (New York: Oxford University Press, 2012), 103.

34 2 Nephi 29:3, 7.

35 2 Nephi 2:26.

36 3 Nephi 27:19, 15:9. See Terryl Givens, *Wrestling the Angel: The Foundations of Mormon Thought: Cosmos, God, Humanity* (New York: Oxford University Press, 2015), 195–197.

37 1 Nephi 15:35; revelation ca. Summer 1829, in *A Book of Commandments, for the Government of the Church of Christ* (Zion [Independence, Mo.]: W.W. Phelps, 1833), 39–40 [D&C 19:6–7]. I am quoting from the earliest extant copies of Joseph Smith's revelations, as categorized by the Joseph Smith Papers Project (josephsmithpapers.org). For the convenience of readers, when applicable I provide citations to the contemporary Doctrine and Covenants of the Church of Jesus Christ of Latter-day Saints.

38 In an argument that the Book of Mormon coheres with some Arminian and some Universalist positions, Clyde Ford observes that the Book of Mormon departs from most varieties of Arminianism by making allowance for those who have not been taught the gospel to be saved. As he notes, however, John Wesley had expressed doubts that God would damn heathen and Muslims. See Ford, "The Book of Mormon, the Early Nineteenth-Century Debates over Universalism, and the Development of the Novel Mormon Doctrine of Ultimate Rewards and Punishments," *Dialogue* 47 (Spring 2014): 1–23.

39 Mosiah 15:2–4; 16:15; Ether 3:4.

40 See Melodie Moench Charles, "Book of Mormon Christology," in Brent Metcalfe, ed., *New Approaches to the Book of Mormon: Explorations in Critical Methodology* (Salt Lake City: Signature Books, 1993), 81–114.

41 Givens, *By the Hand of Mormon*, 200–201.

42 See Richard W. Fox, *Jesus in America: Personal Savior, Cultural Hero, National Obsession* (New York: HarperOne, 2004), 113.

43 William Ellery Channing, *Discourses, Reviews, and Miscellanies* (Boston: Gray and Bowen, 1830), 303.

44 3 Nephi 18:19, 19:18.

45 Moroni 10:32–33.

46 Martin Harris quoted in Joseph Knight Sr., "Reminiscences," in Dean Jessee, ed., "Joseph Knight's Recollection of Early Mormon History," *BYU Studies* 17 (Fall 1976): 37. On the Book of Mormon's early publishing and sales history, see David

J. Whittaker, "'That Most Important of All Books': A Printing History of the Book of Mormon," *Mormon Historical Studies* 6 (Fall 2005): 105–107.

47 Alexander Campbell, "Delusions," *Millennial Harbinger* [Bethany, Va.], 7 Feb. 1831, 90, 87, 93. Campbell repeated these criticisms in *Delusions: An Analysis of the Book of Mormon* (Boston: Benjamin H. Greene, 1832). See Philip L. Barlow, *Mormons and the Bible: The Place of the Latter-day Saints in American Religion* (New York: Oxford University Press, 1991), 35–38.

48 On radical Methodists, see Stephen J. Fleming, "'Congenial to Almost Every Shade of Radicalism': The Delaware Valley and the Success of Early Mormonism," *Religion and American Culture* 17 (Summer 2007): 129–164. On the Reformed Baptists, see Mark Lyman Staker, *Hearken, O Ye People: The Historical Setting for Joseph Smith's Ohio Revelations* (Salt Lake City: Greg Kofford Books, 2009), chap. 7.

49 Joseph Smith History, [1838–], A-1, 2.

50 Brown's retrospective complaint probably reflects the Book of Mormon's teaching that the one baptizing should "stand in the water."

51 "Diary of Mary Brown Pulsipher," n.d., HBLL. See Rhonda Seamons, "'That We May All, in Glory Well': Mary Ann Brown Pulsipher," in Richard E. Turley, Jr., and Brittany A. Chapman, eds., *Women of Faith in the Latter Days* (Salt Lake City: 2011), 1:263–265.

52 Pratt discourse of 7 Sept. 1856, JD, 5:194–195. See Terryl L. Givens and Matthew J. Grow, *Parley P. Pratt: The Apostle Paul of Mormonism* (New York: Oxford University Press, 2011), chap. 1.

53 Eli Gilbert to Oliver Cowdery, 24 September 1834, printed in *Messenger and Advocate* [Kirtland, Ohio], October 1834, 9–10. See Givens, *By the Hand of Mormon*, 186.

54 "Apple of my eye" in McLellin to James T. Cobb, 14 August 1880, in Larry C. Porter, "William E. McLellan's Testimony of the Book of Mormon," *BYU Studies* 10 (Summer 1970): 485–487; other quotes in William McLellin, "1831 Journal," in Jan Shipps and John W. Welch, eds., *The Journals of William E. McLellin, 1831–1836* (Provo, Utah, and Urbana: BYU Studies and University of Illinois Press, 1994), 29–35, 82–83, 177. Emphasis in original.

55 See Barlow, *Mormons and the Bible*, 44–45.

56 Ether 2:3.

57 Grant Underwood, "Book of Mormon Usage in Early LDS Theology," *Dialogue: A Journal of Mormon Thought* 17 (1984): 35–74, esp. 56–61.

58 A searchable database of General Conference talks reveals only stray references to Book of Mormon characters such as Alma and Lehi in the nineteenth century, whereas discussion of such figures became common and then abundant over the course of the twentieth century. See http://www.lds-general-conference.org/.

59 "Bible-drenched" from Barlow, *Mormons and the Bible*, 11.

60 Boyd Packer, "Scriptures," *Ensign*, November 1982, 51–53. See Givens, *By the Hand of Mormon*, 194.

61 Robert E. Wells, "Be a Friend, a Servant, a Son of the Savior," *Ensign*, Nov. 1982, 69–70.

62 Ezra Taft Benson, "Come unto Christ," *Ensign*, November 1987, 83–85; Benson, "The Book of Mormon—Keystone of Our Religion," *Ensign*, November 1986, 4–7. See Patrick Q. Mason, "Ezra Taft Benson and Modern (Book of Mormon) Conservatism," in Mason and John G. Turner, eds., *Out of Obscurity: Mormonism since 1945* (New York: Oxford University Press, forthcoming).

63 *Preach My Gospel*, 106.

64 Benson, "The Book of Mormon—Keystone of Our Religion."

2. JESUS MEETS GENESIS

1 See Paul C. Gutjahr, *An American Bible: A History of the Good Book in the United States, 1777–1880* (Stanford, Calif.: Stanford University Press, 1999), 89–99.

2 *The Sacred Writings of the Apostles and Evangelists of Jesus Christ, Commonly Titled the New Testament*, 2nd ed. (Bethany, Va.: Alexander Campbell, 1828), esp. preface.

3 Quoted in Leroy Garrett, "Alexander Campbell," in Douglas A. Foster, et al., eds., *The Encyclopedia of the Stone-Campbell Movement* (Grand Rapids, Mich.: Eerdmans, 2004), 123.

4 "Gold from the dross" in Edwin S. Gaustad, *Sworn on the Altar of God: A Religious Biography of Thomas Jefferson* (Grand Rapids, Mich.: Eerdmans, 1996), chap. 5.

5 1 Nephi 13:28.

6 Digital images of Smith's "Genesis" manuscript (Old Testament Manuscript 1) are available at http://josephsmithpapers.org/paperSummary/old-testament-revision-1. A transcript has been published by Scott H. Faulring, Kent P. Jackson, and Robert J. Matthews, eds., *Joseph Smith's New Translation of the Bible: Original Manuscripts* (Provo, Utah: Religious Studies Center of Brigham Young University, 2004).

7 "Genesis," page 1 [Moses 1:2, 6]. The words "the Savior" were inserted into a copy of the revelation made beginning in 1831.

8 "Genesis," pages 1–3 [Moses 1:13, 21, 32–33, 39].

9 John 1:3.

10 "Genesis," page 8 [Moses 5:7, 9].

11 Genesis 5:24.

12 Hebrews 11:5.

13 "Genesis," page 15 [Moses 7:3–4].

14 "Genesis," pages 14–15 [Moses 6:52–54, 59, 62, 68].

15 "Genesis," page 15 [Moses 7:13, 18].

16 "Genesis," pages 18 and 19 [Moses 7:55, 62].

17 Kent P. Jackson, "Joseph Smith's Cooperstown Bible: The Historical Context of the Bible Used in the Joseph Smith Translation," *BYU Studies* 40 (2001): 41–70.

18 Joseph Smith, Sidney Rigdon, and F. G. Williams to church leaders in Jackson County, Missouri, 2 July 1833, in JSP D3, 167. For an analysis of the project in its entirety, see Philip L. Barlow, *The Mormons and the Bible: The Place of the Latter-day Saints in American Religion* (New York: Oxford University Press, 1991), 46–61.

19 "First Presidency Statement," *Ensign*, August 1992, https://www.lds.org/ensign /1992/08/news-of-the-church/first-presidency-statement-on-the-king-james -version-of-the-bible.

20 On Smith as a translator, see Samuel M. Brown, *In Heaven as It Is on Earth: Joseph Smith and the Early Mormon Conquest of Death* (New York: Oxford University Press, 2012), 10–11.

21 See Chapter 7 in this volume.

3. SEEING THE SAVIOR'S FACE

1 Newel Knight Autobiography, ca. mid-1840s, Box 4, MS 767, CHL.

2 "Articles and Covenants" printed in *Painesville Telegraph* [Painesville, Ohio], 19 April 1831, 4 [D&C 20:47]; Joseph Smith History [1838–], A-1, pages 40–42, CR 100 102, CHL. See the analysis in William G. Hartley, *Stand by My Servant Joseph: The Story of the Joseph Knight Family and the Restoration* (Salt Lake City: Joseph Fielding Smith Institute for LDS History and Deseret Book, 2003), 68–70.

3 My understanding of visionary experience and its criticism is most strongly shaped by T. M. Luhrmann, *When God Talks Back: Understanding the Evangelical Relationship with God* (New York: Knopf, 2012); and Ann Taves, *Fits, Trances, & Visions: Experiencing Religion and Explaining Experience from Wesley to James* (Princeton, N.J.: Princeton University Press, 1999).

4 Ezekiel 1:1, 26–27. See Paul M. Joyce, *Ezekiel: A Commentary* (New York: T&T Clark, 2007), 72–74.

5 Acts 9:3–4; Acts 26:13.

6 2 Corinthians 12:3–4. For example, see Frank J. Matera, *II Corinthians: A Commentary* (Louisville, Ky.: Westminster John Knox Press, 2003), 276–281.

7 See, for example, Revelation 1:10, 21:10.

8 Quintilla in Frank Williams, trans., *The Panarion of Epiphanius of Salamis, Books II and III* (Leiden, The Netherlands: Brill, rev. ed. 2013), 22. On the conflict between

the new prophets and their opponents, see Elaine Pagels, *Revelations: Visions, Prophecy, & Politics in the Book of Revelation* (New York: Viking, 2012), 103–107; Pagels, *Beyond Belief: The Secret Gospel of Thomas* (New York: Random House, 2003), chap. 3.

9 See Barbara Newman, "What Did It Mean to Say 'I Saw'? The Clash between Theory and Practice in Medieval Visionary Culture," *Speculum* 80 (Jan. 2005): 25–33.

10 John Calvin, *Commentary upon the Acts of the Apostles*, trans. Christopher Fetherstone, ed., Henry Beveridge, vol. 2 (Edinburgh: Calvin Translation Society, 1844), 23.

11 John Wesley to Samuel Wesley, Jr., 4 April 1739, in *The Works of John Wesley*, ed. Frank Baker (New York: Oxford University Press, 1980), 623; Wesley Journal, 9 and 15 August 1850, in *The Works of John Wesley*, eds. W. Reginald Ward and Richard P. Heitzenrater (Nashville, Tenn.: Abingdon Press, 1990), 20:356. See Taves, *Fits, Trances, & Visions*, 15–19.

12 Journal of Nicholas Gilman, quoted in Douglas L. Winiarski, "Souls Filled with Ravishing Transport: Heavenly Visions and the Radical Awakening in New England," *William and Mary Quarterly* 61 (January 2004): 17.

13 Winiarski, "Souls Filled," 28–29. See Taves, *Fits, Trances, & Visions*, 34–41.

14 See Taves, *Fits, Trances, & Visions*, chap. 1.

15 *Connecticut Evangelical Magazine* [Hartford, Conn.], 1 March 1805, 349. Emphasis in original.

16 Garth M. Rosell and Richard A. G. Dupuis, eds., *The Original Memoirs of Charles G. Finney* (Grand Rapids, Mich.: Zondervan, 1989), 16–23. Emphasis in original.

17 Rosell and Dupuis, *Memoirs of Charles G. Finney*, 39 (emphasis in original); John Samuel Thompson, *The Christian Guide to a Right Understanding of the Sacred Scriptures* (Utica, N.Y.: A. G. Dauby, 1826), 71.

18 For a discussion of the multiple accounts of Smith's vision, see Steven C. Harper, *Joseph Smith's First Vision: A Guide to the Historical Accounts* (Salt Lake City: Deseret Book, 2012).

19 See Isaiah 29:13; Mark 7:6; Matthew 15:8.

20 Joseph Smith, ca. 1832 History, JSP H1, 12–13.

21 Joseph Smith to Emma Smith, 6 June 1832, JSP D2, 249–251.

22 Joseph Smith History [1838–], A-1, page 3, CR 100 102, CHL. See Jan Shipps, *Mormonism: The Story of a New Religious Tradition* (Urbana: University of Illinois Press, 1985), 10.

23 Smith, 1832 History.

24 "Hevnly" in Smith, 1832 History; "devil" in Joseph Smith History [1838–], A-1, pages 3–4.

25 Rosell and Dupuis, *Memoirs of Charles G. Finney*, 23. Emphasis in original.

26 Joseph Smith History [1838–], A-1, page 4.

27 Larry C. Porter, ed., "Solomon Chamberlain—Early Missionary," *BYU Studies* 12 (Spring 1972): 316.

28 Joseph Smith History [1838–], A-1, page 3; "Church History," *Times and Seasons* [Nauvoo, Ill.], 1 March 1842, 707.

29 Alexander Neibaur Journal, 24 May 1844, MS 1674, CHL.

30 See Richard S. Van Wagoner, *Sidney Rigdon: A Portrait of Religious Excess* (Salt Lake City: Signature Books, 1994), chap. 2; Mormon population in Kirtland in Stephen C. Taysom, "Development: 1831–1844," in W. Paul Reeve and Ardis Parshall, eds., *Mormonism: A Historical Encyclopedia* (Santa Barbara, Calif.: ABC-CLIO, 2012), 12.

31 Minutes of 18 March 1833, JSP D3, 42. See the discussion in Richard Lyman Bushman, *Joseph Smith: Rough Stone Rolling* (New York: Knopf, 2005), 202–205.

32 Revelation of 6 May 1833, JSP D3, 85–86 [D&C 93:1].

33 Revelation of 2 January 1831, JSP D1, 233 [D&C 38:32]; Luke 24:49.

34 Kirtland Council Minute Book, 21 February 1835, in Fred C. Collier and William S. Harwell, eds., *Kirtland Council Minute Book* (Salt Lake City: Collier's Publishing, 1996), 81. Spelling corrected from manuscript minutes.

35 Joseph Smith Journal, 12 November 1835, JSP J1, 99.

36 Oliver Cowdery Journal, 16 January 1836, in Leonard J. Arrington, ed., "Oliver Cowdery's Kirtland, Ohio, 'Sketch book,'" *BYU Studies* 12 (Summer 1972): 414–415; Joseph Smith Journal, 21 January 1836, in JSP J1, 167.

37 Joseph Smith Journal, 21 January 1836, in JSP J1, 167–168.

38 Benjamin Brown letter of spring 1836 (undated), in Steven C. Harper, ed., "Pentecost Continued: A Contemporaneous Account of the Kirtland Temple Dedication," *BYU Studies* 42 (2003): 4–22. "Holy season" is from Samuel Morris Brown, *In Heaven as It Is on Earth: Joseph Smith and the Early Mormon Conquest of Death* (New York: Oxford University Press, 2012), chap. 6.

39 *Messenger and Advocate* [Kirtland, Ohio], March 1836, 274–281.

40 Joseph Smith Journal, 30 March 1836, in JSP J1, 215–216. See David J. Howlett, *Kirtland Temple: The Biography of a Shared Mormon Sacred Space* (Urbana: University of Illinois Press, 2014), 21–24.

41 Joseph Smith Journal, 3 April 1836, in JSP J1, 219–220.

42 Truman Coe, "Mormonism," *Ohio Observer* [Hudson, Ohio], 11 August 1836.

43 2 Peter 1:10; Ephesians 1:13–14; minutes of 25 October 1831, in Donald Q. Cannon and Lyndon W. Cook, eds., *Far West Record: Minutes of the Church of Jesus Christ*

of Latter-day Saints, 1830–1844 (Salt Lake City: Deseret Book, 1983), 20. See Brown, *In Heaven*, 146–149.

44 2 Peter 1:4; Willard Richards, "Pocket Companion," pages 17–22, Box 2, MS 1490, CHL. Emphasis in original. I have modernized the spelling and punctuation.

45 Parley Pratt discourse of 10 July 1853, JD, 1:307; Brigham Young discourse of 6 April 1853, George D. Watt transcript, Box 2, Folder 6, CR 100 317, CHL.

46 Azariah Smith Journal, 27 March and 29 April 1853, MS 1834, CHL.

47 Patience Loader autobiography in Sandra Ailey Petree, ed., *Recollections of Past Days: The Autobiography of Patience Loader Rozsa Archer* (Logan: Utah State University Press, 2006), 51–54, 72.

48 "Vision of the Redemption of the Dead," *Improvement Era*, December 1918, 166–170 [D&C 138].

49 John Widtsoe, *Joseph Smith as Scientist: A Contribution to Mormon Philosophy* (Salt Lake City: General Board of the Young Men's Mutual Improvement Associations, 1908), 37; Lund quoted in Thomas Alexander, *Mormonism in Transition: A History of the Latter-day Saints, 1890–1930* (Urbana: University of Illinois Press, 1986), 297. See also chap. 14 in that book.

50 See Matthew Avery Sutton, *Aimee Semple McPherson and the Resurrection of Christian America* (Cambridge, Mass.: Harvard University Press, 2007).

51 Boyd K. Packer, "The Spirit Beareth Record," *Ensign*, June 1971, 87–88.

52 David B. Haight, "The Sacrament—and the Sacrifice," *Ensign*, November 1989, 59–61.

53 Denver Snuffer, *The Second Comforter: Conversing with the Lord through the Veil* (Salt Lake City: Mill Creek Press, 2006), 405; Snuffer, *Passing the Heavenly Gift* (Salt Lake City: Mill Creek Press, 2011), 452.

54 See Peggy Fletcher Stack, "Mormon Writer Who Says Church Always Caves to Mainstream May Be Cast Out," *Salt Lake Tribune*, 6 September 2013, accessed 19 July 2015, http://www.sltrib.com/56835902.

55 Joseph Smith Journal, 9 November 1835, JSP J1, 88.

56 Orson Pratt, "Are the Father and the Son Two Distinct Persons?" *Millennial Star*, 15 October 1849, 310. I am grateful to Steven Harper for pointing me to this reference.

57 *Improvement Era* [Salt Lake City], April 1937, 240–241. See Michael Hicks, *Mormonism and Music: A History* (Urbana: University of Illinois Press, 1989), 117–118.

58 See Richard H. Cracroft, "Rendering the Ineffable Effable: Treating Joseph Smith's First Vision in Imaginative Literature," *BYU Studies* 36 (1996–1997): 93–116.

59 Joseph F. Smith, *Two Sermons by President Joseph F. Smith* (Chattanooga, Tenn.: Southern States Mission, 1906), quoted in Kathleen Flake, *The Politics of American*

Religious Identity: The Seating of Senator Reed Smoot, Mormon Apostle (Chapel Hill: University of North Carolina Press, 2004), 120; see also chap. 5 in that book.

60 *The Systematic Program for Teaching the Gospel* (Salt Lake City: Church of Jesus Christ of Latter-day Saints, 1952), 40; *Preach My Gospel: A Guide to Missionary Service* (Salt Lake City: Church of Jesus Christ of Latter-day Saints, 2004), 38. See Jay Edwin Jensen, "Proselyting Techniques of Mormon Missionaries" (M.A. thesis, Brigham Young University, 1974), 81–83.

61 David O. McKay, *Gospel Ideals: Selections from the Discourses of David O. McKay, Ninth President of the Church of Jesus Christ of Latter-day Saints* (Salt Lake City: Improvement Era, 1954), 85; Gordon B. Hinckley, "What Are People Asking about Us?" *Ensign,* November 1998, 70–72; Hinckley, Jan. 2007 interview, accessed 26 August 2015, http://www.pbs.org/mormons/interviews/hinckley.html#2.

62 James B. Allen, "The Significance of Joseph Smith's 'First Vision' in Mormon Thought," *Dialogue* 1 (Autumn 1966): 29–45.

63 See Howlett, *Kirtland Temple*, 160–165.

4. THE WORDS OF THE LORD

1 See Jonathan H. Moyer, "Dancing with the Devil: The Making of the Mormon-Republican Pact" (Ph.D. diss., University of Utah, 2009), 88–97; Thomas G. Alexander, *Things in Heaven and Earth: The Life and Times of Wilford Woodruff, a Mormon Prophet* (Salt Lake City: Signature Books, 1993), chap. 11.

2 L. John Nuttall Journal, 24 November 1889, in Jedediah S. Rogers, ed., *In the President's Office: The Diaries of L. John Nuttall, 1879–1892* (Salt Lake City: Signature Books, 2007), 393.

3 WWJ, 24 November 1889, 9:67–69.

4 Abraham H. Cannon Journal, 19 December 1889, in Edward Leo Lyman, ed., *Candid Insights of a Mormon Apostle: The Diaries of Abraham H. Cannon, 1889–1895* (Salt Lake City: Signature Books, 2010), 38–39.

5 Joseph H. Dean Journal, 24 September 1890, in Moyer, "Dancing," 98.

6 *Deseret Evening News,* 25 September 1890.

7 *Deseret Evening News,* 14 November 1891.

8 Max Weber, *The Theory of Social and Economic Organization,* trans. A. M. Henderson and Talcott Parsons (New York: Free Press, 1947), 363ff. Weber himself used Smith as an example of charismatic authority, though he was uncertain exactly how to classify the Mormon prophet, "since there is a possibility that he was a very sophisticated type of deliberate swindler."

9 Rodney Stark, "A Theory of Revelations," *Journal for the Scientific Study of Religion* 38 (June 1999): 304.

10 See Michael Scott, *Delphi: A History of the Center of the Ancient World* (Princeton, N.J.: Princeton University Press, 2014), chap. 1.

11 2 Samuel 16:23.

12 Jeremiah 1:9.

13 Anne Hutchinson, John Winthrop ("comely" and "delusion"), and Cotton quoted in "The Examination of Mrs. Anne Hutchinson at the court at Newtown," November 1637, in David D. Hall, *The Antinomian Controversy, 1636–1638: A Documentary History* (Durham, N.C.: Duke University Press, 1990, 2nd ed.), 337, 312, 340, 343.

14 Thomas Paine, *The Age of Reason, Part the Second, Being an Investigation of True and Fabulous Theology* (London: Daniel Isaac Eaton, 1796, 2nd ed.), 76. See Leigh Eric Schmidt, *Hearing Things: Religion, Illusion, and the American Enlightenment* (Cambridge, Mass.: Harvard University Press, 2000), 6.

15 Ralph Waldo Emerson, "Self-Reliance," in *Essays* (Boston: James Munroe and Company, 1841), 63–64. See the discussion in Terryl Givens, *By the Hand of Mormon: The American Scripture that Launched a New World Religion* (New York: Oxford University Press, 2002), 217.

16 Schmidt, *Hearing Things*, chap. 2.

17 Nancy Towle, *Vicissitudes Illustrated, in the Experience of Nancy Towle, in Europe and America* (Portsmouth, N.H.: John Caldwell, 1833), 38.

18 Lorenzo Dow, *History of Cosmopolite, or the Four Volumes of Lorenzo's Journal* (New York: John C. Totten, 1814), 20. See Schmidt, *Hearing Things*, 11, 51.

19 Ralph Waldo Emerson, *An Address Delivered before the Senior Class in Divinity College, Cambridge* (Boston: James Munroe and Company, 1838), 17. See Benjamin E. Park, "'Build, Therefore, Your Own World': Ralph Waldo Emerson, Joseph Smith, and American Antebellum Thought," *Journal of Mormon History* 36 (Winter 2010): 41–72.

20 Joseph Smith to Silas Smith, 26 September 1833, in JSP D3, 303–308.

21 Joseph Smith, ca. 1832 History, JSP H1, 13; revelation of 16 February 1832, in Revelation Book 2, page 3, in JSP MRB, 419 [D&C 76:23]; Joseph Smith Journal, 3 April 1836, in JSP J1, 219.

22 Parley Parker Pratt, *The Autobiography of Parley Parker Pratt* (New York: Russell Brothers, 1874), 65.

23 William E. McLellin, "Revelations," *Ensign of Liberty* [Kirtland, Ohio], August 1849, 98.

24 See Givens, *By the Hand of Mormon*, chap. 8.

25 Revelation, ca. early 1830, in Revelation Book 1, page 31, in JSP, MRB, 33. This revelation was never included in any published edition of commandments and revelations.

26 Revelations of April and May 1829, in *Book of Commandments, for the Government of the Church of Christ* (Zion [Independence, Mo.]: W.W. Phelps, 1833), 14–17 [D&C 6] and 28–30 [D&C 11].

27 Revelation, ca. Spring 1829, in Revelation Book 1, page 11, in JSP, MRB, 13 [D&C 10:57].

28 Revelation of September 1830, Revelation Book 1, page 36, in JSP MRB, 43 [D&C 29:1].

29 Revelation of July 1830, Revelation Book 1, pages 34–35, in JSP MRB, 39–40 [D&C 25]. See John 8:21, 13:33.

30 William McLellin, 1831 Journal, in Jan Shipps and John W. Welch, eds., *The Journals of William E. McLellin, 1831–1836* (Provo, Utah, and Urbana: BYU Studies and University of Illinois Press, 1994), 39–46; *Ensign of Liberty*, January 1848, 61.

31 See, for example, revelation of 8 March 1833, JSP D3, 27–32 [D&C 90: 29].

32 Eber Dudley Howe, *Mormonism Unvailed: Or, A Faithful Account of that Singular Imposition and Delusion* (Painesville, Ohio: published by the author, 1834), 226, 145.

33 Jonathan B. Turner, *Mormonism in All Ages: Or the Rise, Progress, and Causes of Mormonism* (New York: Platt & Peters, 1842), 20.

34 Howe cited this phrase, as did John C. Bennett, *The History of the Saints; or, an Exposé of Joe Smith and Mormonism* (Boston: Leland & Whiting, 1842), 144. Emphasis is Bennett's. See revelation of 30 August 1831, Revelation Book 1, page 106, in JSP MRB, 185 [D&C 63:29]. The revelation added that the Saints were "forbidden to shed blood," and another revelation dictated several weeks earlier called upon church members to purchase land so that Zion could be obtained without bloodshed. See revelation of 1 August 1831, Revelation Book 1, page 97, in JSP MRB, 167 [D&C 58:53].

35 See the discussion in David F. Holland, *Sacred Borders: Continuing Revelation and Canonical Restraint in Early America* (New York: Oxford University Press, 2011), 150.

36 Smith to Edward Partridge and William Phelps, 30 March 1834, in JSP D3, 491. Emphasis in original.

37 Revelation of 1 November 1831, in Revelation Book 1, page 113, in JSP MRB, 199 [D&C 68:4].

38 *Messenger and Advocate* [Kirtland, Ohio], March 1836, 277.

39 Joseph Smith Journal, 27 March 1836, JSP J1, 204.

40 Smith remarks, ca. Summer 1839, in Willard Richards, Pocket Companion, pages 75 ("privilege"), 78–79 ("respecter" and "same"), and 21 ("pure"), Box 2, Folder 6, MS 1490, CHL.

41 Revelation of April 1829, in *Book of Commandments*, 16 [D&C 6:25]; revelation of April 1829, in *Book of Commandments*, 21 [D&C 9:8, 10].

42 David Whitmer, *An Address to All Believers in Christ* (Richmond, Mo.: David Whitmer, 1887), 54.

43 Revelation of September 1830 to Oliver Cowdery, Revelation Book 1, pages 40–41, in JSP D1, 185 [D&C 28:2]. See John L. Brooke, *The Refiner's Fire: The Making of Mormon Cosmology, 1644–1844* (Cambridge: Cambridge University Press, 1994), 189.

44 Edward Partridge to Joseph Smith Jr., 19 November 1833, Joseph Smith Papers, Box 3, Folder 1, MS 155, CHL.

45 William Clayton Journal, 23 June and 29 May 1843, in George D. Smith, ed., *An Intimate Chronicle: The Journals of William Clayton* (Salt Lake City: Signature Books, 1991), 108, 106. See Linda King Newell and Valeen Tippetts Avery, *Mormon Enigma: Emma Hale Smith* (Urbana: University of Illinois Press, 1994, 2nd ed.), chap. 10; Todd Compton, *In Sacred Loneliness: The Plural Wives of Joseph Smith* (Salt Lake City: Signature Books, 1997), esp. chaps. 18 and 19.

46 William Clayton to Madison M. Scott, 11 November 1871, MS 4681, CHL.

47 Revelation of 12 July 1843, copy in handwriting of Joseph Kingsbury, Box 1, Folder 75, MS 4583, CHL [D&C 132].

48 William Clayton Journal, 12 July 1843, in George D. Smith, *An Intimate Chronicle*, 110.

49 Lucy Walker, "A Brief Biographical Sketch," typescript by Maureen Ursenbach Beecher, copy in author's possession. See Compton, *In Sacred Loneliness*, chap. 20.

50 On Strang, see Vickie Cleverley Speek, *"God Has Made Us A Kingdom": James Strang and the Midwest Mormons* (Salt Lake City: Signature Books, 2006); Robin Scott Jensen, "Mormons Seeking Mormonism: Strangite Success and the Conceptualization of Mormon Ideology, 1844–50," in Newell G. Bringhurst and John C. Hamer, eds., *Scattering of the Saints: Schism within Mormonism* (Independence, Mo.: John Whitmer Books, 2007), 115–140.

51 WWJ, 18 August 1844, 2:445.

52 Young discourse of 25 August 1844, Thomas Bullock shorthand, transcription by LaJean Purcell Carruth, copy in author's possession.

53 Brigham Young discourse of 29 June 1845, Thomas Bullock minutes, Box 1, Folder 35, GCM.

54 Brigham Young Journal, 31 January 1846, Box 71, Folder 4, BYP. See Reuben Miller, *James J. Strang: Weighed in the Balance of Truth, and Found Wanting* (Burlington, Wisc. Terr.: n.p., 1846).

55 Revelation of 14 January 1847, transcript by Thomas Bullock, in Box 1, Folder 76, MS 4583, CHL; Heber C. Kimball Journal, 19 January 1847, typescript in HBLL; Willard Richards in minutes of 1 August 1847, Box 1, Folder 56, GCM.

314 ÷ NOTES TO PAGES 108–113

56 "Wrote some" in WWJ, 28 May 1847, 3:186; "did not care" in Willard Richards Journal, 28 May 1847, vol. 18, MS 1490, CHL; text of revelation in https://history.lds.org/overlandtravels/trailExcerptMulti?lang=eng&sourceId=4473.

57 William Clayton Journal, 29 May 1847, in George D. Smith, *An Intimate Chronicle*, 324–331.

58 Young discourse of 7 April 1850, transcript by William Clayton, Box 2, Folder 18, GCM.

59 "So and so" and "not the word" in Samuel W. Richards Journal, 11 March 1856 (emphasis in original), vol. 11, MS 1841, CHL; Genesis 2:7; "written revelations" in minutes of 20 April 1856, Box 3, Folder 11, GCM; "living oracles" in discourse of 30 March 1856, transcript by George D. Watt, Box 3, Folder 15, CR 100 317, CHL. See Philip L. Barlow, *Mormons and the Bible: The Place of the Latter-day Saints in American Religion* (New York: Oxford University Press, 1991), chap. 3. See also Gary James Bergera, *Conflict in the Quorum: Orson Pratt, Brigham Young, Joseph Smith* (Salt Lake City: Signature Books, 2002), 126–127. For a recent example of the privileging of ongoing revelation, see Ezra Taft Benson, "Fourteen Fundamentals in Following the Prophet," 26 Feb. 1980 discourse, accessed 20 July 2015, https://www.lds.org/liahona/1981/06/fourteen-fundamentals-in-following-the-prophet.

60 Young discourse of 29 March 1874, in James Bleak, *Annals of the Southern Utah Mission*, Box 1, Folder 9, CHL.

61 Young discourse of 9 August 1874, in JD, 17:154.

62 Richard N. Holzapfel and Christopher C. Jones, "'John the Revelator': The Written Revelations of John Taylor," in Mary Jane Woodger, ed., *Champion of Liberty: John Taylor* (Provo, Utah: BYU Religious Studies Center, 2009): 272–307.

63 George Reynolds, "Revelation—Inspiration," *Juvenile Instructor*, 1 March 1902, 131.

64 See Holzapfel and Jones, "'John the Revelator,'" 307, n. 99.

65 Revelation of 17–18 May 1884, in Holzapfel and Jones, "'John the Revelator,'" 291.

66 Revelation of 13 October 1882, in Holzapfel and Jones, "'John the Revelator,'" 284.

67 WWJ, 26 and 27 January 1880, 7:546–547, 615–621.

68 John W. Taylor quoted in Abraham H. Cannon Journal, 28 Sept. 1890, in Lyman, *Candid Insights*, 137.

69 See Kathleen Flake, *The Politics of American Religious Identity: The Seating of Senator Reed Smoot, Mormon Apostle* (Chapel Hill: University of North Carolina Press, 2004), chap. 2; "The Manifesto and the End of Plural Marriage," accessed 30 August 2015, https://www.lds.org/topics/the-manifesto-and-the-end-of-plural-marriage?lang=eng.

70 This and the several paragraphs following are informed by Flake, *The Politics of American Religious Identity*, esp. chaps. 2–4.

71 *Proceedings before the Committee on Privileges and Elections of the United States Senate in the Matter of the Protests against the Right of Hon. Reed Smoot . . . to Hold His Seat* (Washington, D.C.: Government Printing Office, 1904), 1:143.

72 *Proceedings*, 1:99.

73 *Proceedings*, 1:99, 314–315.

74 *Salt Lake Tribune*, 9 March 1905. Reprinted testimonies in *Salt Lake Tribune*, 19 and 26 February 1905; 5 March 1905.

75 William James, *The Varieties of Religious Experience: A Study in Human Nature* (New York: Longmans, Green, and Co., 1903), 482.

76 McLellin, "Revelations," 99.

77 Revelation of 27 Sept. 1886, in Fred C. Collier, ed., *Unpublished Revelations of the Prophets and Presidents of The Church of Jesus Christ of Latter Day Saints* (Salt Lake City: Collier's Publishing, 1981, 2nd ed.), 145. See the discussion in Brian C. Hales, *Modern Polygamy and Mormon Fundamentalism: The Generations after the Manifesto* (Salt Lake City: Kofford, 2006), 37–41.

78 Taylor quoted in Abraham H. Cannon Journal, 1 April 1892, in Lyman, *Candid Insights*, 319.

79 See "The Manifesto and the End of Plural Marriage," n. 14, accessed 31 August 2015, https://www.lds.org/topics/the-Manifesto-and-the-end-of-plural-marriage.

80 First Presidency Message of 17 June 1933, in James R. Clark, ed., *Messages of the First Presidency* (Salt Lake City: Bookcraft, 1965–1975), 5:327.

81 See Hales, *Modern Polygamy*, 147, 159–161.

82 Official Declaration 2 (in Doctrine and Covenants); Bruce R. McConkie, "The New Revelation on Priesthood," in Spencer W. Kimball, *Priesthood* (Salt Lake City: Deseret Books, 1981), 127–128.

83 Ezra Taft Benson, "Seek the Spirit of the Lord," *Ensign*, April 1988, 4; Boyd Packer, "Personal Revelation," *Ensign*, November 1994, 60. Emphasis in original.

84 Max Weber, "Wissenschaft als Beruf," in *Gesammelte Aufsätze zur Wissenschaftslehre* (Tübingen: J. C. B. Mohr, 1985 [1922]), 612.

5. I COME QUICKLY

1 Joseph Smith, 1832 History, JSP H1, 13; "Church History," *Times and Seasons*, March 1842, 710.

2 While some scholars make distinctions between "millenarianism" and "millennialism," I understand them as interchangeable terms.

3 Mark 13:26, 30, 33.

4 Martin Luther, "Preface to the Revelation of St. John," 1522, in LW, 35:399.

5 See Elaine Pagels, *Revelations: Visions, Prophecy, & Politics in the Book of Revelation* (New York: Viking, 2012), chaps. 1 and 2.

6 Irenaeus, *Against Heresies*, 5.30.4, in Alexander Roberts and James Donaldson, eds., *The Ante-Nicene Fathers*, vol. 1 (Buffalo, N.Y.: Christian Literature Publishing Company, 1885), 560. See Brian E. Daley, *The Hope of the Early Church: A Handbook of Patristic Eschatology* (Cambridge: Cambridge University Press), 28–32.

7 Niceno-Constantinopolitan Creed in Jaroslav Pelikan and Valerie Hotchkiss, eds., *Creeds and Confessions of Faith in the Christian Tradition*, vol. 1 (New Haven, Conn.: Yale University Press, 2003), 163.

8 On the Taborites, see Norman Cohn, *The Pursuit of the Millennium: Revolutionary Millenarians and Mystical Anarchists of the Middle Ages* (New York: Oxford University Press, rev. ed. 1970), 205–223. On Münster, see George Huntston Williams, *The Radical Reformation* (Philadelphia: Westminster Press, 1962), chap. 13.

9 Richard Eburne, *A Plaine Path-Way to Plantations* (London: G.P., 1624), 7.

10 See Zachary McLeod Hutchins, *Inventing Eden: Primitivism, Millennialism, and the Making of New England* (New York: Oxford University Press, 2014); Reiner Smolinski, "Apocalypticism in Colonial North America," in Stephen J. Stein, ed., *The Encyclopedia of Apocalypticism*, vol. 3, *Apocalypticism in the Modern Period and Contemporary Age* (New York: Continuum, 2000), 36–71.

11 Bradford King Journal, Nov. 28, 1830, University of Rochester, Rush Rhees Library, Special Collections. See Paul E. Johnson, *A Shopkeeper's Millennium: Society and Revivals in Rochester, New York, 1815–1837* (New York: Hill and Wang, 2004, rev. ed.), 109. King was a real estate agent who, he explained, went over "to the Lord's side" during the early weeks of the revival.

12 Catherine Wessinger, ed., *The Oxford Handbook of Millennialism* (New York: Oxford University Press, 2011), 721. Scholars further divide evangelical premillennialists into *futurists*, who believe that all of the major prophecies about the "last days" will be fulfilled in a short time before Christ's return, and *historicists*, who believe that the Bible reveals a much longer prophetic timetable and that many key events have already been fulfilled. The Latter-day Saints more closely resemble the historicist position. See Timothy P. Weber, *Living in the Shadow of the Second Coming: American Premillennialism, 1875–1925* (New York: Oxford University Press, 1979), esp. 9–11.

13 See the summary in Stephen J. Stein, "Apocalypticism Outside the Mainstream in the United States," in Stein, *Encyclopedia of Apocalypticism*, vol. 3, esp. 108–117.

14 "Memoir of William Miller," in Joshua V. Himes, *Views of the Prophecies and Prophetic Chronology* (Boston: Joshua V. Himes, 1842), 12.

15 William Miller to Anna and Joseph Atwood, 31 May 1831, in David L. Rowe, *God's Strange Work: William Miller and the End of the World* (Grand Rapids, Mich.: Eerdmans,

2008), 96. On Miller's meteoric rise and fall, see Rowe, *God's Strange Work*, chaps. 5–8.

16 In the following paragraphs, I rely heavily on the research of Grant Underwood, *The Millenarian World of Early Mormonism* (Urbana: University of Illinois Press, 1993); and Dan Erickson, *As a Thief in the Night: The Mormon Quest for Millennial Deliverance* (Salt Lake City: Signature Books, 1998).

17 Ether 13:5; 2 Nephi 30:7; Lucius Fenn to Birdseye Bronson, 12 February 1830, in William Mulder and A. Russell Mortensen, *Among the Mormons: Historic Accounts by Contemporary Observers* (Lincoln: University of Nebraska Press, 1958), 28.

18 "Genesis," page 19, in Scott H. Faulring, et al., eds., *Joseph Smith's New Translation of the Bible: Original Manuscripts* (Provo, Utah: Religious Studies Center of Brigham Young University, 2004), 109 [Moses 7:62, 64–65].

19 Revelation of February 1829 ("field is white"), in JSP D1, 13 [D&C 4:4]; revelation of September 1830 ("magots"), in JSP D1, 18 [D&C 29:18–19]; revelation of July 1830 ("declare"), JSP D1, 159 [D&C 24:12].

20 Nancy Towle, *Vicissitudes Illustrated, in the Experience of Nancy Towle, in Europe and America* (Portsmouth, N.H.: John Caldwell, 1833), 153, 158.

21 Underwood, *The Millenarian World*, chap. 6.

22 Ibid.

23 Terryl L. Givens and Matthew J. Grow, *Parley P. Pratt: The Apostle Paul of Mormonism* (New York: Oxford University Press, 2011), 46–47.

24 Revelation of 6 June 1831, in JSP D1, 332 [D&C 52:43–44]; revelation of 20 July 1831, in JSP D2, 7–8 [D&C 57:3].

25 Orson Hyde Journal, 23 September 1832, MS 1386, CHL; *Painesville* [Ohio] *Telegraph*, 13 March 1832.

26 *Evening and Morning Star* [reprinted in Kirtland, Ohio], June 1832. The reprint of the June 1832 issue included Phelps's February 1832 prospectus.

27 "Hymns," *The Evening and the Morning Star* [Independence, Mo.], June 1832. See the analysis in Michael Hicks, *Mormonism and Music: A History* (Urbana: University of Illinois Press, 1989), 12–14.

28 "Present Age of the World," *The Evening and the Morning Star* [Independence, Mo.], August 1832.

29 "Explanation of the Plat of the City of Zion," circa 25 June 1833, in JSP D3, 128. Spelling and punctuation corrected.

30 Letter from "the Undersigned Citizens of Jackson County" to Missouri Governor Daniel Dunklin, printed in *Evening and Morning Star* [Kirtland, Ohio], December 1833, 114.

31 Joseph Smith, 13 November 1833 Journal, JSP J1, 16–17.

32 Parley Pratt, *A Voice of Warning and Instruction to All People* (New York: W. Sandford, 1837), 20, 88, 190, 140. See Givens and Grow, *Parley P. Pratt*, 118–120.

33 Edward Leo Lyman, et al., eds., *No Place to Call Home: The 1807–1857 Life Writings of Caroline Barnes Crosby, Chronicler of Outlying Mormon Communities* (Logan, Utah: Utah State University Press, 2005), 41–42.

34 Joseph Smith Sr. blessing of Lovina Wilson, 25 April 1836, in H. Michael Marquardt, ed., *Later Patriarchal Blessings of the Church of Jesus Christ of Latter-day Saints* (Salt Lake City: Smith-Pettit Foundation, 2012), 531.

35 Joseph Smith Sr. blessings of Hyrum Smith and Joseph Smith Jr., 9 December 1834, in H. Michael Marquardt, ed., *Early Patriarchal Blessings of the Church Of Jesus Christ of Latter-day Saints* (Salt Lake City: Smith-Pettit Foundation, 2007), 12, 14–15.

36 Joseph Smith Journal, 19 May 1838, JSP J1, 271 (D&C 116); Smith remarks, ca. Summer 1839, in Willard Richards, Pocket Companion, pages 63–64, Box 2, Folder 6, MS 1490, CHL.

37 Leland H. Gentry and Todd M. Compton, *Fire and Sword: A History of the Latter-day Saints in Northern Missouri, 1836–39* (Salt Lake City: Kofford Books, 2011).

38 Hyde to Hirschell, n.d., in Hyde to Joseph Smith, 15 June 1841, in *Times and Seasons* [Nauvoo, Ill.], 1 October 1841, 551–555.

39 Orson Hyde, *A Voice from Jerusalem, or a Sketch of the Travels and Ministry of Elder Orson Hyde* (Boston: Albert Morgan, 1842), 27, 29, 32.

40 For an account of Hyde's mission to Jerusalem, see Steven Epperson, *Mormons and Jews: Early Mormon Theologies of Israel* (Salt Lake City: Signature Books, 1992), chap. 6.

41 William Clayton Journal, 2 April 1843, in JSP J2, 403–404 [D&C 130: 15–16]. Spelling corrected.

42 WWJ, 10 March 1844, 2:365.

43 A revelation dictated by Joseph Smith in 1832 identified "Ahman" or "Awman" as the "name of God in pure Language," in the language of heaven spoken on earth prior to the Tower of Babel. See revelation of ca. March 1832, in Revelation Book 1, JSP MRB, 264–265.

44 William Clayton Journal, 1 January 1845 and 11 April 1844, 153, 129.

45 Joseph Smith Journal, 8 April 1844, JSP J3, 223.

46 Revelation 6:8.

47 See Noel A. Carmack, "Of Prophets and Pale Horses: Joseph Smith: Benjamin West, and the American Millenarian Tradition," *Dialogue* 29 (Fall 1996): 165–176; Alex Beam, *American Crucifixion: The Murder of Joseph Smith and the Fate of the Mormon Church* (New York: Public Affairs, 2014), 128–130.

48 Alexander Ross hymn in *Sacred Hymns and Spiritual Songs for the Church of Jesus Christ of Latter-day Saints in Europe* (Liverpool: F. D. Richards, rev. and enlarged 1851), 361–362; *Zion's Trumpet*, January 1849 ("plagues" and "signs"), November 1849 ("wrath"),

and March 1849 ("no veil"), all in Ronald D. Dennis, trans. and ed., *Zion's Trumpet: 1849 Welsh Mormon Periodical* (Provo, Utah: Religious Studies Center of Brigham Young University, 2001), 15, 7, 216, 54. Ross's hymn ("The Shepherds Have Raised Their Sweet Warning Voice") used the same refrain as Cyrus Wheelock's "Ye Elders of Israel." The latter remains a popular Latter-day Saint hymn.

49 Young discourse of 6 April 1845, *Times and Seasons*, 1 July 1845, 956; "not going to wait" in discourse of 23 February 1862, JD, 9:284.

50 See the analysis in Douglas J. Davies, *The Mormon Culture of Salvation: Force, Grace, and Glory* (Adlershot, U.K.: Ashgate, 2000), 231–233.

51 Joseph Smith Journal, 2 April 1843, JSP J2, 324.

52 WWJ, 23 August 1862, 6:71.

53 Minutes of Nineteenth Ward Ladies Prayer Meetings, 13 October 1875, LR 6092 31, CHL.

54 "The Coming of the Messiah," *Millennial Star*, 7 April 1879, 218; minutes of the Eastern Arizona Stake, 28 June 1879, quoted in Charles S. Peterson, *Take Up Your Mission: Mormon Colonizing Along the Little Colorado River, 1870–1900* (Tucson: University of Arizona Press, 1973), 228, n. 18; Charles Lowell Walker Journal, 14 August 1881, in A. Karl Larson and Katharine Miles Larson, eds., *Diary of Charles Lowell Walker* (Logan: Utah State University Press, 1980), 2:564. See the long list of examples of such prophecies in Erickson, *As a Thief*, chap. 8.

55 Abraham H. Cannon Journal, 6 October 1890, in Edward Leo Lyman, ed., *Candid Insights of a Mormon Apostle: The Diaries of Abraham H. Cannon, 1889–1895* (Salt Lake City: Signature Books, 2010), 144.

56 See M. James Penton, *Apocalypse Delayed: The Story of the Jehovah's Witnesses* (Toronto: University of Toronto Press, rev. ed. 1997), esp. chaps. 1–4.

57 Matthew Avery Sutton, *American Apocalypse: A History of Modern Evangelicalism* (Cambridge, Mass.: Harvard University Press, 2014), 283.

58 Anthony W. Ivins Journal, 2 July 1899, in Elizabeth Oberdick Anderson, ed., *Cowboy Apostle: The Diaries of Anthony W. Ivins, 1875–1932* (Salt Lake City: Signature Books, 2013), 210; GCR, October 1897, 68. See the analysis in Thomas Alexander, *Mormonism in Transition: A History of the Latter-day Saints, 1890–1930* (Urbana: University of Illinois Press, 1986), 5–6, 288–289.

59 R. Jean Addams, "The Church of Christ (Temple lot) and the Reorganized Church of Jesus Christ of Latter Day Saints: 130 Years of Crossroads and Controversies," *Journal of Mormon History* 36 (Spring 2010): 54–127.

60 See Sutton, *American Apocalypse*, chap. 1.

61 Timothy E. W. Gloege, *Guaranteed Pure: The Moody Bible Institute, Business, and the Making of Modern Evangelicalism* (Chapel Hill: University of North Carolina Press, 2015), 29.

62 *Millennial Star*, 15 September 1921, 584.

63 Joanna Brooks, *The Book of Mormon Girl: A Memoir of an American Faith* (New York: Free Press, 2012), 30–37.

64 Ezra Taft Benson, "Prepare for the Days of Tribulation," *Ensign*, November 1980, 32–34.

65 Harry Truman Diary, 25 July 1945, quoted in Paul S. Boyer, *When Time Shall Be No More: Prophecy Belief in Modern American Culture* (Cambridge, Mass.: Harvard University Press, 1992), 116. See Sutton, *American Apocalypse*, 296–303.

66 Joseph Fielding Smith, *Doctrines of Salvation: Sermons and Writings of Joseph Fielding Smith*, vol. 3, ed. Bruce R. McConkie (Salt Lake City: Bookcraft, 1956), 1, 17. Emphasis in original.

67 Ibid., 13, 58.

68 Bruce R. McConkie, *Mormon Doctrine* (Salt Lake City: Bookcraft, 1958), 661.

69 Ibid., 656.

70 See http://www.pewresearch.org/daily-number/jesus-christs-return-to-earth/, accessed 11 May 2015.

71 *Jesus Christ and the Everlasting Gospel* (Salt Lake City: The Church of Jesus Christ of Latter-day Saints, 2015), 94, 100.

72 Underwood, *Millenarian World*, 141.

73 Gordon Shepherd and Gary Shepherd, *A Kingdom Transformed: Themes in the Development of Mormonism* (Salt Lake City: University of Utah Press, 1984), 253.

74 *Gospel Principles* (Salt Lake City: The Church of Jesus Christ of Latter-day Saints, rev. ed. 2009), 261.

75 WWJ, 15 March 1857, 5:33.

6. ELDER BROTHER

1 Creed of Nicaea and Chalcedonian definition in Jaroslav Pelikan and Valerie Hotchkiss, eds., *Creeds and Confessions of Faith in the Christian Tradition*, vol. 1 (New Haven, Conn.: Yale University Press, 2003), 159, 181. For a concise but very useful history, see Diarmaid MacCulloch, *Christianity: The First Three Thousand Years* (New York: Viking, 2009), chaps. 5 and 6.

2 Thirty-Nine Articles in Philip Schaff, *The Creeds of Christendom* (New York: Harper & Brothers, 1877), 3:487–488. For a discussion of how Mormons dissented from the idea of an immaterial and impassible God, see Terryl Givens, *Wrestling the Angel: The Foundations of Mormon Thought: Cosmos, God, Humanity* (New York: Oxford University Press, 2015), 85–86.

3 Articles and Covenants in "The Mormon Creed," *Painesville Telegraph* [Painesville, Ohio], 19 April 1831, 4 [D&C 20].

4 "The Mormon Creed."

5 Brigham Young discourse of 3 July 1870, JD, 14:279–280.

6 In the paragraphs that follow, I rely most heavily on Givens, *Wrestling the Angel*. On the materialist basis of Mormon metaphysics and christology, see Stephen H. Webb, *Mormon Christianity: What Other Christians Can Learn from the Latter-day Saints* (New York: Oxford University Press, 2013). For early developments within Mormon thought, see also Charles Harrell, *"This Is My Doctrine": The Development of Mormon Theology* (Salt Lake City: Greg Kofford, 2010).

7 Revelation of 16 February 1832, in JSP D2, 183–192.

8 Irenaeus, *Against Heresies*, 5.36.1–2, in Alexander Roberts and James Donaldson, eds., *The Ante-Nicene Fathers*, vol. 1 (Buffalo, N.Y.: Christian Literature Publishing Company, 1885), 567. See Colleen McDannell and Bernhard Lang, *Heaven: A History* (New Haven, Conn.: Yale University Press, 1988), esp. chaps. 4, 6, and 7; Peter Brown, *The Ransom of the Soul: Afterlife and Wealth in Early Western Christianity* (Cambridge, Mass.: Harvard University Press, 2015), introduction.

9 Joseph Bellamy quoted in Kathryn Gin Lum, *Damned Nation: Hell in America from the Revolution to Reconstruction* (New York: Oxford University Press, 2014), 40; *Deseret News Extra* [Salt Lake City], 14 September 1852, 24. See Grant Underwood, *The Millenarian World of Early Mormonism* (Urbana: University of Illinois Press, 1993), chap. 3.

10 "Sample of Pure Language," ca. March 1832, JSP D2, 215. See Zachery McLeod Hutchins, *Inventing Eden: Primitivism, Millennialism, and the Making of New England* (New York: Oxford University Press, 2014), chap. 5.

11 2 Peter 1:4.

12 Revelation of 6 May 1833, JSP D3, 86–89 (spelling corrected) [D&C 93]. See Colossians 1:15; 2 Peter 1:4.

13 See Matthew Stewart, *Nature's God: The Heretical Origins of the American Revolution* (New York: Norton, 2014).

14 Thomas Dick, *The Philosophy of a Future State* (New York: Carvill, 1829), 100, quoted in *Messenger and Advocate* [Kirtland, Ohio], Dec. 1836, 423. See Givens, *Wrestling the Angel*, 55.

15 See Benjamin E. Park, "'Reasonings Sufficient': Joseph Smith, Thomas Dick, and the Context(s) of Early Mormonism," *Journal of Mormon History* 38 (Summer 2012): 210–224.

16 Parley P. Pratt, "Materiality," *The Prophet* [New York], May 24, 1845, reprinted in Benjamin E. Park and Jordan T. Watkins, eds., "The Riches of Mormon Materialism: Parley P. Pratt's 'Materiality' and early Mormon Theology," *Mormon Historical Studies* 11 (Fall 2010): 125.

17 John Taylor discourse of 19 February 1860, JD, 8:1.

18 Revelation 12:3, 7, 9. See Elaine Pagels, *The Origin of Satan* (New York: Random House, 1995), chap. 2; Boyd Petersen, "'Not One Soul Shall Be Lost': The War in Heaven in Mormon Thought," *Journal of Mormon History* 38 (Winter 2012): 1–50.

19 "Genesis," page 6, in Scott H. Faulring, et al., eds., *Joseph Smith's New Translation of the Bible: Original Manuscripts* (Provo, Utah: Religious Studies Center of Brigham Young University, 2004), 90 [Moses 4:1–4]. See Givens, *Wrestling*, 133–134.

20 *Times and Seasons* [Nauvoo, Ill.], 15 March 1842, 720 [Abraham 3–4].

21 William Clayton Journal, 17 May 1843, in George D. Smith, ed., *An Intimate Chronicle: The Journals of William Clayton* (Salt Lake City: Signature Books, 1991), 102; Revelation of 12 July 1843, copy in handwriting of Joseph Kingsbury, Box 1, Folder 75, MS 4583, CHL [D&C 132:19–20].

22 *Nauvoo Neighbor* [Nauvoo, Ill.], 20 March 1844.

23 "Secret" and "God was God" from minutes of William Clayton, 7 April 1844, Box 1, Folder 19, GCM; all other quotes from minutes of Thomas Bullock, 7 April 1844, Box 1, Folder 20, GCM. Clerks Clayton and Bullock both recorded Smith's sermon; an amalgamated account then appeared in an August 1844 church periodical. I have expanded their abbreviations and corrected the text slightly.

24 Joseph Smith, discourse of 16 June 1844, Box 4, Folder 6, Joseph Smith Papers, MS 155, CHL.

25 William Clayton Journal, 16 May 1843, in George D. Smith, *An Intimate Chronicle*, 103–104 [D&C 131:7]. See Stephen H. Webb, *Mormon Christianity: What Other Christians Can Learn from the Latter-day Saints* (New York: Oxford University Press, 2013), 83ff.

26 Joseph Smith, discourse of 16 June 1844.

27 Brigham Young to Willard Richards, 8 July 1844, Box 3, Folder 22, MS 1490, CHL.

28 Pratt, "Materiality," 125–126.

29 William Phelps, "The Answer," *Times and Seasons* [Nauvoo, Ill.], 1 January 1844, 758. See Samuel Morris Brown, *In Heaven as It Is on Earth: Joseph Smith and the Early Mormon Conquest of Death* (New York: Oxford University Press, 2012), 275.

30 Eliza R. Snow, "My Father in Heaven," *Times and Seasons*, 15 November 1845, 1039.

31 Phelps, "The Answer," 758.

32 See Corbin Volluz, "Jesus Christ as Elder Brother," *BYU Studies* 45 (2006): 141–158. On the language and ritual of adoption for Latter-day Saints, see Samuel M. Brown, "Early Mormon Adoption Theology and the Mechanics of Salvation," *Journal of Mormon History* 37 (Summer 2011): 3–52; Jonathan A. Stapley, "Adoptive Sealing Ritual in Mormonism," *Journal of Mormon History* 37 (Summer 2011): 53–117.

33 Minutes of 16 February 1849, GCM, Box 2, Folder 8, CHL.

34 Eliza R. Snow, *Biography and Family Record of Lorenzo Snow* (Salt Lake City: Deseret News, 1884), 10.

35 Athanasius, *Against the Gentiles*, trans. Archibald Robertson, in Philip Schaff and Henry Wace, eds., *A Select Library of Nicene and Post-Nicene Fathers of the Christian Church* (New York: Christian Literature Company, 1892), 4:65.

36 See the discussion in Givens, *Wrestling*, 256–264.

37 Martin Luther in Kurt E. Marquart, "Luther and Theosis," *Concordia Theological Quarterly* 64 (July 2000): 182–205.

38 See Taylor G. Petrey, *Resurrecting Parts: Early Christians on Desire, Reproduction, and Sexual Difference* (New York: Routledge, 2016), 74.

39 Young discourse of 9 April 1852, Box 2, Folder 37, GCM.

40 Ibid.

41 Parley P. Pratt, *The Key to the Science of Theology* (Liverpool: F. D. Richards, 1855), 50. See Givens, *Wrestling*, 156–163.

42 Wilford Woodruff Journal, 9 April 1852, WWJ, 3:129.

43 L. John Nuttall Journal, 7 February 1877, typescript, MSS 790, HBLL.

44 Thomas Evans Jeremy Journal, 30 September 1852, MS 1249, CHL.

45 Young discourse of 8 February 1857, JD, 4:217. See Gary James Bergera, *Conflict in the Quorum: Orson Pratt, Brigham Young, Joseph Smith* (Salt Lake City: Signature Books, 2002), chaps. 5 and 6.

46 Young discourse of 8 October 1854, transcript by George D. Watt, Box 2, Folder 25, CR 100 317, CHL. For "one eternal round," see also D&C 3:2, D&C 35:1.

47 Minutes of 2 September 1849, Box 2, Folder 14, GCM.

48 Jill M. Derr and Karen L. Davidson, eds., *Eliza R. Snow: The Complete Poetry* (Provo, Utah: Brigham Young University Press, 2009), 842.

49 Tullidge in "Leaders in the Mormon Reform Movement," *Phrenological Journal*, July 1871, 31; Amasa Lyman, discourse of 16 March 1862, *Millennial Star*, 24 May 1862, 323; Brigham Young comment in WWJ, 26 December 1866, 6:308; Wilford Woodruff comment in WWJ, 21 January 1867, 6:321; minutes of Lyman ecclesiastical trial, 6 April 1867, Box 70, Folder 21, BYP. See Edward Leo Lyman, *Amasa Mason Lyman, Mormon Apostle and Apostate: A Study in Dedication* (Salt Lake City: University of Utah Press, 2009), chaps. 8 and 9.

50 "Transgressors" in Young discourse of 21 September 1856, JD, 4:53; other quotes in Young discourse of 8 February 1857, JD, 4:219–20.

51 *The Doctrine and Covenants of the Church of Jesus Christ of Latter Day Saints* (Nauvoo, Ill.: John Taylor, 1844), 444 [D&C 135]; Young discourse of 27 June 1854, George D. Watt shorthand notes, papers of George D. Watt, CHL, transcript by

LaJean P. Carruth, copy in author's possession; "be crowned" in Young discourse of 8 October 1854.

52 The argument here is congruent with Stephen Prothero, *American Jesus: How the Son of God Became a National Icon* (New York: Farrar, Straus and Giroux, 2003), 183–186.

53 William Phelps, "Joseph Smith," *Times and Seasons*, 1 August 1844, 607.

54 George Q. Cannon Journal, 17 January 1878, excerpted in *Instructor* 80 (June 1945): 259.

55 See Matthew Bowman, "The Crisis of Mormon Christology: History, Progress, and Protestantism, 1880–1930," *Fides et Historia* 40 (Summer/Fall 2008): 11–23.

56 James E. Talmage, *The Articles of Faith* (Salt Lake City: Deseret News, 1899), 73, 66, 41. See Givens, *Wrestling*, 313–314.

57 "Should be understood" and "more advanced" in Charles Penrose, "A Piece of Impertinence," *Deseret Evening News*, 21 March 1900, 4; "single sermon" in Penrose, "Our Father Adam," *Improvement Era* [Salt Lake City], September 1902, 873, 878–879; Penrose, discourse of 6 April 1916, *Eighty-Sixth Annual Conference April 6, 7, and 9, 1916* (Salt Lake City: Deseret News, 1916), 17. See David John Buerger, "The Adam-God Doctrine," *Dialogue: A Journal of Mormon Thought* 15 (Spring 1982): 38–40.

58 James Talmage Journal, 30 June 1916, MSS 229, HBLL.

59 James Talmage, *Jesus the Christ: A Study of Messiah and His Mission According to Holy Scriptures both Ancient and Modern* (Salt Lake City: Deseret News 1915), 613, 669, n. 8, 718. On the significance of Gethsemane within Latter-day Saint thought, see Douglas Davies, "Gethsemane and Calvary in LDS Soteriology," *Dialogue* 34 (Fall–Winter 2001): 19–29.

60 "The Father and the Son," *Improvement Era*, August 1916, 934–942.

61 The following paragraphs are influenced by Bradley Kime, "Exhibiting Theology: James E. Talmage and Mormon Public Relations, 1915–20," *Journal of Mormon History* 40 (Winter 2014): 208–238.

62 See Gaines Foster, *Moral Reconstruction: Christian Lobbyists and the Federal Legislation of Morality, 1865–1920* (Chapel Hill: University of North Carolina Press, 2002), 82–84.

63 James Talmage, *The Vitality of Mormonism: Brief Essays on Distinctive Doctrines* (Boston: Gorham Press, 1919), 26.

64 "Immoral purposes" from James Talmage, "Christianity Falsely So-Called," *Improvement Era*, January 1920, 196–205; other quotes from "Report of World Commission on Mormonism," *The World's Moral Problems: Addresses at the Third World's Christian Citizenship Conference* (Pittsburgh: National Reform Association, 1920), 224, 228, 231.

65 "Flays Mormons at Citizenship Conference in Mosque Session," *Pittsburgh Press*, 12 November 1919, 1.

66 Talmage, "Christianity Falsely So-Called."

7. THE JEHOVAH OF THE TEMPLE

1 Boyd K. Packer, *The Holy Temple* (Salt Lake City: Bookcraft, 1980), 11.

2 Douglas Davies distinguishes between ward, domestic, and temple Mormonism. See *The Mormon Culture of Salvation: Force, Grace and Glory* (Aldershot, U.K.: Ashgate, 2000), esp. chaps. 3 and 5.

3 Gordon B. Hinckley, "Keeping the Temple Holy," *Ensign*, May 1990, 49–52. Hinckley's words came just before the church introduced significant revisions to the ordinance. See John-Charles Duffy, "Concealing the Body, Concealing the Sacred: The Decline of Ritual Nudity in Mormon Temples," *Journal of Ritual Studies* 21 (2007): 13, n. 10.

4 Mircea Eliade, *The Sacred and the Profane: The Nature of Religion*, trans. Willard R. Trask (New York: Harcourt, 1959), 20.

5 For a useful overview of the development of Christian sacred space and the power dynamics surrounding it, see Jeanne Halgren Kilde, *Sacred Power, Sacred Space: An Introduction to Christian Architecture and Worship* (New York: Oxford University Press, 2008).

6 For example, on the need for the ordination of "apostles," see "R" [Sidney Rigdon], "The Ancient Order of Things," *Messenger and Advocate* [Kirtland, Ohio], September 1835, 182–185.

7 "Explanation of the Plat of the City of Zion," ca. 25 June 1833, in JSP D3, 127.

8 Revelation of 16 April 1830, in *Painesville Telegraph* [Ohio], 19 April 1831, JSP D1, 138 [D&C 22].

9 See David G. Hackett, *That Religion in Which All Men Agree: Freemasonry in American Culture* (Berkeley: 2014), esp. 26–27; John L. Brooke, *The Refiner's Fire: The Making of Mormon Cosmology, 1644–1844* (Cambridge: Cambridge University Press, 1994), chap. 4; Catherine L. Albanese, *A Republic of Mind and Spirit: A Cultural History of American Metaphysical Religion* (New Haven, Conn.: Yale University Press, 2007), 51–53.

10 William Morgan, *Illustrations of Masonry* (Batavia: n.p., 1826), 63–94 (quotes on 76–77, 94).

11 [Thomas Smith Webb], *The Freemason's Monitor . . . By a Royal Arch Mason* (Albany, N.Y.: Spencer and Webb, 1797), 153–180, 244–261 (quotes on 170, 154, 244–245). For overviews of both the Master Mason degree and the Royal Arch degree, see Hackett, *That Religion*, 85–94; and Albanese, *A Republic of Mind and Spirit*, 133–136.

12 On the relationship between Masonry and Christianity, see Steven C. Bullock, *Revolutionary Brotherhood: Freemasonry and the Transformation of the American Social Order, 1730–1840* (Chapel Hill: University of North Carolina Press, 1996), chap. 6; Hackett, *That Religion*, 77–83, 94–103.

13 "Genesis," pages 9–10, in Scott H. Faulring, Kent P. Jackson, and Robert J. Matthews, eds., *Joseph Smith's New Translation of the Bible: Original Manuscripts* (Provo, Utah: Religious Studies Center of Brigham Young University, 2004) [Moses 5:29–31, 49–51].

14 On Lucinda Pendleton Harris's possible earthly marriage to Joseph Smith, compare Todd Compton, *In Sacred Loneliness: The Plural Wives of Joseph Smith* (Salt Lake City: Signature Books, 1997), 49–51; and Brian C. Hales, *Joseph Smith's Polygamy*, vol. 1, *History* (Salt Lake City: Kofford Books, 2013), 58–67.

15 Joseph Smith Journal, 15 October 1843, JSP J3, 115.

16 See Michael W. Homer, *Joseph's Temples: The Dynamic Relationship between Freemasonry and Mormonism* (Salt Lake City: University of Utah Press, 2014), chap. 6.

17 Joseph Smith Journal, 4 May 1842, JSP J2, 53.

18 Willard Richards, draft of history (for 4 May 1842), ca. 1845, accessed 23 October 2015, http://josephsmithpapers.org/paperSummary/history-draft-1-january-30-june-1842. When church clerk Thomas Bullock wrote out Richards's notes, he revised this passage to read "in the presence of the Eloheim," reflecting the Latter-day Saint belief in a plurality of gods. See History, Vol. C-1, 1328, CR 100 102, CHL.

19 L. John Nuttall Journal, 7 February 1877, typescript, MSS 790, HBLL. Spelling and punctuation corrected.

20 "J's Lodge" is from the journal of William Clayton, 21 November 1843, quoted in Andrew Ehat, "Joseph Smith's Introduction of Temple Ordinances and the 1844 Mormon Succession Question" (M.A. thesis, Brigham Young University, 1982), 104; Heber Kimball Journal, later reference to June 1842, in Stanley B. Kimball, ed., *On the Potter's Wheel: The Diaries of Heber C. Kimball* (Salt Lake City: Signature Books, 1987), 55; Brigham Young Journal, 30 October and 1 November 1843, Box 71, Folder 3, BYP; numbers of initiates in Devery S. Anderson and Gary James Bergera, *Joseph Smith's Quorum of the Anointed, 1842–1845: A Documentary History* (Salt Lake City: Signature Books, 2005), 75–77.

21 Heber Kimball to Parley Pratt, 17 June 1842, MS 897, CHL; Joseph Fielding Journal, ca. 1843, in Andrew F. Ehat, ed., "'They Might Have Known That He Was Not a Fallen Prophet': The Nauvoo Journal of Joseph Fielding," *BYU Studies* 19 (1979): 145.

22 Mr. & Mrs. McGee [Increase and Maria Van Deusen], *The Mormon Endowment: A Secret Drama, or Conspiracy, in the Nauvoo-Temple* (Syracuse, N.Y.: N. M. D. Lathrop, 1847), 4. The Van Deusens published subsequent editions of this work in their own name.

23 Genesis 3:7.

24 Samuel M. Brown, *In Heaven As It Is on Earth: Joseph Smith and the Early Mormon Conquest of Death* (New York: Oxford University Press, 2012), 183–188, 195–201.

25 WWJ, 21 January 1844, 2:341.

26 William Clayton Journal, 16 May 1843, in George D. Smith, ed., *An Intimate Chronicle: The Journals of William Clayton* (Salt Lake City: Signature Books, 1991), 102 [D&C 131:1–2].

27 Revelation of 19 January 1841, in Book of the Law of the Lord, page 6, accessed 17 May 2015, http://josephsmithpapers.org/paperSummary/revelation-19-january -1841-dc-124 [D&C 124:40–41]; Joseph Smith discourse of 8 April 1844, report by William Clayton, in GCM, Box 1, Folder 19. I have expanded the abbreviations in Clayton's notes.

28 Minutes of 8 August 1844, Box 1, folder 23, GCM.

29 William Clayton Journal (kept for Heber C. Kimball), 13 December 1845, typescript at HBLL.

30 John Hyde Jr., *Mormonism: Its Leaders and Designs* (New York: W. P. Fetridge & Co., 1857), 93. Emphasis in original.

31 Brigham Young discourse of 8 October 1854, transcript by George D. Watt, Box 2, Folder 35, CR 100 317, CHL.

32 Hannah Tapfield King, "Women of the Scriptures," *Woman's Exponent*, 1 November 1903, 41. See Boyd Jay Petersen, "'Redeemed from the Curse Placed upon Her': Dialogic Discourse on Eve in the *Woman's Exponent*," *Journal of Mormon History* 40 (Winter 2014): 135–174.

33 George Miller in William Clayton Journal, 21 Dec. 1845, in Devery S. Anderson and Gary James Bergera, eds., *The Nauvoo Endowment Companies, 1845–1846: A Documentary History* (Salt Lake City: Signature Books, 2005), 117; Catherine Lewis, *Narrative of Some of the Proceedings of the Mormons* (Lynn, Mass.: n.p., 1848), 9; Brigham Young in Nuttall Journal, 7 February 1877; John Taylor, *An Examination into and an Elucidation of the Great Principle of the Mediation and Atonement of Our Lord and Savior Jesus Christ* (Salt Lake City: Deseret News, 1882), 112.

34 Abraham 3:24, originally published in *Times and Seasons* [Nauvoo, Ill.], 15 March 1842, 720.

35 See Robert J. Wilkinson, *Tetragrammaton: Western Christians and the Hebrew Name of God: From the Beginnings to the Seventeenth Century* (Leiden, The Netherlands: Brill, 2015), esp. chaps. 1 and 2, 212, 354–359.

36 *A Collection of Sacred Hymns for the Church of the Latter Day Saints, Selected by Emma Smith* (Kirtland, Ohio: F. G. Williams & co., 1835), 19 and 73; *Proclamation of the Twelve Apostles of the Church of Jesus Christ of Latter-day Saints* (n.p., 1845), 1. See Thomas G. Alexander, "The Reconstruction of Mormon Doctrine: From Joseph Smith to

Progressive Theology," *Sunstone*, July/August 1980, 28; and Douglas Davies, *Joseph Smith, Jesus, and Satanic Opposition: Atonement, Evil and the Mormon Vision* (Aldershot, U.K.: Ashgate, 2010), 69–70.

37 Brigham Young discourse of 9 April 1852, JD 1:51.

38 Brigham Young comments recorded in Joseph F. Smith Journal, 17 June 1871, Box 2, Folder 9, MS 1325, CHL. See David John Buerger, "The Adam-God Doctrine," *Dialogue* 15 (Spring 1982): 19.

39 Brigham Young discourse of 8 February 1857, JD 4:217, 216.

40 On shifting Mormon views of Jehovah, see Boyd Kirkland, "Elohim and Jehovah in Mormon Thought," *Dialogue* 19 (Spring 1986): 77–93.

41 *Juvenile Instructor*, 30 September 1871, 155; Franklin Richards discourse of 30 August 1885, JD 26:300.

42 Colossians 1:16; John 8:58; Exodus 3:14. See the discussion in Wilkinson, *Tetragrammaton*, 105–108.

43 Irenaeus, *Against Heresies*, 4.10.1, trans. John Keble (London: James Parker and Co., 1872), 333. See Elaine Pagels, *Beyond Belief: The Secret Gospel of Thomas* (New York: Random House, 2005), esp. chaps. 4 and 5.

44 Justin, *Dialogue with Trypho* 127, trans. G. J. Davie (Oxford: J. H. and James Parker, 1862), 228.

45 Irenaeus, *Demonstration of the Apostolic Preaching*, 44, trans. J. A. Robinson (London: SPCK, 1920), 110. For an argument that these passages reflect the influence of premonotheistic Israelite religion on early Christianity, see Margaret Barker, *The Great Angel: A Study of Israel's Second God* (Louisville, Ky.: Westminster / John Knox Press, 1992).

46 Genesis 32:30; Martin Luther, *Lectures on Genesis*, in LW, 6:144.

47 Book I, chapter 13, section 10, in John Calvin, *Institutes of the Christian Religion*, trans. Henry Beveridge (Grand Rapids, Mich.: Eerdmans, 1989), 1:118.

48 John Edwards, "Blank Bible," in Stephen Stein, ed., *Works of Jonathan Edwards*, vol. 24 (New Haven, Conn.: Yale University Press, 2006), 1137. On Edwards, see Douglas Sweeney, *Edwards the Exegete: Biblical Interpretation and Anglo-Protestant Culture on the Edge of the Enlightenment* (New York: Oxford University Press, 2015), esp. chap. 5.

49 Ethan Smith, *Treatise on the Character of Jesus Christ, and on the Trinity* (Boston: R. P. & C. Williams, 1814), esp. chap. 6; Ethan Smith, *Key to the Revelation* (New York: J. & J. Harper, 1833), 55. See Terryl Givens, *Wrestling the Angel: The Foundations of Mormon Thought: Cosmos, God, Humanity* (New York: Oxford University Press, 2015), 118.

50 Wilford Woodruff discourse of 7 April 1895, *Millennial Star*, 6 June 1895, 355.

51 James Talmage, *Jesus the Christ: A Study of Messiah and His Mission According to Holy Scriptures Both Ancient and Modern* (Salt Lake City: Deseret News, 1915), iii, 9.

52 Talmage, *Jesus the Christ*, 10, 38, 32, 39.

53 Charles Penrose discourse of 6 April 1916, *Eighty-Sixth Annual Conference . . . April 6, 7, and 9, 1916* (Salt Lake City: Deseret News, 1916), 18–19; "The Father and the Son," *Improvement Era* [Salt Lake City], August 1916, 934–942.

54 Bruce R. McConkie, "Fireside Address," Brigham Young University, 1 June 1980, accessed 23 October 2015, https://speeches.byu.edu/talks/bruce-r-mcconkie_seven-deadly-heresies/.

55 Genesis 2:25; Jonathan Z. Smith, "The Garments of Shame," *History of Religions* 5 (Winter 1966): 217–238. Compare Laurie Guy, "'Naked Baptism' in the Early Church: The Rhetoric and Reality," *Journal of Religious History* 27 (June 2003): 133–142.

56 On the changes in the initiatory, see John-Charles Duffy, "Concealing the Body, Concealing the Sacred: The Decline of Ritual Nudity in Mormon Temples," *Journal of Ritual Studies* 21 (2007): 1–21.

57 See Devery Scott Anderson, ed., *The Development of LDS Temple Worship, 1846–2000: A Documentary History* (Salt Lake City: Signature Books, 2011), 218.

58 See John Dart, "Mormons Modify Temple Rites," *Los Angeles Times*, 5 May 1990.

59 For an overview, see Edward L. Kimball, "The History of LDS Temple Admission Standards," *Journal of Mormon History* 24 (Spring 1998): 135–176.

60 Brigham Young, Heber C. Kimball, and Jedediah M. Grant to Stake Presidents and Bishops in Iron and Washington Counties, 2 March 1856, in Parowan Historical Record, excerpted in Anderson, *The Development of LDS Temple Worship*, xxix. See David John Buerger, *Mysteries of Godliness: A History of Mormon Temple Worship* (San Francisco: Smith Research Associates, 1994), 100.

61 "Oath-bound" in Edward L. Kimball, "The History of LDS Temple Admission Standards," 155; *General Handbook of Instructions* (Salt Lake City: Church of Jesus Christ of Latter-day Saints, 1976), in Anderson, *The Development of LDS Temple Worship*, 419.

62 Hinckley, "Keeping the Temple Holy"; Temple recommend questions (from 2000) in Anderson, *The Development of LDS Temple Worship*, 477–478.

63 Packer, *The Holy Temple*, 4–5; 1998 handbook in Anderson, *The Development of LDS Temple Worship*, 476.

64 *Times and Seasons*, 15 October 1841, 577; Obadiah 21; Revelation 11:1; WWJ, 21 January 1843 ("how are they"), 2:341–342; WWJ, 28 December 1843 (Young), 2:333.

65 Statistics from Lisle Brown, *Nauvoo Sealings, Adoptions, and Anointings* (Salt Lake City: Smith-Pettit Foundation, 2006), 361. See Richard E. Bennett, "'The Upper Room' The Nature and Development of Latter-day Saint Temple Work, 1846–1855," *Journal of Mormon History* 41 (April 2015): 1–34.

66 Eliza R. Snow, "Temple Song," in Jill Mulvay Derr and Karen Lynn Davidson, *Eliza R. Snow: The Complete Poetry* (Provo and Salt Lake City: Brigham Young University Press and University of Utah Press, 2009), 896.

67 "Vision of the Redemption of the Dead," *Improvement Era*, December 1918, 166–170 [D&C 138].

68 Gordon B. Hinckley, "Closing Remarks," *Ensign* [Salt Lake City], November 2004, 105.

69 Robert Bruce Flanders, *Nauvoo: Kingdom on the Mississippi* (Urbana: University of Illinois Press, 1965), 209–210.

70 Walter Martin, *The Kingdom of the Cults* (Minneapolis: Bethany House, rev. ed. 2003), 232; Armand L. Mauss, "Culture, Charisma, and Change: Reflections on Mormon Temple Worship," *Dialogue* 20 (Winter 1987): 77–83.

8. THE GREAT BRIDEGROOM

1 John 2:1–11.

2 Maurice F. Wiles, *The Spiritual Gospel: The Interpretation of the Fourth Gospel in the Early Church* (Cambridge: Cambridge University Press, 1960), 42–45; Frederick Dale Bruner, *The Gospel of John: A Commentary* (Grand Rapids, Mich.: Eerdmans, 2012), 134–135.

3 Orson Hyde discourse of 6 October 1854, *Deseret News*, 19 October 1854.

4 1 Peter 2:21–25.

5 Chalcedonian definition in Jaroslav Pelikan and Valerie Hotchkiss, eds., *Creeds and Confessions of Faith in the Christian Tradition*, vol. 1 (New Haven, Conn.: Yale University Press, 2003), 181.

6 1 Corinthians 7:9, 32; Clement, *Stromateis*, 3:49, 4, 82, in *Alexandrian Christianity*, trans. and eds., John Ernest Leonard Oulton and Henry Chadwick (Philadelphia: Westminster Press, 1954), 62–63, 42, 78.

7 Tertullian, *To His Wife*, 3, and *On Monogamy*, 5, both in William P. Le Saint, trans. and ed., *Tertullian: Treatises on Marriage and Remarriage* (Westminster, Md.: Newman Press, 1951), 12, 80. See the discussion of Clement and Tertullian in Anthony Le Donne, *The Wife of Jesus: Ancient Texts and Modern Scandals* (London: Oneworld, 2013), 139–142.

8 See the discussion in Karen L. King, "The Place of the Gospel of Philip in the Context of Early Christian Claims about Jesus's Marital Status," *New Testament Studies* 59 (October 2013): 565–587.

9 For the story of John Hartmann, see Robert E. Lerner, *The Heresy of the Free Spirit in the Later Middle Ages* (Berkeley: University of California Press, 1972), 134–139.

10 See Hans Boersma, *Embodiment and Virtue in Gregory of Nyssa: An Anagogical Approach* (Oxford: Oxford University Press, 2013), esp. chap. 3. On early Christian understandings of sexuality and the resurrected body, see Taylor G. Petrey, *Resurrecting Parts: Early Christians on Desire, Reproduction, and Sexual Difference* (New York: Routledge, 2016).

11 Revelation 19:9, 21:9.

12 *Hadewijch: The Complete Works*, trans. Columba Hart (New York: Paulist Press, 1980), 281. See Caroline Walker Bynum, *Holy Feast and Holy Fast: The Religious Significance of Food to Medieval Women* (Berkeley: University of California Press, 1987), 153–160.

13 Bernard, *Canticles*, 20.2, in Jaroslav Pelikan, *Jesus through the Centuries: His Place in the History of Culture* (New Haven, Conn.: Yale University Press, 1985), 126. On the Moravian devotion to Jesus's side wound, see Jon Sensbach, *Rebecca's Revival: Creating Black Christianity in the Atlantic World* (Cambridge, Mass.: Harvard University Press, 2005), 179–182.

14 Joseph Smith discourse of 7 April 1844, minutes of Thomas Bullock (abbreviations expanded), Box 1, Folder 20, GCM; WWJ, 11 June 1843, 2:240; revelation of 12 July 1843, copy in handwriting of Joseph Kingsbury, Box 1, Folder 75, MS 4583, CHL [D&C 132:19–20].

15 Minutes of 9 December 1847, Box 12, Folder 4, transcript by Edyth Romney, Leonard J. Arrington Papers, MSS 10, Special Collections, Merrill-Cazier Library, Utah State University, Logan, Utah.

16 Heber C. Kimball Journal, 1 February 1844 and 1 April 1844 (one entry in Vilate Kimball's handwriting), in Stanley B. Kimball, ed., *On the Potter's Wheel: The Diaries of Heber C. Kimball* (Salt Lake City: Signature Books, 1987), 56–57.

17 The latter phrase is from Heber C. Kimball Journal, 7 December 1845, in Kimball, *On the Potter's Wheel*, 164.

18 Heber C. Kimball Journal, Diary, 26 December 1845, kept by William Clayton, typescript at HBLL, 126.

19 Joseph Smith quoted in WWJ, 10 March 1844, 2:361–362. See Glen Leonard, *Nauvoo: A Place of Peace, A People of Promise* (Salt Lake City: Deseret Book, 2002), 260–261.

20 See Devery S. Anderson, *The Development of LDS Temple Worship, 1846–2000: A Documentary History* (Salt Lake City: Signature Books, 2011), xli–xlv.

21 Heber C. Kimball Journal, 1 February 1844 and 1 April.

22 Mark 14:3–9; Matthew 26:6–13; Luke 7:36–50; John 12:1–8.

23 John Pack, autobiography, reference to 13 January 1847, accessed 1 April 2015, https://picasaweb.google.com/johnpackfamily.com/JohnPackJournal#5733587139 085234594.

24 Ruth Page Rogers Journal, 6 August 1879, typescript in author's possession; Samuel H. Rogers Journal, 22 September 1879, MS 1134, HBLL. On the Rogers family, see Paula Kelly Harline, *The Polygamous Wives Writing Club: From the Diaries of Mormon Pioneer Women* (New York: Oxford University Press, 2014), chap. 2.

25 Joseph F. Smith to Susa Young Gates, 8 Jan. 1889, Susa Young Gates Papers, MS 7692, Box 54, Folder 1, CHL. Emphasis in original.

26 Jacob 2:27, 30.

27 Revelation of 12 July 1843 [D&C 132:66].

28 Brigham Young discourse of 8 October 1861, Box 4, Folder 24, CR 100 317, CHL.

29 Augusta Adams to Brigham Young, 20 January 1846, Box 66, Folder 7, BYP.

30 Augusta Adams, last will and testament, 21 February 1848; certificate of sealing in handwriting of Thomas Bullock, 14 April 1848, both in Box 66, Folder 7, BYP.

31 Brigham Young discourse of 27 December 1847, Box 1, Folder 61, GCM. Abbreviations expanded.

32 John W. Gunnison, *The Mormons or, Latter-Day Saints, in the Valley of the Great Salt Lake* (Philadelphia: Lippincott, Grambo, & Co., 1852), 68–69; "Br. Holly and the Sentinel," *Frontier Guardian*, 26 December 1851.

33 See the documents in B. Carmon Hardy, *Doing the Works of Abraham: Mormon Polygamy, Its Origin, Practice, and Demise* (Norman, Okla.: Arthur H. Clark, 2007), chap. 3.

34 Jedediah Grant discourse of 7 August 1853, transcript by George D. Watt, in CR 100 317, CHL. See JD 1:345–346. On Grant's sermon, see Le Donne, *The Wife of Jesus*, 77–80.

35 See Gary James Bergera, *Conflict in the Quorum: Orson Pratt, Brigham Young, Joseph Smith* (Salt Lake City: Signature Books, 2002), chaps. 1 and 2.

36 See Ronald W. Walker, "The Salt Lake Tabernacle in the Nineteenth Century: A Glimpse of Early Mormonism," *Journal of Mormon History* 31 (Fall 2005): 198–240.

37 *Deseret News Extra*, 14 September 1852, 14–23.

38 *The Seer* [Washington, D.C.], October 1853, 158. Emphasis in original. On Pratt and a married Jesus, see Le Donne, *The Wife of Jesus*, 74–77.

39 *The Seer*, November 1853, 172.

40 Brigham Young to Orson Pratt, 29 July 1853 (emphasis in original), retained draft in Box 17, Folder 9, BYP.

41 Orson Hyde discourse of 6 October 1854, *Deseret News*, 19 October 1854.

42 Brigham Young discourse of 6 October 1854, *Deseret News*, 26 October 1854.

43 *New York Times*, 27 December 1854. Emphasis in original.

44 Orson Hyde discourse of 18 March 1855, *Deseret News*, 28 March 1855.

45 John Hanson Beadle and Ovando James Hollister, *Polygamy: Or, The Mysteries and Crimes of Mormonism* (Philadelphia: The National Publishing Co., 1882), 306.

46 Young discourse of 10 February 1867, JD 11:328.

47 Young discourse of 13 November 1870, JD 13:309.

48 Joseph F. Smith Journal, 13 November 1870, MS 1325, Box 2, Folder 8, CHL.

49 WWJ, 22 July 1883, 8:187; Joseph F. Smith, 20 March 1899 discourse, in *Millennial Star*, 15 February 1900, 97.

50 Abraham H. Cannon Journal, 5 April 1894, in Edward Leo Lyman, ed., *Candid Insights of a Mormon Apostle: The Diaries of Abraham H. Cannon, 1889–1895* (Salt Lake City: Signature Books, 2010), 491.

51 Anthony W. Ivins Journal, 2 July 1899, in Elizabeth Oberdick Anderson, ed., *Cowboy Apostle: The Diaries of Anthony W. Ivins, 1875–1932* (Salt Lake City: Signature Books, 2013), 211. See also Rudger Clawson Journal, 2 July 1899, in Stan Larson, ed., *A Ministry of Meetings: The Apostolic Diaries of Rudger Clawson* (Salt Lake City: Signature Books, 1993), 72. The fact that Clawson and Ivins recorded Cannon's statement, with nearly identical wording, suggests that they regarded the teaching as very significant.

52 Josiah Edwin Hickman, patriarchal blessing of 4 December 1900 (with Hickman's comments), in Journal I, typescript accessed 26 October 2015, http://hickmansfamily.homestead.com/files/JEH_I_ocr.pdf.

53 Hickman Journal, 24 June 1917, Journal H, accessed 26 October 2015, http://hickmansfamily.homestead.com/files/JEH_H_ocr.pdf.

54 James Talmage, *Jesus the Christ: A Study of Messiah and His Mission according to Holy Scriptures both Ancient and Modern* (Salt Lake City: Deseret News 1915), 682.

55 "The Origin of Man," *Improvement Era*, November 1909, 78.

56 James Talmage, "The Eternity of Sex," *Young Woman's Journal* [Salt Lake City], October 1914, 600–604; Joseph F. Smith, *Doctrines of Salvation*, ed. Bruce R. McConkie, vol. 2 (Salt Lake City: Bookcraft, 1955), 287–288; Bruce R. McConkie, *Mormon Doctrine* (Salt Lake City: Bookcraft, 1958), 238–239, 522–523.

57 "Peculiar Questions Briefly Answered," *Improvement Era* [Salt Lake City], September 1912, 1042.

58 B. H. Roberts, "Answer Given to Ten Reasons Why 'Christians' Can Not Fellowship with Latter-day Saints," *Liahona, The Elders' Journal* [Independence, Mo.], 30 August 1921, 95.

59 Letter from J. Ricks Smith to Joseph Fielding Smith, 17 March 1963, with the latter's comments, copy in author's possession. See Mosiah 15:10–12.

60 Bruce R. McConkie, *New Testament Doctrinal Commentary*, vol. 1, *The Gospels* (Salt Lake City: Bookcraft, 1965), 135–136.

61 Wayne Lynn, "I Have a Question," *Ensign*, June 1997, 60–61.

62 Nikos Kazantzakis, *The Last Temptation of Christ*, trans. P. A. Bien (New York: Simon & Schuster, 1960), 3.

63 "Film on Christ Brings Out Pickets," *New York Times*, 21 July 1988.

64 William Phipps, *Was Jesus Married?* (New York: Harper & Row, 1970); Phipps, "The Case for a Married Jesus," *Dialogue* 7 (1972): 44–49.

65 Ogden Kraut, *Jesus Was Married* (Salt Lake City: Ogden Kraut, 1969), 16 ("against the traditional"), 32 ("caused the persecution"), 61 ("law of procreation"). See Vern G. Swanson, *Dynasty of the Holy Grail: Mormonism's Sacred Bloodline* (Springville, Utah: Cedar Fort, 2006), 406, n. 52.

66 Joseph W. Musser, "Did Jesus Marry, and Did He Live the Patriarchal Law?" *Truth* [Salt Lake City], January 1949, 197–209.

67 Jan Karel van Baalen, *The Chaos of Cults: A Study in Present-Day Isms* (Grand Rapids, Mich.: Eerdmans, 1947, 6th ed.), 139; J. Oswald Sanders, *Heresies Ancient and Modern* (London: Marshall, Morgan, & Scott, 1948), 112–113; Anthony A. Hoekema, *The Four Major Cults* (Grand Rapids, Mich.: Eerdmans, 1963), 56.

68 Ed Decker, *Decker's Complete Handbook on Mormonism* (Eugene, Or.: Harvest House, 1995), 255–259.

69 Bills quoted in "Claims of a Married Jesus Aren't LDS Church Doctrine," *Deseret News*, 18 May 2006.

70 Daniel Peterson and Stephen Ricks, *Offenders for a Word: How Anti-Mormons Play Word Games to Attack the Latter-day Saints* (Salt Lake City: Aspen Books, 1992), 129–130, n. 439.

71 Richard Holzapfel, Andrew Skinner, and Thomas Wayment, *What Da Vinci Didn't Know: An LDS Perspective* (Salt Lake City: Deseret Book, 2006), chap. 3, quotes at 49, 50.

72 See J. Spencer Fluhman, *"A Peculiar People": Anti-Mormonism and the Making of Religion in Nineteenth-Century America* (Chapel Hill: University of North Carolina Press, 2012), 1.

9. THE GREAT WHITE GOD

1 See Bruce A. Van Orden, *Prisoner for Conscience' Sake: The Life of George Reynolds* (Salt Lake City: Deseret Books, 1992); and Sarah Barringer Gordon, *The Mormon Ques-*

tion: Polygamy and Constitutional Conflict in Nineteenth-Century America (Chapel Hill: University of North Carolina Press, 2002), chap. 3.

2   George Reynolds, "Man and His Varieties," *Juvenile Instructor*, 15 October 1868, 157.

3   Reynolds, "Man and His Varieties," *Juvenile Instructor*, 15 August 1868, 125 ("Patagonia"); 15 October 1868, 157 ("pure Negro" and "Egypt was discovered"); 15 November 1868, 173 ("day will come").

4   Genesis 9:22, 25.

5   David M. Goldenberg, *The Curse of Ham: Race and Slavery in Early Judaism, Christianity, and Islam* (Princeton, N.J.: Princeton University Press, 2003), chap. 12.

6   Phyllis Wheatley, quoted in Goldenberg, *The Curse of Ham*, 178; Adam Clarke, *The Holy Bible, Containing the Old and New Testaments . . . with a Commentary and Critical Notes*, vol. 1 (Baltimore, Md.: John J. Harrod, 1834), 61. See Stephen R. Haynes, *Noah's Curse: The Biblical Justification of American Slavery* (New York: Oxford University Press, 2002); Thomas Virgil Peterson, *Ham and Japheth: The Mythic World of Whites in the Antebellum South* (Metuchen, N.J.: Scarecrow Press, 1978). On black conversion leading to lighter skin, see Jon F. Sensbach, *Rebecca's Revival: Creating Black Christianity in the Atlantic World* (Cambridge, Mass.: Harvard University Press, 2005), 166, 197–199.

7   2 Nephi 5:21 ("exceeding"); 2 Nephi 5:23 ("mixeth"); 2 Nephi 30:6 ("scales of darkness"); 2 Nephi 26:33 ("all are alike"). See Armand Mauss, *All Abraham's Children: Changing Mormon Conceptions of Lineage and Race* (Urbana: University of Illinois Press, 2003), 117.

8   3 Nephi 19:25 ("countenance"), 30 ("even as Jesus"); Mark 9:3 ("white as snow"); 1 Nephi 11:13 ("fair and white").

9   Moses 7:22; Abraham 1:21, 27. See Ryan Stuart Bingham, "Curses and Marks: Racial Dispensation and Dispensation of Race in Joseph Smith's Bible Revision and the Book of Abraham," *Journal of Mormon History* 41 (Summer 2015): 34–56.

10   Spencer Kimball, discourse of 7 Oct. 1960, *One Hundred and Thirtieth Semi-Annual Conference . . . October 7, 8, and 9, 1960* (Salt Lake City: Church of Jesus Christ of Latter-day Saints, 1960), 34.

11   Brigham Young discourse of 5 Feb. 1852, George D. Watt typescript, Box 1, Folder 17, CR 100 317, CHL.

12   See W. Paul Reeve, *Religion of a Different Color: Race and the Mormon Struggle for Whiteness* (New York: Oxford University Press, 2015), chaps. 4 and 5.

13   First Presidency statement in Newell G. Bringhurst, *Saints, Slaves, and Blacks: The Changing Place of Black People within Mormonism* (Westport, Conn.: Greenwood Press, 1981), 230.

14   Joseph Fielding Smith, *Doctrines of Salvation*, vol. 1 (Salt Lake City: Bookcraft, 1954), 65–66.

15 *Letter from Publius Lentulus, to the Senate of Rome Concerning Jesus Christ* (Boston: n.p., 1834). See the discussion in David Morgan, *Protestants & Pictures: Religion, Visual Culture, and the Age of American Mass Production* (New York: Oxford University Press, 1999), 283–286; and Edward L. Blum and Paul Harvey, *The Color of Christ: The Son of God and the Saga of Race in America* (Chapel Hill: University of North Carolina Press, 2012), 19–20, 82–83.

16 "Personal Appearance of Jesus," *Improvement Era* [Salt Lake City], September 1898, 820–825.

17 W. J., "Our Savior," *Juvenile Instructor*, 1 November 1882, 326.

18 Spencer W. Kimball discourse of 8 April 1956, in *One Hundred Twenty-Sixth Annual Conference . . . April 6, 7, and 8, 1956* (Salt Lake City: Church of Jesus Christ of Latter-day Saints, 1956), 118–119. For the above references I am indebted to Noel Carmack, "Images of Christ in Latter-day Saint Visual Culture," *BYU Studies* 39 (2000): 26–27.

19 "Popish idolatry" in Anonymous ("A Layman"), *Puseyite Developments, or Notices of the New York Ecclesiologists* (New York: Berford & Co., 1850), 9. On the legacy of Protestant iconoclasm in America and on the Moravian exception, see Blum and Harvey, *The Color of Christ*, chaps. 1 and 2. On the Protestant aversion to and mid-to-late-nineteenth-century embrace of the cross, see Ryan K. Smith, "The Cross: Church Symbol and Contest in Nineteenth-Century America," *Church History* 70 (December 2001): 705–734.

20 Kent P. Jackson, "Joseph Smith's Cooperstown Bible: The Historical Context of the Bible Used in the Joseph Smith Translation," *BYU Studies* 40 (2001): 52.

21 Parley Pratt, "Celestial Family Organization," *Millennial Star*, October 1844, 192. See Douglas J. Davies, *Joseph Smith, Jesus, and Satanic Opposition: Atonement, Evil and the Mormon Vision* (Aldershot, U.K.: Ashgate, 2010), 37.

22 Noel A. Carmack, "'One of the Most Interesting Sceneries That Can Be Found in Zion': Philo Dibble's Museum and Panorama," *Nauvoo Journal* 9 (Fall 1997): 25–38; Terryl L. Givens, *People of Paradox: A History of Mormon Culture* (New York: Oxford University Press, 2007), chap. 10.

23 "Death by Crucifying," *Juvenile Instructor*, 1 January 1866, 2.

24 George Reynolds, *The Story of the Book of Mormon* (Salt Lake City: Joseph Hyrum Parry, 1888). See Noel A. Carmack, "'A Picturesque and Dramatic History': George Reynolds's *Story of the Book of Mormon*," *BYU Studies* 47 (2008): 115–141.

25 Broadside advertisement quoted in Van Orden, *Prisoner for Conscience' Sake*, 152.

26 J. Leo Fairbanks, "Picture Study in the Sunday School," *Juvenile Instructor*, January 1913, 4. See Carmack, "Images of Christ," 32.

27 On the general popularity and influence of Hofmann and Plockhorst's paintings, see David Morgan, *Protestants and Pictures: Religion, Visual Culture, and the*

Age of American Mass Production (New York: Oxford University Press, 1999), chaps. 7–9.

28 George Reynolds, "The Personal Appearance of the Savior," *Juvenile Instructor*, 15 Aug. 1904, 498–499. See Carmack, "Images of Christ," 21–22.

29 Janne Sjodahl, "Supposed Likeness of Our Lord," *Improvement Era*, January 1925, 253.

30 Clifford Putney, *Muscular Christianity: Manhood and Sports in Protestant America, 1880–1920* (Cambridge, Mass.: Harvard University Press, 2001), 11 ("health and manliness").

31 R. Warren Conant, *The Manly Christ: A New View* (Chicago: n.p., 1904), 8 ("Feminizing"), 24 ("strenuous age"), and 11 (*"virile man"*). Emphasis in original. On Conant, see his obituary, *Chicago Tribune*, 11 July 1930. Conant published an expanded edition of *The Manly Christ* a decade later, retitled *The Virility of Christ* (Chicago: n.p., 1915). See also the analysis in David Morgan, *Visual Piety: A History and Theory of Popular Religious Images* (Berkeley: University of California Press, 1998), chap. 3.

32 Henry Emerson Fosdick, *The Manhood of the Master* (New York: Abingdon, 1913), 13, 161. On the Social Gospel and masculinity, see Susan Curtis, "The Son of Man and God the Father: The Social Gospel and Victorian Masculinity," in Mark C. Carnes and Clyde Griffen, eds., *Meanings for Manhood: Constructions of Masculinity in Victorian America* (Chicago: University of Chicago Press, 1990), 67–78.

33 Billy Sunday, Dec. 1916, quoted in Margaret Bendroth, "Why Women Loved Billy Sunday: Urban Revivalism and Popular Entertainment in Early Twentieth-Century American Culture," *Religion and American Culture* 14 (Summer 2004): 251.

34 Bruce Barton, *The Man Nobody Knows: A Discovery of the Real Jesus* (Indianapolis, Ind.: Bobbs-Merrill, 1925), 42–43, 220. See Morgan, *Visual Piety*, chap. 3.

35 Heber C. Kimball discourse of 6 April 1857, JD 5:22.

36 Richard Ian Kimball, "Muscular Mormonism," *The International Journal of the History of Sport* 25 (April 2008): 549–578.

37 Orson Whitney, *Through Memory's Halls: The Life Story of Orson F. Whitney* (Independence, Mo.: Zion's Press, 1930), 82–83. See also Orson Whitney, Autobiography (n.d.), MSS 188, Special Collections and Archives, Utah State University Merrill-Cazier Library, Logan, Utah.

38 Richard Charles Muhlberger, "Sacred Art—A Critique on the Contemporary Situation," *Liturgical Arts* 28 (1960): 71.

39 See the discussion in Colleen McDannell, *Material Christianity: Religion and Popular Culture in America* (New Haven, Conn.: Yale University Press, 1995), 188–193; Morgan, *Visual Piety*, 116–122; and Carmack, "Images of Christ," 37–39.

40 Vern G. Swanson, "The Book of Mormon Art of Arnold Friberg, 'Painter of Scripture,'" *Journal of Book of Mormon Studies* 10 (2001): 28.

41 Arnold Friberg quoted in Robert T. Barrett and Susan Easton Black, "Setting a Standard in LDS Art: Four Illustrators of the Mid-Twentieth Century," *BYU Studies* 44 (2005): 33.

42 Arnold Friberg interview, in Gregory A. Prince and William Robert Wright, *David O. McKay and the Rise of Modern Mormonism* (Salt Lake City: University of Utah Press, 2005), 19.

43 Ted Schwarz, *Arnold Friberg: The Passion of a Modern Master* (Flagstaff, Ariz.: Northland Press, 1985), 142.

44 Marian Ashby Johnson, "Minerva's Calling," *Dialogue* 21 (Spring 1988): 127–143.

45 Carmack, "Images of Christ," 41.

46 Quentin L. Cook, "Choose Wisely," *Ensign*, November 2014, 46–49.

47 www.altusfineart.com/simon-dewey, accessed 20 May 2015.

48 www.gregolsen.com, accessed 20 May 2015.

49 http://www.reparteegallery.com/m-159-liz-lemon-swindle.aspx, accessed 26 October 2015.

50 I am grateful to Colleen McDannell for this insight.

51 See Anne-Mette Gravgaard and Eva Henschen, *On the Statue of Christ by Thorvaldsen* (Copenhagen: The Thorvaldsen Museum and the Church of Our Lady, 1997), chap. 4.

52 George Reynolds, "The Personal Appearance of the Savior," *Juvenile Instructor*, August 15 1904, 497–500.

53 George Cannon Young's collection in George Cannon Young oral interview, transcript by Hugo Olaiz, copy in author's possession. See the discussion of these events in Matthew O. Richardson, "Bertel Thorvaldsen's *Christus*: A Mormon Icon," *Journal of Mormon History* 29 (Spring 2003): 72–83.

54 Stephen L. Richards to Hubert Eaton, 8 July 1957; Eaton to Richards, 16 July 1957; invoice in Hubert Eaton to Lynn S. Richards, 9 July 1959; Richards to Eaton, 26 January 1959, all in Stephen L. Richards Papers, Box 34, Folder 6, MS 4796, CHL. The marble studio that produced the replica was Rebechi Aldo & Gualtiero, in Pietrasanta.

55 Mark E. Petersen to First Presidency, 29 November 1961, Box 22, Folder 22, CR 1/53, First Presidency Temple Square Mission, CHL.

56 See Prince and Wright, *David O. McKay*, 121; Michael G. Reed, *Banishing the Cross: The Emergence of a Mormon Taboo* (Independence, Mo.: John Whitmer Books, 2012), esp. chaps. 7–9.

57 See Nathaniel Smith Kogan, "The Mormon Pavilion: Mainstreaming the Saints at the New York World's Fair, 1964–65," *Journal of Mormon History* 35 (Fall 2009): 1–52, quotes at 38.

58 Stacey Goodliffe, quoted in Richardson, "Thorvaldsen's *Christus*," 98.

59 *Official Report of the One Hundred Fifty-seventh Semiannual General Conference . . . October 3 and 4, 1987* (Salt Lake City: The Church of Jesus Christ of Latter-day Saints, 1988), 78.

60 Blum and Harvey, *The Color of Christ*, 78.

61 McDannell, *Material Christianity*, chap. 6.

62 Ethan Smith, *View of the Hebrews* (Poultney, Vt.: Smith and Shute, 1825 rev. ed.), 207; John Taylor, *An Examination into and an Elucidation of the Great Principle of the Mediation and Atonement* (Salt Lake City: Deseret News, 1892 rev. ed.), 201–205.

63 John Murphy, "Reinventing Mormonism: Guatemala as Harbinger of the Future," *Dialogue* 29 (Spring 1996): 177–192.

64 Mark E. Petersen, "The Great White God Was a Reality," *Improvement Era*, September 1969, 6–10.

65 See Max Perry Mueller, "The Pageantry of Protest in Temple Square," in Patrick Q. Mason and John G. Turner, eds., *Out of Obscurity: Mormonism since 1945* (New York: Oxford University Press, forthcoming).

66 First Presidency statement of 15 December 1969, published in Lester E. Bush Jr. and Armand L. Mauss, eds., *Neither White nor Black: Mormon Scholars Confront the Race Issue in a Universal Church* (Midvale, Utah: Signature Books, 1984), 222–224.

67 Jason Horowitz, "The Genesis of a Church's Stance on Race," accessed 20 May 2015, http://www.washingtonpost.com/politics/the-genesis-of-a-churchs-stand-on-race/2012/02/22/gIQAQZXyfR_story.html?tid=pm_politics_pop; LDS Newsroom, "Race and the Church," accessed 20 May 2015, www.mormonnewsroom.org/article/race-church.

68 Noel Carmack, "Christ Correlated: Institutionally 'Approved' Representations of Jesus in LDS Visual Resources, 1990–2013," unpublished ms., copy in author's possession.

69 Emile Wilson, *Christ Praying in Gethsemane*, accessed 29 August 2015, https://history.lds.org/exhibit/atonement-of-christ?lang=eng#mv11.

70 https://history.lds.org/exhibit/iac-2015-tell-me-the-stories-of-jesus?lang=eng#mv63, accessed 26 October 2015.

71 Howard W. Hunter, "Exceeding Great and Precious Promises," *Ensign*, November 1994, 8.

72 Coleen Menlove, "Living Happily Ever After," April 2000 General Conference, accessed 30 July 2015, https://www.lds.org/general-conference/2000/04/living-happily-ever-after.

73 Anne Pingree, "Choose Ye Therefore Christ the Lord," *Ensign*, November 2003, III.

74 Gordon B. Hinckley, "Welcome to Conference," *Ensign*, November 1999, 5.

CONCLUSION

1 Revelation of ca. Summer 1829, in *Book of Commandments Given for the Church of Christ* (Zion [Independence, Mo.]: W.W. Phelps, 1833), 40 [D&C 19:18].

2 Bruce McConkie, "The Purifying Power of Gethsemane," *Ensign*, May 1985, 9–11.

3 Alma 31:16.

4 Bruce McConkie, *Mormon Doctrine* (Salt Lake City: Bookcraft, 1958), 5.

5 McConkie, *Mormon Doctrine* [1958], 189, 38, 108. Emphasis in original.

6 Armand Mauss, *The Angel and the Beehive: The Mormon Struggle with Assimilation* (Urbana: University of Illinois Press, 1994).

7 McConkie, *Mormon Doctrine* [1958], 359.

8 Marion Romney to David O. McKay, 28 January 1959, copy in author's possession.

9 George W. Pace, *What It Means to Know Christ* (Provo, Utah: Council Press, 1981), 1, 2, 14. Emphasis in original.

10 Bruce McConkie, "Our Relationship with the Lord," 2 March 1982, accessed 16 May 2015, https://speeches.byu.edu/talks/bruce-r-mcconkie_relationship-lord/. See Stephen Prothero, *American Jesus: How the Son of God Became a National Icon* (New York: Farrar, Straus and Giroux, 2003), 191–192.

11 Boyd Packer, "Scriptures," *Ensign*, November 1982, 53.

12 "Media-Missionary-Member Integrated Proselyting Plan," draft, March 1985, copy in author's possession.

13 *Public Affairs Handbook* (Salt Lake City: The Church of Jesus Christ of Latter-day Saints, 1992), in J. B. Haws, *The Mormon Image in the American Mind: Fifty Years of Public Perception* (New York: Oxford University Press, 2013), 165.

14 McConkie, *Mormon Doctrine* [1958], 238–239.

15 Stephen Robinson, *Believing Christ: The Parable of the Bicycle and Other Good News* (Salt Lake City: Deseret Book, 1992), 32, 46, 119.

16 Dieter Uchtdorf, "The Gift of Grace," *Ensign*, May 2015, 107–109.

17 "Are Mormons Christians?" accessed 29 August 2015, https://www.lds.org/topics/christians?lang=eng.

18 Jan Shipps, *Sojourner in the Promised Land: Forty Years among the Mormons* (Urbana: University of Illinois Press, 2000), 11.

19 Douglas J. Davies, *Joseph Smith, Jesus, and Satanic Opposition: Atonement, Evil and the Mormon Vision* (Farnham, U.K.: Ashgate, 2013), esp. chap. 2.

ACKNOWLEDGMENTS

Even when a book bears a single name, scholarship is by its nature a collaborative enterprise, building on the work of women and men from the distant past and relying on the help of archivists, librarians, and colleagues. Mormon Studies is an especially hospitable subfield of academia. While debates over the Mormon past and present are often heated and passionate, the individuals involved are consistently welcoming of outsiders. The best part of writing a second book on Mormonism was that it allowed me to deepen many friendships begun over the past decade.

I am especially grateful to the following persons who read portions of the manuscript: Gary Bergera, Ryan Bingham, Matthew Bowman, Samuel Brown, Noel Carmack, John-Charles Duffy, Spencer Fluhman, Grant Hardy, J. B. Haws, Shon Hopkin, Philip Jenkins, Colleen McDannell, Patrick Mason, Robert Millet, Max Mueller, Benjamin Park, Courtney Jensen Peacock, Jonathan Stapley, Randall Stephens, Joseph Stuart, Matthew Sutton, John Christopher Thomas, Jordan Watkins, and Stephen Webb. Many other persons were unusually generously with their insights and expertise, including Edward Blum, David Campbell, David Howlett, Christopher Jones, David Morgan, Bill Smith, Douglas Sweeney, Bryce Taylor, Richard Turley, and Margaret Blair Young.

Several institutions made their documents and photographs available to me: The Church of Jesus Christ of Latter-day Saints and its Church History Department; Special Collections at the Harold B. Lee Library, Brigham Young University; the Brigham Young University Museum of Art; the International Society Daughters of Utah Pioneers; and the Pennsylvania Academy of the Fine Arts.

My colleagues at George Mason University are a constant source of good humor and encouragement. Also, the Heidelberg Center for American Studies welcomed me for an academic year while I worked on this project. I thank Detlef Junker, Tobias Endler, Jan Stievermann, Anja Schüler, Manfred Berg, and Wilifried Mausbach for that opportunity and for their hospitality.

I am grateful to my editor Joyce Seltzer for her help in turning this idea into a book, and I also thank Brian Distelberg, Lisa LaPoint, and many other individuals at Harvard University Press for their help in bringing it to fruition.

Mormonism teaches that human beings cannot obtain the fullness of salvation on their own. It is a religion of connection, between husbands and wives, parents and children, and across the generations. In this respect, I have at least obtained a fullness of earthly joy.

INDEX